"A GOOD NAME IS RATHER TO BE CHOSEN THAN GREAT RICHES."

PROVERBS (XXII-I)

*Your baby is a joy to behold!
Name her **NARKEASHA** ("pretty")
or call him **INGALL** ("angel").*

He is strong and destined for greatness:
CONLEY ("hero").
She is noble and proud:
ADELLE ("highborn").

*Was your baby born with a distinctive look?
Maybe she's a **KASSIDY** ("curly-haired")
and he's a **GANNON** ("fair complexion").*

*Would you like your **GYASI** ("marvelous baby")
to grow up to be an artist? Name him
KALIQ ("creative"), **KALIDAS** ("poet"),
or **HARPER** ("harp player").*

*Your darling baby girl is one of a kind—
perhaps **CHAPA** ("su*  *("a gift"),*

BABY NAMES

FOR THE NEW GENERATION

PAMELA SAMUELSON

AND

ALBRY MONTALBANO

Produced by The Philip Lief Group, Inc.

(Previously published as *Baby Names for the New Century*)

AVON BOOKS
An Imprint of HarperCollinsPublishers

Portions of this book were previously published as *Baby Names for the New Century*.

AVON BOOKS
An Imprint of HarperCollins*Publishers*
10 East 53rd Street
New York, New York 10022-5299

Copyright © 1994, 2006 by The Philip Lief Group, Inc.
ISBN-13: 978-0-06-082312-2
ISBN-10: 0-06-082312-7
www.avonbooks.com

First Avon Books paperback printing: June 2006

Avon Trademark Reg. U.S. Pat. Off. and in Other Countries, Marca Registrada, Hecho en U.S.A.
HarperCollins ® is a registered trademark of HarperCollins Publishers Inc.

Printed in the U.S.A.

10 9 8 7 6 5 4 3 2 1

CONTENTS

BABY NAMES

FOR THE NEW GENERATION

INTRODUCTION

By choosing the perfect name for your child, you are making the first gesture of helping your child forge an identity. You may want a name for your child that reflects family heritage, an interest in arts or literature, or aspirations that your child will become the next Nobel Laureate in Physics or a future Baseball Hall of Fame athlete. While you are browsing through the thousands of names available, you are searching for that one precious name that conveys a singular meaning you can offer your child as an indication of what his or her future holds.

Ultimately, of course, the person makes the name; as we mature, our personality and character expand to become the ultimate markers of identity, while a name takes on the lesser role of our most familiar label or appendage. In so many instances, however, a name is one's first method of introduction, identification, and presentation. When we enter a new situation, we are usually introduced by our names. One of the most powerful, primal statements we make about ourselves starts with the words "My name is . . ."

Baby Names for the New Generation is designed to give you a comprehensive and pleasurable strategy for choosing your child's very first gift: her or his name. Containing over 10,000 names from all over the world and throughout history, this book offers a careful balance between the contemporary and classic, the exotic and traditional. From time-honored names such as *Adam, Michael, Jacob, Mary, Linda,* and *Elizabeth* to cutting-edge monikers like *Dakota, Rena,* and *Jazlyn* to multicultural names including *Anzu, Mandara,* and *Marar,* this all-new compilation pulls together the widest breadth of choices of any baby-name book available.

HOW TO USE THIS BOOK

The components of each entry are assembled in an efficient, easy-to-read fashion, providing you with fascinating information about a name's pronunciation, derivation, meaning, history, and variations. You'll also find out who has held the name, from ancient Greeks to Renaissance scholars to contemporary movie stars.

Here's how to read an entry:

ALBERT (AL-burt) Germanic: "bright" or "noble." This name became popular in England after the marriage of Queen Victoria and Prince Albert in 1840. Literature: Albert Camus, French novelist and philosopher. Science: Albert Einstein and Albert Schweitzer, scientists. Eng: *Adelbert, Al, Bert, Elbert;* Czech: *Albertik, Ales;* Fr: *Aubert;* Pol: *Albek;* Ital: *Alberto;* Ger: *Albrecht, Bechtel, Bertchen.*

The main (root) name is in bold type. The phonetic pronunciation is in parentheses. All pronunciations are as simple as possible. Rather than employing an arcane system of syllabication, this book spells out the sounds to echo the way we read and speak. The accented syllable appears in capital letters, as in "AL-." The linguistic derivation of the name is followed by a brief meaning. Often, you'll find an informative comment or historical note, followed by a list of noteworthy people, famous or fictional, who have borne that name, giving the book the air of an almanac. Finally, a list of variations appears in bold, italic type, showing you how you can customize a name to reflect your own ethnic heritage or interests.

THE BABY NAME DATA BANK

In searching for the perfect name for your baby, you may become overwhelmed at times—the dazzling array may seem as vast as the universe. To help you along, The Baby Name Data Bank, located at the back of *Baby Names for the New Generation*, provides an innovative and unique tool for sifting through this book's vast selection. The Data Bank enables you to look at names by category, spanning many interests, including "Astrology," "Education," "Mythology," and "Sports." Say, for instance, you have a passion for gardening. Turn to the Data Bank's list of "Botany" names to gain an at-a-glance look at all the entries in this book that are of a horticultural nature, including female names like *Brier* and *Jasmine* or male names like *Florian* and *Waverly*. Thinking about naming your child after a famous painter or sculptor? Browse through the Data Bank's "Arts" list for reference to names contained in the main body that have been held by artistic figures.

Within the Data Bank, you will also find a list of "Most Popular" names. These are names that enjoy current popularity within North American culture. The "Cutting Edge" list refers you to names that have only recently appeared and are just starting to gain widespread use.

Now, not only can you use familiar criteria for name selection, such as the way a name sounds or the appearance of a name within either parent's lineage, but you can also apply this book's imaginative cross-referencing system to uncover a name's rich legacy.

MAKING THE DECISION

Use *Baby Names for the New Generation* to learn about the myriad possibilities that await you and your child. With its unique format and extensive, worldwide selection, this book aims at exposing you to new names, reminding you of old ones, and setting you on your way to the perfect choice. Read through the entries, say names you most favor to yourself, out loud, and to others, and try to project each possible selection into the future—you and your child will be using that name for a long time to come. The intention is to give you all the information you need to think through this delightful decision thoroughly, but in the end, you are urged to pay closest attention to the name by which your heart refers to your new baby.

FEMALE NAMES

FROM $\boxed{A}$ TO $\boxed{Z}$

AALIYAH (ah-LEE-ya) Hebrew: "highly exalted." Arabic: *Aliya*, *Aliyah*.

AARALYN (AIR-a-lin) American: "with song."

ABENI (ah-beh-NEE) Nigeria. Yoruban: "We prayed for a girl, and lo, she arrived!" *Abebi*.

ABIA (ah-BEE-ah) Arabic: "great."

ABIDA (ah-BEE-dah) Arabic: "worshiper."

ABIGAIL (AB-bi-gayl) Hebrew: "father of joy." Anglicized form of Hebrew *Avigayil*. Bible: Wife of David. History: Abigail Adams, wife of John Adams, second president of the United States. Journalism: Abigail van Buren, advice columnist. Eng: *Abagail, Abbe, Abbie, Abby, Abbye;* Gael: *Abbygael, Abigael, Abigal, Abigale, Abigall, Abigil, Abigayl, Gael, Gail, Galla, Gayel, Gayle.*

ABIRA (ah-BEE-rah) Hebrew: "powerful." *Abi, Adi,. Adira.*

ADA (A-dah) Hebrew: "adorned beautifully." Old English: "happy." Latin: "of noble birth." History: Ada Kepley, the first woman to graduate from law school (1870). Literature: Ada Negri, Italian poet. Theater: Ada Rehan, comic actress. Education: Ada Howard, educator, first president of Wellesley College, 1875–82. *Adda, Addi, Addie, Aida.*

ADALIA (a-DAL-lee-ya) Teutonic: "noble."

ADARA (AH-drah) Arabic: "chaste one."

ADELAIDE (A-de-layd) French: Form of the German name Adelhaide: "highborn." Arts: Adelaide Ristori, Italian actress. Literature: Adelaide Procter, birth name of Mary Berwick, poet and author. *Adela, Adella, Adele, Adell, Adelle.*

ADELINE (A-de-line) Variant of Adelaide in the United States. Eng: *Adiline, Adalene, Adelynn, Adalyn, Adelina.*

ADELLE (ah-DELLE) Old German: "royal" or "highborn." Science: Adelle Davis, nutritionist and author of *Let's Eat Right.* Eng: *Addie, Adela, Adelina, Adelia, Aline;* Czech: *Ada, Adelka, Dela;* Fr: *Adele, Adelina;* Hawaiian: *Akela;* Ital: *Adelina;* Pol: *Ada, Adelayda, Ela;* Russ: *Adel, Adaliya;* Span: *Adelita, Dela, Lela.*

ADERES (ah-de-RAYS) Israel. Hebrew: "clothes worn on the outside" or "mantle." *Aderetz.*

ADESINA (ah-DAY-see-nah) Nigeria. Yoruban: "baby who inspires more to follow." Nigerian couples who have had trouble conceiving often choose this name.

ADIE (ah-dee-AY) Hebrew: "decoration." *Ada, Adiella.*

ADILA (AH-dee-lah) Arabic: "equal."

ADITI (ah-DEE-tee) Hindi: "unfettered and without chains." Mythology: In Hindu mythology, mercy, compassion, and protection are granted by Aditi, the mother goddess, who gave birth to gods.

ADOETTE (ah-do-AY-tuh) Native American: "strong as a tree." Native American children given this name were most likely born near a tree or exhibited a spiritual kinship to nature.

ADONCIA (ah-dahn-SEE-ah) Spanish: "sugar." *Doncia.*

ADONIA (ah-DON-nee-ah) Greek mythology: According to Greek myth, the Greek hero Adonis first captured the heart of Aphrodite, goddess of love, through his beauty.

ADRIENNE, ADRIEN (a-DREE-in) French. Derived from the Greek: "girl from Adria." Theater: Adrienne Lecouveur, French stage actress. Literature: Adrienne Rich, American poet. Sports: Adriana Behar, first Olympic double medalist in beach volleyball. Eng: *Adri, Adriena;* Ger: *Adriane;* Ital: *Adria, Adriana.*

AGALIA (ah-gah-LEE-ah) Greek: "brightness, joy."

AGATA (ah-gah-TAH) Greek: "beneficent" or "compassionate." Agata is a beloved name that can be found in disparate cultures around the world, from Russia to Europe to North and South America. Eng: *Agatha, Aggie, Agna, Agnessa, Agnetta;* Fr/Ger: *Agathe;* Hung: *Agi, Agota;* Ital: *Agalina, Agnesina;* Pol: *Aga, Atka;* Port: *Agueda;* Russ: *Agasha, Ganya, Gashka.*

AGATHA (AH-ga-tha) Greek, Latin: "virtuous." Literature: Agatha Christie, best-selling British author of detective stories and plays. Her longest-running play is *The Mousetrap.*

AGNES (AG-ness) Greek, Latin: Derived from the word "lamb," symbolizing purity and chastity. The name became popular due to Saint Agnes, a virgin martyr in the early Christian era. Elizabethan England adored the name. Arts: Agnes de Mille, choreographer. History: Agnes MacPhail, politician, first woman elected to the Canadian legislature. Literature: Agnes Strickland, British biographer and novelist; Agnes Repplier, essayist, "Points of View"; Science: Agnes Robertson Arber, British botanist. Bulg: *Agnessa;* Czech: *Agneska, Anka;* Eng: *Aggie, Agna, Nessa, Nesta;* Fr: *Agnies;* Gk: *Agni;* Ital: *Angella, Agnesca, Agnola;* Lith: *Agne, Agniya;* Pol: *Aga, Agnieszka;* Russ: *Agnessa, Nessia, Nyusha;* Span: *Ines, Necha, Nesho;* Swed: *Agneta.*

AHAVA (ah-HAH-vah) Israel. Hebrew: "cherished one." *Hava, Ahuva.*

AH KUM (ah-KOOM) Chinese: "treasure."

AI (ah-EE) Vietnamese: "tender release."

AIDA (ah-EE-dah) Latin, Old French: "to help." Music: name of the Ethiopian princess in *Aida,* an opera by Verdi.

AILAINA, ALAINE (ah-LAYN-ah) Gaelic: "rock," "noble," "handsome," "harmony," or "cheerful."

AILEEN, AILENE (eye-LEEN) Greek: "celestial ray" or "one who carries the light." Eng: *Ailey, Eileen, Elene, Ileane, Ilene, Leana;* Fin: *Aila, Aili.*

AIMEE (ay-MEE) French: Adaptation of the Latin *amor,* "one who is loved." Eng: *Amy.*

AIN (ah-EEN) Arabic: "apple of one's eye," thus "to be treasured."

A'ISHAH (ah-ee-SHAH) Arabic: "living, prosperous." Wife of Muhammad. Believers of Islam hold that Muhammad, a seventh-century Arab, was last in a line of prophets from God, which included Moses and Jesus. The most popular Islamic names are the names of his wives. *Aishah.*

AKAKO (ah-KAH-ko) Japanese: "red." In ancient times, Japanese once considered the color red as a powerful healing modality, particularly in cases of blood diseases and wily nature spirits.

ALAMEA (ah-luh-MAY-uh) Hawaiian: "ripe" or "precious."

ALANA, ALANNA (ah-LAHN-ah) Hawaiian: "an offering from the soul"; Gaelic: "rock" or "buoyant"; Hebrew: "a little tree." Eng: *Alaina, Alayne, Alene, Allayne, Alenne, Lana.*

ALANI (ah-LAH-nee) Hawaiian: "orange-bearing tree." The most popular reference is to the Oahu tree, whose scented leaves are made into cachets. Often used in the masculine form.

ALAQUA (ah-LAG-quah) Native American: "sweet gum tree." Native Americans often use the names of plants and animals for their babies' names.

ALAUDA (ah-LAW-dah) Gaelic: "bird who sings."

ALAULA (ah-LAW-lah) Hawaiian: "sweet illuminations" at dawn or dusk. Applicable to boys or girls.

ALBERTA (al-BUR-tah) Old English: "highborn genius." Music: Alberta Hunter, blues singer. Dance: Albertina Rausch, ballerina and choreographer. Czech: *Alba, Berta;* Eng: *Albertine, Allie, Bertie, Elberta, Elbi;* Gk: *Alverta;* Ital: *Albertina;* Lat: *Albertine;* Pol: *Albertyna, Alaka;* Span: *Bertunga.*

ALBINA (al-BEEN-nah) Latin: "golden-haired" or "white-skinned." A popular name used worldwide. Czech: *Alva, Bela, Bina;* Eng: *Alba, Albinia, Alvinia;* Ger: *Alwine;* Pol: *Ala, Albinka;* Russ: *Alvina.*

ALBRY (ALL-bree) United States. English: "not so very ordinary girl." Variant of Aubrey.

ALEKA (uh-LEH-kuh) Hawaiian: "noble" or "kind."

ALENA (ah-LEE-nah) Russian: Form of Helen.

ALETEA (ah-leh-TEH-uh) Spanish: contemporary usage for "life's eternal verities."

ALEXANDRA, ALEXANDRIA, ALEXANDRINA (a-lex-AHN-dra) Greek: "protector of humankind." Dance: Alessandra Ferri. Bulg: *Alekko, Aleksi, Sander;* Czech: *Leska;* Eng: *Alexina, Lexie, Lexine, Sandy, Sandra, Zandra;* Fr: *Alexandrie, Alexius;* Ger: *Alexius;* Gk: *Alexiou, Ritsa;* Hung: *Alexa, Eli;* Ital: *Alessandra, Alessio;* Russ: *Alya, Aleksasha, Lelya, Sasha, Shura, Shurka;* Span: *Alejandra, Alejandrina.*

ALI (ah-LEE) Arabic: "highest" or "greatest." A variant form of Allah, title of the Supreme Being in the Muslim faith. History: Ali Mubarak, Egyptian minister of education, 1988–91, who modernized the school system. Movies and Television: Ali Mc-Graw, actress, *Love Story.* Literature: Ali Neva'i, Turkish poet and scholar. Eng: *Alie, Allie, Ally.*

ALICE (AH-liss) Middle English: Derived from Alys and Aeleis, which evolved from the Old French Aliz and Aaliz. Originally the high German name Adelheidis, akin to Adelaide, meaning "noble birth." Arts: Alice Aycock, sculptor. Business: Alice Thomas, first American woman tavern keeper (1670). History: Alice Hathaway Roosevelt, wife of

President Theodore Roosevelt (1901–09). Literature: Alice Wykeham-Martin Pollock, British author who wrote *Portrait of My Victorian Youth;* Alice Lidell, the schoolgirl who inspired Lewis Carroll's *Alice in Wonderland; Alice Adams,* Booth Tarkington's Pulitzer Prize winning novel (1922). Science: Alice Evans, pioneer in milk pasteurization. Eng: *Aletha, Ali, Alicia, Allison, Alissa, Alisha, Ellie, Elsie, Elsa;* Bulg: *Alisa;* Czech: *Alicia;* Fr: *Alix;* Ger: *Adelcia, Alexia, Elschen, Ilse;* Gk: *Alike, Alizka;* Hawaiian: *Alika;* Hung: *Alisz, Alizka, Lici;* Ir: *Ailis;* Pol: *Ala, Alisia;* Span: *Alicia, Elsa, Licha.*

ALIMA (ah-LEE-muh) Arabic: "one whose heart soars in music and dance." Mythology: "goddess of the oceans."

ALMA (AHL-mah) Spanish, Italian: "soul" or "spiritual essence," referring to the spirit power the newborn child brings to his parents.

ALMEDA (al-MAY-dah) Native American: "fields of cottonwood"; Spanish: "avenue for strolling."

ALONA (ah-LO-nah) Basque: reference to the Virgin Mary.

ALTHEA (al-THEE-ah) Greek, Latin: "healer." Sports: Althea Gibson, first African-American woman tennis champion. *Altheda, Altheta, Thea, Theda, Theta.*

ALUMIT (ah-loo-MEET) Hebrew: "sacred mystery" or "female child." Commonly used in contemporary Israel. *Alma, Alumice.*

ALVA (AHL-vah) Latin: "fair complexion." History: Alva Myrdal, Swedish sociologist, diplomat, and political leader who won the Nobel Peace Prize in 1982 for her work with the nuclear disarmament movement.

ALZBETA (ahlz-BAY-tah) Czechoslovakian: "consecrated to God."

AM (uhm) Vietnamese: "moon-empowered" or "divine feminine." Philosophy: According to Asian philosophy, the passive, receptive *yin* energy, together with the male principle *yang,* creates the cosmos.

AMALIE (ah-mah-LEE) Latin: "hard worker." Widely used German name.

AMANDA (ah-MAHN-dah) Latin: "receptive to love" or "one who loves deeply." Regularly used since the seventeenth century, it is still popular today. Literature: Amanda Douglas, author of children's books. Theater: Amanda Prynne, character in Noel Coward's *Private Lives.* Eng: *Amandy, Manda, Mandie, Mandy, Mandaline;* Fr: *Amandine;* Span: *Amata.*

AMARA (ah-MAHR-rah) Greek: "eternal beauty." *Amargo, Amarinda, Mara.*

AMARANTHA (ah-mar-AN-tha) Greek: "beyond death." The name of a plant. Mythology: a mythical plant thought to be immortal. *Amarande, Amaranta, Amarante.*

AMARYLLIS (ah-mah-RILL-iss) Latin: species of flowers, often used in poetry to suggest pastoral life.

AMAUI (uh-MOW-ee) Hawaiian: type of bird similar to a dusty brown thrush, which is known for its docile nature.

AMAYA (ah-MAH-yah) Japanese: "night rain." Surname.

AMAYETA (ah-mah-YEH-tah) Native American. Miwok: "fruit from the manzanita tree."

AMBER (am-BUR) United States: A golden brown semi-precious stone whose name was immortalized in the title of Kathleen Windsor's 1944 best-selling novel *Forever Amber*. ***Ambar, Amberetta, Amberly, Ambur.***

AMELIA (ah-MEEL-ya) Latin: "hard worker." Aeronautics, History: Amelia Earhart, aviatrix, first woman to cross the Atlantic solo; Amelia Adelaide, British queen of William IV; Amelia Jenks Bloomer, suffragette who wore trousers later called "bloomers." Literature: Amelia Sedley, character in Thackeray's *Vanity Fair*; Amelia Bedelia, children's book favorite. ***Amalea, Amalie, Amelita, Amy, Em, Emelina, Emily, Emma, Emmaline, Emmy.***

AMETHYST (am-ih-THIST) Greek: "against intoxication." A purple or violet gemstone used in ancient Greece to protect its owner against the effects of strong drink.

AMINA (ah-MEE-nah) Arabic, Swahili: "beyond reproach." *Amineh, Aminah, Ameena.*

AMIRA (ah-MEE-rah) Hebrew: "princess" or "one who speaks." *Amirah, Ameera.*

AMITA (ah-MEE-tah) Hebrew: "truth."

AMITY (AM-a-tee) English, French: "bound by friendship." One of the virtue names brought by the Puritans to the New World. Other virtue names include Charity, Hope, and Chastity. *Amitie.*

AMY (AY-mee) Latin: "one who is loved." Aeronautics: Amy Johnson, British aviator who flew solo from London to Australia in 1930. Literature: In spite of the prominence given the name by Louisa May Alcott's *Little Women,* it didn't become a favorite until the 1950s; Amy Lowell, poet and Pulitzer Prize winner for *Lilacs* (1926). History: Amy Carter, daughter of President Jimmy Carter. Music: Amy Mann, singer. Eng: *Amish, Amice, Amil, Esma, Esme;* Fr: *Aimee, Aimie;* Span: *Amada, Amata.*

AN (AHN) Chinese: "peace."

ANASTASIA (AHN-ah-STAH-see-ah) Greek: "reborn from the dead." A beloved name in Russia that came out of the Greek Orthodox tradition. History: In 1918, during the Russian Revolution, the Grand Duchess Anastasia, daughter of Czar Nicholas, was rumored to have made a miraculous secret escape after her family was massacred. Movies and Television: Greta Garbo immortalized the duchess in the film *Anastasia.* Eng: *Anastace, Anastyce, Stacy;*

Czech: *Anastazia, Stasa, Staska;* Fr: and Gk: *Anastasie;* Russ: *Anya, Asya, Nastasya, Nastka, Nastusha, Tasenka, Taska, Tasya;* Span: *Tasia.*

ANDREA (AHN-dree-ah) Latin: "feminine grace" or Greek: "ideal woman." Most commonly used in the United States. Arts: Andrea Sansovino, Italian Renaissance sculptor; Andrea Mantegna, Italian Renaissance fresco artist; Andrea Solari, Italian painter. Sports: Andrea Jaeger, tennis champion. Eng: *Andree, Andria, Andriana;* Fr: *Andree;* Ir: *Aindrea; Andrewina, Ohndreea, Ondrea.*

ANDROMEDA (ahn-DRAH-mee-dah) Greek mythology: Name of a beautiful young woman who was saved by Perseus after being tortured by an angry sea creature. It was thought she later ascended to the heavens as a star. Also, the name of a plant that blooms in spring.

ANEMONE (ah-NEH-moh-nee) Greek: "breath." *Ann-Aymone, Anne-Aymone.*

ANGELA (AHN-jell-ah) Greek: "angelic messenger." Popular name worldwide in the twentieth century. Movies and Television: Angela Lansbury, starring actress of the TV series *Murder She Wrote;* Angie Dickinson, actress; Angelica Huston, actress. History: Angela Burdett-Coutts, baroness and British philanthropist who raised Turkish relief funds from 1877–78. Literature: Angela Mackail Thirkell, British novelist who wrote *Coronation Summer.* Fr: *Aingeal, Ange, Angele;* Ital: *Angelica;* Ger: *Angelika, Angelina, Angeline, Angelique, Angelita, Angiola, Anjela, Annijilla, Gelya.*

ANN (ahn) Israel. Hebrew: "blessed with grace." English from Hannah. Inordinately popular until the 1850s when it nose-dived. Later revived in England. Queen Elizabeth II named her daughter Anne in 1950. Literature: Anne Sexton, poet; Anna Sewell, English writer, best known for her popular *Black Beauty*; Anna Akmatova, Russian poet; Anne Brashler, U.S. poet, short story writer. Education: Anne Sullivan, educator of Helen Keller. History: Annie Oakley, sharpshooter in Wild Bill's Wild West Show. Music: Annie Lennox, British pop singer. Journalism: Anne O'Hare McCormick, first female journalist to win the Pulitzer Prize (1937). Science: Anna Comstock, naturalist and science educator. Sports: Annie Smith Peck, mountain climber. Czech: *Andulka, Anicka, Andula;* Eng: *Ana, Annabelle, Annie, Nan, Nancy;* Fr: *Annette;* Ger: *Annchen, Nettchen;* Hung: *Anci, Aniko, Nina, Nusi;* Ital: *Annetta, Annina;* Pol: *Anka, Hania;* Span: *Anita, Nana, Nita;* Russ: *Anninka, Annuska, Anya, Asya, Nyuta;* Span: *Anica, Anita, Nana;* Yiddish: *Chana, Channa, Hanna, Hannah.*

ANNABELLE (ahn-A-bel) French: "grace and beauty."

ANNETTE (ahn-ET) French: "gracious." Movies and Television: Annette Benning, actress (*Being Julia*). Politics: Annette Abbott Adams, first woman Assistant United States Attorney General.

ANONA (ah-NOH-nah) Latin: "seasonal plantings." Astrology: When given to girls born under the earth signs of Virgo, Taurus, or Capricorn, the name reaffirms their spiritual connection to nature.

ANTHEA (ahn-THAY-ah) Greek: "goddess of blossoms."

ANTONETTA (ahn-toh-NETT-ah) Swedish and Slavic: "beyond value." Theater: Antoinette Perry, actress and director who established American Theater Wing (1941) and for whom the Tony Award was named. History: Antoinette Brown Blackwell, first woman pastor (1852); Antonette Bourignon, Flemish religious figure who spread Bourignianism through Scotland and Holland. *Antonella, Antonette, Antonia.*

ANTONIA (an-TOH-nee-ah) Latin: "of exceptional worth." Roman clan name used as a first name. Literature: *My Antonia* (1918), a novel by Willa Cather dealing with Bohemian immigrants in the frontier farmlands of Nebraska. Czech: *Anuska;* Eng: *Netta, Nettie, Toni, Tonia;* Fr: *Antoinette, Antonie;* Ital: *Antonella, Antonia, Antonieta;* Span: *Antonieta, Antonina;* Welsh: *Anwen.*

ANZU (AHN-zoo) Japanese: "apricot," a symbol of feminine ripeness. Western folklore uses the apricot as a metaphor for shy adoration.

AOLANI (ow-LAH-nee) Hawaiian: "celestial home."

APRIL (A-prill) Latin: "forthcoming." It instantly connotes springtime. Eng: *Aprilete, Aprille, Averell, Averil, Averyl, Avril;* Span: *Abril.*

ARA (AR-ah) Teutonic: "eagle maid."

ARABELLA (ar-ah-BELL-ah) Latin: "yielding to prayer." Possibly from Annabelle, but it may be from the Latin *orabilis*, "capable of being moved by entreaty." Music: *Arabella,* opera by Richard Strauss. Literature: Arabella Allen, character in Dickens's *Pickwick Papers.* Eng: *Ara, Arabel, Arabela, Arbell, Arbella, Bel, Bella;* Fr: *Belle;* Ital: *Orabella, Orbella.*

ARDEN (AR-dinn) Latin: "highly excited, thrilled." Literature, Theater: In Shakespeare's *As You Like It,* the Forest of Arden was full of magic and delightful mystery.

ARELLA (ah-RAY-leh) Israel. Hebrew: "spirit" or "God's helper." *Arela.*

ARETE (ah-RAY-teh) Greek: Modern adaptation of the ancient spelling of grace. Also, "full of grace" or "beautiful." Music: Aretha Franklin, a popular American singer who sold fourteen million single recordings from 1967–73. Eng: *Aretha, Aretta;* Fr: *Arette;* Gk: *Arethi.*

ARIADNE (ah-ree-ODD-nee) Greek mythology: daughter of Cretan King Minos, who rescued Theseus from the Labyrinth after he killed the Minotaur. Music: *Araidne auf Naxos,* an opera by Richard Strauss. *Arene, Araidna, Ariana, Arianie, Arianna, Arianne, Aryana.*

ARIEL (ah-ree-AYL) Israel. Hebrew: "divine feline." Literature: *Ariel, a* collection of poems by the American poet Sylvia Plath. Also a sprite in Shakespeare's *The Tempest*. **Aeriel, Aeriela, Ariela, Arielle, Ariellel.**

ARISTA (ah-REE-stah) Latin: "sowing the fields." Astrology: Refers to a perfect child born under the sign of Virgo, symbolized by the chaste goddess of the harvest.

ARIZA (ah-REE-zah) Hebrew: "doors of cedar." Popular in the Middle East. *Arza, Arzice.*

ARLENE (ahr-LEEN) Old English: "man" or "vow." First noticed in England around the 1850s. *Arla, Arlee, Arlinda, Arline, Arleen, Arlen, Arly, Arlynne, Lena, Lina.*

ARNINA (ahr-NEE-nah) Middle Eastern: "to illuminate," "peak," "one who delivers God's words," or "singer." Popular in Israel and gaining popularity today in the United States. *Arnie, Arnice, Arnit.*

ARTEMIS (AR-te-miss) Greek: "virgin goddess of the moon" or "huntress." Mythology: The equivalent of the Roman Diana.

ARTHA (AHR-tah) Hindi: "personal treasure" or "material wealth." Philosophy: In Hindu philosophy, considered one of the four human goals.

ASA (AH-sah) Japanese: "starting life at dawn."

ASHA (AH-shah) Swahili: "life."

ASHLEY (ASH-lee) Old English: "from the field of ash trees." Originally a surname, now a popular first name for females. Eng: *Ashely, Ashla, Ashlan, Ashlee, Ashleigh, Ashton.*

ASTA (AS-tah) Greek: "bright as a star," or Old Norse: "God's omnipotent power." Also derived from the aster flower. Norw: *Astrid, Astyr.*

ATHENA (ah-THEE-nah) Latin: Variant form of Athena, the Greek goddess of wisdom and war.

ATIDA (ah-TEE-duh) Hebrew: "that which comes tomorrow." Popular in Israel as well as the United States.

AUBERTA (oh-BEHR-tah) French: "noble" or "bright." Eng/Fr: *Aubrey, Aubrie, Aubry, Aubriana, Aubrianne.*

AUDEY (AW-dee) United States. English. Contemporary variant of Audrey in the United States.

AUDRA (AWH-drah) English: From Etheldreda. Old English: "noble strength." Movies and Television: made famous by actress Linda Evans's character in the television series, *The Big Valley;* Audra Lindley, actress. *Audi.*

AUDREY (AW-dree) Old English: "regal force." Movies and Television: Audrey Hepburn, actress, winner of an Academy Award for *Roman Holiday* (1953) and staunch supporter of UNICEF; Audrey Meadows, actress on TV's *The Honeymooners.*

Audy, Audie, Audra, Audree, Audreen, Audria, Audry.

AUGUSTA (aw-GUSS-tah) Latin: "grand" or "splendid." Arts: Augusta Savage, sculptor; Literature: P. G. Wodehouse's hero Bertie Wooser had a terrifying Aunt Augusta. History: Augusta, queen consort of Prussia, 1881–88. Philosophy: Augusta Simmons Stetson, Christian Science clergyman. Dance: Augusta Maywood, prima ballerina. *Augustina, Agustina.*

AULII (OW-lee) Hawaiian: "delicious."

AURELIA (aw-REE-lya) Latin: "golden." *Aurene, Auriel, Aurielle, Arela, Arella.*

AURORA (oh-ROHR-ah) Latin: Aurora was the Roman goddess of dawn, referred to by Homer as "rosy-fingered." Literature: Amandine Aurore Lucie Dupin, the French novelist (1804–76). Dupin (George Sand) is as famous for her novels as she is for her love affairs with prominent artistic figures as Alfred de Musset and Frederick Chopin. Aurora is a character in Manuel Puig's *Kiss of the Spider Woman.* Fr: *Aurore.*

AVA (AY-vah) Hebrew: "life," from *chava;* English: derived from Eve; German pronunciation of Eva, and old Germanic-Norman form of Hedwig. Movies and Television: Ava Gardner, actress. *Avah, Avalee, Avelyn, Avilina, Aviana, Avia, Aviance, Avis;* Heb: *Aviva.*

AVI (AH-vee) Hebrew: "lord of mine" or "father of mine." Popular name in contemporary Israel.

AVIVA (ah-VEE-vah) Hebrew: "joyful spring," referring to the renewal of nature after winter. *Avivah, Avivi, Avivice, Avrit.*

AWANATA (ah-wah-NAH-tah) Native American. Miwok: "original turtle." Mythology: In Native American mythology, the first living being on Earth was the humble turtle who created the rest of existence by diving to the depths of the ocean, grabbing a mouthful of dirt, then spitting out the world into its earthly form.

AWENDELA (ah-wayn-DAY-lah) Native American: "fresh morning." A name especially appropriate for babies who arrive before the sun rises.

AYAME (ah-YA-me) Japanese: "iris." Mythology: In Asian lore, the iris blooms in May and represents the power of the warrior. In Greek mythology, Iris is the Greek goddess of the rainbow and a messenger of the gods.

AYLA (AY-la) Hebrew: "oak tree." Literature: Jean Auel's Cro-Magnon hero Ayla from *The Clan of the Cave Bear.* **Ayala.**

AYOKA (ah-YO-kah) Nigeria. Yoruba: "joy-giver." Often used as an intimate nickname or term of endearment.

AZALEA (a-ZAYL-yah) Latin, Greek: "dry." Name of a flower. *Azalia.* Hebrew: "spared by Jehovah."

AZAMI (ah-ZAH-mee) Japanese: "prickly plant." In the Far East plants such as thistles represent a stubborn and hard-nosed nature.

AZIZA (ah-ZEE-zah) Arabic: "beloved." Swahili: "very beautiful." Business: Aziza cosmetics.

AZIZE (ah-ZEEZ) Swahili: "highly valued" or "uncommonly exquisite."

BABETTE (bab-ETT) French: "stranger, lovely." Movies and Television: *Babette's Feast*, movie directed by Gabriel Axel, won 1986 Academy Award for Best Foreign Film.

BADU (ba-DEW) African: "tenth born child." Music: Erykah Badu, popular American singer.

BAHIRA (ba-HEE-rah) Arabic: "electrifying."

BAILEY (BAY-lee) English, French: "steward" or "public servant." *Baylee, Bayley, Baylie, Bailee, Baylee;* Ir: *Bailie.*

BAINA (BAY-e-nah) African: "sparkling."

BAKA (BAH-kah) Hindi: "crane." In Hindu lore, the crane represents long life and good health.

BAKARNE (BAK-ar-neh) Basque: "solitude."

BAKULA (BA-koo-lah) Hindi: "flower." Hindu legends describe a magical flower called bakula whose blossoms are brought to life when watered with wine dripping from a pretty girl's mouth.

BALLARI (bal-LAR-E) Hindi: "walking quiety."

BAMBI (BAM-bee) Italian: "child." Short for *bambino*. Movies and Television: Bambi, a lovable deer with soulful eyes in Walt Disney's animated film, *Bambi*. **Bambie, Bamby.**

BARA (BAR-ah) Hebrew: "to choose."

BARBARA (BAR-bah-rah) Greek: "strange" or "not from here." Term originally referred to non-Greek-speaking people. Popularized by St. Barbara, who was kept in a tower by her father and later made the patron saint of architects and mines. History: Barbara Bush, former First Lady. Literature: Barbara Tuchman (1912–89), Pulitzer Prize-winning author of history books. Movies and Television: Barbara Stanwyck, actress. Music: Barbra Streisand, singer. Eng: *Babb, Babbett, Barb, Barbary, Barbie, Barbette, Bobbi, Bobby, Bonni, Bonnie, Bonny;* Gk: *Voska;* Russ: *Varvara, Varina, Varka, Varya, Vavka.*

BARIKA (ba-REE-ka) Arabic: "win" or "blossom." Popular Swahili name.

BATYA (bah-TEE-ya) Hebrew: "God's precious daughter." Popular in contemporary Israel. *Basia, Basya, Batia.*

BAYO (BAH-yoh) Nigeria. Yoruban: "joy is found."

BEATA (bee-AH-tah) Latin: "happy."

BEATRICE (BEE-a-triss) Latin: "bringer of joy." Beatrix was first used in Medieval England. When Queen Victoria named her daughter Beatrice, it became very popular. History: Beatrice Webb, along with her husband Sidney J. Webb, was a leading figure in the British Fabian Society and Labour Party; Queen Beatrix of the Netherlands. Literature: Beatrice was the ideal love of Dante Alighieri, an Italian poet, which he celebrated in his work, *La Vita Nuova*; Beatrix Potter, British writer and illustrator of children's books such as *Peter Rabbit*. Movies and Television: Bea Arthur, actress. Theater: Beatrice Lillie, entertainer. Eng: *Bea, Bee, Trixie;* Span: *Beatrisa, Beatriz, Bebe, Trisa;* Port: *Beatriz.*

BECCA (BEH-kah) Hebrew: "bound."

BEDELIA (beh-DEL-lee-ah) French: "strength." •

BEHIRA (beh-HEE-rah) Hebrew: "blinding light of truth."

BEL (bell) Hindi: "revered tree known as wood apple." Hindu law prohibits anyone but Brahmins from touching or destroying the wood apple tree.

BELA (BELL-ah) Old French: "lass of the porcelain skin." Popular in Czechoslovakia. Eng: *Blanche.*

BELEN (bay-LEN) Spanish: "Bethlehem." Use of the term as a given name suggests a deep tie to the birthplace of Jesus.

BELICIA (bel-EE-see-ah) Spanish: "devoted to the Lord." Variant of Isabel.

BELINDA (be-LIN-dah) Old Spanish: "pretty." *Bel, Belle, Linda.*

BELITA (bel-EE-tah) Spanish: "beautiful."

BELLE (bell) French: "beautiful." History: Belle Sherwin, suffragette. Literature: Belle Watling, a madam in Margaret Mitchell's novel *Gone with the Wind.* Eng: *Bella;* Lat: *Belloma.*

BELVA (bel-VAH) Latin: "beautiful view."

BENA (BEE-nah) Native American: "pheasant." Scholars cannot verify which tribe invented this name.

BENITA (ben-NEE-tah) Latin: "She whom God has blessed." Spanish adaptation of Benedicta, which itself is derived from Benedict. Eng: *Bena, Bennie, Binnie, Dixie;* Fr: *Benoite;* Span: *Benicia.*

BERDINE (BUR-deen) Teutonic: "bright maiden."

BERNADETTE (BUR-nah-DETTE) French: "courageous like a bear." History: Bernadette of Lourdes, canonized in 1933. Theater: Bernadette Peters, actress and singer. Eng: *Berna, Bernadeena, Bernadene, Bernadett, Bernadine;* Ital: *Bernadetta, Bernadina;* Pol: *Ina.*

BERNICE (bur-NEES) Greek: "bringer of victory." Name of Egyptian princesses. Arts: Berenice Abbott, photographer. *Barri, Barrie, Beranice, Berenice, Berna, Bernicia, Bernelle, Bernetta, Bernette, Bernie, Bunny, Nixie, Veronica, Veronique.*

BERTHA (BUR-tha) Teutonic: "shining one." *Berta, Berthe, Bertie, Berty;* Span: *Bertina.* History: Bertha von Suttner, 1905 Nobel Peace Prize winner.

BERTILLE (bur-TEEL) Teutonic: "heroine."

BERYL (burl) Sanskrit: "cat's eye." From the gem beryl. Aeronautics, History: Beryl Markham, aviator and author of *West with the Night. Berri, Berrie, Berry, Beryla, Beryle.*

BESS See Elizabeth.

BETH See Elizabeth.

BETHAN (BETH-ahn) Welsh: "consecrated to God."

BETHANY (BETH-ah-nee) Hebrew: Place name. Bible: A hamlet close to Jerusalem frequented by Jesus. *Bethanie, Bethani, Bethanee, Bethann, Beth-Ann.*

BETSY (BEHT-see) Hebrew: Derivative of Elizabeth. History: Betsy Ross, seamstress who is said to have designed the first U.S. flag.

BEULAH (BEW-lah) English, Hebrew: "a married woman." Bible: Israel is known as the Land of Beulah. Literature: In *The Pilgrim's Progress,* Beulah is a land of joy.

BEVERLY (BEH-ver-lee) English: "stream where the beavers swim." Place name that started as a last name, then adapted as a given name. Chosen for both sexes. Literature: Beverly Cleary, author of children's books. Music: Beverly Sills, opera star. *Bev, Beverelle, Beverley, Bevlyn, Bevvy, Buffy, Verlee, Verly, Berlye.*

BEYONCE (bay-ON-say) African American: "beyond others." Music: Beyoncé Knowles, American R&B artist.

BIANCA (bee-YAHN-kah) or (BYAN-kah) Italian: "of light complexion" or "white." The Italian counterpart of Blanche. Literature: Bianca is Kate's sister in Shakespeare's *The Taming of the Shrew.* Music: The title of a song by Cole Porter in *Kiss Me Kate. Beanka, Bionca, Bionka, Biancha, Blanca, Blancha.*

BIBI (BEE-bee) Arabic: "woman of honored status." *Bebe, Beebee.*

BIBIANE (bee-bee-ANN) Latin: "lively."

BINA (BEE-nah) Hebrew: "discernment" or "insight." Native American: "crops." Names that cross cultures with various meanings hold particular spiritual power, according to many traditions. *Buna.*

BIRGIT (BEER-jit) Norwegian: "protecting power." Adaptation of Bridgett. Overwhelmingly popular in Scandinavian countries. Music: Birgit Nilsson, international opera star who excelled in the works of Wagner. Den: *Bergitte;* Swed: *Birgitta.*

BLAIR (blair) Celtic: "field with no slope." Scottish place name. *Blaire, Blayre.* Movies and Television: Blair Brown, actress (*Loverboy*).

BLANCHE (blahnche) Old French: "she of the porcelain skin." Aeronautics: Blanche Scott, first woman to break the sound barrier. History: Blanche Castile, thirteenth-century queen of France; Blanche Ames Ames, inventor and illustrator who drew political cartoons depicting women's struggle for suffrage. Music: Blanche Theborn, mezzo-soprano. Czech: *Bela, Blanka;* Eng: *Blanshe;* Ital: *Bianca;* Span: *Blanca, Branca;* Swed: *Blanka, Blenda.*

BLENDA (BLEN-dah) Teutonic: "dazzling."

BLOSSOM (BLAH-suhm) Old English: "flower-like."

BLUEBELL (BLEW-bell) English: The name of a flower. *Bluebelle.*

BLYTHE (blithe) Old English: "happy, free-spirited." Literature, Theater: Noel Coward's play *Blithe Spirit.* Movies and Television: Blythe Danner, actress. *Blithe.*

BO (bow) Chinese: "most treasured." Variant of Bonita. Movies and Television: Bo Derek, actress (*10*).

BO-BAE (bow-BAY) Korean: "treasure, precious."

BOBBI (bah-bee) Old English: Derives from Barbara. More common in the southern states of the United States. Literature: Bobbie Ann Mason, novelist. *Bobbie, Bobby.*

BOGDANA (bawg-DAH-nah) Polish: "celestial present." *Bogna, Bohdana.*

BOHDANA (bow-DAAN-a) Russian: "from God."

BOLADE (BOH-lah-deh) Nigeria. Yoruban: "honor arrives."

BOLANILE (baw-lah-NEE-leh) Nigeria. Yoruban: "our treasured home."

BONA (bow-NAH) Hebrew: "creator of dreams."

BONAMY (bow-NAH-may) French: "good friend."

BONITA (bow-NEE-tah) Spanish: "beautiful." Movies and Television: Bonita Granville, actress. *Bo, Boni, Bonie, Nita.*

BONNIE (BAH-nee) Scottish: "pretty girl," from the Old French *Bonne* meaning "good." Aeronautics: Bonnie Tiburzi, first woman hired as jet pilot by a commercial U.S. airline. Music: Bonnie Raitt, singer, daughter of John Raitt. Sports: Bonnie Blair, speed skater, most decorated female athlete in Olympic Winter Games (five gold medals). *Bonni, Bonny, Bunni, Bunnie, Bunny.*

BRANDY (BRAN-dee) Dutch: "burnt wine." Sports: Brandy Johnson, gymnast. *Brandais, Brande, Brandea, Brandee, Brandi, Brandice, Brandie.*

BRECK (breek) Gaelic: "freckled."

BREE (bree) Gaelic: Short form of names like **Brina** and **Breanna**. Journalism: Bree Walker, TV news anchor. *Bria, Brea, Brielle.*

BREENA (bree-NAH) Gaelic: "fairy land."

BRENDA (BREN-dah) Old English: "beacon on the hill" or "on fire." *Bren, Brendalynn.*

BRETTA (BRET-tah) Celtic: "from Britian."

BRIALLEN (bree-AL-en) Welsh: "primrose."

BRIANA (bree-ON-ah) Celtic: "strong."

BRIDGET (BRIHJ-itt) Celtic: "the high goddess," derived from *brigenti*. Military: Bridget Divers, fought on battlefield during U.S. Civil War. Literature: Title character of British writer Helen Fielding's 1999 novel *Bridget Jone's Diary*. Movies and Television: Bridgitte Bardot, actress; Bridget Fonda, actress *(Single White Female)*, Brigitte Nielsen, actress *(Red Sonya)*. Eng: *Berget, Bergit, Biddy, Bridgid, Brietta, Brigid, Brigit, Brita, Brydie;* Gk: *Bree, Berek;* Ital: *Brigada, Birgita;* Norw: *Birget;* Pol: *Bryga, Brygida, Brygitka;* Span: *Brigida, Gidita;* Swed: *Birgitta, Biddy.*

BRIER (BRY-ar) French: "heather." In English, the word refers to a thorny rose, a symbol of beauty and danger. *Briar.*

BRIGHID (bride) Celtic: "power." Old Irish names are very popular in Ireland now. *Brid, Bride, Breeda, Brigid.*

BRINA (BREE-na) Gaelic: Short form of Sabrina. *Breena, Brena.*

BRISA (BREE-zah or BREE-sah) Spanish: Short form of the Spanish name Briseida. Mythology: from Briseis, the Greek name of Achilles' beloved in Homer's *Iliad.* **Brissa, Bryssa, Briza, Breezy, Brisha, Brisia.**

BRITES (br-EYE-tehs) Celtic: "strength."

BRITTANY (BRIT-'n-ee) English: From Britannia. *Britani, Britany, Britney, Britny, Brittaney, Brittanie, Brittney.* Music: Britney Spears, singer.

BRONA (broh-NAH) Greek: "arriving before triumph." A popular girl's name today in Czechoslovakia. Eng: *Bernice.*

BRONWEN (broh-NAH-wen) Welsh: "dark, pure."

BRONWYN (broh-NAH-win) Welsh: "fair breast."

BROOKE (brooke) Old English: "brook" or "stream." Movies and Television: Brooke Adams, actress *(Days of Heaven),* Brooke Shields, actress *(Pretty Baby).* **Brook.**

BRUNHILDA (broon-HILL-dah) Old Greek: "swordbearing woman." History and Music: Wagner's Ring Cycle features Brunhilda, a woman who goes to war. *Hilda, Hilde, Hildie.*

BRYANNA (bree-AN-nah) Irish Gaelic: "power, fortitude." *Brianna, Briona, Bryana, Bryann, Bryanne.*

BRYNN (brin) Welsh: "hill." *Brinn, Brynne.*

BRYONY (bree-oh-NEE) Latin: A European vine characterized by luxurious leaves and small blossoms. *Bronie, Briony.*

BUA (BOO-uh) Vietnamese: "magic chant" or "anvil." Vietnamese lore attributes powers of good fortune and physical well-being to various metals.

BUENA (boo-A-nah) Spanish: "good."

BURDETTE (ber-DET) Middle English: "small bird."

BUTHAINAH (boo-THA-e-nah) Arabic: "soft sand."

CADENCE (KAY-dintz) Latin: "rhythmic flow" or "final chords." *Cadena, Cadenza, Kadena.*

CADY (KAY-dee) Old English: "the simple happiness of a shepherdess." Short form of Arcadia. *Cade, Cadee, Cadey, Cadie, Cadence, Kade.*

CAELAN (CAY-lan) Gaelic: "victorious people."

CAI (kay) Vietnamese: "fair sex."

CAIA (cay-EE-ah) Latin: "to rejoice."

CAILIDA (kah-LEE-dah) Spanish: "compassionate" or "adoring."

CAILIN (KAY-lin) Gaelic: Meaning uncertain. May be variable form of Cayley. *Caylin, Cailyn, Caelan, Calynn, Caileen, Cayleen.*

CAITLIN (KATE-lin) Irish: Variant form of Katherine. Greek for "pure essence." Literature: Caitlin Thomas, writer. Science: Caitlin Brune, experimental psychologist. *Caitilin, Caitlan, Caitlion, Caitlyn, Catlin, Kaitlan, Katelyn.* See Katherine.

CALA (KAH-lah) Arabic: "castle" or "fortress."

CALANDRA (ka-LAHN-drah) Greek, Italian: "singing bird." *Cal, Calendre, Calandria, Callee, Callie, Calinda.*

CALANTHRA (cal-AN-thrah) Greek: "beautiful blossoms."

CALEDONIA (cale-DOE-nee-ya) Latin: "from Scotland."

CALEY (CALE-ee) Gaelic: "slender."

CALIDA (cal-EE-dah) Latin, Spanish: "ardent, warm and loving."

CALLA (cal-LAH) Greek: "beauty."

CALLAN (cal-LAHN) German: "chatter."

CALLIDORA (kah-lee-DORR-ah) Greek: "beauty's gift."

CALLIGENIA (ka-le-JEN-ee-ah) Greek: "child of a lovely goddess." A subtle compliment to the baby's mother.

CALLIOPE (kah-LYE-oh-pee) Greek: "lyrical voice." Literature: The muse of epic poetry. *Kalliope.*

CALLISTA (kah-LISS-ta) Greek: "beautiful." A saint's name. Astrology, Mythology: A nymph who became first a she-bear, and then the constellation known as the Great Bear. Movies and Television: Calista Flockhart, actress in TV's *Ally McBeal. Calesta, Calista, Calisto, Callie, Cally, Callysta, Calissa, Call, Kala, Kallie.*

CALTHA (cal-THAH) Latin: "yellow flower."

CALYPSO (kah-LIP-soh) Greek: "hidden lady." Mythology: Nymph who beguiled Odysseus for seven years. Music: West Indies style of extemporaneous singing.

CAM (kam) Vietnamese: "sweet citrus."

CAMBRIA (kam-BREE-yah) Latin: "from Wales."

CAMELIA (ka-MEEL-yah) Latin: flower name often associated with the name Camille. Politics: Camilla Parker-Bowles, wife of Prince Charles of Wales. *Camilla, Kamelia.*

CAMEO (KAM-ee-o) Italian: "skin." Arts: Popular jewelry piece consisting of a small picture meticulously carved on a gem or shell. *Cammeo.*

CAMILLE (kah-MEEL) Latin, French: "born without fetters." Literature: Camille is an accomplished warrior in the *Aeneid;* character in Alexander

Dumas's play and story; Camilla Collett, nineteenth-century Norwegian novelist, leader of the feminist movement. Music: Camille Saint-Saens, French organist and composer. Czech: *Kamila;* Eng: *Cam, Cama, Camala, Cami, Camila, Camile, Camilla, Camilia, Cammie, Mille, Millie;* Fr: *Camille;* Hung: *Kamilka;* Pol: *Milla.*

CAMMI (KAH-mee) English: From the Latin for camillus, an attendant at religious services. *Cami, Cammie, Cammy.*

CANA (KAH-nah) Turkish: "beloved."

CANDACE (KAN-diss) Possibly Latin: "gleaming" or "impeccably white." History: Title of ancient Ethiopian queens. Movies and Television: Candice Bergen, actress in TV's *Murphy Brown.* Eng: *Candee, Candi, Candie, Candis, Candy, Dace, Dacey, Kandace.*

CANDIDA (kan-DEE-dah) Latin: "dazzling white." Literature: George Bernard Shaw named one of his most sympathetic characters Candida. *Candide,* a novel by Voltaire. Music: *Candide,* a light opera written by Leonard Bernstein. *Candi, Candide, Candie, Candy.*

CANDRA (KAHN-drah) Latin: "luminescent."

CANTARA (kahn-TAH-rah) Arabic: "small crossing."

CAPRICE (kah-PREESE) Italian: "ruled by whim." *Capricia, Caprie, Capriana.*

CAPUCINE (kah-poo-CHEEN) French: "hood." Derived from Italian term for the hooded cloaks worn by certain Franciscan monks. *Cappucine, Capucina.*

CARA (KAH-rah) Latin: "beloved." Astrology: name of a star in the Orion constellation. *Caralea, Caralee, Caralisa, Carella, Cari, Carita, Caroline, Kara, Karry.*

CARAF (KAH-rahf) Welsh: "love."

CARESSE (kah-RESS) French: "tender touch." *Caress, Caressa.*

CAREY (KARE-ee) Welsh, English: "loving." *Caree, Carree.*

CARI (KAR-ee) Turkish: "flows like water."

CARINA (kah-REE-nah) Spanish, Italian: "little darling." *Carena, Carin, Carinna, Cariana, Karina.*

CARISSA (kah-RISS-ah) Greek: "very dear." *Carisa, Carisse.*

CARLA (KAR-lah) English, Italian: "female strength." See Carly; Karla.

CARLOTTA (kar-LOT-ah) Spanish, Italian: Variant form of Charlotte. Dance: Carlotta Grisi, nineteenth-century Italian dancer who created the role in the ballet *Giselle*. **Calota.**

CARLY (KAR-lee) English: "female strength." History: Carly Hills, Secretary of Housing and Urban

Development under President Gerald Ford. Music: Carly Simon, popular American singer. Eng: *Carlee, Carley, Carli;* Ir: *Carleen;* Span: *Carlena, Carlina, Calita.*

CARMELA (kar-MAY-lah) Latin: "bountiful orchard." Refers to Mount Carmel in Israel. *Carmel, Carmelita, Carmella, Carmelle.*

CARMEN (KAR-min) Latin: "sing out." Bible: derived from Mount Carmel, from which the Virgin Mary hailed. Music: Carmen is the ill-fated titular heroine in Bizet's opera. Movies and Television: Carmen Miranda and Carmen Rae, actresses. *Carmelia, Carmelina, Carmelita, Carmencita;* Ital: *Carmina, Carmine, Carmita, Charmaine, Karmen, Lita, Mina.*

CARNA (KAR-nah) Arabic: "horn."

CARNELIAN (KAR-nee-lee-an) Latin: "red gem."

CAROL (KARE-ill) Greek: "man." A century-old name derived from Caroline. Popularity peaked in the 1960s. Movies and Television: popular during the time of actress Carole Lombard. Also actresses Carol Channing *(Hello, Dolly!)* and Carol Burnett (TV's *The Carol Burnett Show).* Sports: Carol Heiss, Olympic gold medalist in figure skating (1960). *Carel, Carey, Cari, Carla, Carleen, Carlene, Carley, Carlin, Carlina, Carline;* Span: *Carlita, Carlota, Carlotta, Carly, Carlyn, Carlynn, Caro, Carola, Carole, Carolena, Carolin, Carolina, Carolinda, Caroline, Caroll, Carolyn, Carrie, Carroll, Carry, Cary, Caryl, Caryll;* Eng: *Charla, Charleen,*

Charlena, Charlene, Charlotte, Charlotta, Charmain, Charmian, Charmion, Cheryl, Cherlyn; Pol: *Ina;* Finn: *Karel, Kari, Karla, Karleen, Karlina, Karlinka, Karlotta, Karole, Karolina, Karyl, Kerril, Lola, Loleta, Lolita;* Swed: *Lotta, Lotte, Lottie, Sharleen, Sharlene, Sharline, Sharmaine, Sharmian.*

CAROLINE (KARE-oh-line) Latin, French: "little, womanly one." Education: Caroline Spurgeon, British educator and first woman to hold professorship. History: Caroline Kennedy, attorney, author, and daughter of President John F. Kennedy; Carolin Norton, nineteenth-century British author and crusader for marriage reform and infant custody laws. *Ina, Inka, Karoline, Karlinka, Lina, Line, Linchen, Linka, Lottchen, Tota.* See variants for Carol.

CARON (KARE-inn) French: "untarnished" or "crystalline." Variant of Karen.

CAROUN (KAR-ohn) Armenian: "spring."

CARRIE (KARE-ee) United States. English. Popular contemporary form of Caroline. History: Carrie Chapman, reformer who led campaign leading to the Nineteenth Amendment, the vote for women. Movies and Television: Carrie Bradshaw, main character of HBO's series *Sex and the City. Cari, Carri, Cary, Kari, Karie, Kary.*

CARSON (KAHR-sin) Scottish: Surname used as first name for girls. Literature: Carson McCullers, author of the novel *The Heart is a Lonely Hunter.*

CASEY (KAYE-see) Irish: "attentive." Short form of Acacia. *Cacey, Casee, Caycee, Cacia.*

CASSANDRA (kah-SAHN-drah) Greek: "conflicting warriors." Literature: Novelist Jane Austen's sister was named Cassandra. Mythology: Name of the Trojan king Priam's daughter upon whom Apollo bestowed prophetic gifts. When she did not return his love, the god turned the people against her. Very popular during the Middle Ages. *Casandera, Casandra, Cass, Cassandre, Cassaundra, Cassie, Cassondra, Cassy, Kasandera, Sande, Sandee, Sandera, Sandie, Sandy, Saundra, Sondra, Zandra.*

CASSIA (KASH-ah) Greek: "spicy cinnamon."

CATHERINE (KA-thur-inn) Latin, Greek: "without tarnish." One of the most popular names in the world. Sports: Catalina Ponor, Romanian Olympic gold medalist for Artistic Gymnastics. Literature: Catherine Barkley, heroine of Hemingway's *A Farewell to Arms;* Catherine Earnshaw, the beautiful but headstrong protagonist of Emily Brontë's *Wuthering Heights.* History: Catherine the Great, Empress of Russia. *Catharin, Catharine, Catherene, Cathrene, Cathrine, Carhryn;* Gael: *Catriona, Caitrin;* Ital/Port: *Catarina;* Span: *Caterina, Cathy, Cathie, Kate, Katharin, Katharine, Katharyn, Katherin, Katherine, Kathi, Kathie, Kathy, Kathren, Kathryn, Kathryne;* Fr: *Trinette, Trina, Trine;* Ger: *Trinchen;* Hung: *Katica, Kato;* Lith: *Kofryna;* Russ: *Katushka, Katryna, Kotinka, Kisa, Kitti, Yekaterina.*

CATHLEEN See Kathleen.

CECILIA (sah-SEE-lyah) Latin: "unseeing." From a Roman clan name. The blind St. Cecilia is the patron saint of music. Movies and Television: Cicely Tyson, actress (*The Rosa Parks Story*). *Cecelia, Cele;* Swed: *Celia, Celie, Cesia, Cesya, Cicilia;* Eng: *Cicely;* Fr: *Cecile, Cecille, C'Ceal, Ceci, Cecia;* Hawaiian: *Kikelia, Kikylia, Sacilia, Sasilia, Sasilie, Seelia, Seelie, Seely, Seslia, Sessaley, Sesseelya, Sessile, Sessilly, Sile, Sileas, Sisely, Siselya, Siseel, Sisiliya, Sissela;* Eng: *Sissie, Sissy.*

CEDRICA (sed-REE-kah) Welsh: "gift of splendor." From Celtic.

CELESTE (seh-LEST) Latin, French: "from the heavens." Literature: Queen Celeste, wife of Babar the elephant, a character in Jean and Laurent de Brunhoff's children's book *Babar.* Movies and Television: Celeste Holm, actress. Span: *Celesta, Celestina, Celestine, Celestyna, Tyna;* Czech: *Tynka;* Fr: *Celestine, Celeste, Celie;* Ital: *Celestina, Cela, Celek, Celstyna, Celina, Celinka, Celka, Cesia;* Pol: *Inka, Inok, Cela, Celestyn, Celestyna, Celina, Celinka, Cesia;* Russ: *Inka, Selinka, Celestia, Celestiel, Celesse, Celisse.*

CELIA (SEEL-yah) English: Variant form of Cecilia. Fr: *Celie, Ceil, Cele, Celina, Celine, Celinda, Celinna, Celenia, Calenne.*

CERISE (sah-REES) French: "cherry" or "cherry red." *Cherise, Sheriz, Sarise, Sharise.*

CERELLA (sah-RELL-ah) Latin: "of the spring." Astrology: Name for a girl born under one of the spring signs: Aries, Taurus, or Gemini. *Cerelia.*

CERES (SEHR-ees) Latin: "of the spring." Mythology: Roman goddess of agriculture and fertility.

CESARA (SEY-sar-ah) Spanish: "long haired."

CHALONDRA (CHAL-oon-DRA) African: "smart."

CHANAH (HAN-ah) Hebrew: "grace."

CHANDI (CHAHN-dee) Hindi: "wrathful" or "threatening." Variant of Shakti, the Hindu goddess who represents the feminine universal energy.

CHANEL (sha-NELL) French: "canal, channel." Arts: Synonymous in contemporary culture with the fashion designed by Coco Chanel. Suggests by association sophistication and wealth. *Chanelle, Channelle, Shanell, Shanelle, Shannelle.*

CHANTAL (shahn-TAHL) French: "rocky location." Common in France. *Chantalle, Chantel, Chantelle, Chantele, Shantal, Shantalle, Shantel, Shantell, Shantelle.*

CHAO-XING (chau-TSEENG) Burmese: "morning star." In Burma, a girl is more often given a nature name than a boy.

CHAPA (CHA-pah) Native American: "superior."

CHARITY (CHARE-ah-tee) Latin: "love for humankind." First popular among the Puritans in the seventeenth century, due to its status as one of the three cardinal virtues (along with Faith and Hope).

Carissa, Carita, Chareese, Charissa, Charisse, Charita, Charitee, Charitey, Cherri, Cherry, Sharitee.

CHARLIZE (SHAR-leez) French: "womanly." Movies and Television: Charlize Theron, South African actress and Academy Award winner (*Monster*).

CHARLOTTE (SHAR-lott or shar-LAH-tuh) French: "petite beauty." Variant of Charles. History: Due to Goethe's calling his heroine Charlotte in *The Sorrows of Werther*, the name took on a tragic romantic flavor in the eighteenth century. Journalism: Charlayne Hunter Gault: first black woman admitted to the University of Georgia, now an anchorwoman for public television. Literature: Charlotte Brontë, eighteenth-century British author. Science: Charlotte Friend, microbiologist. Sports: Charlotte Dod, British athlete. *Carla, Carlie, Carly, Carlene, Charlene, Charline, Cheryl, Karla, Lota, Loleta, Loetta, Lolita, Sharleen, Sharline, Sheri, Sherri, Sherill, Karla;* Czech: *Karlicka;* Fr: *Lolotte;* Ger: *Karla, Lottchen, Lotte, Lotti;* Gk: *Karlotta;* Hung: *Sarolta;* Lat: *Sarlote;* Pol: *Lottie;* Span: *Carlota.*

CHARMAINE (shar-MAYNE) French: "bountiful orchard." Variant form of Carmel. *Charmayne, Charmian, Charmine.*

CHARO (CHAR-oh) Spanish: Pet name for Rosa. Movies and Television: Charo, singer, ex-wife of Xavier Cougat.

CHASTITY (CHASS-tah-tee) Latin, French: "purity" or "innocence." Movies and Television: Chastity

Bono, daughter of singer Cher and Sonny Bono. *Chastity, Chasta, Chastine, Chastina.*

CHAVA (HA-vah) Hebrew: "life" or "animal." Theater: Chava Theeter, one of Tevya's daughters in *Fiddler on the Roof.* **Chabah, Chaya, Chayka, Eva, Hava, Haya, Kaija.**

CHAVI (HAH-vee) English Gypsy: "female child." *Chavali.*

CHAYA (HA-yah) Israel. Hebrew: "living energy" or "aliveness." *Kaija.*

CHELSEA (CHEL-see) Old English: "harbor" or "dock." English place name. Part of a borough of Greater London on the north bank of the river Thames. Also a popular U.S. name. *Chelsa, Chelsi, Chelsie, Chelsy.*

CHENOA (chay-NO-ah) Native American: "pure dove" or "bird of peace." *Shenandoa, Shonoa.*

CHER (share) French: "dear" or "loved one." Variant of Cherie. Movies and Television: Cher, Academy Award-winning actress and singer. Theater: Cherelle Guilfoye, theater historian. *Chere, Cherie, Charee, Chereen, Cherina, Cherine, Cherell.*

CHERILYN (shar-ee-LIN) United States. English: Combination of Cheryl and Lynn common in the United States. *Charlin, Charalyn, Charlynne, Charelyn, Charelynn, Charilyn, Cherilin, Cherilynn, Cherralynn, Cherylyn, Sherrily.*

CHERRY (CHAYR-ee) Old French: "cherry." *Chere, Cheree, Cherey, Cherida, Cherise, Cherita, Cherrey, Cherri, Cherrie.*

CHERYL (SHER-ill) United States. English: Twentieth-century adaptation of Charlotte in the United States. Peaked in the United States in the 1960s. Theater: Cheryl Crawford, producer. *Charil, Charyl, Cheriann, Cheryll, Sherianne, Sheril, Sherill, Sheryl.*

CHESNA (CHESS-nah) Slavic: "bringing peace and calm." *Chessa, Chessy.*

CHEYENNE (shy-ANN) Native American. Algonquin: Name of Algonquin tribe in the Great Plains and the capital of the state of Wyoming. *Cheyanne, Cheyanna, Chiana, Chianna.*

CHIKA (chee-KA) Japanese: "close" or "intimate." Connotes a sense of dear intimacy.

CHINA (CHY-nah) Chinese: Country name used as a first name. Music: Chynna Phillips, singer. *Chynna, Chyna.*

CHINUE (CHEEN-weh) Nigeria. Ibo: "God's own blessing."

CHIQUITA (CHIK-ee-tah) Spanish: "little girl."

CHIYO (CHEE-yo) Japanese: "thousand years" or "eternal."

CHLOE (KLOH-ee) Greek: "fresh-blooming." Mythology: name is related to Demeter, the goddess of fertility. *Chloe, Clo, Cloe.*

CHLORIS (KLO-riss) Greek: "green." Mythology: Name of a minor goddess of vegetation. Movies and Television: Cloris Leachman, actress (TVs *The Mary Tyler Moore Show*). **Cloris, Clorissa.**

CHO (cho) Japanese: "butterfly."

CHOLENA (ko-LEE-nah) Native American. Delaware: "that which soars."

CHRISANN (kriss-AHN) Greek, English: "golden flower." Variant name of Saint Chrysantus. *Chrisanne, Chrisanna, Chrysann, Crisann;* Span: *Crisann, Chrysanta, Chrysandra.*

CHRISTA (KRISS-tah) Greek: "anointed one" or "denoted to Christ." Sports: Christa Rothenburger, German speed skater. Science: Christa McAuliffe, Challenger astronaut and teacher. *Chrysta;* Span: *Crista, Crysta.*

CHRISTABEL (criss-tah-BELL) Latin: "beautiful Christian." Literature: Title character of Samuel Taylor Coleridge's poem. *Cristabel, Cristabell, Christabella, Christabelle, Christobel, Chrystabel, Chrystalbelle, Chrystobel, Crystabella, Crystabel.*

CHRISTEN (KRISS-tin) English: Variant of Christian. Greek: "christos" or "anointed." Science: Christen Raunkiaer, Danish botanist who developed classifications for plants. *Chris, Christy, Christin, Cristen, Kristen, Krysten, Krystin.*

CHRISTINA (kriss-TEE-nah) English: "Christian." One of the most popular names in the world. Literature: Christina Rossetti, nineteenth-century British poet; Christina Stead, Australian novelist (*The Man Who Loved Children*). Science: Christiane Nüsslein-Volhard, German Nobel Laureate (1995) for her genetic discoveries. Sports: Chris Evert, tennis champion. Eng: *Chrissy, Christie, Christy, Chrystal, Crystal, Cristina, Krissi, Krissie, Krissy, Tina, Crystina, Krista, Krystin, Kristina, Kristinka*; Czech: *Tyna*; Finn: *Kristia*; Fr: *Christiane, Christel*; Ger: *Christa, Christiane, Chrystel, Stina, Tine*; Ir: *Cristin, Crisiona*; Ital: *Cristina*; Lat: *Krista, Kristine*; Pol: *Krysta, Krystyna, Krystnka*; Port: *Cristina*; Russ: *Khristina, Khristyna, Tina*; Scan: *Kirsten, Kirstin, Christiana, Crystina, Crystine, Khristeen, Kit, Kris, Kristi.*

CHRISTMAS (KRISS-miss) Old English: The day of Christ's birth, adapted as a given name in the 1800s, but later replaced by Noel, the French translation.

CHRYSEIS (kriss-ICE) Latin: "daughter with the golden tresses." Literature: name of a girl with great beauty in *The Iliad* by Homer. *Chrysille.*

CHU HUA (chu-WHO-ah) Chinese: "rainbow blossom." Flowers in East Asian lore are often symbols of magic and transformation.

CHUKI (CHOO-kee) Swahili: "a blessing among enemies."

CHUMANI (shoo-MAHN-ee) Native American. Sioux: "drops of dew."

CHUN (chwen) Burmese: "eternal return" or "nature's renewal."

CINDY See Cynthia.

CIRA (CHEE-rah) Italian: "sun."

CLAIBORNE (CLAY-born) Old English: "born of the earth." Business: Liz Claiborne, one of the original founders of Liz Claiborne, Inc, which designs clothing for men and women.

CLAIRE (klaire) English: "bright, shining, and gentle." A popular name in the United States and France. Aeronautics: Claire Chennault, aviator who formed "Flying Tigers" group to aid China. Business: Claire Giannini Hoffman, first woman to serve on Board of Directors of Sears, Roebuck and Co. (1963). Theater: Claire Luce, actress in Ziegfield Follies. Eng: *Clair, Clarita, Clare, Clarie, Clarina, Clarice, Clarissa, Clarisse;* Fr: *Clairette, Clarette;* Ger: *Clarissa, Klarissa;* Hung: *Klarika;* Ital: *Chiara, Clarissa;* Slav: *Klara;* Span: *Clareta, Clarisa, Chiara, Ciara, Clair, Claireen, Clairene, Claireta, Clairette, Clerissa, Klaire, Klara, Klaretta, Klarissak, Klaryce, Klayre, Kliara, Klyara.*

CLARA (KLAIR-ah) Latin: "bright" or "clear." History: Clara Barton, founder of the American Red Cross in 1881. Literature: Clara Peeters, a pioneer of still life painting in the early seventeenth century.

CLAUDIA (CLAW-dee-ah) Latin: "limping." Derived from a clan name. Literature: French novelist Colette used the name Claudine in her novels. *Claude, Claudelle, Claudetta, Claudette, Claudie, Claudina, Claudine, Claudey, Claudy.*

CLEMENCE (clem-EN-say) French: "clemency" or "mercy." Mythology: In Roman mythology, Clemence was the goddess of pity. *Clementina, Clementine.*

CLEO (KLEE-oh) Greek: Short form of Cleopatra. Literature, Mythology: Clio is the mythological muse of historic poetry. Music: Cleo Laine, British jazz singer.

COCHETA (co-SHAY-tah) Native American: "that which cannot be fathomed."

COLLEEN (col-LEEN) Irish: "girl." *Colleena, Collene.*

COLUMBIA (co-LUM-be-yah) Old English: "dove."

COMFORT (kome-FORT) French: "strength." *Comforte.*

CONSTANCE: (KAHN-stintz) Latin: "constancy" or "unwavering." Literature: Constance Fenimore Woolson, author of novel *Dorothy*. Music: Connie Francis, singer. Theater: Constance MacKenzie, actress. *Connie;* Span: *Constancia;* Ital: *Constantina;* Lat: *Constantia, Constancy, Constanta, Constanza.*

CONSUELO (kon-SWAY-loh) Spanish: "comfort from the heart." Variation of Dolores. Literature: Consuelo is the beautiful Venetian singer in George Sand's 1842 novel of that title. A gypsy girl raised in the streets of Venice, she becomes a successful opera singer.

CORA (KOR-rah) English, Greek: "maiden." Literature: Cora Munroe, heroine in James Fenimore Cooper's 1826 novel *The Last of the Mohicans*. Possibly a variant form of Kore. *Coralee, Coralyn, Corlene, Corella, Coretta, Corinne, Corinna, Corissa, Corrissa, Coryn, Corynn, Corrin.*

CORAZON (kor-ah-ZAHN) Spanish: "heart." History: Corazon Aquino, former president of the Philippines. *Corazana.*

CORBY (KOR-bee) English: Place name.

CORDELIA (KOR-deel-ee-yah) Latin: "rope," "heart," or "a sea jewel." Literature: Cordelia, character in William Shakespeare's play *King Lear*. She is the youngest and most loyal of Lear's three daughters.

CORINTHIA (ko-RIN-thee-ah) Greek: "woman of Corinth."

CORLISS (KOR-lihs) Old English: "cheerful and generous."

CORNELIA (cor-NEEL-ee-ah) Latin: "hornlike." Very common in ancient Rome. Education: Cornelia Clapp, zoologist and teacher.

COURTNEY (KORT-nee) Old French: "noble bred" or "lady-in-waiting." Movies and Television: Courtney Gibbs, Miss U.S.A. (1988); Courteney Cox, actress (TV's *Friends*).

COVENTINA (KOVE-en-tina) Celtic: "water goddess."

COZETTE (koh-ZET) French: "little pet." Literature: In Victor Hugo's *Les Misérables*, Cosette is Jean Valjean's beloved adopted daughter. *Cosette.*

CRESENT (KRES-sent) Old French: "one who creates."

CRYSTAL (kriss-TAHL) Latin: "brilliantly transparent." Like Sapphire, names relating to precious or semi-precious stones denote high value and great healing powers. *Chrystal, Cristel, Cristol, Krystal, Kristol.*

CWEN (kwen) Celtic: "queen." *Cwene.*

CYBELE (si-BELL) Greek, Roman: "mother." Mythology: An Asiatic nature goddess known as the Great Mother.

CYBIL (SIH-bull) Latin: Variant form of Sibyl. Movies and Television: Cybill Shepherd, actress. Mythology: In Greek myth, Cybil can foresee the future. *Cybill, Cybilla, Cybilene.*

CYNTHIA (SINN-thee-ah) Greek mythology: One of the names of Artemis, the goddess of the moon. Her birthplace was Mount Cynthus. Arts: Cindy

Sherman, photographer. History: Edmund Spenser gave Queen Elizabeth I that name. Dance: Cynthia Gregory, ballerina. Literature: Cynthia Freeman, novelist. Eng: *Cindi, Cindie, Cindy, Cinthia, Cyndi, Cynth, Cynthie;* Gk: *Kynthia;* Port: *Cintia;* Span: *Cintia, Cyntia.*

CYRAH (SEER-ah) African: "enthroned." Cyrene is the name of an ancient city on the north coast of Africa. *Cyra, Cyrena, Cyrina, Cyrene.*

CYRILLA (SEER-ill-lah) Greek: "lordly and proud."

CZARINA (zar-REE-nah) Latin, Russian: "empress."

DABRIA (DAB-ree-yah) Latin: "name of an angel."

DACEY (DAY-see) Gaelic: "from the south" or "down below." Girls in the United States today have appropriated this once-male name. *Dacie, Dacy, Dasi, Dasie, Dasy.*

DAGMAR (DAHG-mar) Scandinavian: "day maid"; Old German: "brilliant mind" or "day to remember." A strong-sounding name that has infiltrated many countries, particularly Germany, Scandinavia, and Eastern Europe. Czech: *Dagmara, Dasa;* Est: *Dagi, Dagmara;* Pol: *Daga.*

DAGNY (DAG-nee) Old Norse: "release from darkness." A Norwegian adaptation of the masculine Dag.

DAHLIA (DAL-yah) Swedish: "valley." The flower was named for botanist Anders Dahl. Afr: *Dalia;* Isr: *Daliah.*

DAI (dye) Japanese: "great."

DAISY (DAY-zee) Old English: "day's eye." A flower used as a first name. Literature: Daisy Buchanan, character in F. Scott Fitzgerald's *The Great Gatsby*; Heroine of Henry James's novelette *Daisy Miller*. *Daisie, Daisi, Daisey, Daizy, Daysi, Deysi, Daisha, Dacia, Dacey, Dacy, Deyci.*

DAKOTA (dah-KOH-tah) Native American: "friend, ally." Tribal name.

DALE (dayl) English: "small valley." Movies and Television: Dale Evans, actress and wife of Roy Rogers. *Dalena, Dalenna (short forms for Madeleine), Dayle, Dalene, Dalena, Dalina, Dalenna;* Dutch: *Dael, Daly, Daelyn;* Scand: *Dahl, Dallana.*

DALILA (dah-LEE-lah) Hebrew: "twig" or "water bearer." *Dalice.*

DALLAS (DA-liss) Scottish: "of the dales and meadows." Name of Texas city used as given name. *Dallis.*

DAMALI (dah-MAH-lee) Arabic: "beautiful vision."

DAMARA (dah-MAR-ah) Greek: "gentle girl."

DAMHNAIT (DEV-nat) Irish: "poet." Old Irish names are very popular in Ireland now. *Devnet, Downet, Dympha.*

DAMIA (dah-MEE-ah) French: "untamed." *Damiana, Damiane, Damien.*

DAMITA (dah-MEE-tah) Spanish: "baby princess."

DANA (DAY-nah) Polish: "gift"; Celtic: "great womb." She who gave birth to the pantheon of gods was called Dana in Celtic lore. Sports: Dana Zatopkova, javelin thrower and oldest Olympic medalist. *Dane, Denia, Daney.*

DANAE (da-NAY) Greek mythology: The daughter of Acrisius who was seduced by Zeus in a golden rain and gave birth to Perseus. Variants follow the "De—" name pattern. *Danay, Danaye, Danee, Denae, Denay.*

DANICA (DAN-i-kah) Slavic: "morning star." *Dannica, Danika, Dannika.*

DANIELLE (dan-YELL) French: "divine judgments." Since the name originally derived from the biblical Daniel, who was a prophet, it can symbolize great psychic powers of insight. Sports: Danielle Goyette, Canadian gold medalist for ice hockey (2002). Literature: Danielle Steel, novelist who had at least one book on the best-seller lists for a record of 393 consecutive weeks. Span: *Daniela;* Heb: *Danika;* Russ: *Danikla;* Eng: *Danilla, Daniella, Daniele, Danyelle, Donielle.*

DANNA (DAH-nah) Hebrew: Place name. Bible: A village in Judea. Variant of Daniel and Danny. Span/Ital: *Dani, Dannee, Danni, Dany, Danelle, Dannell, Dannelle, Dannon, Danitza, Danice,*

Danise, Danette, Danita, Dannia, Danya, Dania, Dannalee, Dantina, D'Anna, Dannah.

DAPHNE (DAFF-nee) Greek: "laurel tree." Mythology: The gods changed Daphne into a laurel tree to shield her from Apollo, who loved her. Literature: Daphne DuMaurier, British writer (*Rebecca*). *Daphney;* Isr: *Dafne, Daphna.*

DARA (DARE-rah) Hebrew: "wise." The name of a descendant of Judah noted for his wisdom. Also a Gaelic name meaning "strong." *Dahra, Darah, Darra, Darrah, Dareen, Darissa, Darice.*

DARBY (DAR-bee) English: Place name. Derived from Derby, a surname used as a first name.

DARCY (DAR-see) Gaelic: "O Dorchaidhe" or "dark man's descendant." An English place name and surname. Dance: Darci Kistler, ballerina. *Darcie, Darci, Darcey, D'Arcy, Darcia, Darcel, Darcell, Darcelle, Darchelle.*

DARIA (DAH-ree-ah) Greek: "luxurious." *Darielle, Dariele, Darrelle, Darian, Darienne, Darianna.*

DARLENE (dahr-LEEN) English: Modern adaptation of the Old English "dearling," or "darling." *Darla, Darline, Darleen, Darlena, Darlina, Darleena, Darleane.*

DARNELL (dahr-NELL) English: "disguised." Place name and surname. *Darnelle, Darnae, Darnisha, Darnetta.*

DARYL (DARE-ill) Old French: "small and dear." Movies and Television: Daryl Hannah, actress. *Daryll, Darryll, Darrill, Darylene, Darylyn, Darolyn, Darrylynn.*

DARYN (DARE-inn) Greek: "gift." *Daryan, Darynne.*

DASHA (DAH-shah) Greek: "divine display." Slavic variant of Dorothy.

DAVIDA (da-VEE-dah) Israel. Hebrew: "beloved." *Davita, Davina, Davia, Davonna, Davy, Davynn, Daveen, Davine, Davianna.*

DAWN (dawn) Middle English: "fresh light." Literature: Dawn Powell, novelist (*The Golden Spur*). Movies and Television: Dawn Steel, Hollywood producer. Sports: Dawn Fraser, Australian Olympic gold medalist. *Dawna, Dawne, Dawnika, Dawnette, Dawnetta, Dawnelle, Dawnielle.*

DAYO (DAH-yoh) Nigeria. Yoruba: "joy arrives."

DEANDRA (dee-AN-dra) Contemporary American blend of Deanne plus variants of Andrea and Sandra. *Deandrea, Deandria, Deeandra, Diandra, Diandre, Dianda, Deanda.*

DEANNA (dee-AN-nah) Old English: Variant form of Diana. *Deanne, Deann, Deeana, Deeann, Deeanna, Deana, Deena, Deane, Deonna, Deonne, Deona, Deondra.*

DEBORAH (DEH-bor-rah) Hebrew: "stinger" or "bee." Name of great power, indicating penetrating effect and industriousness. Bible: Name of the Hebrew judge who rallied the Israelites to freedom from the Canaanites. The victory song she wrote is part of the Book of Judges. Dance: Debbie Allen, choreographer and actress. Journalism: Deborah Norville, TV and radio reporter. Music: Deborah Harry, singer for the rock group Blondie. Movies and Television: Debra Messing, actress (TV's *Will and Grace*). *Debra, Debbie, Debrah, Debby;* Span: *Debora;* Eng: *Debra, Debralee;* Heb: *Devora;* Ger: *Deboran;* Yiddish: *Dwora.*

DEGULA (deh-GOO-lah) Israel. Hebrew: "of wide renown" or "marvelous."

DEIDRE (DEE-dra) Gaelic: "sadness." History: Legendary Irish heroine with a beauty comparable to that of Helen of Troy and a story as tragic. Literature: Title of two plays by William Butler Yeats. Sports: Deidre Dionne, 2002 Canadian medalist in freestyle skiing. *Dee, Deedee, Deirdre, Deidra, Deedra, Diedra, Diedre.*

DEKA (DEE-kah) Somalian: "pleasing."

DELANEY (de-LAY-nee) Irish: Surname. Eng: *Delayne, Delayna;* Fr: *Delaina, Delaine.*

DELANNA (del-AHN-nah) Italian: "soft as wool."

DELFINA (del-FEEN-ah) Latin: "dolphin." Variant form of Delphine, the name of a thirteenth-century French saint.

DELIA (DEE-lee-ah) English, Greek: "visible"; "of Delos." Place name. Mythology: The island of Delos was the birthplace of Artemis. Delia is also a short form of Cordelia and Adelia. History: Delia Akely, first Western woman to lead an expedition across the African continent. Literature: Delia Salter Bacon, nineteenth-century writer who headed an attempt to prove that Francis Bacon wrote Shakespeare's plays. *Del, Delise, Delys, Delyse.*

DELICIA (de-LEE-sha) Latin: "pleasure-giver." *Delisa, Delisha, Dalisha, Delissa, Delyssa, Deliza, Delight.*

DELILAH (dee-LYE-lah) Hebrew: "craving love." Bible: Woman who discovered the source of Samson's strength was his hair. *Delia, Dalila.*

DELLA (DELL-ah) Variant form of Adelle meaning "of the nobility." Music: Della Reese, singer. *Dell.*

DELMA (DELL-mah) Spanish: "of the sea." *Delmar, Delmare, Delmara.*

DELMELZA (de-MELL-zah) English: Fortified place name in Cornwall, England.

DELTA (DEL-tah) Greek: Fourth letter of the Greek alphabet. Also, an alluvial deposit at the mouth of a river, such as the Mississippi Delta.

DELU (day-LOO) Africa. Hausa: "female blessing in a family of men."

DEMETRIA (de-MEE-tree-ah) Greek: "of Demeter." Movies and Television: actress Demi Moore (*Ghost*). Mythology: Demeter was the goddess of corn and harvest. *Demetra, Demitra, Dimetria, Demitras, Demeter, Demi.*

DENA (DAY-nah) Native American: "low-lying meadow." *Dene, Denia, Deneen, Denny, Denica.*

DENISE (de-NEES) French: "Dionysian." Arts: Denise Scott Brown, architect. *Denice, Deniece, Dennisha;* Span: *Denisa.*

DERICA (dare-EE-kah) German, English: Contemporary: "beloved leader." *Dereka, Derrica, Dericka.*

DERORA (de-ROH-rah) Israel. Hebrew: "running streams" or "free bird." *Derorice, Derorit.*

DERRY (DARE-ee) Irish: Surname also used as a short form of names like Derica. *Deri, Derrie.*

DERVAL (dehr-VAL) Irish: "true desire." *Dervla, Dervilia.*

DESIREE (dez-a-RAY) French: "ardently desired." *Desirae, Diseraye, Desarae, Dsaree, Diziree, Dezarae, Dezirae;* Eng: *Desire, Desyre.*

DESSA (DESS-ah) Greek: "roaming nomadically."

DESTINY (DESS-tah-nee) English, French: "one's fortune" or "fate." *Destinee, Destinie, Destini, Destanee, Destine,* Span: *Destina.*

DEVA (DEE-vah) Hindi: "celestial spirit." In Hindu tradition, a *deva* is a shining or dazzling being of light whom devotees invoke for various blessings.

DEVAKI (dah-vah-KEE) Hindi: "dark." The mother of the enlightened Krishna, and so highly revered as a goddess herself.

DEVANY (DEV-a-nee) Gaelic: "dark-haired." *Devenny, Devaney, Davanie, Devinee, Devony.*

DEVI (DAY-vee) Hindi: "goddess." One of the many names for Shakti, the creative power of the Divine and personified by a goddess.

DEVON (deh-VAHN) English: Name of a country in England noted for its beautiful farmland and thick cream. An English place name. *Devan, Devyn, Devynn, Devana, Devanna, Devonna, Devonne, Devona, Devondra, Devonette;* Eng/Fr: *Devin.*

DEVORA (deh-VOR-ah) See Deborah.

DEWANDA (deh-WAHN-dah) United States. English: Contemporary African-American creation, a blend of De and Wanda.

DIAMOND (DYE-mund) Greek, English: "of high value." The April birthstone was first introduced as a female name in the 1890s. *Diamonique, Diamante, Diamanda, Diamontina.*

DIANA (dye-AHN-ah) Latin: "celestial" or "god-like." Arts: Diane Arbus, photographer. History: the late Princess Diana, ex-wife of Prince Charles of

Britain. Journalism: Diane Sawyer, TV anchor woman. Music: Diana Ross, popular singer; Diahann Carroll, actress and singer. Mythology: As the Roman goddess of the moon and the chase, she was the counterpart to Artemis and Phoebe in Greek mythology. Science: Dian Fossey, studied mountain gorillas in their natural environment. *DeeDee, Di, Didi, Dian, Dianna, Dianne, Diane, Diahna, Diahann, Diandra, DiAnne, Dee, Deanna, Dede, Dyanna, Dyann, Dyana.*

DIANTHA (dye-ANN-tha) Contemporary blend of Diana and Anthea.

DIANTHE (dye-ANN-tha) Greek: "flower of the gods." *Diandre, Diantha.*

DIATA (dy-AH-tah) African: "lion."

DIDO (DYE-do) Greek: Name. Literature: In Vergil's *Aeneid,* she is the queen of Carthage who receives the shipwrecked Aeneas, falls in love with him, then kills herself after he rejects her. Music: Dido Armstrong, popular British singer in America.

DIELLE (dee-ELL) French: "god." *Diella.*

DILYS (de-LEES) Welsh: "perfection."

DINA (DEE-nah) Hebrew: "God has judged. God has vindicated." Bible: Jacob's only daughter. *Deena.*

DINAH (DYE-nah) English: Variant of Dina. Literature: Dinah Mulock Craik, nineteenth-century novelist and author of children's stories. Movies and Television: Dinah Shore, TV entertainer. *Dyna, Dinorah, Diondra;* Span: *Dina, Denora.*

DIONNE (dee-ON) Greek: "devotee of Dionysus." Music: Dionne Warwick, popular singer. Mythology: Name of the mother of the Greek goddess Aphrodite. *Deonne, Dione, Diona, Dionia, Dionna.*

DIOR (dee-ORR) French: "golden." *D'Or.*

DIVINA (dah-VEE-nah) Italian: "divine one." Also a variant of Davina; Israel. Hebrew: "loved one." *Divinia.*

DIXIE (DIX-ee) French: "tenth." Refers to the states below the Mason-Dixon line. Science: Dixy Lee Ray, marine biologist. *Dixee, Dixy.*

DODIE (do-DEE) Hebrew: "beloved." Familiar form of Dora and Dorothy. *Dodee, Dodey, Dodi, Dody.*

DOLLY (DOLL-ee) American: familiar form of Dorothy. History: Dolly Madison, First Lady. Music: Dolly Parton, country singer. *Dollee, Dolley, Dollie.*

DOLORES (dah-LORR-us) Latin, Spanish: "weeping heart" or "sorrow." History: Dolores Huerta, co-founder of the United Farm Workers. *Delores, Doloris.*

DOMINIQUE (dah-mi-NEEK) Latin, French: "of the Lord." Music: "Dominique" was a popular song performed by the Singing Nun during the sixties. *Dominica;* Span: *Domenica, Domenique, Dominee.*

DONATELLA (doh-NAH-tel-lah) Italian: "beautiful star."

DONNA (DAHN-ah) Latin, Italian: "lady." A title akin to Don for men. Music: Donna Summer, singer. *Donni, Donnie, Donielle, Donelle, Donella, Donisha, Donetta, Donya, Dahnya, Dahna, Donnalee, Donnalyn, Donna-Marie;* Span: *Dona.*

DORA (DORR-ah) Greek: "present" or "talent." Literature: Popularized as the given name of a character in Charles Dickens's novel *David Copperfield. Dodee, Dodi, Dodie, Dody, Doralia, Doralyn, Doralynn, Doreen, Dorelia, Dorelle, Dorena, Dorenne, Dorette, Dori, Dorie, Dorita, Dorrie, Dory.*

DOREEN (dorr-EEN) Gaelic: "mourning." French: "gold-laid." One of the most popular British names during the twenties. *Dorene, Doreyn, Dorine, Doryne.*

DORETTA (door-ETT-ah) Greek: "gift from God." Variant of Dora.

DORIA (DORR-ee-ah) Greek: Place name. A city in Greece called "Doris." Also variant of Dora, Dorothy, and Theodora. Military: Doric Miller, Navy hero during Pearl Harbor attack. Awarded the Navy Cross. Sports: Doriane Vidal, 2002 Olympic medalist for snowboarding. *Dori, Dorian, Doriane, Dorianne, Dorice, Dory.*

DORINDA (dorr-IN-dah) Greek, Spanish: Elaborate adaptation of Dora.

DORIS (DORR-iss) Greek: "overflowing graces." Doris was the gray-eyed wife of Nereus and the mother of at least fifty sea nymphs. Dance: Doris Humphrey, choreographer. Literature: Doris Lessing, English novelist who resided for many years in Southern Rhodesia and wrote *The Golden Notebook*. Movies and Television: Doris Day, actress. *Dora, Dorris, Dorice, Dorisa, Dotty;* Hawaiian: *Dorisa;* Heb: *Dorit;* Eng: *Dorita;* Czech: *Dorka.*

DOROTHY (DORR-uh-thee) Greek: "divine present." Arts: Dorothea Lange, photographer. Movies and Television: Heroine of the book and movie *The Wizard of Oz.* Politics: Dorothy Day, founder of the Catholic worker movement; Dorothea Dix, crusader for humane care of the mentally ill. Science: Dorothy Hodgkin, Nobel Prize-winning chemist. Sports: Dorothy Hamill, ice skater. *Dorothea; Dorothee, Dorotha, Dortha, Doro, Dorrit, Dory, Dotty, Dolly, Dollie, Theodora;* Span: *Dorotea.*

DORRIT (DORR-it) Greek: Variant of Dorothy. Literature: Titular protagonist of Charles Dickens's novel *Little Dorrit*. **Doria, Doritt.**

DORY (DORR-ee) French: "golden." Also diminutive form of Dorothy.

DOUCE (doose) French: "sweet."

DREA (DREH-ah) Greek: "courageous."

DREW (dru) Old French: "sturdy." Greek: "vision." Movies and Televison: Drew Barrymore, actress (*Charlie's Angels*).

DRINA (DREE-nah) Spanish: "fighter for justice." Short form of Alexandra. *Dreena.* See Alexandra.

DRUSILLA (dru-SILL-ah) Latin: "mighty." Bible: Paul referred to Drusilla in the Book of Acts. *Drucie, Drucilla, Drucy, Druscilla, Drusy, Drew.*

DUANA (d'WAH-nay) Irish: "dark." *Duna, Duayna, Dwana.*

DUENA (d'WAY-nah) Spanish: "protect the companion."

DULCE (DOOL-cee) Latin: "sweet" or "sweetness." Literature: Dulcinea del Toboso is a character in Cervantes's *Don Quixote*. *Delcina, Delcine, Delsine, Dulce, Dulcea, Dulci, Dulcia, Dulciana, Dulcibella, Dulcibelle, Dulcine, Dulcinea, Dulcina.*

DURENE (DUR-een-eh) Latin: "everlasting."

DUSCHA (DOO-shah) Russian: "divine spirit." An independent name often used as a term of endearment or in intimate encounters.

DUSTY (DUST-ee) English: Place name. Music: Dusty Springfield, singer. *Dustee.*

DYLANA (dah-LAHN-ah) Welsh: "ocean-born." Literature: Popularized by the poet Dylan Thomas.

DYANI (dah-YAHN-ee) Native American: "gazelle." Indian lore posits the deer or gazelle as a powerful animal, but one whose real strength lay hidden behind a graceful docility.

EADLIN (eh-DLYN) Irish: "princess."

EADOIN (eh-DEEN) Irish: "blessed with many friends."

EARLINA (ear-LYNA) English: "noble woman." *Earline.*

EARTHA (ER-tha) Old English: "earth's daughter." Astrology: Best for girls born under an earth sign. Music: Eartha Kitt, jazz singer. *Erta, Hertha.*

EASTER (EE-ster) English: Holiday name adapted as a given name in the 1800s. Related to French version Pascale.

EAVAN (ee-VON) Celtic: "fair one." Literature: Eavan Boland, renowned Irish poet.

EBBA (EHB-bah) German: "strength."

EBERTA (ee-BUR-tah) Teutonic: "shiny."

EBONY (EBB-ah-nee) Greek, Egyptian: "black." Very dark, black wood. *Eboni, Ebonee, Ebonique.*

ECHO (EK-oh) Greek: "sound returned." Mythology: A nymph whose unrequited love for Narcissus led her to disappear, leaving only her voice behind. *Ekko.*

EDA (EHD-ah) Old English: "rich." Possibly a variant of Edith. *Ede.*

EDANA (eh-DAHN-ah) Gaelic: "tiny flame." History: St. Aidan was a seventh-century Irish monk. *Aidana, Aydana, Ede.*

EDDA (EDD-ah) German: "with clear goals." Variant form of Hedda or Hedwig. *Eda.*

EDELINE (EDD-ah-leen) Old Greek: "high born" or "royal." Variation of Adeline.

EDEN (EE-den) Hebrew: "pleasing delights." Place name. The name of Adam and Eve's original garden of paradise. History: Eden Gomez, Nicaraguan rebel leader. Literature: Eden Phillpotts, British novelist who describes Devonshire. Span: *Edenia, Edana.*

EDENA (ee-DEE-nah) Hawaiian. Kahuna: Variation of Edna. See Edna.

EDITH (EE-dith) Old English: "precious treasure." Arts: Edith Head, Hollywood designer. Literature: Edith Wharton, author of the novel *Age of Innocence*. Eng: *Eda, Edia, Editha, Ediva, Edyth, Edythe, Eyde;* Czech: *Dita, Edita;* Ger: *Editha;* Hawaiian: *Edi;* Hung: *Duci, Edit;* Ital: *Edita;* Pol: *Edka, Edda, Ita.*

EDMONDA (ed-MON-dah) Anglo-Saxon: "wealthy defender."

EDNA (EDD-nah) Hebrew: "renewal of spirit." Literature: Poet Edna St. Vincent Millay, Pulitzer Prize-winning poet noted for her verse of the 1920s celebrating life. *Edena.*

EDLYN (EDD-lin) Old English: "noble one."

EDREA (ed-DREE-ah) Old English: "rich and strong." *Edra, Eidra, Eydra.*

EDWARDINE (EDD-wer-dyne) Old English: "rich protector." *Edwarda, Edwardeen, Edwardene, Edwardyne.*

EDWIGE (ED-wig) French from Old Greek: "pleasing strife." *Edvig, Edwig, Hedvig, Hedwibe.*

EDWINA (ed-WEE-nah) Old English: "prosperous friend." *Edina, Edween, Edwiena, Edwena, Edwyna.*

EFFIE (EFF-ee) Greek: "melodious talk." Peaked as an independent name in the middle of the nineteenth century. Theater: Character in the Broadway musical *Dreamgirls*. **Effi, Effy, Ephie, Eppie, Euphemia, Euphemie, Euphie.**

EGA (AY-guh) Nigeria. Yoruban: "palm bird." Refers to a saying: "Those who do not fathom the palm bird's cry merely criticize its shriek."

EGLANTINE (EGG-lin-teen) Old French: "sweet-briar." *Eglantyne.*

EIBBLIN (ebb-LIN) Gaelic: "luminescent glow." Like Evelyn, Helen, or Eileen.

EILEEN (eye-LEEN) Irish: "brillantine light." Derived from Helen. Popular Irish name made trendy in Britain in the early 1900s. Business: Eileen Ford, owner of modeling agency. Music: Eileen Farrell, opera star. *Aileen, Ailene, Alene, Aline, Ayleen, Eilleen, Eiley, Eily, Ileana;* Slav: *Lina.*

EILIS (AY-lis) Celtic: "God's oath."

EIRENE (ee-REH-nee) Old Norse: "eternal calm." Popular in Scandinavian countries.

EITHNE (ith-NEE) Irish: "fiery." *Aine, Aithnea, Eithne, Ethnah, Ethnea, Ethnee.*

ELA (EHL-lah) Portuguese: "she." Music: Ella Fitzgerald, jazz singer.

ELAINE (ee-LAYNE) French: Variant form of Helen. Mythology: In the tales from the Round Table, Elaine is a young woman who pines achingly for Sir Lancelot, and in some versions gives birth to his son Galahad. Literature: Tennyson's version of this tale ends tragically in her death. *Alaina, Alayna, Alayne, Allaine, Elaina, Elana, Elane, Elanna,*

Elayne, Ellaina, Ellaine, Ellane, Ellayne, Lainey, Layney.

ELATA (eh-LAH-ta) Latin: "lofty" or "elevated."

ELBERTA (el-BUR-tah) Teutonic: "nobly brilliant."

ELDA (ell-DAH) Anglo-Saxon: "wise."

ELDORA (ell-DORR-ah) Spanish: "gold-laden." *Eldoree, Eldoria, Eldoris.*

ELEANOR (ELL-ah-norr) Greek: "light." Variant of Helen. History: Eleanor of Aquitaine, name of one of the strongest queens in English history and wife of Henry II; Eleanor Roosevelt, wife of President Franklin Delano Roosevelt, was one of the most politically active First Ladies in the United States. Literature: Eleanor Trent, character in Dickens's *The Old Curiosity Shop;* Elinor Devine, author of *You're Standing in My Light.* Eng: *Elaine, Eleanore, Elen, Elenor, Elenora, Elenore, Eleonora, Eleonare, Elianore, Elinor, Elinore, Elia, Elleanor, Elleaora, Elleanor, Elleanora, Elli, Ellie, Ellinor, Ellinore, Elnora, Enora, Helenora, Lena, Lenora, Lenore, Leonora, Leonore, Leora, Lina, Nelda, Nelle, Nelley, Nelli, Nellie, Nelly, Nonnie, Nora, Norah, Norina;* Czech: *Elena.*

ELECTRA (eh-LEK-trah) Greek: "brilliant light." The name has the same roots as the word "electricity." Mythology, Theater: The heroine of Greek tragedies about the House of Atreus, told by Aeschylus, Euripides, and Sophocles, and retold by

Eugene O'Neill in the play *Mourning Becomes Electra*. **Elektra.**

ELENI (eh-LAY-nee) Greek: "illumination" or "light-bearer." Variant of Helen. Ger: *Elenitsa;* Czech: *Elenka;* Eng: *Elenora;* Span: *Eleonor;* Heb: *Eleora;* Hawaiian: *Elese.* See Helen.

ELDORIS (el-DOOR-is) Greek: "of the sea."

ELESE (eh-LEZ-ee) Old German: "noble." Hawaiian form of Elsie.

ELFRIDA (ell-FREE-dah) Old English: "magic of the elves." Literature: Elfriede Jelinek, Austrian winner of the Nobel Prize for Literature (2004). *Elfie, Elfre, Elfredah, Elfredda, Elfreeda, Elfrieda, Elfryda, Elfreyda, Ellfreyda, Elva, Elvah, Freda, Freddi, Freddy, Freeda, Frieda, Friedah, Fryda.*

ELGA (ELL-gah) Slavic: "holy." *Elgiva, Heiga.*

ELIDI (eh-LEE-dee) Derivation unknown: "solar graces." Astrology: Excellent name for a child born under a fire sign or at the peak of summer.

ELIORA (eh-LEE-oh-rah) Hebrew: "God illuminates the soul." Popular in contemporary Israel. *Eleora.*

ELISA (el-IS-ah) Spanish: "dedicated to God."

ELISHA (el-ESH-ah) Hebrew: "Jehovah is God." Movies and Television: Elisha Cuthbert, actress (TV's *24*).

ELITA (eh-LEE-tah) Latin: "chosen one."

ELIZABETH (eh-liz-ah-BETH) Hebrew: "joined with God." Bible: Elizabeth was the mother of John the Baptist, remembered for her healing of the poor. Business: Elizabeth Arden, Canadian founder of cosmetics company. History: Elizabeth Stanton, suffrage pioneer; Elizabeth Peabody, founder of first kindergarten in 1860. Literature: Elizabeth Barrett Browning, poet; Elizabeth, character in Jane Austen's *Pride and Prejudice*. Movies and Television: Elizabeth Taylor, actress and humanitarian. Eng: *Bessie, Bessy, Beth, Betsy, Bett, Bette, Betty, Elsa, Elsi, Elsie, Elisa, Elisaveta, Elissa, Eliza, Elyse, Elyssa, Libbie, Libby, Lisa, Lisbet, Lisbeth, Liz, Liza, Lizabeth, Lizbeth, Lizzi, Lizzie, Lizzy;* Bulg: *Elisveta;* Czech: *Betka, Betuska, Eliska;* Fr: *Babette, Elise;* Ger: *Betti, Elisabet, Elsbeth, Elschen, Else, Ilse, Lise, Liese, Lieschen, Liesel;* Gk: *Elisavet;* Hung: *Boski, Liszka, Zizi;* Ir: *Eilis;* Ital: *Bettina, Elisa, Lisettina;* Lat: *Lisbete;* Lith: *Elzbieta;* Port: *Elis, Elisabeta;* Rum: *Elisabeta, Betti;* Russ: *Lizka, Yelizaveta;* Scot: *Elspeth;* Span: *Isabel, Isabelita, Ysabel.*

ELLA (EL-lah) Old English: "beautiful fairy woman." Music: Ella Fitzgerald, nicknamed the First Lady of Song, was a popular American Jazz singer.

ELLAMA (EL-lah-mah) Hindi: "she who rules her children." Protecting deity of southern India. *Elamma.*

ELLEN (ELL-in) Greek: "luminous light." A favorite choice in the United States since the 1950s, especially for middle names. Education: Ellen Putter, youngest college president, Barnard, 1981; Ellen Pendleton, President of Wellesley College, 1911–36. Literature: Ellen Glasgow, novelist who won the Pulitzer Prize for *In This Our Life,*1941. Movies and Television: Ellyn Burstyn and Ellen Barkin, actresses. Music: Ellen Beach Yaw, soprano who reportedly sang the highest note ever sung. Science: Ellen Richards, first woman professional chemist in the United States. *Elan, Elen, Elena, Lene, Eleni, Elenyl, Elin, Ellan, Ellin, Ellene, Ellie, Ellon, Elly, Ellyn, Ellon, Elyn.*

ELMA (ELL-mah) Turkish: "sweet fruit."

ELMIRA (ell-MYE-rah) Arabic: "noble lady." *Allmera, Allmeera, Almeria, Almira, Almyra, Elmerya, Elmyrah, Merei, Meera, Mira, Mirah, Myra, Myrah.*

ELOISA (ell-o-WEE-sa) Spanish, Italian: "acclaimed battler." Variant form of Louise. *Eloiza;* Eng: *Eloise.*

ELORA (eh-LORR-ah) Indian: "God bestows the laurel to the victor." *Ellora.*

ELSE (AYL-se) Old German: "regal." Very popular in Denmark.

ELSPETH (ells-PETH) Hebrew: "devoted to god." English: variation on Elizabeth.

ELVIRA (ell-VYE-ra) Teutonic, Spanish: "sprite" or "gnomish." Movies and Television: Character in

TV's *Mistress of the Dark*. Elva, Elvia, Elvera, Elvie, Elvina, Elvinia, Elvita, Ela, Wira, Elwira, Lira; Pol: *Wirke;* Ger: *Elvire.*

ELVITA (el-VEE-tah) Spanish: "truth."

ELYSIA (ee-LEE-see-ah) Latin: From "Elysium Fields," the blessed home happiness at the end of the world. *Ellese, Eliese, Elise, Elisia, Elyse, Ileesia, Iline, Ilysa, Ilysia, Ilyse.*

EMALIA (em-ah-LEE-ah) Latin: "flirt."

EMANUELE (ee-MAHN-yu-ell) Hebrew: "God in humankind." Bible: Name applied to the Messiah. Refers to the child about to be born. *Emmanuelle, Emanuelle.*

EMBER (EMM-bur) Old English: "smoldering remains of fire."

EMELINE (EMM-el-een) Teutonic: "industrious."

EMILY (EMM-ah-lee) Latin: "admiring." Gothic clan name: "hard worker." Enormously popular name in the nineteenth century that lost status after 1900 and is now again in favor. Arts: Emily Carr, Canadian painter of western landscapes and Indians. Literature: Emily Dickinson, reclusive nineteenth-century poet; Emily Brontë, author of *Wuthering Heights;* Emily Post, author on manners. Science: Emily Blackwell, first woman physician in the U.S. *Aimil, Amalea, Amalia, Amalie, Amelia, Amelie, Ameline;* Eng: *Amy, Ema, Emile, Em, Emalee, Emalia, Emelda, Emma, Emmalee, Em-*

maline, Emmalynn; Hawaiian: *Emele, Emely, Emelyne, Emera, Emila, Emilea, Emlyn, Emlynne;* Bulg: *Emilia;* Czech: *Emilka, Milka;* Fr: *Emilie;* Ger: *Amalie, Amma, Amilia, Emmi;* Iran: *Emmali;* Ir: *Eimilie;* Ital: *Emilia;* Scot: *Aimil;* Span: *Amelita, Nenca, Nuela.*

EMMA (EMM-ah) English, German: "whole" or "complete." Education: Emma Willard, pioneered higher education for women (1787–1870). Literature: Emma Southworth, novelist of *Hidden Hand;* Emma Lazarus, poet and essayist who penned "The New Colossus" on the base of the Statue of Liberty. Movies and Television: Emma Thompson, Oscar-winning actress in *Howards End* (1992). Hawaiian: *Ema;* Fr: *Emmaline, Emeline, Em, Emmaline, Emmalyn, Emmalynn.*

ENA (ENN-ah) Old English: "wife" or "soul."

ENID (EE-nid) Welsh: "living soul." *Eanid, Enidd, Enyd, Enydd.*

ENOLA (eh-NOH-lah) English: Contemporary use, origin unknown. Some say it is a respelling of "alone."

EOSTRE (ee-OH-stray) Anglo-Saxon: "goddess of the dawn."

ERICA (ayr-REE-kah) Scandinavian: "eternally royal." Literature: Erica Jong, author of *The Fear of Flying.* Music: Erica Morini, concert violinist. Sports: Erika Holst, Swedish Olympic medalist for ice hockey (2002). *Airica, Airika, Ayrika, Enrica, En-*

rika, Ericka, Erika, Enricka, Errika, Eyrica, Rickee, Ricki, Rikki, Rikky.

ERIKO (ayr-REE-koh) Japanese: "child with a collar." "Ko" means child.

ERIN (AYR-inn) Gaelic: "Irish born." Popular name in the United States. *Eri, Erina, Erinn, Erinna, Erienne, Eryn.*

ERITH (AYR-ith) Irish: "flower."

ERMA (ER-mah) Old Greek: "cosmic whole." Most popular in the first half of the twentieth century. Literature: Erma Bombeck, humorist. *Ermina, Erminia, Erminie, Irma, Irminia, Hermia, Hermine, Hermione.*

ERNA (er-NAH) German: "serious."

ERWINA (er-WEE-nah) Old English: "boar" or "friend."

ESHE (EH-sheh) Swahili: "life."

ESMA (EZ-mah) French: "esteemed." History: A French cousin of James VI brought this name to Scotland. Today, it is usually a female name. Literature: J. D. Salinger titled a short story *For Esmé— with Love and Squalor.* **Esmee.**

ESMERALDA (ez-mer-AHL-da) Spanish: "emerald." *Emerald, Emerant, Emeraude, Esma, Esmaralda, Esmarelda, Esmiralda, Esmirelda, Ezmeralda.*

ESPERANZA (ess-per-AHN-za) Spanish: "hope." Literature: Main character in *The House on Mango Street* by American writer Sandra Cisneros.

ESTEFANY (ess-STEFF-ah-nee) Spanish: "crown" or "wealth." *Estefania, Estephanie, Estefani.*

ESTELLA (ess-TELL-ah) Latin: "star." Movies and Television: Estelle Parsons, actress (*Bonnie and Clyde*); Estelle Getty, actress (TV's *The Golden Girls*). Business: Estée Lauder, cosmotologist who started her own cosmetics company in 1946. Today the company is synonomous with innovation and sophistication. *Essie, Essy, Estella;* Fr: *Estelle, Estee, Estela, Estelita, Estrella;* Span: *Estrelita, Estrellita, Stella, Stelle.*

ESTHER (ESS-ter) Persian: "myrtle leaf" or "star." Bible: Persian ruler Xerxes's wife, who persuaded Haman not to annihilate her people. Movies and Television, Sports: Esther Williams, actress and Olympic gold medal swimmer. *Essie, Essy, Esta;* Span: *Ester, Etti, Ettie, Etty, Hester, Heather, Hettie, Hetty, Hittie.*

ETANA (eh-TAHN-ah) Israel. Hebrew: "resolve" or "determination."

ETHEL (ETH-ell) Old English: "noble." Derived from elongated names like Etheldra. Peaked in popularity in 1870s. History: Ethel Andrus, founder of the American Association of Retired People (AARP). Theater: Ethel Merman and Ethel Barrymore, actresses. Music: Ethel Waters, singer. *Ethelda, Eth-*

lin, Ethelinda, Etheline, Ethelyn, Ethelynne, Ethille, Ethyll.

EUDOCIA (yu-DOH-see-ah) Greek: "highly considered." *Docie, Doxie, Doxy, Eudosia, Eudoxia.*

EUDORA (yu-DORR-ah) Greek: "gift without limits." Literature: Eudora Welty, novelist known for the perceptive depiction of small-town life in the South. Mythology: Eudora was a minor goddess. *Dora, Dorey, Dorie, Eudore.*

EUGENIA (yu-JEEN-ee-ah) Greek: "fortunate birth." History: Napoleon III's wife, the Empress Eugenie. *Eugenie, Eugena, Eugina.*

EUNICE (YU-nihs) Latin: A female name derived from the Greek name Eunike, meaning "happy victory."

EVA (AY-vah) Israel. Hebrew: "she who bestows life." Movies and Television: Eva Gabor, Eve Arden, and Eva Marie Saint, actresses. History: Eva Perón, better known as Evita, first female politician in Argentina and wife of President Juan Perón. Eng: *Ebba, Eve, Evelina, Eveline, Evelyn;* Czech: *Evicka, Evka;* Fr: *Evaine;* Ger: *Evchen, Evy;* Gk: *Evathia;* Hung: *Evi, Evike, Vica;* Pol: *Ewa, Ina, Lina;* Russ: *Yeva, Yevka;* Span: *Evita, Chava, Evonne, Evy.*

EVANGELIA (eh-vahn-GEE-lee-ah) Greek: "angel" or "God's messenger." *Angela, Evangelina, Lia, Litsa.*

EVELINA (eh-vee-LEE-nah) Old French: "hazelnut." Literature: Title character of Fanny Burney's nineteenth-century novel *Evelinay*. **Eveleen, Evelene, Eveline, Evelyn.**

EVELYN (EH-veh-linn) Old Greek: Derived from Evalina. Some popularity as a boy's name in the past. History: Evelyn Ruggles-Brise, British penologist who reformed treatment of juveniles. Literature: Evelyn Waugh, British satirist who wrote *Brideshead Revisited*. Sports: Evelyn Ashford, Olympic gold medalist in track. *Aveline, Evelene, Eveline, Evelyne, Evelynn, Evelynne, Evlin, Evline, Evlyn, Evlynn.*

EZRELA (ehz-RAY-luh) Hebrew: "God is my protector." Common in contemporary Israel.

FABIANA (fay-BEE-yan-ah) Latin: "bean." Sports: Fabienne Reuteler, Swiss Olympic medalist in snowboarding (2002). *Fabienne.*

FAIDA (FAY-dah) Icelandic: "folded wings."

FAINA (FAY-ee-nah) Anglo Saxon: "joyful."

FAITH (fayth) Latin, Greek: "trust" or "conviction." A virtue name. Middle English: "loyalty." Used by the Puritans. Arts: Faith Ringwold, artist. Literature: Faith Popcorn, futurist. Theater: Faith Prince, actress who starred in the Broadway revival of *Guys and Dolls.* Music: Faith Hill, popular country singer. *Fae, Fay, Faye, Fayth.*

FAIZAH (FAH-ee-zah) Arabic: "winning."

FALLON (FA-linn) Gaelic: "of a ruling family." Surname used as a first name. *Falon.*

FANNY (FA-nee) Latin: "from France." Sports: Fani Halkia, Greek Olympic gold medalist for Track and Field. Literature: Fannie Flagg, novelist and actress. Theater: Fanny Brice, star of "Ziegfeld Follies." *Fannee, Fanney, Fannie, Fani.*

FANTINE (F'AN-teen) French: "childlike."

FARICA (fah-REE-kah) Old German: "chief of peace." Diminutive of Fredericka.

FARIDEH (fahr-ee-DEH) Persian: "wonderful."

FARRAH (FAIR-uh) Middle English: "delightful." Movies and Television: Farrah Fawcett, actress (TV's *Charlie's Angels, Extremities*). *Fara, Farah, Farra.*

FATIMA (FAH-tee-mah) Arabic: "one who weans her infant" or "chastity." Mohammed's favorite daughter. According to the Koran, she was one of only four perfect women of the world. Swahili: *Farimah, Fatma, Fatuma.*

FAUNA (FAW-nah) Greek: "goddess of fertility."

FAUSTINE (faws-TEEN) Latin: "auspicious" or "lucky." History: Two Roman emperors were named Faustina. Literature: Johann Wolfgang von Goethe completed his play *Faust, the First Part of the Tragedy* about the Faust legend in 1808. Music: The Faust legend has inspired operas: Berlioz's *La Damnation de Faust* (1893); Busoni's *Doktor Faust* (1925); and Charles Gounod's *Faust* (1859), which is based on Goethe's play. *Fausta, Fauste, Faustina.*

FAWN (fahn) Old French: "baby deer." History: Fawn Hall, infamous secretary for Oliver North. *Faina, Fanya, Faun, Fauan, Faunia, Fawna, Fawne, Fawnia, Fawnya.*

FAY (faye) Old French: "elf" or "fairy." Diminutive of Faith. First used in significant numbers in the 1920s. Movies and Television: Fay Wray, Faye Dunaway, actresses. *Fae, Faye.*

FAYETTE (fay-ETT) Old French: "baby fairy."

FE (faye) Spanish: "faith."

FELDA (FELL-dah) German: "from the field."

FELICIA (feh-LEE-shah) Latin: "happy." One of the virtue names. History, Literature: Felicia Hemans, poet. *Falecia, Falicia, Falisha, Falishia, Felice, Feliciana, Felicidad, Falicie, Felicienne, Felicitas, Felicita, Felicity, Felise, Felita, Feliz, Feliza.*

FEMI (fay-ME) African: "love me."

FERN (fern) Old English: A plant that thrives in shade. Literature: Fern Arable, character in E.B. White's *Charlotte's Web. Ferne.*

FERNANDA (fer-NAHN-dah) Spanish: "adventurous."

FERYAL (fair-YAL) Arabic: "beauty of light."

FIA (FEE-ah) Scottish: "dark of peace."

FIALA (fee-AH-lah) Czechoslovakian: "violet."

FIAMMETTA (FEE-a-MET-tah) Italian: "a flutter-ing flame." *Fia.*

FIDELIA (fee-DAYL-yah) Latin: "faithful." *Fidelina, Fidess.*

FIFI (FEE-fee) French: "he shall add."

FILIPA (fee-lee-PAH) Spanish: form of Philipa, meaning "loves horses."

FIONA (fee-OH-nah) Gaelic: "pretty" or "porce-lain skin." Invented by a British novelist in the early 1900s and still popular in England. Literature: Char-acter in Len Deighton's *Berlin Match*; Fiona Macleod, eighteenth-century Scottish author who wrote stories about the mystical Celtic world. Music: Fiona Apple, American singer. Sports: Fiona Mac-Donald, English Olympic gold medalist in curling. *Fionna.*

FIONNULA (fee-oh-NOO-lah) Gaelic: "pale shoulders." *Fenella, Finella, Finola, Fionneuala, Nola, Nuala.*

FLANA (FLAHN-ah) Latin: "yellow hair." Origi-nally a Latin clan name in the Roman Empire. *Flavie, Flavienne, Flavyere.*

FLAVIA (FLAH-vee-ah) Latin: "golden tresses." It was common in the Roman empire. *Flavie, Raviere, Flavyere.*

FLEUR (flure) French: "flower." Literature: Character in John Galsworthy's *The Forsyte Saga*. *Fleurette, Fleurine.*

FLORA (FLORR-ah) Latin: "flower." History: Flora Macdonald was a nineteenth-century Scottish heroine who helped Prince Charlie escape the English. Mythology: Roman goddess of springtime. Popular in the nineteenth century. Theater: Title character of a 1960s musical *Flora, the Red Menace*, starring Liza Minnelli. *Flora, Fiore, Fiori, Fleur, Flor, Flore, Florella, Florelle, Floria, Florida, Florie, Florine, Floris, Floriese, Florrie, Florry.*

FLORAMARIA (FLORR-ah ma-REE-yah) Spanish: "flower of Mary."

FLORENCE (FLORR-intz) Latin: "blossoming." History: Florence Nightingale gave wings to its usage. She herself was named for Florence, Italy, where she was born. Military: Florence Blanchfield, U.S. nurse and military officer. Science: Florence Merriam Bailey, ornithologist. Sports: Florence Griffith Joyner (Flo-Jo), sprinter, three-time Olympic gold medalist (1988). Span: *Fiorentina, Fiorenza, Flora, Florencia, Florentia, Florentyna, Florenze, Flori, Floria, Floriana, Florie, Florina, Florinda, Florine, Floris, Florrie, Florry, Floss, Flossey, Flossie, Flossy.*

FOLA (FAW-lah) Nigeria. Yoruba: "honor."

FOLAYAN (faw-LAH-yahn) Nigeria. Yoruba: "to walk in dignity."

FONTANE (fawn-TAN) French: "source of water."

FORTUNA (for-TOO-nah) Latin: Goddess. Mythology: Roman goddess of fortune, chance.

FRANCES (FRAN-siss) Latin: "without fetters" or "of France." Education: Frances Willard, educator, reformer, first president of the National Council of Women. History: Frances Folsom Cleveland, wife of President Grover Cleveland; Frances Perkins, first female cabinet member, Secretary of Labor, 1933. Literature: Fran Lebowitz, humorist; Fran Podulka, novelist and poet who wrote *The Wonder Jungle*. Music: Frances Alda, operatic soprano. Eng: *Fan, Fancy, Fannie, Fran, Franci, Francie, Frank, Frankie, Franni, Frannie, Franny;* Fr: *Francette, Francee, Franceline, Francene, Francette, Francey, Francine, Francoise;* Russ: *Fanechka, Fanya, Fania;* Ital: *Francesca;* Span: *Francisca,* Ger: *Franzetta, Franzi, Franziska.*

FREDA (FRAY-day) Old German: Diminutive of Alfreda, Frederica, Winifred. Arts: Frida Kahlo, artist. *Freada, Freeda, Freida, Frida, Frieda.*

FREDERICA (fred-REE-kah) German: "peace." Music: Frederica von Stade, mezzo-soprano. *Farica, Federica, Fred, Fredalena, Freddi, Freddie, Freddy, Fredericka, Frederickina, Frederika, Fredrika, Frederine;* Fr: *Frederique, Frederica, Fredi, Freda, Fredia, Fredie, Fredda, Fredricia;* Norw: *Fredrika, Ferika, Friederike;* Pol: *Freyderyka, Rica, Ricki, Rickie, Ricky, Rikki, Rikky.*

FREYA (FREE-ya or FRAY-ah) Scandinavian mythology: Freeya was the goddess of fertility, parallel to Venus in Roman lore. The name gave the word Friday to the weekly calendar. *Fraya.*

FUJITA (foo-JEE-tah) Japanese: "a field."

FUKAYNA (foo-KEH-ee-nah) Arabic: "knowledgeable" or "scholarly."

GABRIELLE (gah-bree-ELL) Israel. Hebrew: "God's servant" or "divine heroine." Popular for the last century worldwide. Arts: Gabrielle "Coco" Chanel, fashion designer. Bible: Gabriel is one of God's four archangels in the Hebrew tradition. Literature: Gabrielle Campbell Long, prolific British historian, specialist on the Renaissance. Sports: Gabriela Sabatini, tennis star. *Gabbe, Gabbi, Gabi, Gabriela, Gabriellia, Gabrila, Gaby, Gavra, Gavrielle;* Fr: *Gabrielle, Gigi.*

GADA (GAH-dah) Hebrew: "good fortune" or "well-pleased." Popular in the Middle East.

GAEA (GYE-ah) Greek: "the planet earth." The Greek goddess of the earth thought to have given birth to sea, mountain, and sky. *Gaia, Gaiea, Gala.*

GAIL (gayl) Hebrew: Very popular in the United States during the 1950s. Literature: Gail Hamilton, nineteenth-century author who wrote on women's worth. Science: Gail Borden, nineteenth-century inventor of condensed milk who started company that bears her name. *Gael, Gaila, Gaile, Gale, Gayel, Gayelle, Gayle, Gayleen, Gaylene, Gayline, Gali, Gaylie.* See Abigail.

GALA (GALL-ah) Swedish: "singer."

GALATEA (gah-lah-TEE-ah) Greek mythology: Pygmalion prayed that Galatea, his statue, would come to life. Aphrodite granted his wish, and the sculptor married his work of art. Literature: George Bernard Shaw's play *Pygmalion,* on which the musical *My Fair Lady* was based. Music: Gal Costa, one of Brazil's top singing stars. *Gal, Galatee.*

GALENIA (gall-EEN-ee-yah) Spanish: "small intelligent one."

GALIENA (gah-lee-AYN-yah) Old German: "supreme one." *Galiana, Galianna.*

GALYA (GAHL-yah) Israel. Hebrew: "saved by God's love." *Galia, Gailia, Gallya.*

GAMADA (GAHM-ah-dah) African: "glad, pleased."

GANA (GAHN-ah) Hebrew: "garden."

GARDA (GAR-dah) Teutonic: "protected."

GARDENIA (gar-DEEN-yah) Scottish: Name of a sweet-smelling flower. Science: Alexander Garden, an eighteenth-century botanist, coined the name.

GARLAND (GAR-lind) Old French: "necklace of flowers." *Garlanda, Garlande, Garlandera.*

GARNET (GAR-nitt) Middle English: Birthstone of the month of January.

GASHA (GAY-sha) Russian: "good."

GAVILA (gah-VEE-lah) Israel. Hebrew: "divine heroine." *Gavrilla, Gavryla, Gavrylla.*

GAVINA (gah-VEE-nah) Latin: "of Gabio." From Gabinus, saint's name.

GAVRILLA (gahv-REEL-lah) Hebrew: "heroine."

GAY (gaye) Old French: "cheerful" or "free-hearted." Medieval surname fashionable again in this century. *Gae, Gai, Gaye.*

GAYNOR (GAYE-nor) Welsh: Variant of Guinevere. Popular in England. *Gaenor, Gayna, Gayner.*

GAZIT (gah-ZEET) Israel. Hebrew: "carved stone." Popular in Israel and adapted throughout the world. *Gazita.*

GELASIA (ghel-AAS-ee-ah) Greek: "predisposed to laughter."

GELLA (GHEL-lah) Hebrew: "one with golden hair."

GELSEY (GHEL-see) Persian: "a flower." Arts: Gelsey Kirkland, renowned American ballarina. *Gelsi, Gelsy.*

GEMINI (jeh-mah-NYE) Greek: "twin." Astrology: Appropriate for a girl born under the sign of Gemini, represented by a set of twins. *Gemine, Geminia, Geminine, Mini.*

GEMMA (JEM-ah) Italian: "valuable gem." History: Made fashionable by the canonization in 1940 of St. Gemma, known for her extraordinary display of stigmata and holy wounds. *Jemma.*

GENA (JEE-nah) Diminutive variant form of Regina. *Geena, Genelle, Geneene, Genina, Genie, Genalyn, Genaye, Geana, Geanndra, Genette.*

GENERVA (jen-NERV-ah) English: Variant form of Guinevere. Arab: *Genna;* Eng: *Genn;* Ital: *Ginevra;* Welsh: *Gwenhwyfar.*

GENESIS (JEN-eh-siss) Israel. Hebrew: "the beginning" or "origin." Bible: First of the Five Books of Moses. *Genessa, Genisa, Genisia, Genisis, Jenessa.*

GENEVA (jen-NEE-vah) Old French: "juniper tree." Place name. A city and lake in Switzerland, as well as a city in central New York. *Gena, Genever, Genevra, Genoveva, Ginebra, Ginevra, Ginevre, Janeva;* Fr: *Janevra.*

GENEVIEVE (jEN-ah-VEEV) Celtic: "female lineage." Arts: Genevieve Boullogne, still-life painter. Literature: Genevieve Taggard, poet and critic. History: St. Genevieve protected the city of Paris against the invasion of Attila the Hun, then later became its patron. Movies and Television: Genevieve Bujold, actress. *Gena, Genavieve, Geneva, Geneve, Geneveeve, Genivieve, Gennie, Genny, Genovera, Genoveva, Gina, Janeva, Jenevieve.*

GEORGIA (JOR-jah) Latin: "farmer" or "one who sows the earth." Arts: Georgia O'Keefe, painter of abstract floral and desert scenes. Business: Georgette Mosbacher, author, former cosmetics entrepreneur and wife of former U.S. Secretary of Commerce Robert Mosbacher. History: Georgiana Cavendish, eighteenth-century British duchess. *George, Georgeann, Georgeanne, Georgeina, Georgena, Georgene;* Fr. *Georgette;* Eng: *Georgetta, Georgiana, Georgianne, Georgie, Georgienne, Georgina, Georgine, Georgyann, Georgyanne, Giorgia, Giorgina, Giorgyna, Jorgina.*

GEORGIHA See Georgia.

GERALDINE (JER-all-deen) French: "one who rules by the spear." First appeared in the 1500s. Feminine form of Gerald, popular in the first half of this century. History: Geraldine Ferraro, onetime U.S. vice-presidential candidate. Movies and Television: Geraldine Page and Geraldine Chaplin, actresses. *Deena, Dina, Dyna, Geralda, Geraldeen, Geraldene, Geraldina, Geralyn, Geralynne, Geri, Gerianna, Gerianne, Gerilynn, Geroldine, Gerry, Geralda, Jeraldeen, Jeraldene, Jeraldine, Jeralee, Jere, Jeri, Jerilene, Jerrie, Jerrileen, Jerroldeen, Jerry.*

GERDA (GAIR-dah) Old Norse: "safe barrier." Popular in Latvia today as a variant of Georgia.

GERMAINE (jer-MAYNE) Celtic: "loud voicings," "German-born." Literature: Germaine Greer, feminist and author. *Germain, Germana, Germane, Germayne, Jermaine, Jermane, Jermayn, Jermayne.*

GERTRUDE (GER-trood) German, French: "power of the sword." Business: Gertrude Thompson, first woman to head Board of Directors of a U.S. railroad (1930). History: In the seventh century, the name of Saint Gertrude. The name found fashion in the mid-nineteenth century. Literature: Gertrude Stein, American poet, novelist, and critic. Science: Gertrude Elion, shared Nobel Prize for medicine (1988) for work on AZT, drug used to combat AIDS. Sports: Gertrude Ederle, first woman to swim the English Channel, breaking existing men's record in 1926. Theater: Gertrude Lawrence, actress. *Geltruda, Gerda, Gert, Gerta, Gertie, Gertina, Gertraud, Gertrud, Gertruda, Gerty, Trude, Trudi, Trudie, Trudy.*

GEVA (GAY-vah) Israel. Hebrew: "small mount." Bible: Originally a biblical location. Fashionable today in Israel.

GHISLAINE (zhee-LAYNE) German, French: "loyal vow."

GHITA (GEE-tah) Italian: "pearl-like."

GIACINTA (jah-SEEN-tah) Italian: "hyacinth."

GIANINA (jee-AHN-ee-ah) Italian: "god is gracious."

GIANNA (jee-AHN-ah) Italian: Version of Jane. *Gia, Giana, Gianina, Giannina, Gianella, Gianara, Gionna, Geonna.*

GIGI (JEE-jee or ZHEE-zhee) French: Pet name for Gabrielle. Movies and Television: *Gigi*, a famous musical of the 1950s starring Leslie Caron. See Gabrielle.

GILANA (jee-LAHN-ah) Israel. Hebrew: "great happiness." *Gila, Gilah, Gilal, Gilala, Gilat.*

GILBERTE (jil-BURT) Old German: "shining vow." *Berta, Bertie, Berty, Gigi, Gilberta, Gilbertina, Gilbertine, Gill, Gillie, Gilly.*

GILDA (JILL-da or GEEL-da) English: "golden." Movies and Television: Gilda Radner, actress and comedian (TV's *Saturday Night Live*). *Gildie, Gildy.*

GILLIAN (GILL-ee-ahn) Latin: "Jove's child." Movies and Television: Gillian Anderson, actress (TV's *X-Files*). *Gilian, Gill, Gillan, Gillianne, Gillie, Gillyanne, Jillian, Jillianne, Jillyan, Zhilian.*

GINA (GEE-nah) Japanese: "silvery." Movies and Television: Geena Davis and Gina Gershon, actresses. *Geena.*

GINESSA (JIN-ess-ah) Celtic: "white as foam."

GINGER (JIN-jer) English: "ginger spice" or "peppy." Movies and Television: Ginger Rogers, actress who danced in many films with Fred Astaire.

Ginnie, Genny, Ginnette, Ginnelle, Ginna, Gin-nilee, Ginnelle, Gineen.

GIOVANNA (jo-VAHN-ah) Italian: "bountiful God." *Giovana, Giavanna, Geovana, Geovanna.*

GISELLE (jeh-ZELL) French: "vow." Dance: Title character in Gautier's ballet. Span: *Gisela, Gisell, Gisele, Gizelle, Gisella, Giselda, Gizi;* Hung: *Gizike.*

GITANA (je-TAN-ah) Spanish: "gypsy." *Gitane, Gitanna.*

GITTA (GITT-ah) Gaelic: "forcefulness." Diminutive of Brigitte.

GIULIA (JOO-lee-ah) Italian: From Latin "young and refreshing." *Guila, Guiliana, Guiletta, Julia, Juliana, Julie, Juliet, Julietta, Juliette.*

GIULIANA (JOO-lee-AHN-nah) Italian: "child of Jove." *Guilia.*

GIZANE (GEE-zhan-ay) Basque: "Christ's incarnation."

GLADYS (GLAD-iss) Welsh: Variant form of Claudia. Music: Gladys Knight, popular singer; Gladys Swarthout, operatic soprano. *Glad, Gladdie, Glad-dys, Gladi, Gladis, Gladyss.*

GLENDA (GLEN-dah) Welsh: "mild and kind." Movies and Television: Glenda Jackson, actress.

GLENNA (GLEN-ah) Gaelic: "glen" or "narrow valley." Movies and Television: Glenn Close, actress (*The Big Chill*). *Glenda, Gleneen, Glenene, Glenine, Glen, Glenn, Glenne, Glennene, Glennie.*

GLORIA (GLOW-ree-ah) Latin: "glory" or "glory-born." Business: Gloria Vanderbilt, inventor of designer jeans. Literature: Edmund Spenser used the name Gloriana in the *Faerie Queene* to praise Elizabeth I; Gloria Steinem, feminist writer. Movies and Television: Gloria Swanson added to the name's popularity in the 1920s through the 1960s. Theater: George Bernard Shaw used the name in his play *You Never Can Tell*. *Gloree, Glorie, Gloriana, Gloriane, Glorria, Glory.*

GLYNIS (GLYN-iss) Welsh: "small glen." Popular in Britain in the middle of the twentieth century. Movies and Television: Glynis Johns, actress (*Mary Poppins*). *Glinnis, Glinyce, Glinys, Glinyss, Glynnis.*

GODIVA (gode-EYE-vah) English: "gift from God." History: Lady Godiva, English noblewoman in the eleventh century who is famous for her ride through the marketplace while clothesless. While the woman is real, the story is most likely a myth. Business: Godiva Chocolatier, renowned maker of quality chocolates.

GOLDA (GOLD-ah) Old English: "of gold." History: Golda Meir, former U.S.-born Israeli prime minister. Movies and Television: Goldie Hawn, actress. *Goldarina, Goldarine, Goldi, Goldie, Goldina, Goldy, Goldia.*

GORDANA (goor-DAAN-ah) Serbian: "proud."

GRACE (grayse) Latin: "favor" or "blessing." Dance: Graciele Danielle, choreographer. History: Grace Goodhue Coolidge, wife of President Calvin. Military, Science: Grace Hopper, naval officer, pioneer in computer technology. Movies and Television: Grace Kelly, actress who won an Oscar for *The Country Girl* (1954). *Engracia, Gracielle, Gracella, Gracelynn, Gracelynne;* Span: *Grecia, Gracia, Gracie, Gracee, Grayce, Graciana, Gratia, Grazia, Grazyna.*

GRANIA (GRAN-ee-ah) Gaelic: "love."

GRAZIA (GRAH-zee-ya) Italian: "from grace." Literature: Grazia Deledda, 1936 Nobel Prize winner for her writing about her homeland of Sardinia, Italy.

GREER (Greer) Scottish: From Latin "ever-watching." Diminutive of Gregory. Movies and Television: Greer Garson, actress. Greer was her mother's maiden name. *Grier.*

GRESSA (GRAY-sah) Norwegian: "earthly carpet" or "grassy land."

GRETA (GRETT-ah) Greek: "pearlescent." Nickname for Margaret. Movies and Television: Popular name in the 1930s inspired by Greta Garbo. Sports: Grete Waitz, Norwegian runner who won the New York City Marathon women's title a record nine times. Literature: Gretel, title character in the popular German fairy tale *Hansel and Gretel* who saves her brother and herself. *Greeta, Gretal, Gretchen,*

Grete, Gretel, Grethel, Gretna, Gretta, Grette, Gryta.

GRETCHEN (GRETT-shin) Greek: "pearly luster." Diminutive of Margaret.

GRISELDA (gri-ZELL-dah) Latin, German: "gray-haired one." Literature: Used in Boccaccio's tale about an exceptionally patient wife in the *Decameron*. **Gricelda, Grizelda, Gryzelda, Gryselda, Griselle, Grisella**; Scot: *Grizel*.

GRYTA (GREH-tah) Greek: "a pearl."

GUADALUPE (gwah-dah-LOO-pay) Spanish, Arabic: "valley of wolves."

GUDRUN (goo-DROON) Scandinavian: "battle." Literature: Character in D. H. Lawrence's novel *Women in Love*. **Gudren, Gudrin, Gudrinn, Gudruna.**

GUIDA (GYE-dah) Italian: "one who guides."

GUILLERMINA (gwee-EER-mee-nah) Spanish: "loving."

GUINEVERE (GWIN-ah-veer) Welsh: "fair one." Literature, Music: King Arthur's Queen Guinevere, popularized by Rodgers and Hammerstein's musical *Camelot*. The modern form of the name is Jennifer. **Gaenna, Gaynor, Genevieve, Guenevere;** Ital: *Ginevra; Gueniveer, Guenna.* See Jenny.

GUNDA (GOON-dah) Norwegian: "female warrior." Used in contemporary Norway. *Gundala.*

GURIT (goo-REET) Israel. Hebrew: "baby creature," suggesting the innocence of the newborn. *Gurice.*

GUSTAVA (goo-STAV-ah) Spanish: "staff of the Gods."

GWENDOLYN (GWIN-do-linn) Welsh: "fair-haired." According to a few legends, Gwendolyn was the wife of Merlin, the great magician of Avalon. Dance, Theater: Gwen Verdon, dancer and actress. Music: Gwen Stefani, singer. Movies and Television: Gwenyth Paltrow, Academy Award-winning actress (*Shakespeare in Love*). *Guendolen, Guenna, Gwen;* Welsh: *Gwenda;* Eng: *Gwendaline, Gwendolen, Gwendolene, Gwendolin, Gwendoline, Gwendolynne, Gwenna, Gwenette, Gwenyth, Gwyn, Gwyneth, Gwynn, Gwynna, Gwynne, Gwenda, Gwendi, Gweneth, Gwenyth, Gwinn, Wendi, Wendy, Win, Winnie, Wynne.*

GYPSY (JIP-see) Old English: Refers to the tribe of Romany, which originated in India. *Gipsy.*

GYTHA (GITH-ah) English: "gift."

HABIBAH (hah-BEEB-ah) Arabic: "beloved."

HABIKAH (hah-BEEK-ah) African: "sweetheart."

HADARAH (hah-DAR-ah) Hebrew: "bedecked in beauty."

HADASSAH (hah-DAHS-ah) Israel. Hebrew: "myrtle tree." Bible: Hebrew name of Esther, Queen of Persia.

HADIYA (hah-DEE-ah) Swahili: "present."

HADLEY (HAD-lee) English: "field of heather." Surname used as a girl's name. Literature: Name of Hemingway's first wife.

HAIDEE (HAY-dee) Greek: "with propriety." *Haydee.*

HALCYONE (HAHL-see-ohn) Greek: "King fisher." Mythology: In ancient myth, "halcyon days" were a two-week period for calm before the winter solstice when the eggs of the fisher king could germinate peacefully in the ocean. *Halcie, Haley, Halcyonth.*

HALDANA (HAHL-dah-na) Old Morse: "half-Danish." Name connotes "fierceness" as the Danes were invaders of foreign lands. *Haldane.*

HALEY (HAY-lee) English: "clearing of hay." Sports: Hayley Wickenheiser, Canadian Olympic gold medalist in ice hockey (2002). Movies and Television: Hayley Mills, actress. *Hayley, Hailey, Haylee, Haylie, Hailee, Haleigh.*

HALFRIDA (hal-FREE-dah) German: "peaceful heroine." *Halfrid*

HALIA (hah-LEE-ah) Hawaiian: Paraphrase of "remembrance of loved one."

HALIMA (hah-LEE-mah) Swahili: "caressing nature."

HALLIE (HAL-ee) Old English: "From the hall." *Halli, Hailey.*

HALONA (hah-LONE-ah) Native American: "fortunate."

HANA (ha-NAH) Japanese: "bud" or "blossom."

HANAKO (hah-NAH-koh) Japanese: "flower child."

HANNAH (HAH-nah) Israel. Hebrew: "grace." Bible: Mother of the prophet Samuel, who was barren until God answered her prayers. Inspired variants of Ann. Education: Hanna Gray, first woman president of a major university (University of Chicago, 1978). History: Hannah Arendt, historian. *Ann, Anna, Anne, Annie, Hana;* Hebrew: *Hanah, Hanna, Hanne, Hannele, Hannelore, Hannie, Hanny, Honna, Nan, Nanney, Nannie, Nanny.*

HARELDA (har-ELD-ah) Teutonic: "mighty in battle."

HARIKA (har-EE-kah) Turkish: "wonderful."

HARLEEN (har-LEEN) English: "meadow of the hares." Feminine of Harley. *Harlie.*

HARMONY (HAR-moh-nee) Latin, Greek: "musical consonance" or "in tune." *Harmonic, Harmoni, Harmonee, Harmonia.*

HARRIET (HARE-ee-ett) Greek: "lady of the hearth." Variant of Henrietta very popular in the eighteenth and nineteenth centuries. History: Harriet Tubman, abolitionist who helped 300 slaves escape via the Underground Railroad. Literature: Harriet Beecher Stowe, author of *Uncle Tom's Cabin;* Harriet Stratemeyer Adams, author of children's books and young adult novels. *Harrie, Harrietta, Harriet, Harrietta, Harriette, Harriot, Harriott, Hatsie, Hatsy, Hattie, Hatty.*

HASANA (hah-SAH-nah) Nigeria. Hausa: "she who arrives first." An old Nigerian custom is to name the first-born female of twins Hasana. If the second twin is male, he is called Husseini; if female, Huseina.

HATEYA (hah-TEH-yah) Native American. Miwok: "footprint in the sand." The name was inspired by the practice of tracking animals from their footprints.

HAVA (ha-VAH) Hebrew: "life."

HAYLEY See Haley.

HAZEL (HAY-zill) Old English: Name of a tree. Popular in the late nineteenth century during the botanical name craze. Sports: Hazel Hotchkiss Wightman, tennis player who won forty-five national titles. *Hazal, Hazell, Hazelle, Hazle.*

HAZINA (ha-ZEEN-ah) African: "treasure."

HEATHER (HEH-thur) Middle English: Name of a flower. Its Scottish flavor intensified its trendiness in the 1970s. It has since become very popular.

HEDDA (HED-ah) Greek: "given to battle." Anglicized adaptation of Hedwig. Journalism: Hedda Hopper, gossip columnist. Theater: Hedda Gabler, title character in Ibsen's play. *Heda, Heddi, Heddie, Hedi, Hedvig, Hedvige, Hedwig, Hedwiga, Hedy, Hetta.*

HEDWIG (HED-wig) Greek: "battling." Movies and Television: Hedy Lamarr, actress. *Hadoig, Hadwig;* Czech: *Hedmck, Hedoig, Hedoiga, Hedvige, Hedwiga, Hedwige, Hedy.*

HEIDI (HYE-dee) German, Swiss: "honorable." Short form of Adelheide. Literature, Movies: made famous by Johanna Spyri's novel *Heidi,* which was later made into a number of films and a television series. Arts: Heidi Brandt, designed Christmas seals in 1956 and 1961. *Hedie, Heidie, Hydie.*

HELEN (HELL-in) Greek: "illuminated one." Education: Helen Keller, author and teacher. Mythology: Helen of Troy is the most famous Helen, the wife of Menelaus, who ran off with Paris, thus causing the downfall of Troy. Theater: Helen Hayes, actress, the first lady of the American stage. Journalism: Helen Gurley Brown, publisher. Sports: Helen Wills Moody, tennis champion. Ellen is the most popular variant. *Aileen, Ailene, Aleanor, Alene, Eileen, Elaina, Elaine, Elana, Elayne, Eleanor, Elanore;* Bulg: *Elena; Eleni, Elenora, Elenore, Eleonore, Elianora, Elinor, Ella, Elladine, Elleanora, Elle, Ellen, El-lette, Elite, Ellin, Ellinor, Elly, Ellyn, Galina, Halina, Helena, Helene, Hellena, Hellene, Ileana, Ilene, Ilona, Jelena, Lana, Leanora;* Eng: *Lenore, Leonora, Leonore, Leora, Lienor, Lina, Nelda, Nell, Nelly, Nonnie, Nora;* Ger: *Lena, Lene;* Russ: *Yelena, Olenka, Olena, Nelya, Lili.*

HELGA (HEL-gah) Old German: "pious" or "religious." Very popular today in Norway and Iceland.

HELIA (HEEL-ee-ya) Greek: "of the sun."

HELKI (HELL-kee) Native American. Mowak: "to touch." Derived from the habit of slender-billed birds who dig holes with their beaks during the winter months.

HELMA (HELL-mah) German: "protective."

HELOISE (HEL-oh-ees) French: "renowned fighter." History: The secret lover of the twelfth-century theologian Pierre Abelard who later disavowed their alliance and became a nun. He joined a monastery after her uncle emasculated him out of revenge. Literature: The pen name of a professional advice-giver and author of the book and newspaper column *Hints from Heloise*. *Aloysia, Eloisa, Eloise, Heloisa, Lois.*

HELSA (HELL-sah) Hebrew: "devoted to God."

HENRIETTA (hen-ree-ETT-ah) Greek: "household manager." Business: Hetty Green (1834–1919), financier, called the "witch of Wall Street," richest woman in the United States in her day. Politics: Henrietta Szold, Zionist leader. Science: Henrietta Leavitt, astronomer who discovered four novas. *Enrichetta, Enrichette, Enriqueta, Etta, Ettie, Etty, Hattie, Hatty, Hendrika, Henka, Henna, Hennie, Henrie, Henrieta, Henriette, Henrika, Hetta, Hettie, Yetta, Yettie.*

HERA (HARE-oh) Greek mythology: Hera was the Queen of the Heaven, wife of Zeus and the goddess of marriage.

HERMINIA (ayre-MEE-nee-ah) Latin: "army member." Herminia is the name of a saint. *Hermaine, Hermione.*

HERMOSA (ERR-mose-ah) Spanish: "beautiful."

HESPER (HESS-per) Greek: "evening star."

HILA (HILL-ah) Hebrew: "aura."

HILDA (HILL-dah) German: "virgin warrior." Power name that has inspired many variants such as Hildegarde and Hildebranth. Sports: Hilde Pedersen, Norwegien Olympic medalist in cross-country skiing. History: Hilda, a famous guru in the United States during the sixties. Literature: Hildegarde Knef, author; Hilda Doolittle, imagist poet. *Hilde, Hildi, Hildie, Hildy*.

HILLARY (HILL-ah-ree) Greek, Latin: "filled with pleasure." History: Hillary Rodham Clinton, wife of former U.S. President Bill Clinton and health-care activist. Due to her popularity the name is becoming trendy. *Hilary;* Fr: *Hilaire*.

HINDA (HIN-dah) Yiddish: "deer" or "gazelle." Hinda was the name of one of Muhammed's many wives.

HOA (ho) Vietnamese: "blossom" or "calm heart."

HOLA (HO-lah) Native American. Hopi: "rainstick." Derived from a Hopi ceremonial stick filled with seeds.

HOLIDAY (HAH-li-dae) English: "festive day."

HOLLIS (HAH-lis) English: "near the valley."

HOLLY (HAH-lee) English: "holly tree or shrub." Traditional Christmas wreath. First used as a name at the turn of the century and peaked during the

1960s. Good for babies born in December. Literature: Character in Galsworthy's *The Forsyte Saga*. Movies and Television: Holly Hunter, actress. *Hollie, Holli, Hollee, Holice;* Eng: *Hollis, Hollyann.*

HONEY (HUH-nee) English: "nectar."

HONOR (AH-ner) Latin: "integrity." *Honora;* Fr: *Honore,* Eng: *Honore.*

HOPE (hope) English: "expectation." A virtue name.

HORTENCIA (horr-TEN-see-ah) Latin: "garden." Variant form of Hortense. Literature: Hortense Kalisher, novelist. *Horsensia, Hortense, Ortensia.*

HOSANNA (ho-ZAN-ah) Greek, Hebrew: A prayerful cry of adoration. *Hosannie.*

HOSHI (HO-shee) Japanese: "nightlight" or "shining star." Used for centuries in Japan. *Hoshie, Hosiko, Hoshiyo.*

HUBERTA (hue-BER-tah) Teutonic: "bright mind."

HULDA (HUL-dah) Old German: "greatly loved" or "full of grace." Bible: Hulda was a prophet in the Bible. *Huldi, Huldie, Huldy.*

HUSNIYAH (hoos-NEE-yah) Arabic: "beautiful."

HYACINTH (HYE-a-cinth) Greek: "alas." Name of a violet flower. Name of third-century saint. Mythology: According to Greek lore, Apollo loved a beautiful youth named Hyacinth, who was killed by the god's rival Zephyr. The flower sprung from the youth's blood. *Cinthia, Cinthie, Cinthy, Giacinta, Giacintia, Hyacintha, Hyacinthe, Hyacinthia, Hyacinthis, Hyacintia, Jacenta, Jacinda, Jacinta, Jacintha, Jackie, Jacky, Jacynth.*

HYPATIA (HYE-pat-ee-ya) Greek: "surpassing."

I

IANTHE (ee-AHNTH) Greek: "violet flower." Mythology: Ianthe was the daughter of Oceanus, a sea nymph. *Ianthia, Ianthina, Janthia.*

IDA (EYE-dah) Old English: "wealthy" or "fulfilled." Journalism: Ida Wells, journalist who established the United Negro College Fund. Literature: Ida Tarbell, author of *Life of President Lincoln.* Movies and Television: Ida Lupino, actress and director; Ida Kaminska, actress. Politics: Ida Saxton McKinley, wife of U.S. President William McKinley. *Idia, Idalene;* Ital: *Idalia, Idalina, Idaline, Idalya, Idalyne, Ide, Idell;* Eng: *Idelle, Idella, Idell, Idetta;* Ger: *Idette;* Pol: *Itka;* Yiddish: *Ita.*

IDANIA (eye-DAHN-eye-ya) Slavic: "hardworking" or "prosperous."

IDELLE (eye-DELL) Celtic, Welsh: "bountiful." *Idella, Idelisa.*

IDOIA (ee-DOE-ee-ah) Spanish reference to the Virgin Mary.

IDOLA (eye-DOL-ah) Greek: "idolized."

IDONA (eye-DOHN-ah) Teutonic: "industrious worker."

IDRA (eye-DRAH) Hebrew: "fig tree."

IGNATIA (ihg-NAA-shee-ya) Latin: "fiery."

ILANA (ee-LAHN-ah) Israel. Hebrew: "tree." *Elana, Elit, Ilanit.*

ILARIA (eye-larh-ee-ya) Latin: "one who is merry."

ILIMA (eye-LEE-mah) Hawaiian: "flower of Oahu."

ILKA (ILL-kah) Slavic: "admiring" or "committed to success." Variant of Helen. Popular in Hungary.

ILONA (eye-LO-nah) Hungarian: "lovely" or "pretty." Related to Helen.

ILSE (ILL-sah) German: Short form of Elizabeth. *Ilsa, Ilsie.*

IMA (EE-mah) Japanese: "in the moment" or "eternal present."

IMAN (eye-MON) Arabic: "faith" or "belief." Movies and Television: Iman, actress and supermodel.

IMELDA (ee-MEL-dah) Italian: "one who battles forcefully." Name of a fourteenth-century Italian saint. History: Imelda Marcos, wife of deposed Philippine ruler. *Melda.*

IMOGENE (EYE-mah-jeen) Latin: "without blame" or "innocent." Literature: Heroine of Shakespeare's *Cymbeline.* Movies and Television: Imogene Coca, comedian. *Imogen.*

IMPERIA (eem-PARE-ee-ah) Latin: "imperial" or "royal."

INA (EYE-nah) Greek: "pure" or "chaste." Derived from the Irish Agnes. Sports: Ina Kleber, German swimmer who set world record for the 200-meter backstroke (1984). *Ena.*

INDIA (IN-dee-ah) Indian: The name of the country, often used as a first name. *Inda, Indee, Indiana.*

INDIGO (IN-dee-go) Latin: The color of dark blue used as a first name.

INDIRA (in-DEER-ah) Hindi mythology: Indira is the god of heaven and thunderstorms. History: Indira Gandhi, Indian leader. *Indra, Indria.*

INEZ (eye-NEZ) Spanish: "unadulterated." Variant form of Agnes. Ital: *Ines, Inesita;* Russ: *Inessa; Inetta, Ynes, Ynesita, Ynez.*

INGA (ING-ah) Scandinavian: "protected by Ing." Ing was a powerful god of fertility and peace, according to Norse mythology. The modern name comes from the name of an ancient Germanic deity and hero known by the different names of Inge, Ingo, Invaar, Ingvio, and Ingwi. History: First appears in *Ingaevones* as the name of an ancient German tribe mentioned by the Roman historian Tacitus. Music: Inge Borkh, renowned dramatic soprano. Theater: Inga Swenson, actress. *Ingaberg, Ingaborg, Inge, Ingeberg, Ingeborg.*

INGRID (ING-rid) Scandinavian: "Ing rides." Ing, the god of fertility, rides the land each year to prepare it for spring planting. Movies and Television: Ingrid Bergman, Swedish actress who won the Oscar for *Gaslight* (1944). Sports: Ingrid Kristiansen, Norwegian who set women's marathon world record (1985). *Inge, Inger, Ingmar.* See Inga.

INOCENCIA (ee-no-SEN-see-ah) Spanish: "innocence." *Inocenta, Inocentia.*

IOLA (eye-OH-lah) Greek: "violet-colored dawn."

IOLANA (ee-oh-LAH-nah) Hawaiian: "to soar like the hawk."

IORWEN (eye-or-WHEN) Welsh: "beautiful."

IPHIGENIA (iff-ah-ZHEN-ee-ah) Greek mythology: The eldest child of Agamemnon and Clytemnestra. She was sacrificed by her father in order to get favorable winds for the Greek fleet on its way to Troy. Her mother used this act as an excuse for murdering Agamemnon. *Iffy, Iphigene.*

IRENE (eye-REEN) Greek: "bestowing peace." First appeared in English-speaking countries in the mid-nineteenth century. Popular during the Roman Empire. Movies and Television: Irene Dunne, actress. Sports: Irena Szwinski, Polish athlete who won record seven Olympic medals in track and field. Theater: Irene Worth, actress. Slav: *Eirena, Eirene, Erena, Irayna, Ireen, Irena;* Eng: *Iren, Irena, Irin, Irine, Rene;* Russ: *Irenee, Irenka, Ira; Irina;* Lat: *Irka, Irisha;* Rum: *Irini, Arinka, Ira, Irena, Irina, Irishka, Rina, Yarina, Yaryna.*

IRISA (ee-REE-sah) Greek: "from the flower iris." Astrology: Symbolic flower of the moon. Literature: Iris Murdoch, British author (1919–1999) known for witty and sensitive novels. Mythology: In Greek mythology, it is the rainbow deity. Eng: *Iris;* Russ: *Irisa, Irisha.*

IRMA (ERR-mah) Latin: "nobel."

IRVETTE (er-VETT) Old English: "friend of the sea." Also a Scottish place name.

ISABEL (ee-sah-BELL) Hebrew: "sworn to the Almighty." Arts: Isabel Bishop, painter. Literature: Isabel Archer, the protagonist in Henry James's *Portrait of a Lady*. History: Isabella Baum Free, abolitionist who raised funds during the Civil War for black education. Movies and Television: Isabella Rossellini and Isabel Sanford, actresses. *Bel, Bella, Belicia, Belita, Bell, Gelle, Ibbie, Isa, Isabeau, Isabelita, Isabella, Isabelle, Isobel, Isobella, Isobelle, Issie, Issy, Izabella, Izabelle, Izzie, Izzy, Ysabel, Ysobel.*

ISADORA (iz-ah-DORR-ah) Latin: "gift of Isis." Dance: Isadora Duncan, 1878–1927, modern dancer. Mythology: Isidore was a popular name among the Greeks because of the goddess Isis. *Isidora.*

ISATAS (EE-stahs) Native American: "snow."

ISHA (EE-shah) Israel. Hebrew: "woman."

ISHI (ee-SHEE) Japanese: "rock." *Ishiko, Ishiyo, Shiko, Shiyo.*

ISIS (EYE-siss) Egyptian mythology: Sister of Osiris and the most powerful of all the female goddesses.

ISLA (ees-LAH) Celtic: "island."

ISMAELA (ees-mah-AY-lah) Israel. Hebrew: "God listens." *Isma, Maela, Maella.*

ISOKA (ee-SOH-keh) Nigeria. Benin: "satisfying gift from God." *Soka.*

ISOLDE (ee-ZOHL-dah) Origins unclear, though some sources offer the Welsh "fair lady." The name of a legendary Irish princess beloved by Tristan, but forced to marry her royal uncle. Music: The most famous version of this tale is Wagner's opera *Tristan and Isolde. Iseult, Isold, Isolda, Isolt, Isolte, Ysolda, Ysolde.*

ISTVAN (EESHT-vahn) Greek: "crowned with laurels." Popular in Hungary. *Pista, Pisti.*

ITA (ee-TAH) Italian: "thirsty."

ITALIA (ee-TAL-ya) Latin: "from Italy." *Talia.*

IVANA (ee-VAH-na) Hebrew: "Jehovah's generosity." Business: Made famous by Ivana Trump, corporate executive, novelist, and former wife of Donald Trump. *Ivanka, Ivanna, Ivania, Ivannia.*

IVEREM (ee-VEH-rem) Hebrew: "blessing and favor."

IVONNE (eye-VAHN) Russian: Variant form of Yvonne. *Ivonna.*

IVORY (EYE-vree) Latin: The creamy-white color, or the hard tusk of an elephant.

IVRIA (ee-VREE-ah) Hebrew: Variant of *Ivri,* meaning "across the banks of the Euphrates River" or "home of Abraham." Bible: Name for the tribe of Israel. *Ivriah, Ivrit.*

IVY (EYE-vee) Old English: "crawling ivy." Literature: Ivy Compton-Burnett, nineteenth-century English novelist. Mythology: The plant was revered as a holy object. *Ivey, Ivie, Iva, Ivalyn, Ivyanne.*

IWILLA (eye-WILL-ah) United States. English: "I will arise again." Invented name used by African-Americans in the 1800s.

IYABO (ee-YAH-boh) Nigeria. Yoruba: "mother has returned."

JACINDA (jah-SINN-dah) Greek: "hyacinth flower." Mythology: The beloved of Apollo; the flower sprang up in his blood when he died. *Giacinda, Giacintha;* Span: *Giancinthia, Jacenda, Jacenta;* Eng: *Jacey, Jade, Jacindia, Jacinna, Jacinta, Jacinth, Jacinthe, Jacinthia, Jacy, Jacynth.*

JACINTA (hah-SIN-tah) Spanish: "purple."

JACKIE (JAK-ee) French: Used as an independent name in the twentieth century. Jacqueline Bouvier Kennedy, widow of President John F. Kennedy, is known as Jackie. Eng: *Jackee, Jacki, Jacky, Jacqui, Jacquie, Jacquetta.* See Jacqueline.

JACOBINA (JAK-ko-BEE-nah) Israel. Hebrew: "the hard supplies." Scottish people use this feminization of Jacob. Eng: *Jackee, Jackie, Jacky;* Fr: *Jacoba, Jacobette.*

JACQUELINE (JAK-ka-lin; jak-LEEN) French: "one who replaces others." Aeronautics: Jacqueline Cochran, first woman to break the sound barrier. History: Noticed in England as early as the 1600s, peaking in the 1960s with the appearance of First Lady Jacqueline Bouvier Kennedy. Literature: Jacqueline Suzanne, novelist, *The Valley of the Dolls*. Movies and Television: Jacqueline Bisset, actress *(The Deep)* and Jaclyn Smith, actress (TV's *Charlie's Angels)*. Sports: Jackie Joyner-Kersee, Olympic gold-medalist in track and field. *Jacalyn, Jackalin, Jackelyn,* Fr: *Jackette, Jacketta,* Eng: *Jacki, Jackie, Jacklin, Jaclyn, Jacolyn, Jacqualine, Jacquelyn;* Span: *Jackquenetta, Jacquenette, Jacquetia, Jacquelynne, Jacqui, Jacquine, Jacaline, Jaquette, Jaqueline, Jaquelyn, Jaquith.*

JADE (jayd) Spanish: The jade stone. Healing gem in Buddhist countries of Burma and Tibet where it was used to cure heart disease and avert storms. Movies and Television: Jada Pinkett Smith, actress (*Collateral*). *Jada, Jadira, Jadee, Jady, Jaida, Jaide, Jaydra.*

JADZIE (JAD-zee) Polish: "princess."

JAE (jaye) Latin: "jaybird." Span: *Jaclana, Jacleah, Jacleen, Jacna;* Fr: *Jacnelle, Jacnette, Jaya, Jayleen, Jaylene, Jaylee, Jaylynn.*

JAEL (ya-AYL) Israel. Hebrew: "she-goat who runs untamed." Used for both sexes in Israel. Astrology: Excellent for those born under Capricorn, symbolized by the goat. Bible: Wife of the Kenite Heber, and slayer of Sisera, Canaanite chieftain.

JAFIT (ya-FEET) Israel. Hebrew: "fair" or "profoundly attractive." *Jaffi, Jaffice.*

JAHA (JAH-ha) East Africa. Swahili: "dignity."

JAHZARA (jahz-ARE-ah) African: "blessed princess."

JAINA (JAY-nah) Hindu: "good character."

JAIONE (JAY-own-ay) Basque: nativity."

JAIRA (JAI-rah) Spanish: "Jehovah teaches."

JALA (JA-lah) Arabic: "charity."

JALENA (jah-LEEN-ah) Slavic: "light."

JALILA (jah-LIE-lah) Arabic: "great."

JAMAICA (ja-MAY-ka) English: Place name. The name of West Indies island used as given name.

JAMIE (JAY-mee) Scottish, Spanish: Variant forms of James. Used for both sexes. *Jaime, Jaimee, Jaimelynn, Jamee, Jamey, Jaymie, Jaymee, Jamia, Jamielee, Jamilyn, Jamison, Jamesina,* Eng: *Jamie-Lee, Jamie-Lynn;* Arab: *Jamell, Jamila,* Heb: *Jametta.*

JAN (jahn) Israel. Hebrew: "Lord full of grace." *Jana, Janina, Janine, Jann, Janna.*

JANAE (ja-NAY) Hebrew: A popular "Ja" name. Bible: Janai is a Biblical male name meaning "God has replied." *Janay, Janai, Janaye, Jannae, Jeanae, Jeanay, Jenae, Jenay, Jenee, Jenai, Jennae, Jennay, Jenaya, Janaya, Janais.*

JANE (jayne) Israel. Hebrew: "God's grace." Multicultural variations. Education: Jane Addams, American social settlement worker, co-founder of Hull House in Chicago (1889). Journalism: Jane Pauley, TV news anchor. Literature: *Jane Eyre*, the classic novel by Charlotte Brontë; Jane Austen, author of *Pride and Prejudice*. Movies and Television: Jane Fonda, actress, Oscar for *Klute* (1971). Science: Jane Wright, cancer researcher. Sports: Janine Aiello, athlete who set women's record for stair-climbing. *Jan, Jana, Janae, Janeen, Janela, Janelle, Janean, Janesa, Janessa, Janet, Janeta, Janetta, Janette, Janey, Janice, Janie, Janina, Janine, Janis, Janna, Jayne, Jaynelle;* Eng: *Jean, Jeanette, Jeanie, Jeanine, Jeanne, Jenni, Jennie, Jenny, Jess, Jessy, Jinni, Joan, Joana, Joanna, Joanne, Joann, Joanny, Joeann, Johanna, Joni, Jonie;* Braz: *Joana;* Czech: *Jana, Janka, Janica, Jenka, Johanka;* Fr: *Jeanne, Jeanette;* Ger: *Hanna, Johanna, Jutta;* Gk: *Ioanna;* Hung: *Zsanett;* Ir: *Sheena, Shena;* Ital: *Gianina, Giovanna;* Pol: *Joanka, Zannz;* Russ: *Ivanna, Ioanna;* Slav: *Iva, Ivanka;* Span: *Juana, Juanita.*

JANEETA (JAHN-ee-tah) Islamic: "gift of God."

JANESSA (jah-NESS-ah) Contemporary blend of Jan and Vanessa. *Janesse, Janissa, Jannessa.*

JANET (jah-NETT) Scottish: Variant form of Jane, from the French Jeanette. Journalism: Janet Ranner, journalist who wrote biweekly "Letter from Paris" in *The New Yorker* magazine from 1925–75. Literature: Janet Rosenburg, author of *Reinventing Home.* Movies and Television: Janet Leigh, actress. Music: Janet Jackson, pop singer. Sports: Janet Guthrie, first woman to compete at the Indianapolis 500. *Janette, Jannet, Janett, Jannetta, Janeth, Janneth.*

JANICE (JA-niss) Variant form of Jane. Literature: Character in Paul Ford's novel *Janice Meredith. Janiece, Jannice, Janise, Janicia, Janis, Jannis.*

JANINE (jah-NEEN) Variant form of Jane. *Janina, Jannee, Janene, Jannine, Jannina.*

JANNA (jahn-NAH) Hebrew: "flourishing."

JARDENA (yar-DAY-na) Israel. Hebrew: "running downhill."

JARVINA (jar-VIN-ee-yah) German: "keen intelligence."

JASMINE (JAZ-min) Persian: "jasmine flower." In botany lore, jasmine represents kindness and affability. Used by the upper class at the turn of the century, it became fashionable among the masses in the 1930s. *Jasmin, Jasmina, Jazmin, Jessamine, Jessamyn, Jessi;* Eng: *Jessie;* Hindi: *Yasman, Yasmine.*

JAVIERA (HA-vee-ER-ah) Spanish: "shining." *Javeera, Xaviera.*

JAYNE (jayne) Sanskrit "triumphant."

JAZLYN (JAZ-lin) Contemporary: Variant form of Jasminea. *Jazzlyn, Jazlynn, Jaslyn, Jaslynn, Jasleen, Jazzalyn;* Fr: *Jasmaine, Jazmaine, Jasminique;* Eng: *Jazmina, Jazma, Jazzy.*

JEAN (jeen) French: "divine grace is falling." Scottish variant of Joan and popular worldwide. Astrology: Jeanne Dixon, psychic. Movies and Television: Jean Stapleton, actress (TV's *All in the Family*). Eng: *Jeane, Jeanette, Jeanie, Jeanine, Jenica, Jennine;* Finn: *Janne;* Fr: *Jeanne;* Hawaiian: *Kini;* Hung: *Janka, Johanna;* Ital: *Giovanna, Vanna;* Pol: *Janina, Janka, Janeska, Nina;* Slav: *Ivana.*

JEANELLE (ja-NELL) Contemporary: Variant form of Jean. *Jeannelle. Jeanette, Jenelle, Jenella.*

JEANETTE (ja-NETT) Diminutive of Jean. A favorite name in France and Scotland, frequently used in the United States. Arts: Jeanette Kastenberg, fashion designer. Movies and Television, Music: Jeanette MacDonald, singing actress. Politics: Jeanette Rankin, member of Congress. *Jeannette, Jeanetta, Jenette;* Scot: *Jennet.*

JEEVIKA (JEV-ee-kah) Hindu: "water."

JELENA (yay-LAY-nah or juh-LAY-nah) Russian: "illumination" or "candle." Variant of Helena. See Helen.

JEMINA (jay-MEE-nuh) Israel. Hebrew: "favoring the right side." *Jem, Jemi, Jemma, Jemmi, Jemmie, Jemmy, Mina.*

JEMIMA (jah-MYE-mah) Israel. Hebrew: "dove" or "bright as day." Jemima was one of Job's three stunning daughters. The Puritans brought the name to the United States. History: Jemima Wilkinson, nineteenth-century religious leader who established a colony near Seneca Lake, New York. *Jamima, Jemimah, Jemmimah, Jemmie, Jemmy, Mima, Mimma.*

JEMMA (JEM-ah) Short form of Jemima.

JENDAYA (jen-DAH-ya) Zimbabwe. Shona: "give thanks." *Daya.*

JENICA (zhye-NEE-ka or anglicized to jah-NEE-kah) Russian: Contemporary variant of Jane. See Jane.

JENNA (JENN-ah) Variant form of Jenny. *Jennah, Jennabel, Jennalee, Jennalyn, Jannarae, Jennasee, Jenesi.* See Jenny.

JENNIFER (JENN-ah-fer) Old Welsh: "white frothy waves" or "pale ghost." Widely used in United States, it was originally a Cornish variant of Guinevere, King Arthur's unfaithful wife. *Genn, Gennifer, Genny, Ginnifer, Jenefer, Jeni, Jenifer, Jeniffer, Jenn, Jenni, Jennica, Jennie, Jenniver, Jenny, Jeny.*

JENNY (JEN-ee) English: Diminutive form of Jane and Jennifer. Music: Jenny Lind, Swedish soprano. *Jennie, Jenni, Jeni, Jinny, Jen, Jennyann, Jennylee, Jenilee, Jenalee, Jennilyn, Jenilynn, Jenalyn, Jena, Jeneen, Jenene, Jenetta, Jenita, Jen-*

nis, Jenice, Jeniece, Jenise, Jenarae, Jennessa, Jennika.

JEOVANA (joh-VAN-nah) Variant of Jovana. *Jeovanna.*

JERALYN (jer-ah-LINN) Contemporary: Blend of Jerry and Marilyn. *Jerelyn, Jerilyn, Jerilynn, Jerralyn, Jerrilyn.*

JERICA (JARE-ah-kah) Contemporary: "strong, gifted ruler." Blend of Jeri and Erica. *Jerrica, Jerika, Jerrika.*

JERUSHA (jer-YU-shah) Hebrew: "inheritance."

JESSICA (JESS-sah-kah) Israel. Hebrew: "wealthy." Literature: Character in Shakespeare's *The Merchant of Venice*. Movies and Television: Jessica Tandy, actress who won an Oscar for her role in *Driving Miss Daisy* (1989). Music: Jessica Simpson, popular American singer, best known for her TV show, *The Newlyweds*. *Jess, Jessi, Jessie, Jessy;* Eng: *Jessalyn, Jesslyn;* Hung: *Janka, Gessica.*

JEWELL (jew-ELL) French: "precious gem." Music: Jewel Kilcher, popular American singer.

JEZEBEL (JEZ-ah-bel) Israel. Hebrew: "lost prince." Bible: Phoenician princess, wife of Israel's King Ahab. *Jez, Jezzie.*

JIANA (jee-ANN-ah) Contemporary: Phonetic form of Gianna, an Italian form of Jane. *Jianina, Jianna, Jianine.*

JIERA (geh-ERA) Lithuanian: "living."

JILL (jill) Latin: "youthful." Diminutive of Gillian. Popular before 1600, then revived after the 1920s. Movies and Television: Jill Ireland, Jill St. John, and Jill Eikenberry, actresses. Sports: Jill Trenery, figure-skating world champion (1990). *Jilian, Jilan, Jillana, Jilane, Jillayne, Jilleen, Jillene, Jilli, Jillian, Jillie, Jilly, Jillyan, Jyl.*

JILLIAN (JILL-ee-ahn) Latin: "pure babe." *Gilli, Gillian, Gillie, Jill, Jillianna.*

JIN (gin) Japanese: "better than best." Japanese parents avoid this name out of fear it will demand too much of the child.

JISELLE (ji-ZELL) Contemporary: "allegiance."

JOAN (jone) Israel. Hebrew: "Lord full of graces." Popular in the early twentieth century, though rarely used today. History: Joan of Arc, the maid of Orleans, patron saint of France. Movies and Television: Joan Crawford and Joan Collins, actresses; Joan Rivers, comedian. Music: Joan Baez, folk singer. *Joane, Joanie, Jonee, Joni.*

JOANNA (jo-AH-nah) Variant of Jane or Joan. Popular in the nineteenth century until the 1950s. Literature: Joanna Southcott, nineteenth-century British religious fanatic who wrote *Book of Wonders;* Joanne Kathleen (J. K.) Rowling, famous British author who wrote the *Harry Potter* series; Joanna Bailli, nineteenth-century British dramatist and poet. Movies and Televison: Joanna Gleason,

Tony Award-winning actress. Music: Title of a Stephen Sondheim song ("Johanna"). *Jo, Joana, Joann, Jo Ann, Joanne, Jo Anne, Joeann, Johanna, Johannah.*

JOAQUINA (wah-KEE-nah) Spanish: "Jehovah's decision."

JOBY (JO-bee) Israel. Hebrew: "tormented" or "diseased." Originally a nickname for Jobina, but used today as an independent name in the United States. *Jobi, Jobie.*

JOCASTA (jo-KASS-tah) Latin: "cheerful." Mythology: Jocasta was the mother of the tragic Oedipus who marries her unknowingly.

JOCELYN (JOSS-lin or JOS-sa-lyn) English, French: "light-hearted." Music: cellist Jocelyn DuPre. *Jocelynn, Joceline, Jocelina, Joscelyn, Josalyn, Josalynn, Josilyn, Joslyn, Joslin, Jozlin, Josalind.*

JODELLE (jo-DELL) French: Surname used as a given name. *Jodell, Jo Dell.*

JODI (JO-dee) Israel. Hebrew: "glorified." Recently transformed into independent name but originally nickname for Judith. Movies and Television: Jodie Foster, Academy Award-winning actress for *The Accused* (1988) and *Silence of the* Lambs (1991). History: Jodi Bilinkoff, historian. Jody Williams, 1997 Nobel Peace Prize winner for her work banning anti-personnel mines. *Jodie, Jody.*

JOELLE (jo-ELL) French: "Jehovah is God." *Joella, Joellen, Joellyn, Joell.*

JOKLA (JOH-klah) East African. Swahili: "robe of adornment."

JOLAN (YOH-lahn or jo-LAHN) Greek: "purple flower." Popular in Hungary as variant of Yolanda.

JOLIE (JOH-lee) French: "pretty to behold." Popular since the 1960s. *Jolee, Joley, Joli, Joly.*

JOLINE (yo-LEEN) Israel. Hebrew: "she whose fortunes shall multiply." *Joleen, Jolene.*

JONINA (yo-NEE-nah) Israel. Hebrew: "bird of paradise" or "dove of peace." *Jona, Jonati, Jonit, Yona, Yonit, Yonita.*

JONQUIL (JAHN-quil) Flower name. Member of the amaryllis family known for its yellow or white fragrant leaves. Popular in England. *Jonquille.*

JORA (YO-rah) Israel. Hebrew: "fall mists." Astrology: Excellent for females born under the sign of Scorpio. *Jorah.*

JOSEPHINE (JO-sah-FEEN) Israel. Hebrew: "God augments." History: The nickname of Napolean's empress, born Marie Josepheo. Literature: Josephine Tey, mystery writer, author of *Singing Sands.* Music: Josephine Baker, cabaret star. Theater: Josephine Peabody, playwright. Fr: *Fifi, Fifine;* Ital: *Fina, Guiseppina, Jo, Joette, Joey, Joline, Josee, Josefa, Josefina, Josefine, Josepha,*

Josephe, Josephina, Josetta, Josette, Josey, Josie, Jozsa.

JOVITA (joh-VEE-tah) Latin: Originated during the Middle Ages. May be considered a shortening of Joyce. *Gioia, Joi, Joie, Joya, Joyann, Joye.*

JOYCE (joice) Latin: "joyous." Trendy in the early twentieth century. Literature: Joyce Gary, British novelist; Joyce Carol Oates, short-story writer and novelist; Science: Joyce Brothers, psychologist and advice columnist. *Joice, Joycelyn, Joyoua.*

JOY (joy) Latin: "joy." Literature: Joy Williams, writer. Science: Joy Gessner Adamson, British naturalist who wrote *Born Free. Gioia, Joi, Joie, Joya, Joyann, Joye.*

JOYITA (hoy-EE-tah) Hispanic: "jewel."

JUANITA (wah-NEE-tah) Spanish: Diminutive form of Juana. *Juana, Juanetta, Juanisha, Nita.*

JUDITH (JOO-dith) Israel. Hebrew: "glorified one" or "from Judah." Arts: Judy Chicago, painter and sculptor. Bible: Old Testament name that came into fashion from the 1920s to the 1960s. Movies and Television: Judith Anderson, Australian actor; Judith Ann Ford, Miss America 1969. Music: Judith Blegen, opera singer. Eng: *Jodi, Jodie, Jody, Judy, Judi, Judie;* Bulg: *Judita;* Czech: *Jitka;* Fr: *Judithe;* Gk: *Ioudithe;* Hung: *Jucika, Jutka;* Ital: *Guila;* Port: *Judite;* Lith: *Judita;* Russ: *Yudif, Yudita;* Swed: *Judit, Judeana, Juditha.*

JULIA (JOO-lee-ah) Latin: "young" or "freshly sown." An international name. Literature: Julia Moore, poet; Julia Peterkin, Pulitzer Prize-winning novelist *(Sister Mary,* 1928). Movies and Television: Julia Roberts, actress *(Steel Magnolias);* Julia Child, author, TV host *(The French Chef).* Eng: *Gillie, Julie, Juliet, Julietta, Julina, Juline, Julissa, Julica, Juliana;* Czech: *Juliska, Julka;* Fr: *Juliane, Juliette, Juli, Julianna;* Hung: *Julinka, Juiska;* Ir: *Sile;* Pol: *Julia, Julicia;* Russ: *Yulinka, Yuliya, Yulka, Yulya;* Scot: *Sileus;* Serb: *Jula, Yula;* Span: *Julieta, Julita.*

JULIANA (JOO-lee-AHN-ah) Latin: Clan name "young spirit." Early Christian saint name. During medieval times it was shortened to Gillian (and eventually to Jill). Movies and Televison: Julianne Moore, actress *(The Hours);* Julianna Margulies, actress (TV's *ER). Juliane, Julianna, Julianne, Julieanna, Julieanne, Julyana.*

JULIET (JOO-lee-ett) English, French: Variant form of Julia. Dance: Juliet Prowse, Broadway dancer. Education: Juliet Corson, established New York cooking school. Literature: Shakespeare used the name in *Romeo and Juliet* and *Measure for Measure.* Span: *Julieta;* Fr: *Juliette;* Ital: *Julietta.*

JUN (joon) Japanese: "respectful surrender" or Chinese: "verities of life."

JUNE (joon) Latin: "young." June is the bridal month, probably because Juno was the god of marriage. The name was popular during the 1950s. Literature: June Brindel, novelist, *Ariadne.* Movies and

Television: June Allyson, actress. *Junel, Junelle, Junette, Junae.*

JUNO (JOO-noh) Latin: "goddess of heaven." See June.

KAATJIE (kaht-JEE) Dutch: "pure."

KABIBE (KAHB-ee-bay) African: "little lady."

KABIRA (KAHB-ee-rah) African: "powerful."

KACHINA (kah-CHEE-nah) Native American: "sacred dancer."

KACIA (kah-SEE-yah) Greek: "thorny."

KACIE (KAY-see) Irish: "eagle-eyed." It started out as initials "K.C." and recently became popular as the phonetic spelling. *Kacey, Kaci, Kaycee, Kaycie, Kacy, Kacee, K.C. Kacia, Kaesha.*

KADY (KAY-dee) English: Rhyming variant of Katy or Cady. *Kadie, Kadi, Kadee, Kaedee, Kadia, Kadian, Kadienne.*

KAELYN (kay-LIN) Old English: "meadow."

KAETHE (KAY-thee) Greek: "pure."

KAGAMI (kah-GAE-mee) Japanese: "true reflection" or "pure mirror."

KAI (kay) Hawaiian: "deep blue seas."

KAIA (kay-AH) Greek: "earth."

KAIDA (KY-dah) Japanese: "little dragon."

KAIE (KAY-ee) Celtic: "combat."

KAIMI (KAI-mee) Polynesian: "the seeker."

KALA (KAH-la) Hindi: "dark-skinned" or "time." Otherwise known as Shiva, the Hindu principle of masculine energy.

KALANI (kah-LAH-nee) Hawaiian: Paraphrase of "the sky," or "the chieftain." *Kaloni, Kalanie, Kailani.*

KALANIT (kah-lah-NEET) Israel. Hebrew: "rainbow flower." Refers to a common Israeli flower that profusely dots the hillsides.

KALARE (KAH-lar-ay) Latin: "bright" or "clear."

KALEI (kah-LAY-ee) Hawaiian: "The flower wreath" or "the beloved."

KALI (ka-LEE or KAH-lee) Hindi: "the black one." The wrathful form of the Hindu goddess Shakti, known for her fearful appearance and bloodthirsty habits. In Bengal she is worshiped as the divine mother.

KALIKA (kah-LEE-kah) Greek: "rosebud."

KALILA (kahl-EE-lah) Arabic: "beloved."

KALINA (ka-LEE-na) Polish, Czechoslovakian: Flower name and place name. Kalena is the Hawaiian equivalent of Karen. *Kalena, Kaleen, Kalene, Kaleena.*

KALINDA (ka-LIN-da or ka-LEEN-da) Hindi: "solar power" or "shining source." Mythology: In Hindu lore, the mountains of Kalinda were thought to be sacred and the source of transcendent experiences. *Kaleenda.*

KALISKA (ka-LEE-ska) Native American. Miwok: "coyote on the tail of a doe." Mythology: According to Miwok legend all the animals of the Great Forest met one day to make the first man. Each one wanted to create man according to his own best qualities. But the coyote tricked everyone, and that night created man as the combination of all these qualities. Hence, man is strong like a bear, fearless as a fox, and crafty as a coyote.

KALISTA (kah-LIS-tah) Greek: "most beautiful one."

KALLAN (KAL-lin) Scandinavian: "stream."

KALLI (ka-LEE) Greek: "singing lark." Formerly used for Calandra, now a nickname in the United States. *Cal, Calli, Colli, Kal, Kallie, Kally.*

KALONICE (KAHL-ohn-ee-say) Greek: "beauty's victory."

KALYCA (ka-LEE-ka) Greek: "budding rose." *Kali, Kaly, Kalica, Kalika.*

KAMA (kah-MAH) Hawaiian: "babe who nurses"; Hindi: "one who incites love." Mythology: The Hindu god Kama is similar to Cupid who also used a bow and arrow to inspire love.

KAMALI (KA-ma-lee) Zimbabwe. Mahona: "spirit guide" or "protector." When plagues or disasters threaten a village, newborn babies are saved by the spirit named Kamali.

KAMARIA (kham-ARE-ee-yah) Swahili: "like the moon."

KAMBRIA (KAM-bree-a) Welsh: "of Wales." Variant of Cambria.

KAMEA (kah-MAY-ah) Hawaiian: "the one and only."

KAMEKO (KA-may-ko) Japanese: "turtle daughter." Since turtles are a symbol of longevity, this name bestows long life on the child.

KAMILA (ka-MEE-la) Hungarian: "sacred helper"; Arabic: "immaculate." Polish and Latvian variant of Camille. *Kamilah, Kamilla, Kamillah.*

KANANI (kah-NA-nee) Hawaiian: "beautiful lady." *Ani, Nani.*

KANDE (KAHN-dee) African: "first born daughter."

KANE (kayne) Japanese: "two right hands." From *Kaneru*, which refers to the ability to do many things at one time.

KANI (KAH-nee) Hawaiian: "sound." The Hawaiian equivalent of Sandy.

KAPRI (KAH-pree or kah-PREE) Italian: "arbitrary chooser." *Kaprice, Kapricia, Kaprisha.*

KAPUA (ka-POO-uh) Hawaiian: "flowering buds."

KARA (KAH-rah) Latin: "dear one." Eng: *Kara, Karah, Karalyn, Karalynn, Karalee, Kaira, Kari, Karie, Karrie, Kary, Karianne, Karianna, Kariana;* Fr: *Karielle;* Ir: *Karrah, Karrie.*

KARASI (kar-ASE-ee) African: "life and wisdom."

KAREN (KARE-inn) Greek: "without stain" or "immaculate." Education: Karen Horney, psychoanalyst and teacher. Literature: Karen Blixen (Isak Dinesen), author of *Out of Africa.* Eng: *Caren, Caron, Caryn, Karon, Karyn;* Latin: *Katina;* Russ: *Karina, Karyna;* Swed: *Karin.*

KARIMA (KARE-ee-mah) Arabic: "noble."

KARIS (KARE-iss) Greek: "grace."

KARISMA (ka-RIZ-ma) Origin unknown: "favor" or "gift."

KARISSA (kah-RISS-ah) Greek: "very dear."

KARLA (KAR-lah) Australian aborigine: "fire." German, Czech, and U.S. version of Charlotte. In aboriginal lore, one is forbidden to speak a deceased person's name. Hence, when the first Karla passed on, his name was eliminated from the language. Another word was chosen for fire. Literature: John Le Carre named George Smiley's Russian nemesis with the code name "Karla"; Karla Jay, author. *Karly, Karli, Karlie, Karlee, Karley, Karleigh, Karlesha, Karleen, Karlene, Karline, Karlina, Karlyn, Karlen, Karlin.*

KARLYN (KAR-lyn) Greek: "little and womanly."

KARMA (KAR-mah) Hindi: "just due" or "destiny." According to the Hindu doctrine of Karma, one's future is directly affected by one's present and past actions.

KARMEL (kar-MELL) Israel. Hebrew: "garden of grapes." A place name referring to Mount Carmel. Modern Israeli name. *Carmel, Carmi, Carmia, Karmeli, Karmi, Karmia, Karmiel;* Fr: *Karmielle.*

KARMINA (KAR-mee-nah) Hebrew: "song."

KAROLINA (kare-oh-LEE-nah) Russian: "tiny lady." Also variant of Caroline. History: Karoline Mikkelsen, first woman to set foot in Antarctica, 1935. Literature: Karolina Muzakova, Czech novelist; Karoline Pichler, Austrian novelist. See Caroline.

KARYAN (KARE-yee-ann) Armenian: "the dark one."

KASI (KA-shee) Hindi: "from the holy city." Banaras, a holy Hindu city, is commonly called Kasi.

KASINDA (ka-SEEN-dah) Africa. Umbundu: "earth closes up behind the last one." A wish-fulfilling name used by the Ovimbundu of Africa after many children have already been born.

KASMIRA (kas-MIR-ah) Old Slavic: "bringing peace."

KASSIDY (KASS-ee-dee) Irish: "curly-haired."

KATA (KAT-ah) Japanese: "worthy."

KATE (kayte) Greek: "chaste." Short form of Katherine. Aeronautics: Katherine Stinson, first woman to fly at night (1915); Literature: Kate Millet, feminist author; Kate Chopin (1851–1904), American short-story writer and novelist, known for her portrayal of Creole life in Louisiana in *The Awakening*. Movies and Television: Kate Mulgrew and Kate Melligan, actresses. *Cait, Caitie, Cate;* Ir: *Catey, Kaethe, Kait, Kaitlin;* Eng: *Kati;* Czech: *Katica, Katie, Katy;* Afr: *Kateke;* Russ: *Katka, Katerinka.*

KATHERINE, KATHLEEN, KATHRYN (KATH-rin, KATH-leen, KATH-rin) Greek: "chaste." Since the end of the Middle Ages, this name has been one of the most fashionable worldwide. Journalism: Katherine Graham, publisher of the *Washington Post.* Literature: Katherine Ann Porter, author *(Ship of Fools);* Katharine Mansfield, author; Kathleen Coyle, Irish novelist *(A Flock of Birds).* Movies and Television: Katharine Hepburn, actress. Science: Katherine Blodgett, inventor of non-reflecting glass. Eng: *Cari, Cass, Cassie, Catarina, Caterina, Catherine, Cathelina, Cathie, Kate, Kathie, Kathy, Katie, Katy, Kay, Kaye, Kit, Kittie, Kitty;* Czech: *Kata, Katarina, Katica, Katka, Katuska;* Est: *Katharina, Rina;* Fr: *Trinette;* Ger: *Katchen, Trinchen;* Hung: *Kata, Katinka, Kato, Katoka;* Ice: *Katrin;* Ir: *Caitlin;* Ital: *Katerina;* Lith: *Kofryna;* Norw: *Karena, Karin, Katia;* Pol: *Kasienka, Kaska;* Port: *Catarania;* Russ: *Katenka, Katerinka, Katinka, Katka, Katya, Kiska, Kotinka, Yekaterin, Yekaterina;* Span: *Catalina;* Swed: *Kajsa, Kolina.*

KATRIEL (ka-tree-ELL) Israel. Hebrew: "my crown is God."

KATRIEN (kat-REE-en) Dutch: "pure."

KATRINA (KAT-reen-ah) German: "pure."

KAULA (kawh-LAH) Polynesian: "prophet."

KAVERI (ka-VAIR-ee) Hindi: "the sacred Kaveri River." Hindu devotees cleanse their souls by bathing in this river, one of seven sacred ones in the religion. Such nature names are now popular, but once were considered base by families in high caste.

KAVITA (kav-EE-tah) Hindu: "poem."

KAY (kai) English, Scandinavian: "keeper of the keys." First appeared in the early 1900s. Sports: Kaye Hall, American Olympic medalist in swimming (2004). Literature: Kay Boyle, expatriate novelist who lived in France. *Caye, Kai, Kayanna, Kayana, Kaye.*

KAYA (KA-ya) Ghana: "don't leave, but live"; Native American. Hopi: "old babysitter," meaning the infant has great wisdom, despite its age.

KAYLA (KAY-lah) Hebrew: "crown of laurels." Popular variant of Kay. *Kaila, Kaylee, Kaylyn, Cayley.*

KAYLEE (kay-LEE) Variant of Kay. *Kayleigh, Kaylie, Kayley, Kayli, Kaylea, Kayleen, Kaylene, Kailee, Kailey, Kaley, Kalie, Kaleigh, Kalee, Kaeli, Kaeleigh, Kaelee, Kaelie.*

KAYLYN (kay-LINN) Variant combination of Kay and Lynn. *Cailin, Caylynne, Kaylynn, Kaylan, Kalyn, Kalin, Kalen, Kalan, Kaelyn, Kaelin, Kailynne, Kailin, Kailan, Kayleen, Kaelene, Kaileen, Kailene.*

KEALA (kay-AH-lah) Hawaiian: "the route."

KEELY (KEE-lee) Irish: "lively" or "aggressive." Variant form of Kelly. *Keeley, Keelie, Keelyn, Keila, Keilah.*

KEENA (KEE-nah) Irish, English: "quick" or "brave."

KEEYA (KEE-yah) African: "garden flower."

KEI (kay) Japanese: "respect" or "ecstasy." Popular in Japan.

KEIDA (KAY-dah) Old Norse: "flowing water." *Keli, Kelie, Kelli, Kelley, Kelly.*

KEIKI (ke-EE-kee or KAY-kee) Hawaiian: "child."

KEIKO (KAY-ko) Japanese: "adored one."

KEILANI (kay-ee-LAH-nee) Hawaiian: "glorious chief."

KEIRA (KEER-ah) Celtic: "black haired." Movies and Television: Keira Knightly, actress (*Pirates of the Caribbean*).

KEISHA (KEE-sha) Latin: Short form of Lakeisha, developed from Leticia, derived from the eighteenth-century name Letitia. *Keshia, Kisha, Kesha, Keesha, Kiesha, Kecia.*

KEITHA (keth-AH) Gaelic: "woodland." Variant of Keith.

KEKONA (ke-KO-nuh) Hawaiian: "second born."

KELBY (KELL-bee) Scandinavian, Gaelic: "place by the flowing water."

KELILA (ke-LEE-lah) Hebrew: "crown" or "laurel." Symbol of victory and beauty. Popular in Israel. *Kaele, Kayle, Kelilah, Kelula, Kyla, Kyle.*

KELLA (KEL-lah) Gaelic: "warrior."

KELLEN (KELL-lin) German: Possible derivative of Charles. *Kellyn, Kellan.*

KELLY (KELL-ee) Gaelic: "defender of justice." Music: Kelly Clarkson, singer who made her debut as the first winner of TV's American Idol. Sports: Kelley Law, Canadian Olympic medalist in curling (2002). *Keli, Kelia, Kellen, Kelley, Kelli, Kellia, Kellie, Kelilna, Kellisa.*

KELSI (KELL-see) Gaelic: "warrior"; Scandinavian: "from the ship island." *Kelci, Kelcie, Kelsy, Kelsie.*

KENDA (KEN-dah) English: "child of clear, cool water." Contemporary U.S. name. Astrology: excellent for water signs: Cancer, Scorpio, or Pisces. *Kendi, Kendie, Kendy, Kennda, Kenndi, Kenndie, Kenndy.*

KENDALL (KEN-dahl) Celtic: "ruler of the valley." Business: Kendall-Jackson, popular American wine from the vineyards in California.

KENDRA (KEN-drah) Contemporary: "regal protector." *Kenna, Kindra, Kenndrea, Kendria, Kyndra.*

KENISHA (ke-NEE-sha) Contemporary: "gorgeous woman." Blend of Ken and Iesha. *Kennesha, Keneisha, Keneshia.*

KENNIS (KEN-iss) Gaelic: "beautiful."

KENYA (KEN-yah) Africa: Name of the mountain and country in Africa, used as a given name.

KENZIE (KEN-zee) Scottish: "light one."

KEREN (KER-in) Israel. Hebrew: Name. Bible: One of the three daughters of Job. *Kerrin, Keryn.*

KERRY (KER-ee) Gaelic: "dusky." Literature: Keri Hume, author; Kerry Tucker, mystery writer. *Keri, Kerri, Kerrie, Kera, Keriann, Kerianne, Keriana, Kerianna, Kerra, Kerrianne.*

KESHIA (KESH-ah) Africa. "Most beloved." Movies and Television: Made famous by Keshia Knight Pulliam, child actress who played Rudy on TV's *The Cosby Show. Kesha, Shia.*

KETURA (ke-TOO-rah) Israel. Hebrew: "sacrifice." Bible: Second wife of Abraham.

KETZIA (ket-ZEE-ah) Israel. Hebrew: "bark that smells of cinnamon." *Ketti, Kezia, Kezi.*

KEVINA (KEV-i-nah) Contemporary: "beautiful person." *Keva, Kevia.*

KEZIA (ke-ZYE-ah) Israel. Hebrew: "cassia" or "sweet-scented spice." Cassia is a genus of trees and shrubs, one species of which produces cinnamon. Bible: One of Job's three daughters. *Kazia, Keziah, Kissie, Kizzy, Kesiah.*

KHALIDAH (kah-LEE-dah) Arabic: "immortal."

KIA (kay) African: "hill."

KIAH (KEY-ah) Australian. Aboriginal: "from the beautiful place."

KIANA (KEY-anah) Hawaiian: "moon goddess."

KIANGA (kay-OHN-gah) African: "sunshine."

KIARA (kee-AH-rah) Contemporary variation of Ciara and Tiara. *Kierra, Keira, Kiarra.*

KICHI (KEY-chee) Japanese: "fortunate."

KIELE (kee-EL-e) Hawaiian: "gardenia" or "fragrant blossom."

KIKI (KEE-kee) Spanish: Pet form of Enriqueta, from Henrietto.

KIKILIA (ke-ke-LEE-ah) Hawaiian: "dimsighted." Variant of Cecilia.

KIKU (kee-KOO or KEE-koo) Japanese: "chrysanthemum." The flower of September, it stands for longevity.

KILEY (kye-LEE) Gaelic: "good-looking." *Kilee.*

KIM (kim) Old English: "king" or "chief." Movies and Television: Kim Novak, actress (*Vertigo*); Kim Basinger, actress (*Batman*).

KIMANA (ke-MA-na) Native American. Shoshone: "butterfly." Mythology: According to native lore, God searched the earth as a butterfly to find the perfect location to fashion the first human.

KIMATRA (kim-AH-trah) Hindu: "seduce."

KIMBERLY (KIM-bur-lee) Old English: "from the king's fields." Common in the United States. *Kim, Kimberlee, Kimberlei, Kimberlie, Kimmie, Kimmy, Kym, Kymberley.*

KIMI (KEE-mee) Japanese: "uncomparable" or "supreme." *Kim, Kimiko, Kimiyo, Miko.*

KINA (KEE-nah) Hawaiian: "China." Equivalent of Tina.

KINETA (kee-NET-tah) Greek: "energetic player." From the same root as "kinetic."

KIOKO (kee-OH-koh) Japanese: "child who meets the world with happiness."

KIRA (KEE-rah) Russian: "lady." *Kiri, Kirra, Kiran, Kirana.*

KIRAN (KEY-rahn) Hindi: "ray."

KIRBY (KIR-bee) English: "farm associated with a church."

KIRIMA (kerr-ee-MAH) Eskimo: "a hill."

KIRSI (KEER-see) India. Dravidian: "amaranth blossoms." Amaranth flowers are known for never fading. The Todas of India use this name widely.

KIRSTEN (KEER-stin) Scandinavia: "one who follows Christ." Popular in Norway. Music: Kirsten Flagstad, Norwegian opera star. *Keerstin, Kersten, Kerstin, Kirstin, Kiersten, Kierstin, Kirsty,*

Kirstyn, Kirstynn, Kyrstin, Kierstin, Kirstine, Kirstie.

KISHI (KEE-shee) Japanese: "beside the shore." This name bestows long life on the child.

KISKA (KISS-ka) Russian: "chaste." Popular variant of Katherine.

KISMET (KIZ-met) Turkish: Contemporary: "fate" or "destiny."

KITA (KEE-tah) Japanese: "northward." In Japanese lore, the different directions of the compass hold sacred meanings.

KITRA (KEY-trah) Hebrew: "a crown."

KIZZY (KIZ-ee) Israel. Hebrew: "cinnamon," a coarse cinnamon bark. Literature: Character in Alex Haley's *Roots*. *Kissie, Kizzie.*

KLARIKA (klar-EE-kah) Hungarian: "brilliant."

KLAUDIA (KLAW-dee-ah) Latin: "limping." *Claudia.*

KOHANA (KO-han-ah) Japanese: "little flower."

KOKO (KO-ko) Japanese: "stork." In East Asian mythology, the stork symbolizes long, healthy life.

KOLINA (ko-LEE-na) Swedish: "chaste." Variant of Katherine. See Katherine.

KOMALA (KOM-ah-lah) Hindi: "delicate."

KONA (KO-nah) Hindi: "hard curves." Astrology: good for child born under the sign of Capricorn. Mythology: Alternate name Saturn, a divinity of Hindu lore.

KONANE (koh-NAH-nee) Hawaiian: "lunar glow."

KORA (KOH-rah) Greek: "lithe maid." Literature: Author James Fenimore Cooper began a trend by inventing the name in *The Last of the Mohicans*. *Cora, Corabel, Corabella, Corabelle;* Span: *Corabellita, Corella, Corena, Coretta, Corey, Cori, Corilla, Corrie, Corry, Coryna, Korabell, Koree, Koreen, Korella, Korena, Korenda, Korette, Korey, Korilla, Korina, Korinna, Korinne, Korissa, Korrina, Korynna, Koryssa.*

KOREN (KORE-en) Greek: "maiden."

KORI (KO-ree) Greek: "lass." United States. English: Adaptation of Cora. *Cori, Corie, Cory, Corri, Corrie, Corry, Korie, Kory, Korri, Korrie, Korry.*

KOSTYA (KO-stya) Russian: "faithful" or "persistent." Contemporary usage in Russia.

KOTO (KO-to) Japanese: "string jewel" or "harp."

KRISTIN (KRISS-tin) Scandinavia: "follower of Christ." Variant of Christina, popular in the United States for half a century. Arts: Kristin Morrow, furniture designer. Education: Kristin Kold, nineteenth-century Danish educator who established basic pattern for the residential high school. Sports: Kristi Yamaguchi, Olympic gold medalist in figure skating (1990). *Krissie, Krissy, Krista, Kristan, Kristeen, Kristel, Kristelle, Kristi, Kirstyna, Kristina, Kristine, Kristyn, Kristyna, Krisztina, Krystyna.*

KRITI (KRIH-tee) Hindu: "a work of art."

KRYSTA (KRISS-tah) Polish: Form of Christina.

KRYSTAL (KRISS-tal) United States. English: Variant of Christina. Also, variant of crystal, a healing gem. *Cristalle, Cristel, Crysta, Khristalle, Khristel, Khrystle, Khrystalie, Kristel, Krystalle, Khrystale.*

KSENA (KHES-ee-nah) Polish: "praise to god."

KUAI HUA (kwigh-KHWAH) Chinese: "mallow flower." Oriental healers use the mallow flower to destroy demons and ward off evil.

KUMIKO (KOO-mee-koh) Japanese: "girl with braids." Short form is Kumi meaning "braided locks."

KUMUDA (kuh-MOO-da) Sanskrit: "lotus flower." A sacred flower in both Hindu and Buddhist practices.

KUNIKO (KOO-nee-koh) Japanese: "child from the countryside." Short form is Kuni meaning "from the countryside."

KURI (KOO-ree) Japanese: "chestnut." A magical tree in Japanese lore, the chestnut is rarely cut down out of fear of displeasing the gods.

KUSA (KOO-sah) Hindi: "God's grass." Devoted Hindus offer the needlelike kusa grass during seasonal rituals to obtain immortal life for their ancestors. Jewelry made of kusa grass wards off demons.

KYA (KI-ah) African: "diamond in the sky."

KYLA (KI-lah) Yiddish: "wreath" or "royal crown"; Irish Gaelic: "beside the church" or "attractive."

KYLAR (KI-lahr) Celtic: "chapel."

KYNA (KI-nah) Gaelic: "wise."

KYOKO (kee-OH-ko) Japanese: "mirror."

KYRA (KEER-rah or KYE-rah) Greek: "enthroned" or "madame." Variant form of Cyra. Gk: *Kryie, Kyria, Kyrene, Keera, Keira, Kira.*

LAASYA (laah-SIGH-ah) Hindi: "dance."

LABDHI (LAHB-dee) Indian: "heavenly power."

LACEY (LAY-see) United States. English: Variant of Larissa. Highly popular. *Lacee, Lacie*.

LADA (LAH-dah) Slavic: "goddess of love and fertility."

LADONNA (LAH-doe-nah) Spanish: "the woman."

LAEL (LAY-el) Israel. Hebrew: "of God."

LAHELA (lah-HAY-luh) Hawaiian: "sheep." Variant of Rachel.

LAILA (LAY-lah) Persian, Arabic: "night's child." Music: famous song by Eric Clapton. *Leila;* Swahili: *Layla, Laylah.*

LAINA (LAY-nah) English: "route" or "path." *Layna, Layne, Laine, Laney, Lanie, Lainie, Lania.*

LAINEY (LAY-neeh) English: "sun ray."

LAKA (LA-kah) Hawaiian: "pacify" or "seduce." The goddess associated with the traditional hula dance is called Laka.

LAKEISHA (lah-KEE-shah) Contemporary: Variants of Leticia. African-American creation. *Lakeesha, Lakecia, Lakesha, Laketia, Lakeyshia, Lakisha, Lakeshia, Lakiesha, Lakitia, Lekeisha, Lekisha, Laquisha.*

LAKSHA (lahk-SHA) Hindi: "white rose."

LALA (lah-LAH) Slavic: "flower" or "tulip."

LALI (LAH-lee) Spanish: Short form of Eulalie. Lala is the Hawaiian equivalent of Lara. Also a form of Helen. *Lalai, Lala, Lalla, Lally.*

LALO (LAH-loe) Latin: "to sing a lullabye."

LANA (LAN-ah or LAHN-ah) Hawaiian: "appealing to the eye." Short form of Alana. *Lanna, Lannette, Lanae, Lanice, Lanni.*

LANDRA (lahn-DRAH) German: "counselor."

LANI (LAH-nee) Hawaiian: "heavens" or "celestial home."

LANZA (LAHN-sah) Italian: "noble and eager."

LARA (LAR-ah) Latin: "protection." Mythology: In Roman mythology, Lares were spirits that guarded crossroads, and then became household gods. *Lara-laine, Laramae, Larinda, Larina, Larita, Lari.*

LARAINE (la-RAIN) Variant form of Lorraine. *LaRayne, Larraine.*

LAREINA (la-RAIN-ah) Spanish: "the queen." *Larena.*

LARISSA (lah-REE-sah) Greek: "happy girl" or "smiling heart." Variant form of Lara. Russ: *Larisa, Larochka, Laryssa, Laressa.*

LARK (lahrk) Middle English: Name of a bird known for its playful song. Nature name used since the 1950s in the United States.

LATANYA (lah-TAHN-yah) Contemporary blend of La and Tanya. An African-American creation. *Latania, Latonia, Latonya.*

LATASHA (la-TAH-sha) Contemporary blend based on Natasha meaning "birthday." *Latashia, Latoshia.*

LATEEFAH (lah-TEE-fah) North Africa. Arabic: "calm" or "sweet." Music: Queen Latifah, popular hip hop artist. *Latifa.*

LATICIA (LAAH-tee-see-ah) Modern form of the medieval name Leticia, meaning "joyful."

LATIKA (lah-TEE-kah) Hindi: "elegant."

LATISHA (la-TEE-sha) United States. English: Contemporary African-American combination name based on Letitia. *Lakeisha, Leticia, Tisha.*

LATOYA (lah-TOY-ya) Spanish: "victorious one." An African-American combination of La and Toya. Music: LaToya Jackson, singer, sister of Michael Jackson. *Latoia, Latoyla.*

LAURA (LAU-rah) Latin, English: "laurel tree." Laura has been used for more than 800 years. In the Greek and Roman era, valiant soldiers were given wreaths of laurels to honor their victory. The fourteenth-century Italian, Petrarch, wrote many of his sonnets to his beloved Laura. Literature: Laura Ingalls Wilder, author (*Little House on the Prairie*). Movies and Television: *Laura,* classic film of the 1940s; Laura Dern, actress (*Ramblin' Rose*). Sports: Laura Baugh, youngest winner of U.S. Women's Amateur Golf Championship. Eng: *Lari, Larel, Larella, Lauren, Laureen, Laurena, Laurene, Laretta, Laurette, Laurice, Laurie, Lauriett, Lora, Loreen, Loren, Lorena, Lorene, Loretta, Lorette, Lorie, Lorinda, Lorita, Lorna, Lorri, Lory;* Bulg: *Lora;* Fr: *Lauretee;* Hawaiian: *Lola;* Ital: *Lauretta;* Pol: *Laurka;* Port: *Laurinda;* Russ: *Lavra;* Span: *Laureana, Laurita, Lauraine, Lauralee, Laure, Lauriane, Laurentine, Lauretta, Laurice.*

LAUREN (LAWH-ren) Variation of Laura, introduced by Lauren Bacall, actress (*The Big Sleep*). Popular in the 1940s. Designer Ralph Lauren has extended its popularity to the present time. Movies and Television: Lauren Hutton, model and actress (*American Gigolo*). *Laurin, Lauryn, Laurynn,*

Loren, Lorin, Lorrin, Loryn, Lorynne, Lorne, Lorren, Lorrie.

LAUSANNE Arthurian Legend: "Lake Geneva."

LAVEDA (lah-VEE-dah) Latin: "innocent one."

LAVERNE (lah-VERN) Latin: Roman goddess of minor criminals. *Laverine, Lavern, Laverna, Verne.*

LAVINIE (lah-VEEN-ee) Latin: "cleansed" or "born in Latium." Modern French form of Lavinia. Literature: In Shakespeare's play *Titus Andronicus*, Lavinia is Titus's tragic daughter who represents beauty and sacrifice. *Lavena, Lavenia, Lavina, Lavinia, Levinia, Levenia, Lovina, Lovinia, Vinnie.*

LAVONNE (la-VAHN) Old French: "yew wood." Combination of La and Yvonne.

LAYNA (LAY-nah) Greek: "light" or "truth."

LEA (LEE-ah) Israel. Hebrew: "fatigued." Popular in the United States, Sweden, and Hungary. Eng: *Lee, Leigh, Liah;* Fr/Ital/Port: *Lia;* Ger: *Lean;* Yiddish: *Leah.*

LEALA (lee-AL-ah) French: "devoted" or "faithful." *Leola, Lealia, Lealie.*

LEANDRA (lee-AHN-drah) Latin: "brave as a lion." Astrology: Excellent for those born under the sign of Leo, symbolized by a lion. *Leodora, Leoine,*

Leoline, Leonanie, Leona, Leonelle, Leonette, Leonice, Leonissa.

LEANNA (lee-AHN-ah) Gaelic: "with great affection." The name of a flowering tropical vine. *Leann, Leanne, Leana, Leeanne, Leianna.*

LEBA (LEE-bah) Yiddish: "beloved."

LECIA (LEE-sha) Latin: Short form of Alicia or Felecia, used as an independent name. *Lecy, Lisha, Lishia.*

LEDA (LEE-da) Greek mythology: Wife of Tyndareus, mother of Helen of Troy and Clytemnestra. *Leyda, Leida, Lyda, Leta.*

LEDAH (LEE-dah) Israel. Hebrew: "born alive." Also a form of Letitia meaning "happiness." *Leda, Lida, Lidah.*

LEE (lee) Old English: "dweller of the fields"; Irish Gaelic: "rhyming child"; Chinese: "purple plum."

LEEBA (LEE-bah) Israel. Hebrew: "heartfelt" or "full of emotion." Popular in Israel.

LEENA (LEE-nah) Estonian: "illumination" or "flaming candle." Variant of Helen. *Hele, Lenni.*

LEHUA (le-HOO-uh) Hawaiian: "divinely blessed." Also the name of a Hawaiian flower.

LEI (lay) Chinese: "bud."

LEILANI (lay-LAH-nee) Hawaiian: "blossom from the gods."

LELA (LEE-lah) Spanish: "lofty" or "high born." Spanish variant of Adelle.

LEMUELA (lay-MUEL-lah) Hebrew: "dedicated to God."

LENA (LEE-nah) Israel. Hebrew: "dwelling." Popular name in Israel. Also a nickname for the German Magdalene and the Russian Galina. Movies and Television: Lena Ashwell, actress, organized entertainment for World War II troops; Lena Olin, actress; Una Wertmuller, film producer and director. Eng: *Lenah, Lina, Linah;* Latin: *Liene.*

LENKA (LEHN-kah) Czechoslovakian: "illumination" or "flaming candle." Variant of Helen.

LEOLA (LEI-o-lah) French: "loyal."

LEONARDA (lee-oh-NAR-dah) Old German: "lion's roar." *Lenda, Leonarde.*

LEONIE (LAY-o-nee or lay-OH-nee) French: "lioness." Science: Leona Baumgartner, physician and public health administrator. *Leona, Leonela, Leondra, Leondrea, Leonda.*

LEONORA (LEE-o-NOR-ah) Greek: "illumination." History: Leonora Kearney Barry, labor leader, real name of Mother Lake. Literature: Lenore made famous in America from Edgar Allan Poe's poem "The Raven." Music: Name of heroine in three major operas—*Fidelio, Il Trovatore,* and *La Favorita. Leanor, Leonara, Leanore, Lenore, Leonore, Norah.*

LEOPOLDA (LEE-o-poll-dah) German: "of the people."

LEORA (LEE-or-ah) Israel. Hebrew: "She who brings light." *Liora, Leorah.*

LEOTIE (leh-oh-TEE or anglicized to lay-O-tee) Native American: "blossom on the prairies."

LERATO (luh-RAH-toh) Botswana. Tswana: "love."

LESLIE (LESS-lee or LEZ-lee) Scottish Gaelic: "living in a gloomy castle." Once a place name in Scotland. Alternately used for girls and boys. Fashionable in the United States. Literature: Sir Stephen Leslie, British biographer *(English Men of Letters).* Military: Leslie Groves, commanded atomic bomb project, 1942–47. Movies and Television: Leslie Caron, French actress *(Gigi). Lesli, Lesley, Lesly, Lesya, Lezli, Lezly.*

LETA (LEE-tah) Swahili: "creating." Excellent first name which can be sacred with a variety of second names such as "peace" or "love." Also a nickname meaning "happiness."

LETICIA (le-TEE-sha) Latin: "great joy." In the Middle Ages, the name was spelled Letitia. Eng: *Leda, Tish;* Ital: *Letizia;* Pol: *Letycia, Letitia, Letisha, Letty, Laetitia.*

LEVANA (le-VAHN-ah) Latin: "uplift." Roman mythology: Levana was the goddess of the newborn.

LEVIA (leh-VEE-uh) Israel. Hebrew: "to combine forces." Masculine adaptation is Levi.

LEWANA (leh-WAN-ah) Israel. Hebrew: "shining white one: the moon." *Levana, Levanna, Lewanna, Livana.*

LEXANDRA (lex-ANN-dra) Variant form of Alexandra. *Lexann, Lexi, Lexine;* Czech: *Lexa.*

LEXIA (LEX-ee-ah) Greek: "protector of humanity." Diminutive of Alexandra. *Lexa, Lexie, Lexina, Lexine.*

LEYA (LEH-ya) Spanish: "lover of justice." Astrology: Often used to represent the sun sign of Leo.

LEYNA (LEH-nah) Old German: "little angel."

LIA (LEE-ah) Greek: "news-bearer"; Hebrew: "fatigued." Popular in Portugal, Greece, United States, and France.

LIAN (LEE-an) Chinese: "willow that sways like a dancer."

LIANA (lee-AHN-ah) French: Short form of names like Jillian and Juliana. *Lia, Lianna, Lianne, Liane, Liann, Lian, Li.*

LIBBY (LIB-ee) United States. English: Short form of Elizabeth. Movies and Television: Libby Holmon, actress; Libby Morris, comedian. *Libbie.*

LIBERTY (LIB-ur-tee) English: "freedom." Span: *Libertina, Librada.*

LIBRA (leeb-RAH) Latin: "equality."

LICIA (LIS-ee-yah) Latin: "happy."

LIDA (LEE-dah or LYE-dah) Russian. Diminutive name ending used as an independent name. Also, variant of Lydia.

LIDIA (LEE-dee-ah) Greek: "she who comes from Lydia," an ancient Asiatic country. Science: Lydia Shattuck, botanist. Eng: *Lydia, Lydie;* Czech: *Lidka;* Fr: *Lydie;* Hung: *Lidi;* Pol: *Lidka;* Russ: *Lidka, Likochka.*

LIDOINE (li-DOE-neh) Daughter of Cavalon, from Arthurian Legend.

LIEN (LEE-in) Chinese: "lotus." In Chinese lore, the lotus symbolizes eternity and pure, realized consciousness.

LIENE (LI-eh-ne) Latvian: Adapted from Lena.

LIESBET (liz-BET) Hebrew: "devoted to God."

LIESL (LEES-ul or LEE-zul) German: Short form of Elizabeth. *Liezel, Leizl.*

LILA (LEE-luh) Hindi: "whimsical dance of God"; Persian: "lilac bush"; Polish: "brave protector." Short for Leopoldine.

LILAC (LIE-lak) Latin: "purple."

LILAH (LIE-lah) Arabic: "night."

LILIA (lee-LEE-uh) Hawaiian: "lilies." Science: Lilia Vladislavovna Minina, reached the North Pole in 1977 via Russian atomic icebreaker.

LILIHA (lee-LEE-huh) Hawaiian: "angry disregard." Female governor of Oahu during the 1920s.

LILITH (LIL-ith) Arabic: "from the darkness." According to Eastern lore, Lilith was Adam's original spouse. When she quarreled with Adam about household matters, Adam balked and she departed. Then God fashioned Eve from the rib of Adam and they nearly lived happily ever after.

LILLIAN (LILL-ee-an) Latin: "lily blossom." Literature: Lillian Hellman, writer (*The Little Foxes*). Movies and Television: Popularized by actress Lillian Gish. Music: Lillian Nordica, soprano, first opera singer to achieve fame in Europe. Sports: Lillian Leitzel, circus aerialist. Eng: *Lila, Lilie, Lilia, Liliana, Liliane, Lilie, Lilli, Lillia, Lillianne, Lillie, Lilly;* Est: *Lilli;* Ger: *Lieschen, Liesel;* Gk: *Lilika;* Hawaiian: *Lilia, Lileana;* Hung: *Boske Lilike;* Latin: *Lilana;* Russ: *Leka, Lelya, Lena, Lenka, Olenka;* Serb: *Liljana;* Span: *Lilia, Lillyan, Lillyanna, Lily, Lilyan, Lilyann.*

LIMBER (LIMB-ur) Nigeria. Tiv: "joyfulness."

LINA (LEE-nah) Russian: Short form of various names, such as Adelina, Carolina, and Angelina.

LINDA (LIN-dah) Spanish: "pretty." Science: Linda B. Buck, winner of the 2004 Nobel Prize in Medicine. History: Lynda Bird Johnson, daughter of President Lyndon Johnson. Journalism: Linda Ellerbee, journalist and news anchor. Music: Linda Ronstadt, pop singer. *Lin, Lindee, Lindey, Lindi, Lindie, Lindy, Linn, Lynda, Lynde, Lyndy, Lyn, Lynn, Lynnda, Lynndie.*

LINDSEY (LIND-zee) Old English: "island of linden trees." Place name. Until the middle of this century, more popular as a boy's name. Now trendy for girls. *Lind, Lindsea, Lindsee, Lindsy, Linzee, Linzy, Lyndsay, Lyndsey, Lyndsie, Lynnsey, Lyundsie, Lynnzey, Lynsey.*

LINETTE (lin-ETTE) Welsh: "honored model." *Lanette, Linet, Linnet, Linnetta, Lynette, Lynnet, Lynnette.*

LINN (lyn) Anglo-Saxon: "a cascade."

LINNEA (LYN-ay) Norweigan: "lime tree." National flower of Sweden.

LIOLYA (lee-OHL-yah) Russian: Popular adaptation of Helen.

LIONA (lee-O-nuh) Hawaiian: "roaring lion." Good name for those born under the sign of Leo, represented by the lion.

LIRIT (leer-RIT) Israel. Hebrew: "with musical grace," "lyrical charm," or "poetical." Popular in Israel today.

LISA (LEE-sah) Israel. Hebrew: "divine vow." Diminutive of Elizabeth. Arts: Lisa Del Giocondo, subject of Leonardo da Vinci's "Mona Lisa." Music: Lisa Stansfield, singer. *Leesa, Leeza, Liesa, Liesebet;* Fr: *Lise, Liseta, Lisetta, Lisette, Liszka.*

LISANDRA (le-SAN-dra) Greek: "one who frees others." *Linzanne, Lissandra, Lizandra, Lizann, Lysandra.*

LISETTE (LEE-set-te) French: "she who fights with honor"; German: nickname for Elizabeth.

LISSA (LIS-sah) Greek: "bee"; Arabic: "reborn" or "renewed life"; United States. English: Derived from Melissa, a plant symbolizing sympathetic love. *Elissa, Elyssa, Lyssa.*

LITSA (LIT-sah) Greek: From *evangelia,* meaning "heavenly messenger" or "angelic spirit."

LIV (live) Norweigan: "life." Movies and Television: Liv Tyler, actress (*The Lord of the Rings*).

LIVANA (lee-VAH-nah) Israel. Hebrew: "lunar" or "moon glow." Astrology: Good for children born under the sign of Cancer, ruled by the moon.

LIVIA (LIV-ee-yah) Latin: "the olive."

LIVIYA (li-VEE-ya) Israel. Hebrew: "brave lion" or "royal crown." Adaptations of Levia or Livia. *Levia, Leiya, Livia.*

LIVONA (li-VO-nah) Israel. Hebrew: "sacred aroma" or "divine spices." *Levina.*

LIZA (LI-zah) Russian: "devoted to the Lord." Nickname for Elizabeth. Common in the United States. Music: Liza Minnelli, singer, actress, and daughter of Judy Garland.

LIZINA (li-ZEE-nah) Latvian: Melodic adaptation of Elizabeth.

LOIS (LO-iss) Old German: "famous warrior." Bible: The name of Timothy's grandmother. Science: Lois Gibbs, environmentalist who fought to close Love Canal chemical waste dump. Literature: Lois Lane, secret crush of Superman in *Superman* comic series.

LOKELANI (loh-ke-LAH-nee) Hawaiian: "rose blossom that falls from heavens." Name of a Hawaiian flower.

LOLA (LO-lah) Hawaiian: "honored"; United States. English: Adaptation of Charlotte and Lolita. Music: "Lola," a song by the rock group Kinks in the 1960s.

LOLITA (lo-LEE-tah) Spanish: "of the sorrows." Diminutive of Lola. Literature: Title character in *Lolita*, Vladimir Nabokov's 1958 novel.

LOLOTEA (loh-loh-TEH-ah) Native American. Zuni: "blessing from God." Adaptation from the Spanish Dolotea.

LOMASI (lo-MAH-see) Native American: "beautiful blossom."

LONNA (LOHN-nah) Slavic: "light."

LORE (LOR-eh) Basque: "flower."

LORELEI (lor-ah-LYE) German: Place name. Name of a rock that juts out of the Rhine River. Mythology: Name of a siren who sat on the rock combing her hair and singing sailors to their untimely demise. *Loralee, Loralie, Loralyn, Lorilee, Lorilyn, Lura, Lurette, Lurleen, Lurlene, Lurline.*

LORELLE (lor-RELL) Latin: "laurel tree." Diminutive of Laurel.

LORETTA (lo-REH-tah) Spanish: "untainted." The name is also a form of Laura. Military: Loreta Velazquez, raised and equipped a Confederate infantry unit. Movies and Television: Loretta Young, actress. Music: Loretta Lynn, country singer. *Loret, Larette, Lauret, Laureta, Lauretta, Lorita, Lorette.*

LORI (LOR-ee) Latin: "laurel." Sports: Lori McNeill, tennis player. *Lorri, Lorrie, Lorry.*

LORNA (LOR-nah) Scottish: Place name. Literature: Female character in the nineteenth-century novel *Lorna Doone.* Music: Lorna Luft, singer. *Lorrna.*

LORRAINE (lor-RAIN) French: "born or made in Lorraine," an area in eastern France. History: Joan of Arc was from Lorraine, so the name is associated with her. Journalism: Lorraine Adams, Pulitzer Prize-winning journalist. *Laraine, Laurraine, Lorain, Loraine, Lori, Lorine, Lorrayne.*

LOTTA (LAH-tah) Swedish: "petite lady." Variant of Caroline.

LOTUS (LOH-tus) Greek: "lotus flower." The Egyptians consider this flower a water lily, while the Greeks consider it a shrub. In Hindu philosophy, there is a legend about Brahma seated on a lotus floating on the sea in deep contemplation.

LOUANNA (LU-ann-ah) German: "gracious warrior."

LOUISE (loo-EASE) Old German: "she who fights with honor." Literature: Louisa May Alcott, novelist (*Little Women*). Eng: *Alison, Alyson, Eloise, Lois, Lou, Louisa;* Fr: *Aloyse, Lisette;* Ger: *Aloisa, Luise;* Gk: *Eloisa;* Ital: *Eloisa;* Pol: *Iza, Lilka, Lodoiska, Ladka, Ludwika;* Russ: *Luyiya;* Span: *Eloisa, Luisa.*

LOURDES (lords) Section of France where the Virgin Mary was seen.

LOVE (luv) Old English: "love." Surname used as a first name. Movies and Television: Jennifer Love Hewitt, actress (*The Truth about Love*). *Loveday, Lovey.*

LOVETTE (luv-ETT) English: "little loved one."

LOVISA (luv-IS-ah) German: "renowned warrior."

LUANA (lew-AHN-nah) Old German: Combination of Louise and Anne. *Lewanna, Louanna, Luane, Luann, Luannie, Luwana.*

LUCERNE (lew-SERN) Latin: "lamp." Also the name of a city in Switzerland. A place name. *Lucerna.*

LUCETTE (LEW-sett) French: "illumination."

LUCIA (lew-CHEE-ah) Italian: "light."

LUCINA (lew-SEE-nah) German: "illumination." Mythological Roman goddess of childbirth and giver of first light to newborns.

LUCINDA (lew-SIN-dah) Latin: "beautiful light." Journalism: Lucinda Frank, Pulitzer Prize-winning journalist. *Cinda, Cindy, Lucetta, Lucille, Lucy.*

LUCITA (loo-SEE-tah) Spanish: "Mother Mary of Light." Short form of Maria de la Luz.

LUCRECE (lew-CRE-say) French, from the Latin "Lucretia." History: A Roman matron who committed suicide as a protest against dishonor.

LUCY (LOO-see) Latin: "clear light." The name prophesies that the child's life will be illuminating. St. Lucy is considered the patroness of sight. Movies and Television: Lucille Ball, actress (TV's *I Love*

Lucy). Theater: Lucy Clifford, English playwright and novelist and friend of Henry James and George Eliot. Eng: *Lou, Lu, Lucette, Laciana, Luciane, Lucille*; Bulg: *Lucine;* Czech: *Lucia;* Fr: *Lucienne;* Ger: *Luzi;* Hawaiian: *Luke;* Hung: *Luca;* Ital: *Lugia;* Latin: *Luciya;* Pol: *Lucya;* Russ: *Luziya;* Slav: *Lucika, Lucka;* Span: *Luciana, Lucila.*

LUELLA (lew-EL-lah) Old English: "elfin."

LULANI (loo-LAH-nee) Hawaiian: "heaven's peak." Name of high spiritual powers for both sexes in Hawaiian culture.

LULU (LOO-loo) Anglo-Saxon: "calming"; Native American: "hare"; Swahili: "a pearl."

LUMINA (lew-MEE-nah) Latin: "of the light."

LUNA (LOO-nah) Spanish: "lunar" or "planet." Zuni parents often choose this name. Astrology: Good for children born under the sign of Cancer.

LUNETTE (loon-ETT) French: "little moon."

LURLEEN (lur-LEEN) German: Place name. Modern variant of Lorelei. *Lura, Lurette, Lurlene, Lurline.*

LUSELA (loo-SAY-lah) Native American. Miwok: "bear licks swinging toe." Bear names are most often chosen in the Miwok tribe.

LUYU (LOO-yoo) Native American. Miwok: "shaking the beak." One of many animal names preferred in the Miwok tribe.

LUZ (looz) Spanish: "light." Spanish: This popular Spanish name is a shortened form of Maria de la Luz, "Mary of the Light."

LYDIA (LID-ee-ah) Greek: "hailing from Lydia." An area in Asia ruled by King Midas, famed for his riches. Bible: Businesswoman in Phillipi and first Christian convert. Science: Lydia Pulsifier, cultural geographer. *Lidia, Lidya, Lydie.*

LYNN (lin) Old English: "falling water" or "waterfall lake." Used variously as an independent name, a nickname, a middle name, or as part of a combination. This name is very popular in the twentieth century. *Lin, Linell, Linelle, Linette, Linn, Linne, Linnette, Lyn, Lyndall, Lyndel, Lyndell, Lyndelle, Lynell, Lynelie, Lynette, Lynna, Lynne, Lynnelle, Lynnette;* Span: *Lina.*

LYRIS (LEER-iss) English: "from Lyra." Literature: Lyrius Hyatt, poet.

LYSSA (LI-sah) English: "honey."

LYVIA (liv-EE-ah) English: "life."

MABBINA (MAY-bee-nah) Irish: "happiness."

MABEL (MAY-bel) English: "worthy of love." Short form of Amabel. Latin: "lovable." Literature: Mabel Dodge Luhan, novelist (*Lorenzo in Taos*). Movies and Television: Mabel Normand, silent film actress (*Mabel's Strange Predicament*). *Mable, Maybelle, Mabelle.*

MABLI (mahb-LEE) Welsh: "beautiful one."

MACARIA (MAH-kar-ee-yah) In Greek mythology, Macaria was the daughter of Hercules and Deianara.

MACHIKO (mah-CHEE-koh) Japanese: "enlightened child." History: Empress Michiko, currently on Japan's throne.

MACKENZIE (mac-KEN-zee) Scottish: "fair" or "favored one."

MADA (MAH-dah) Arabic: "the end of the path."

MADDIE (MAD-ee) United States. English: Variation of Madeline often used in the United States.

MADELINE (MAD-a-lin) Greek: "of Magdala," a village in Palestine where Mary Magdalene resided, near the Sea of Galilee. Literature: Title character of a popular children's book. Arts: Madeleine Boullongne, seventeenth-century French still-life painter. Movies and Television: Madeline Kahn, actress (*Young Frankenstein*); Madeline Carroll, British actress. *Lena, Lenna, Lina, Linn, Lynn, Lynne, Mada, Madalena, Madelina, Madge, Mady, Magda, Magdalena;* Ger: *Magda, Marlene, Lena;* Hung: *Magdolna;* Ital: *Maddelina;* Pol: *Lena, Magdelina, Magda;* Russ: *Madelina, Magdalina, Magda;* Span: *Magaly, Magda, Magola, Lena.*

MADGE (MAHD-gih) Greek: "pearl."

MADIERA (mah-DIE-era) Spanish: "sweet wine."

MADISON (MAH-duh-son) English: Surname currently popular as first name. Movies and Television: Madison, the mermaid heroine in the film *Splash.*

MADONNA (mah-DON-nah) Latin, Italian: "my lady." Arts: a maternal representation of the Virgin Mary. Music: Madonna Louise Ciccone, pop star.

MADY (MAH-dee) English: "maiden."

MAEKO (mah-EE-koh) Japanese: "honest child."

MAEMI (mah-AY-mee) Japanese: "honest smile."

MAERTISA (mair-TEE-sah) English: "famous."

MAEVE (ma-EEVE) Irish: Name. Queen of Ireland in the first century, renowned for her might and strong will.

MAGAN (MAI-gan) Teutonic: "powerful."

MAGANHILDI (MAI-gan-hill-dee) German: "strong battle maiden."

MAGDA (MAHG-dah) Greek: "one who is elevated."

MAGDALENA (mahg-dah-LEEN-ah) Spanish, Czechoslovakian: "woman from Magdala," an area in the Middle East near the Sea of Galilee, Mary Magdalene's place of origin. *Magdalen, Magdalene.*

MAGENA (mahg-EN-ah) Native American: "the coming moon."

MAGGIE (MAG-ee) Greek: "essence of pearl." Popular in the 1850s. Nickname for Margaret. Literature: Maggie Tulliver, character in George Eliot's *The Mill on the Floss.* Theater: Maggie Smith, Tony Award-winning actress. *Maggey, Maggy, Maggi.*

MAGNOLIA (mag-NOHL-yah) French: Honors the magnolia flower. Named after Pierre Magnol, an eighteenth-century French botanist. Strong Southern women are called "steel magnolias."

MAHA (ma-HAH) African: "beautiful eyes."

MAHALA (ma-HAH-lah) Native American: "feminine power." *Mahalia.*

MAHALIA (mah-HAH-lee-ah) Hebrew: "affection."

MAHINA (mah-HEE-nah) Hawaiian: "lunar glow." Hawaiian equivalent of Diana, the Roman goddess of the hunt.

MAILLE (MAY-lee) Irish: "pearl."

MAIOLAINE (may-EY-oh-lan-ay) French: "flower."

MAIREAD (may-READ) Irish: "pearl." History: Mairead Corrigan, 1976 winner of the Nobel Peace Prize for her work as founder of the Northern Ireland Peace Movement, later renamed Community of Peace People.

MAIRWEN (may-ER-wen) Welsh: "fair Mary."

MAISHA (my-SHA) African: "life."

MAISIE (MAY-zee) Scottish: Nickname for Margaret or Marjorie; Greek: "pearl." Literature: *What Maisie Knew*, a novel by Henry James showing the small, expanding consciousness of a child. *Maisey, Maisy, Maizie.*

MAITANE (may-TAIN) English: "dearly loved."

MAITILDA (mah-TIL-dah) Irish: "strong battle maiden."

MAIZA (MAH-ee-zah) North Africa. Arabic: "discerning."

MAJA (mah-JAH) Arabic: "splendid."

MAJESTA (mah-JESS-tah) Latin: "royal" or "bearing dignity." *Majesty, Maja.*

MAKANA (mah-KAN-nah) Hawaiian: "prize" or "gift from the heart."

MALANA (ma-LAH-nah) Hawaiian: "buoyant" or "light."

MALCAH (MAAL-kah) Hebrew: "queen."

MALINA (ma-LEE-nah) Hawaiian: "soothing" or "calm."

MALINDA (MAH-lyn-dah) Greek: "honey."

MALINI (MAH-li-nee) Hindi: "gardener."

MALISSA (MAH-lis-sah) Greek: "honeybee."

MALKA (MAL-kah) Israel. Hebrew: "spritely."

MALLORY (MAL-oh-ree) French: "lacking good fortune." *Mal, Malorie, Malori, Malory, Mallorie.*

MALMUIRA (mahl-MUE-rah) Scottish: "dark skinned." *Malmuirie*

MALVINA (MAL-vee-nah) Irish: "sweet."

MANA (MAH-nuh) Hawaiian: "psychic gifts."

MANDA (MAHN-dah) Spanish: "battle maid."

MANDARA (mahn-DAH-rah) Hindi: "the mythical mandara tree." Mythology: In Hindu lore, if one sits under the mandara tree, one's worries will disappear. It is also believed all trees and plants have spirits that must be appeased. When tree spirits are happy, it's thought they will bestow many blessings on children.

MANDY (man-DEE) Latin: "worthy of love."

MANETTE (man-ETT) French: "bitter."

MANGENA (mahn-GEE-nah) Hebrew: "melody."

MANIDISA (mahn-DEE-sah) Xhosa: "sweet as sugar."

MANISHA (mahn-EE-sha) Hindu: "sharp intellect" or "genius."

MANOELA (man-OH-el-lah) Spanish: "with us is God." Varient of Manuel.

MANSI (MAHN-see) Native American. Hopi: "cut blossom." *Mancey, Manci, Mancie, Mansey, Mansie, Mansy.*

MANTREH (MAHN-trah) Persian: "pure."

MANUELA (man-WEL-ah) Hebrew: "God is among us."

MANYA (MAHN-yah) Russian: Nickname commonly used today. See Mary.

MARA (MAHR-rah) Czechoslovakia: "palm branch." Commonly used worldwide, particularly in Slavic countries. Variant of Mary. *Maralinda, Maraquina, Tamara.*

MARCELLA (mahr-CEL-lah) Latin: "of Mars." Mythology: Mars was the Roman god of fertility, for whom the month of March was named. He was identified with the Greek god Ares, the god of war. Fr: *Marcelle, Marchelle;* Ital: *Marcelina, Marcelyn, Marcellin, Marcellina, Marcelinda.*

MARCI (MAR-see) United States. English: Cotemporary name that was once a nickname for Marcia, meaning "military might." *Marcie, Marcy, Marsi, Marsie, Marsy.*

MARCIA (MAR-sha) Latin: "of Mars." First appeared in the Roman Empire, later revived in the 1800s. Journalism: Marcia Kramer, journalist for the *Washington Post.* Science: Marcia Mayer, physicist who developed the theory of the structure of atomic nuclei. *Marci, Marcie, Marcena, Marciana, Marcianne, Marcila, Marcine, Marcy, Marsha.*

MARDEA (mar-DEE-ah) African: "last."

MARDI (MAR-dee) French: "Tuesday."

MARELDA (mar-ELL-dah) German: "famous battle maiden."

MARELLA (mar-ELL-lah) Irish: "shining sea."

MAREN (MAHR-en) Latin: "sea."

MARENDA (MAHR-en-dah) Latin: "admirable."

MARGANIT (mahr-gah-NEET) Israel. Hebrew: "marganit flower." An Israeli flower with multicolored blossoms.

MARGARET (MAHR-gah-ret) Greek, Latin: "pearl." Name to many queens, Margaret has been consistently popular throughout the West for centuries. History: Margaret Thatcher, former British prime minister, known for her conservative agenda. Literature: Margaret Truman, mystery writer (*Murder at the Kennedy Center*). Movies and Television: Meg Ryan, actress. Music: Peggy Lee, singer. Science: Margaret Mead, anthropologist; Margaret Sanger, birth control pioneer. Eng: *Daisie, Daisy, Madge, Mararet, Maggie, Maggy, Marga, Margery, Marget, Margie, Marguerite, Margy, Marjorie, Marjory, Meg, Megan, Meggy, Meghan, Peg, Peggy, Rita;* Armenian: *Margarid;* Bulg: *Marketa;* Czech: *Gitka, Gituska, Margareta, Marka, Marketa;* Est: *Marga, Margarete, Mari, Meeri, Reet;* Fin: *Marjatta;* Fr: *Margot, Marguerite;* Hung: *Grete, Gretel, Gretchen, Margareta, Margarete, Margot;* Ital: *Margarita;* Latin: *Margrieta;* Pol: *Margits, Margisia, Rita;* Port: *Margarida;* Slav: *Perla;* Norw: *Margrete;* Span: *Margarita, Rita, Tita.*

MARGAUX (MAR-go) French. Contemporary derivative of Margaret, the spelling said to have come from the famous Margaux champagne. Movies and

Television: Margaux Hemingway, actress and grand-daughter of novelist Ernest Hemingway. *Margo, Margot.*

MARHILDA (mar-HIL-dah) German: "famous battle maiden." *Marhildi.*

MARI (MAR-ee) Variant of Mary. See Mary.

MARIA (mah-REE-ah) Latin: This is the most common Spanish name in the world, derived from the Virgin Mary, mother of Jesus. Can be used with other names and suffixes, as in Annmarie, Rosemarie, and Anna Maria. Mariah (ma-RYE-ah) is also popular today. Journalism: Maria Henson, Pulitzer Prize-winning journalist. Literature: Maria Zayas, seventeenth-century Spanish novelist; Marie Corelli, English romantic novelist (*A Romance of Two Worlds*). Music: Mariah Carey, pop singer. Philosophy: Maria Mitchell, first woman elected to the American Philosophical Society (1869). Science: Maria Mayer, Nobel Prize winner for Physics (1963); Marie Curie, Nobel Prize winner for Physics (1903). Span: *Carmen, Dolores, Jesusa, Lucita, Luz;* Fr: *Marie, Maree;* Slav: *Marya;* Czech: *Mariah, Marielena, Marialena, Marialinda, Marialisa, Marieanne, Mariko.*

MARIABELLA (mah-REE-ah-bell-ah) Italian: "my beautiful Mary."

MARIAM (mar-EE-ahm) Bible: Mariam is the wife of Herod. Literature: Title character in Elizabeth Cary's play *The Tragedy of Mariam*, which was the first English play written by a woman to be published (1613).

MARIAMNE (mah-REE-ah-meh-nee) Hebrew: "rebellious."

MARIGOLD (mahr-EE-gold) English: "Mary's gold." Refers to both the flower and the mother of Jesus.

MARIKA (mar-EE-kah) Hebrew: "bitter."

MARILYN (MER-ah-lin) Israel. Hebrew: "bitterness." Diminutive of Mary. Movies and Television: popularized in the 1950s by Marilyn Monroe, actress in *Gentlemen Prefer Blondes*. Music: Marilyn Home, opera star. Philosophy: Marilyn Pearsall, philosopher. *Maralin, Maralynn, Marelyn, Marilee, Marilin, Mariliyn, Marilynne, Marralynn, Marrilin, Marrilyn, Marylin, Marylyn.*

MARINA (mar-REE-nah) Latin: "sea-born." Mythology: Derived from Mars, god of war. *Marena, Marine, Marinna, Marna, Marne, Marni, Marnie.*

MARION (MER-ee-un) French: Derived from Mary. Adapted to Marion in England during medieval times. History: Robin Hood's Maid Marion; Marion Folsum, Secretary of Health, Education and Welfare under President Dwight D. Eisenhower. Science: Marion Dorset, chemist. *Marian, Maryon, Maryonn.*

MARIPOSA (mahr-EE-pose-ah) Spanish: "butterfly."

MARISHA (mah-REE-sha) Russia: Beloved nickname. See Mary.

MARISOL (mar-EE-sol) Spanish: "sunny sea."

MARISSA (mah-RISS-ah) Latin: "sea-born." Span: *Maris, Marisa;* Ger: *Marysa, Maritza;* Russ: *Mariza, Marisha;* Dutch: *Maryssa, Maryse, Mari, Merisa, Merissa.*

MARJA (MAHR-ja) Scandinavian: "sadness from the sea."

MARJAN (MAHR-jan) Polish: Variant form of Mary. *Marjanne, Marjon.*

MARJORIE (MAR-jeh-ree) English: Variant form of the French Margerie, derived from Margaret. *Marji, Marja, Marjo, Margerie, Margery.*

MARLA (MAR-lah) Variant form of Marlene or Mario. Also used as a prefix for other variants. Movies and Television: Marlee Matlin, deaf actress. *Marlette, Marlisa, Marlise, Marlissa, Marlo, Marlyssa, Marlyse, Marlys.*

MARLENE (mar-LEEN or mar-LAYNE) Variant of Madeline. Movies and Television: Marlene Dietrich, actress (*The Blue Angel*). *Marlena, Marleen, Marleene, Marleena, Marlina, Marline, Marleina, Marlaina, Marlayna, Marlayne, Marlinda, Marlana.*

MARLO (MAR-low) United States. English: Short form of Marlene. Movies and Television: popular in the 1970s because of the TV career of actress Marlo Thomas. *Marlon, Marlow, Marlowe.*

MARMARA (mar-MAH-rah) Greek: "effervescent" or "brilliantine."

MARNA (MAR-nah) Hebrew: "rejoice."

MARNI (MAR-nee) Israel. Hebrew: "proclaim with joy." Used independently in the United States, but also a nickname for Marinna. Music: Marnie Nixon, singer.

MARTA (MAR-tah) Variant of Martha used copiously throughout the world, particularly in Sweden.

MARTHA (MAR-tha) Aramaic: "madame" or "honored lady." Bible: Martha is the woman who cooked while Jesus addressed her sister Mary. Martha is the patron saint of social workers, nurses, and doctors. The Puritans revived the name, though it's rarely used now. Dance: Martha Graham, choreographer and dancer. History: Martha Washington, wife of President George Washington; Martha (Calamity) Jane Burke, gun-fighter. Business: Martha Stewart, the founder and front person of *Martha Stewart Living. Marlet, Marit, Mart;* Span: *Marta, Martell, Marth, Marthe, Marthena, Marite, Marti, Martina, Martita, Matti, Marty, Martynne, Martyne, Mattie, Martus;* Hung: *Martuska, Macia;* Pol: *Masia;* Eng: *Pat, Patty.*

MARTINA (mar-TEA-nah) Spanish: "warring." Music: Martina McBride, country singer.

MARVEL (MAR-vell) Old French: "worthy of awe." Education: Marva Collins, educator, helped underprivileged children to achieve in school. *Marva, Marvela, Marvele, Marvella, Marvelle.*

MARVINA (mahr-VEE-nah) Celtic: "renowned friend."

MARY (MARE-ee) Israel. Hebrew: "bitter heart" or "rebelliousness." Up until the Middle Ages, its use was considered sacrilegious; today it is used throughout the world. Commonly found in combination, as in Mary Pat and Mary Ann. Arts: Mary Cassatt, impressionist painter (*Women Bathing*). Business: Mary Morton Kehew, first president of the National Women's Trade Union League. History: Queen Marie Antoinette; Mary Queen of Scots. Literature: Mary Shelley, British writer (*Frankenstein*); Mary Mapes Dodge, editor of *St. Nicholas Magazine* and author of classic children's books. Movies and Television: Mary Pickford, actress. Philosophy: Mary Calkins, first woman president of the American Philosophical Society (1918). Sports: Mary Decker Slaney, first woman to run 1500 meters in under four minutes. Eng: *Mame, Mamie, Mara, Marabel, Marella, Maria, Marian, Mariana, Marianne, Marice, Marie, Marietta, Mariquita, Marilee, Marilyn, Marion, Marisha, Marla, Marlo, Marya, Maryanne, Marylin, Maura, Maureen, May, Meri, Meriel, Merrill, Mimi, Minette, Minni, Minny, Mitzi, Mollie, Molly, Muriel, Polly;* Czech: *Marenka, Mariska, Maruska;* Est: *Marye;* Fin: *Maija, Maikki, Marja;* Fr: *Mannette, Manon, Marie, Maryse;* Ger: *Marika, Maroula;* Hung: *Mara, Mariska;* Fr: *Moira, Moya, Muire;* Latin: *Mare;* Lith: *Marije;* Pol: *Macia, Manka, Maryna;* Rum: *Maricara;* Russ: *Mariya, Marya, Manka, Marinka, Marisha, Maruska, Masha, Mashenka, Mashka;* Scot: *Moire, Muire;* Span: *Mart, Marita, Mariquita, Maruca;* Swed: *Mirjim;* Yiddish: *Miriam;* Zuni: *Meli.*

MASAGO (mah-SAH-go) Japanese: "dune." Suggests the ever-changing, but eternal nature of the sand dune.

MASHA (MAH-shah) Russian: Variant of Mary. See Mary.

MASIKA (mah-SEE-kah) Swahili: "baby comes in rain."

MATANA (mah-TAH-nah) Israel. Hebrew: "blessing" or "divine gift." Suggests the infant is a present from the Divine. Popular today in Israel.

MATEJA (maht-EH-jah) French: "gift of God."

MATILDA (mah-TILL-dah) Old German: "chaste warrioress." Popular in Slavic and Scandinavian countries. Nicknames include Tilda and Tilli. William the Conqueror took the name to Britain in the eleventh century when it was pronounced Maude. Literature: Mathilda Serao, Italian novelist. Eng: *Mat, Mathilda, Mattie, Matty, Maud, Maude, Tilda, Tildy, Tillie, Tilly;* Czech: *Tylda;* Fr: *Matilde;* Ger: *Maddy, Malkin, Matty;* Ital: *Matelda;* Pol: *Macia, Mala, Tila;* Span: *Matusha, Matuxa.*

MATRIKA (mah-TREE-kah) Hindi: "divine mother." One of the sacred names of Shakti, the Hindu goddess.

MAUREEN (maw-REEN) Old French: "dark"; Gaelic: "baby Mary" or "bitter child." Movies and Television: Maureen O'Sullivan and Maureen O'Hara, actresses. Music: Maureen McGovern, singer. Sports: Maureen Connolly, tennis great, first woman to win the "Grand Slam." Eng: *Maura, Maurene, Marine, Moira, Mora, Moreen;* Span: *Morena.*

MAUSI (MAW-see or MAU-see) Native American: "plucking blossoms."

MAUVE (mawve) French: "mallow plant," a purplish-petaled plant that gives name to the color mauve. *Malva.*

MAVIS (MAY-viss) English, French: "song-thrush." Common in England in the 1920s and 1930s.

MAXINE (max-EEN) English: "the greatest." Literature: Maxine Kumin, poet, short-story writer, novelist. *Maxi, Maxie, Maximina.*

MAY (mai) Latin: "the month of May." Also used as a short form of Mary. *Mai, Mayleen, Maylene.*

MAYA (MYE-yah) Greek: Contemporary form of *Maia* meaning "maternal one." Arts: Maya Ying Lin, designer of Vietnam Memorial in Washington, D.C. Literature: Maya Angelou, novelist and poet. Mythology: Mother of Hermes or Mercury and the goddess of growth after which the month of May was named. Sports: Maya Chiburdanidz, Russian, youngest chess champion in 1978 at age seventeen. *Maia, Mya.*

MAYDA (MAI-dah) English: "maiden."

MAYSA (MAI-sah) Arabic: "graceful."

MAZEL (may-ZEL) Hebrew: "luck."

MEADOW (MED-oh) American: "beautiful field."

MEDA (MAY-duh) Native American: "prophet," "priestess," or "edible root."

MEDINA (med-EE-nah) Arabic: "city of the Prophet." In Medina, Mohammed began his campaign to establish Islam.

MEENA (MEE-nah) Hindu: "precious stone."

MEGA (MEH-gah) Spanish: "gentle" or "mild and peaceful."

MEGAN (MEG-an or MEE-gan or MAY-gan) Gaelic: "soft" or "gentle." *Meghan, Meagan, Meaghan, Maygan, Maegan, Meeghan, Meggan, Meghann, Meghanne.*

MEGARA (MEG-AR-ah) Greek: "wife of Hercules."

MEI (may) Latin: "great one."

MEIKO (may-EE-koh) Japanese: "a bud."

MEL (mell) Portuguese: "honey."

MELA (MAY-lah) Hindi: "sacred encounter"; Polish: "dark-skinned" or "black." Variant of Melanie.

MELANIE (MEL-uh-nee) Greek: "dark-skinned" or "black." Melanie comes from the name Melanesia, an Australian region full of dark-skinned people. The name is used throughout the world. Literature: The character Melanie Wilkes in Margaret Mitchell's *Gone with the Wind* launched the name in this century. Movies and Television: Melanie Griffith, actress (*Working Girl*). Eng: *Mel, Mela, Melaney, Melani, Melania, Melanney, Melannie, Melantha, Mella, Mellanie, Melli, Mellie, Melloney, Melly, Meloni, Melonie, Melony*; Russ: *Milena, Melasya, Milya*; Slovenian: *Milena*; Pol: *Ela, Melka*; Latin: *Melaina, Melana, Melania*.

MELANTHA (me-LANN-tha) Greek: "dark blossom." A dark violet lily native to the shores of the Mediterranean.

MELBA (MELL-bah) Greek: "thin" or "sensitive"; Latin: "the mallow flower." In China the mallow flower protects against demons. Place name, Melbourne, Australia. Astrology: Symbol of Virgo. *Mellba, Melva, Mellva, Nellie.*

MELCIA (MELT-shuh or anglicized to MEL-shuh) Polish: "ambitious" or "admirer." Variant of Amelia.

MELIA (meh-LEE-ah) Spanish: "dogwood tree" or "yellow-tinted." Variant of Cornelia.

MELINDA (me-LINN-dah) Greek: "calm" or "tender." A seventeenth-century poetic name coined in imitation of Belinda. *Linda, Lindi, Lynda, Malina, Malinda, Malinde, Mallie, Mally, Malina, Melina, Melynda, Melli, Mellie, Melly.*

MELISANDE (mel-a-ZAHND) German, French: "strength" or "determination." Variant form of Millicent. *Melisandra* (mell-a-SAHN-dra).

MELISSA (me-LISS-sah) Greek: "stinging bee " Music: Melissa Manchester, singer; Melissa Etheridge, singer. Dance: Melissa Hayden, ballerina. Movies and Television: Melissa Gilbert, actress (TV's *Little House on the Prairie*). *Lissa, Mel, Melesa, Melessa, Melisa, Melisande, Melise, Melisenda, Melisse, Melita, Melitta, Mettle, Mellisa, Melly, Melosa, Milli, Millicent, Millie, Misha, Missie, Missy.*

MELITA (me-LEE-tah) Greek: "sweet honey." *Malita.*

MELODY (MEL-oh-dee) Greek: "tuneful." The name occurred as early as the thirteenth century. *Melodey, Melodia, Melodia, Melodee, Melodice.*

MELORA (ma-LOR-ah) Latin: "improve."

MELOSA (meh-LO-sah) Spanish: "sweetlike" or "tender."

MELVINA (mell-VEE-nah) Celtic: "Christian." A variation of Malvina. Arts: Malvina Hoffman, sculptor. *Malvina, Melva, Melvena.*

MEMPHIS (mem-FIS) Egyptian: "good place to live."

MERCEDES (mer-SAY-deez) Spanish: "tender mercy" or "compassion." A reference to Our Lady of

Mercies. Business: Mercedes Jellinek, inspiration for the name of the German automobile company. Movies and Television: Mercedes Ruehl, actress (*The Fisher King*). *Merced, Mercede, Mersade.*

MERCIA (mer-SEE-ah) Old English: Place name. Reference to a kingdom in central England called Mercia between 500–1000 A.D.

MERCY (MER-see) Middle English: "compassion." History: A virtue name used frequently by the earliest colonists in the United States. Literature: Mercy Warren, nineteenth-century author of political satires. *Merci, Mercie, Mersey.*

MEREDITH (MARE-uh-dith) Old Welsh: "one who guards the sea." Movies and Television: Meredith Baxter, actress (TV's *Family Ties*). *Merri, Merrie, Merry, Meredath, Meridith, Merridith.*

MERI (MARE-ee) Finnish: "seas"; Hebrew: "one who rebels." Possibly derived from Mary.

MERIEL (MARE-ee-el) Gaelic: "brilliant seas." *Merial, Meriol, Merrill, Meryl.*

MERLE (murle) French: "blackbird." Variation on Men. Movies and Television: Merle Oberon, actress. *Merl, Merla, Merlina, Merline, Merola, Meryl, Myrle, Myrleen, Myrlene, Myrline.*

MERRY (MARE-ee) Old English: "cheery." Also a diminutive of Meredith. *Marrilyn, Marylea, Marylee, Mercy, Merri, Merrie, Merrielle, Merrilee, Merrily.*

MESHA (MAY-shah) Hindi astrology: Name for a child born under the sign of Aries, the ram.

MIA (MEE-ah) Israel. Hebrew: "Who compares to God?" Variant of Michaela, very popular in United States and Israel. Movies and Television: Mia Farrow, actress. Sports: Mia Hamm, American soccer star and Olympic gold medalist.

MICHAELA (mih-kah-AYL-lah) Israel. Hebrew: "Who compares to God?" Music: Character in Bizet's opera *Carmen*. *Micaela, Makaela, Mickayla, Mychaela, Mikella, Mikelle.*

MICHAL (MEE-kal) Israel. Hebrew: "Who is like God?" Bible: Daughter of King Saul and David's first wife. *Mychal, Mical, Michaelyn, Michaeline, Micole.*

MICHELE, MICHELLE (mee-SHELL) Hebrew: "Who is like God?" Derived from Mikhael. Popular name in the United States. The masculine form of this name is Michael. Movies and Television: Michelle Pfeiffer, actress (*Catwoman*). Music: Michelle Phillips, singer in the band The Mamas and the Papas. *Mia, Michal, Michel, Micki, Mickie, Micky;* Ital: *Michaelle.*

MICHIKO (MEE-chee-koh) Japanese: "beautiful, sagacious child."

MIDORI (mee-DO-ree) Japanese: "green." In Asian lore, a color related to precious human birth, suggesting a life of great renown. Sports: Midori Ito, Olympic silver medalist in figure skating (1992). Hawaiian: *Miki;* Japn: *Mika, Mikko, Mikki.*

MIEKO (mee-EH-koh) Japanese: "already prosperous."

MIETTA (mee-ETT-ah) French: "small sweet thing."

MIGINA (mee-GEE-nah) Omaha Indian: "fresh moon." Good for a girl born under a new moon. Astrology: Appropriate for girls born under the sign of Cancer.

MIKA (MEE-kah) Native American: "raccoon with wise heart"; Russian: "God's child." Also a nickname for Dominika meaning "belonging to the Lord" or "Sunday's child."

MIKI (MEE-kee) Japanese: "stalk" or "flower stem."

MILADA (mi-LAH-dah) Czechoslovakian: "my love." Movies and Television: Milla Jovovich, Ukranian actress (*The Fifth Element*). Mythology: Lada is the goddess of procreation and love. *Mila, Milla.*

MILAGROS (meel-AH-gros) Spanish: "miracle." *Milagrosa, Milagritos.*

MILDRED (MIL-dred) English: "gentle strength." Science: Mildred Dresselhaus, physicist.

MILI (MEE-lee or MIL-ee) Israel. Hebrew: "virtuous" or "who is Godlike." Nickname for Millicent.

MILIANI (mee-lee-AH-nee) Hawaiian: "gentle caress." *Miliana, Milana.*

MILICA (MI-lits-uh or mi-LEE-kuh) Old Gothic: "ambitious" or "industrious."

MILLICENT (mill-ee-CENT) Old German: "ambitious" and "faithful." *Lissa, Mel, Mellicent, Melli, Mellie, Melly, Milli, Millie, Milly.*

MIMI (MEE-mee) French: "faithful defender." Variant of Helmine. Related to Mary. Spanish nickname for Maria. Music: Mimi Benzell, opera star; Mimi, hero of Puccini's opera *La Boheme.*

MINA (MEE-nah) German: "love"; Czechoslovakian: "earth child." Worldwide use, particularly in Czechoslovakia with Hermina. Name endings (*mina* and *mena*) and diminutives used as independent names. *Minna, Minnie, Minette, Minnette, Mena, Meena.*

MINAL (mee-NAHL) Native American: "fruits."

MINDA (MIN-dah) Hindi: "profound wisdom" or "deep knowing."

MINDY (MIN-dee) United States. English: Now independent, but also short version of Minna. Music: Mindy Carson, singer. *Mindi, Mindie.*

MINEKO (mee-NEE-ko) Japanese: "summit" or "child of the cliffs."

MINERVA (mi-NER-va) Latin: Mythological name of the goddess of wisdom and civilized life, the Roman equivalent to Athena.

MINETTE (min-ETTE) French: "faithful defender." Variant of Helmine.

MINNIE (MIN-nee) Old German: "will" plus "helmet." Scottish pet form of Mary. Literature and Music: heroine of Belasco's drama *The Girl of the Golden West* and Puccini's opera *Minnie*. Movies and Television: Minnie Driver, British actress popular in the United States (*The Phantom of the Opera*). Music: Minnie Pearl, country singer. Theater: Minnie Fiske, actress who made Ibsen's plays famous in the United States. *Mini, Minie, Minni, Minny.*

MINOWA (mi-NO-wah) Native American: "traveling singer."

MIO (MEE-o) Japanese: "three times strong."

MIRA (MIR-ah) Variant form of Myra and Miranda. *Miri, Miriana.*

MIRANDA (mir-RAN-dah) Latin: "worthy of admiration." Literature: Miranda, Prospero's daughter, is the heroine of Shakespeare's tropical romance, *The Tempest*. Movies and Television: Miranda Richardson, actress. *Maranda, Meranda, Mira, Myranda, Randa, Randi, Randy.*

MIRELLA (mir-ELL-ah) Hebrew: "Jehovah spoke." *Mireille, Mirelle, Myrelle, Mireya.*

MIRI (MEE-ree) Israel. Hebrew: Variant of Miriam. English Gypsy: "my own."

MIRIAM (MIR-ee-ahm) Israel. Hebrew: "she who follows her own way." Variant of Mary in the Bible. Eng: *Mimi, Minni, Minnie, Mitzi;* Finn: *Mirjam.*

MISTY (MISS-tee) English: "full of mist." Music: Song "Misty" from the film *Play Misty for Me. Misti, Mistie, Mystee, Mysti.*

MITA (MEE-tah) Italian: "myth."

MITUNA (mi-TOO-nah) Native American. Miwok: "wrap up." Refers to the tradition of wrapping up freshly caught fish inside large leaves.

MITZI (MIT-see) English: "a mind of her own." Movies and Television: Mitzi Gaynor, dancer and actress. *Mitzy;* Japn: *Mitsu.*

MIWA (MEE-wah) Japanese: "wise eyes." The variant Miwako refers to a child who has great insight.

MIYA (MEE-yah) Japanese: "Shinto temple" or "sacred house."

MIYUKI (mee-YOO-kee) Japanese: "beautiful generations," often varied to Miyoko, "beautiful generations child."

MOANA (moe-ANAH) Hawaiian: "ocean."

MODESTY (MAH-dess-tee) Latin: "without conceit" or "shy." A virtue name. *Modesta, Modestine.*

MOHALA (mo-HAH-luh) Hawaiian: "blooming petals."

MOIRA (MOY-rah) Scottish: Variant form of the Irish Maire, from Mary. *Moyra.*

MOLLY (MOL-lee) Variant of Mary commonly used. History: Molly Pitcher, carried water to wounded soldiers during the American Revolution. *Molli, Mollie.*

MONA (MOHN-nah) Greek: "regal." Arts: *Mona Lisa,* painting by Leonardo da Vinci.

MONICA (MAHN-ee-kah) Latin: Variant form of Mona. Sports: Monica Seles, tennis player. Fr: *Monique;* Ger: *Monika.*

MONIFA (moe-NEE-fah) Egyptian: "I am lucky."

MONIQUE (moe-NEEK) French: "advisor."

MONTANA (mon-TAN-nah) Latin, Spanish: "mountain." The name of a western state used as a name for boys and girls.

MORA (MOH-rah) Spanish: "sweet berry."

MORENA (mo-RAY-nah) Portuguese: "brunette." *Moreen, Morella.*

MORGAN (MOR-gin) Old Welsh: "by the sea." Arts: Morgan Russell, painter who established the synchronist art movement. Military: Morgan Smith, nineteenth-century army officer. Movies and Television: Popularized recently by Morgan Fairchild, actress. Mythology: In the Arthurian tales, Morgan Le Fay was a magical priestess and secret sister of King Arthur. *Morgaine, Morganne, Morgana, Morgayne, Morgen.*

MORIAH (moh-RYE-ah) Israel. Hebrew: "God is my tutor." The name of the mount of the Temple of Solomon in Jerusalem. *Moria, Morice, Moriel, Morit.*

MORISAK (mor-REE-sahk) Spanish: "skin like a Moor." *Morissa.*

MORNA (MOOR-nah) Celtic: "dearly loved."

MOROWA (moh-ROH-wah) Africa. Akhan: "queen."

MORWENNA (mor-WENN-ah) Welsh: "ocean wave."

MOSI (MOH-see) Swahili: "first born."

MOSWEN (MOHSS-when) Botswana. Tswana: "white."

MOYA (MOI-ya) Irish: "bitter."

MOZELLE (mo-ZEH-le or anglicized to mo-ZEL) Israel. Hebrew: "lifted from the dark seas." *Moselle.*

MU LAN (moo-LAHN) Chinese: "magnolia blossom." In China the magnolia is the flower of May and a symbol of sweetness. Movies and Television: Title character of a popular Disney movie.

MUNA (MU-nah) Arabic: "desire."

MUNIRAH (moo-NEE-rah) Arabic: "teacher."

MURA (MOO-rah) Japanese: "countryside or "native village."

MURIEL (MUR-ee-eill) Celtic, Irish: "shining sea." Business: Muriel Siebert, first woman to own a seat on the New York Stock Exchange. Literature: Muriel Spark, Scottish novelist, poet, and critic *(Robinson)*.

MUSETTA (mu-SET-tah) Old French: "ballad."

MUSLIMAH (moose-LEE-mah) Arabic: "pious person."

MU TAN (moo-TAHN) Chinese: "peony flowers." Chinese tradition considers the peony a charm for love.

MYISHA (mye-EE-sha) Arabic: "woman" or "life." Variant form of Aisha. *Myesha, Myeisha, Myeshia, Myiesha.*

MYLA (MYE-lah) Contemporary: "brims with mercy." *Mylene, Myleen, Milena.*

MYRA (MYE-rah) Latin: "scented oil." Literature: Subject of Fulke Greville's seventeenth-century love poems. Music: Myra Dame Hess, pianist, interpreter of Bach, Beethoven, Mozart, and Schumann. *Myrah, Myriah.*

MYRTA (MIR-tah) Latin: Name. In Roman mythology, the evergreen shrub from which this name is derived symbolized love. *Myrtle.*

MYSTIQUE (miss-TEEK) French: "intriguing." A new name derived from Misty. *Mystica, Mistique.*

NAAMAH (nah-MAH) Hebrew: "pleasant."

NAAVAH (nah-VAH) Israel. Hebrew: "delightful."

NABILIA (nah-BEE-lah) Arabic: "of nobility." *Nabeela.*

NADA (NAH-dah) Arabic: "giving."

NADALIA (nah-DAHL-ee-ah) Armenian: "born on Christmas."

NADETTE (nay-DET) German: "the courage of a bear." *Nadetta.*

NADIA (NAH-d'yah) Slavic: "promise"; Arabic: "laden with dew." Sports: Nadia Comaneci, Romanian gymnast, three gold medals, 1976 Olympics. *Nadhia, Nadja, Nadya, Natka.*

NADINE (nay-DEEN) French: Variant form of Nadia. Literature: Nadine Gordimer, Nobel Prize in Literature (1991), author of *My Son's Story*. **Nadeen** (nah-DEEN).

NAEEMAH (nah-EE-mah) Arabic: "generous."

NAEVA (NAH-ee-vah) French: "evening."

NAGIDA (nah-GEE-dah) Israel. Hebrew: "leader" or "prosperous."

NAIDA (nah-DAH) Latin: "sea goddess." Astrology: Good name for child born under Pisces.

NAILAH (NAH-ee-lah) Arabic: "successful person."

NAIYA (NYE-yah) Greek: "water nymph."

NAJWA (nahj-WAH) Arabic: "passionate."

NAKIA (nah-KEE-ah) Egyptian: "pure" or "faithful."

NALA (nah-LAH) African: "successful."

NALANIE (nah-LAHN-EY-ee) Hawaiian: "heaven's calm."

NALDA (nahl-DAH) Spanish: "strong."

NALINI (nah-LYN-ee) Sanskrit: "lovely."

NAMI (nah-MEE) Japanese: "wave."

NANA (NAH-nah) Hawaiian: Spring month. Also a star's name.

NANCY (NAN-cee) Hebrew: "grace." Literature: Nancy Mitford, novelist, *Pursuit of Love*. Politics: Nancy Kassebaum, U.S. Senator; Nancy Davis Reagan, former First Lady; Nancy Hanks, mother of President Abraham Lincoln. Sports: Nancy Lopez, golfer. *Nanci, Nancey, Nancie.*

NANETTE (nan-ETT) French: "favor" or "grace." Variant form of Ann. *Nan, Nanine, Nann, Nannette.*

NANI (NAH-nee) Greek: "charming"; Hawaiian: "lovely." Derived from Ann.

NANNA (nan-NAH) Hebrew: "grace." Sports: Nanna Jansson, Swedish Olympic medalist in ice hockey.

NANON (nah-NOHN) French: "grace."

NANYAMKA (nah-YAHM-ka) Ghana. Ewe: "God's gift."

NAOMI (nay-OH-mee) Israel. Hebrew: "cordiality." Bible: Ruth's mother-in-law. Literature: Naomi Wolf, feminist author (*The Beauty Myth*); Naomi Smith, mystery writer (*Buried Remembrances*). Movies and Televison: Naomi Watts, English-born Australian actress (*King Kong* remake). Music: Naomi Judd, country-western singer. *Noemi* (no-AY-mee); Span: *Neomi, Noemy, Neoma.*

NAPEA (nap-EE-ah) Latin: "of the valley."

NAPUA (nah-PU-ah) Hawaiian: "the flowers."

NARA (NAHR-ah) Japanese: "strong oak tree"; Old English: "nearest and dearest." In Asian lore, the oak represents unwavering fidelity. In Native American traditions, the oak tree sprang from the ashes of the first man. *Nareen, Nareena, Nareene.*

NARCISSA (nar-SISS-ah) Greek: "daffodil." Derived from the masculine Narcisse. Mythology: The Greek legend of the handsome young man who fell in love with his own face. *Narcisa, Narcisse, Narcyssa, Narkissa.*

NAREEN (NAHR-een) Celtic: "contented."

NARIKO (nah-REE-koh) Japanese: "child who is humble" or "gentle child who climbs high." Short form is Nari meaning "thunder booms."

NARILLA (nah-REE-luh) English Gypsy: Unknown origin. *Narrila.*

NARKEASHA (nark-EE-ash-ah) African: "pretty."

NASHA (nah-SHA) African: "born during a rainy season."

NASHOTA (nah-SHO-tah) Native American: "double." Astrology: Good for the second born of twins.

NASHWA (NAH-shwah) Egyptian: "wonderful feeling."

NASNAN (NAHS-nan) Native American. Carrier: "embraced by music."

NASYA (NAH-see-ah or anglicized to NAHS-yuh) Israel. Hebrew: "divine transformation" or "healing." *Nasia.*

NATA (NAH-tah) Native American: "voice of creation"; Hindi: "rope trickster." Also a Polish form of Nadia.

NATALIE (NAT-a-lee) Latin, French: "day of her birth" or "birth of Christ." Movies and Television: Natalie Wood, actress (*West Side Story*); Natalie Portman, actress (*Star Wars*) Music: Natalie Cole, singer, daughter of Nat King Cole. Eng: *Nat, Nati, Natie, Natti, Natty, Netti, Nettie, Netty, Natala, Natalina, Nataline, Nathalia, Nathalie, Noel, Noelle, Novella;* Czech: *Natalia, Natasa;* Ger: *Natalia;* Pol: *Natalia, Nata, Naska, Nacia;* Russ: *Nata, Natalka, Natalya, Natasha, Tasha, Tashka, Taska, Tasya, Tata, Tushka;* Span: *Talia.*

NATANE (nah-TAH-nee) Native American. Arapho: "female child."

NATARA (nat-AR-AH) Arabic: "sacrifice."

NATASHA (nah-TASH-ah) Greek: "rebirth." Russian form of Natalie. Movies and Television: Nastassja Kinski, actress. *Nastassia, Nastassja, Nastassija, Nastassy, Natasia, Natazy.*

NATESA (nah-TAY-shah or anglicized to nah-TE-sah) Hindi: "dance lord." Mythology: A name for the

Hindu god Shiva who, with Vishnu, is one of the two great gods of Hinduism.

NATHIFA (nah-THEEF-ah) Arabic: "clean" or "without taint."

NATKA (NAHT-kah) Russian: "promise" or "looking toward the future." Variant of Nadia.

NAVIT (NAV-it) Hebrew: "pleasant."

NAWAR (nah-WAR) Arabic: "flower."

NAYSA (nye-SAH) Arabic: "miracle of God."

NEALA (NEEL-ah) Gaelic: "victor." *Neila, Neile, Neilla, Neille.*

NECI (NEH-see) Latin: "passionate" or "without limits." Popular in Hungary.

NEDA (NEH-duh) Old English: "wealthy protector"; Slavic: "Christ's day." *Nedda, Neddie, Nedi.*

NEDIVA (neh-DEE-vah) Israel. Hebrew: "high born."

NEDRA (ned-RAH) Latin: "awareness."

NEELY (NEE-lee) Irish Gaelic: "victor." Popular in the United States. *Nealie, Nealy, Neeli, Neelie.*

NEERJA (neer-JAH) Hindu: "lotus flower."

NEHAMA (neh-HAMA) Hebrew: "comfort."

NEITH (nee-ITH) Egyptian: "divine mother."

NEKANA (nek-AHN-ah) Spanish: "sorrow." *Nekane.*

NELDA (NEL-dah) Anglo-Saxon: "from the alder trees."

NELIA (neh-LEE-ah) Spanish: "of the cornel tree." Short form of Cornelia. *Neelia, Neelie, Neelya, Nela, Nila.*

NELKA (NEL-kuh) Latin: "stone" or "fortress." Polish: Short form of Petronella. Pol: *Ela, Nela, Nelka, Petra;* Span: *Petra, Tona.*

NELLIE (NEL-lee) Greek: "one who shines"; English: adapted from Helen. Journalism: Nellie Bly, reporter who wrote articles exposing insane asylums. Music: Nellie Melba, Australian operatic soprano. Literature: Nelly Sachs, Swedish writer who won the Nobel Prize in Literature (1966). Politics: Nellie Taylor-Ross, first woman elected governor of Wyoming (1925). Russ: *Nella, Nelya.*

NENET (neh-NET) Egyptian: "the goddess of the deep." Mythology: Nenet is a goddess who symbolizes the still sea that is home to the Creator.

NEOLA (neh-OH-lah) Greek: "youthful soul."

NEORAH (nee-OR-ah) Hebrew: "light."

NERIA (neh-REE-ah) Hebrew: "lamp of God" or "angel."

NERINE (neh-REEN) Greek: "ocean sprite." *Nerice, Nerida, Nerina, Nerissa, Neryssa.*

NERISSA (ner-RISS-ah) Greek: "ocean's daughter." Astrology: Name for one born under the water signs. *Nerice, Nerise, Nerisse, Rissa.*

NESSA (NEH-sah) Russian: "reborn from the dead." Nickname for Anastasia.

NETIA (NEHT-ee-ah) Israel. Hebrew: "vegetation" or "bush." Popular in Israel today. *Neta, Netta.*

NETIS (NAY-tis) Native American: "one who can be trusted."

NEVA (NEH-vah) Spanish: "snowfall" or "like a snowflake." Short form of Nevada. Port: *Neiva.*

NEVINA (NEV-ee-nah) Gaelic: "saint worshipper."

NEZA (NEH-zhuh) Slavic: "chaste." Variant of Agnes.

NIA (NEE-ah) Swahili: "purpose."

NIABI (nee-AH-bee) Native American: "fawn."

NICIA (nee-SEE-ah) Greek: "victorious army."

NICOLE (nee-COLE) Greek: "triumphant march." Feminine form of Nicolas. Nicola, the Italian form, is more common in Britain. History: Nicole d'Oresme, fourteenth-century French prelate who advised Charles V on tax and coinage; Nicola Pasic, premier of Serbia and Yugoslavia, 1906–26. Movies and Televison: Nicole Kidman, Australian Academy Award-winning actress (*The Hours*). Music: Nicola Porpora, Italian composer and singing teacher. *Colette, Cosette, Nicholle, Nickie, Nicol, Nicola, Nicolette, Nicoline, Nicolle, Nikky, Nikolette;* Gk: *Niki.*

NIGHEAN (NEEG-han) Scottish: "young woman." *Nighinn.*

NIKA (NEE-kah) Russian: "born to God." Short form of Dominique.

NILE (NYE-el) Egyptian: "river nile."

NILI (NEEH-lee) Israel. Hebrew: Shortened representation of the biblical phrase "the glory of Israel will not lie or repent."

NIMEESHA (nim-EE-sha) African: "princess."

NIMIANE (NIM-ee-ahn) Anglo-Saxon. In Arthurian Legend, Nimiane was the Lady of the Lake who gave Arthur his famous sword, Excalibur. She is also known as Vivian. *Nimue, Niniane, Nineve.*

NINA (NEE-nah) Spanish: "girl"; Native American: "powerful." Dance: Dame Ninette de Valois, ballerina. History: Nina was the name of one of Christopher Columbus's three ships. Journalism: Nina Totenburg, journalist who broke the Anita Hill story. *Neena, Ninacska, Nineta, Ninetta, Ninet, Ninette, Ninetta, Ninnette, Ninon;* Russ: *Ninochka, Ninotchka.*

NINON (nih-NAWN) French: Variant form of Anne. History: Ninon de Lenclos, a charismatic seventeenth-century aristocrat. *Ninette, Nynette.*

NIOBE (nye-OH-bee) Greek: "fern." Mythology: Niobe, queen of Thebes, is a tragic figure in Greek mythology. She represents eternal mourning after the gods killed her children.

NIREL (ni-RAYL) Israel. Hebrew: "field of crops" or "divine illumination." Israeli name.

NIRVANA (neer-VAHN-ah) Hindu: "deep silence."

NIRVELI (neer-VAY-li) India: "child of the deep waters."

NITA (NEE-tah) Spanish: Name ending used today as an independent name. In Japanese, Nita means "compassionate one."

NITARA (ni-TAR-rah) Sanskrit: "profoundly grounded" or "connected to the source."

NITSA (neet-SAH) Greek: "light."

NITUNA (nit-UN-ah) Native American: "daughter."

NIXIE (nik-ZEE) German: "little water sprite."

NIYATI (nee-YAH-tee) Hindu: "fate."

NIZANA (nee-ZAH-nah) Israel. Hebrew: "blossom." Hebrew flower name. *Nitza, Nitzana, Zana.*

NOELANI (no-ah-LAH-nee) Hawaiian: "mist of heaven" or "misty rain." *Noe.*

NOELLE (no-ELL) French: "birthday." History: Commonly used in reference to Christmas and Christ's birth. Sports: Noelle van Lottum, athlete who holds the record for the longest junior game of tennis, fifty-three minutes long. *Noel, Noell, Noella, Noelline, Noele, Noeline, Noleen.*

NOGA (NO-gah) Israel. Hebrew: "dawn glow." Also appropriate for boys.

NOICHA (NO-chah) Native American: "sun."

NOLA (noh-LAH) Gaelic: "widely acclaimed." *Nolene, Nolana.*

NOLETTA (noh-LET-tah) Latin: "unwilling."

NONA (NOH-nah) Latin: "nine." In many traditions, nine is a mystical number. Sports: Nona Gaprindashvili, held women's chess title (1962–78).

NORA (NOR-ah) Greek: Short form of names like Eleanor. In Ireland, the diminutive "een" was added to form Noreen. Literature: Character in Ibsen's *A Doll's House.* Movies and Television: Nora Dunn, comedian and actress (TV's *Saturday Night Live*). Theater: Nora Bayes, vaudeville actress. Music: Norah Jones, Grammy Award-winning singer. *Noreen, Norene, Noreena, Norine, Norabell, Norissa, Norah.*

NORBERTA (nor-BERT-AH) German: "bright heroine." *Norberte, Norberaht.*

NORDICA (nor-DIH-kah) German: "from the north." *Nordika.*

NORELL (noh-RELL) Scandinavian: "from the north." Business: Perfume named for U.S. fashion designer Herman Norell. *Narelle.*

NORI (NOR-ee) Japanese: "principle" or "philosophy."

NORIKO (noh-REE-kah) Japanese: "child of ceremony" or "law and order."

NORINA (NOR-ee-nah) English: "light."

NORMA (NOR-mah) English, Latin: "of the north." Movies and Television: Norma Rae, title character in movie starring Sally Field; Norma Jean Baker, birth name of Marilyn Monroe.

NOURA (NO-rah) Arabic: "inner illumination." A propitious name for a child's spiritual growth.

NOVA (NOH-vah) Latin: "new." Science: A nova is a star that suddenly becomes extremely bright and then fades back to its former luminescence.

NOYA (noy-AH) Arabic: "beautiful."

NUALA (NU-alah) Irish: "lovely shoulders."

NUBIA (NU-bee-ah) Egyptian: "from Nubia."

NUDARA (nu-DAHR-ah) Arabic: "gold." *Nudar.*

NUNA (NU-nah) Native American: "land."

NURI (nur-REE) Arabic: "light."

NURIA (noo-REE-ah) Israel. Hebrew: "God's flames." Popular throughout the world, especially Israel. Isr: *Nuri, Nuriel.*

NURIT (noo-REET) Israel. Hebrew: Name of a flower. This perennial flower native to Israel has small yellow blossoms. *Nurice, Nitrita.*

NURU (NOO-roo) Swahili: "in the daylight."

NUSI (NOO-shi) Hungarian: "with grace." Variant of Hannah. *Nusa.*

NYDIA (NYE-dee-ah) Latin: "refuge" or "nest."

NYLA (NYE-lah) Greek: "winner." *Nila.*

NYSA (NYE-sah) Greek: "a new beginning."

NYX (NYE-ks) Greek: "night."

OBA (oh-BUH) Nigeria. Yoruba: "goddess who rules the rivers."

OBELIA (oh-BEEL-ee-ah) Greek: "pillar of strength."

OCEANA (oh-SHAH-nah or oh-see-AHN-ah) Greek: "ocean." In Greek mythology, Oceanus was god of the huge ocean that surrounds all the world's land.

OCTAVIA (ock-TAHV-yah) Latin: "eighth in line." A clan name of Roman emperors. *Octaviana.*

ODA (OH-dah) German: "elfin spear." *Odiana, Odiane.*

ODANDA (oh-DAN-dah) Spanish: "famous land."

ODEDA (oh-DEED-ah) Hebrew: "strong." *Odede.*

ODELE (oh-DELL) German: "wealthy"; Greek: "chant." *Odela, Odelet, Odelette, Odell, Odella, Odelle.*

ODELIA (oh-DEL-ya) Israel. Hebrew: "Praise be the Lord." *Oda, Odeela, Odele, Odelinda, Odile, Odilia, Odila, Odella, Odette.*

ODERA (oh-DAY-ruh) Israel. Hebrew: "tractor."

ODESSA (oh-DESS-ah) Greek: "wandering quest" as in "odyssey." Literature, Mythology: The Russian port of Odessa was supposedly named to honor the Odyssey, recorded in Homer's epic of the same name.

ODETTE (oh-DETTE) French from the German: "riches." Dance: The good swan in *Swan Lake.* Music: Odetta, folk singer. *Odetta.*

ODINA (oh-DEEN-ah) Latin: "mountain."

OFIRA (oh-FEER-ah) Hebrew: "gold."

OFRA (oh-FRAH) Hebrew: "fawn."

OGIN (oh-GEEN) Native American: "rose that grows in the fields."

OHANNA (oh-HAN-nah) Armenian: "God's gracious gift."

OIFA (OY-fah) Celtic. In Celtic mythology, Oifa turned her sister's children into swans out of jealousy.

OKI (OH-kee) Japanese: "ocean depths" or "far out to sea." Good for children born during sea voyages.

OKILANI (oh-keh-LAH-nee) Hawaiian: "descended from the heavens."

OKSANA (oke-SAH-nah) Russian: "glory be to God."

OLABUNMI (aw-lah-BOON-mee) Nigeria. Yoruban: "prize won through honor."

OLATHE (o-LAH-tha) Native American: "lovely."

OLDWIN (OLD-wyn) English: "special friend." *Oldwyn, Oldwina.*

OLEDA (ol-EE-dah) English: "winged." *Oleta.*

OLENA (o-LAY-nah) Russian: "illumination." Variant of Helen.

OLESIA (o-LE-shuh) Polish: "protector of humanity." Variant of Alexandra.

OLETHA (o-LE-thah) English: "light" or "nimble."

OLEXA (oh-LEX-ah) English: "defender of mankind." Variant of Alexandra.

OLGA (OL-gah) Old Norse: "holy one." The name was popularized from Saint Olga, who spread Christianity in Russia during the tenth century. Still a popular name in Russia. *Helga, Olga, Olva;* Czech:

Olina, Olunka, Oluska; Est: *Olli, Olly;* Pol: *Ola, Olenka;* Russ: *Lelya, Lesya, Olenka, Oika, Olya, Olyusha.*

OLIANA (oh-lee-AH-nuh) Hawaiian: "fragrant oleander." An oleander is a poisonous evergreen shrub with aromatic red and white blossoms.

OLINA (oh-LEE-nah) Hawaiian: "filled with happiness." *Oleen, Oline.*

OLINDA (oh-LEEN-dah) Spanish: "protector."

OLISA (o-LEE-sah) Africa. Ibo: "Supreme Spirit." Often attached to other names to create a prayer or proverb.

OLIVIA (oh-LIV-ee-ah) Latin: "olive branch." The olive branch has traditionally been a symbol of peace and friendship. Movies and Television: Olivia de Havilland, Olivia Hussey (*Romeo and Juliet*), actresses. Music: Olivia Newton-John, singer. *Liv, Liva, Livia, Livvie, Olia, Oliva;* Eng: *Elive;* Fr: *Olivet, Olivette, Olivine, Ollie, Olva.*

OLUBAYO (oh-loo-BAH-yah) Nigeria. Yoruban: "greatest pleasure."

OLWEN (OHL-wenn) Welsh: "white footprint." Along with Bronwen, one of the best-known first names in the Welsh language, though quite rare outside Wales. *Olween, Olwin, Olwyn.*

OLYMPIA (oh-LIM-pee-ah) Greek: "from Olympus." Mythology: The Greek gods lived on Mount

Olympus, said to be in Thessaly, northern Greece. *Olimpia.*

OMA (o-MAH) Arabic: "military chief." Derived from the masculine Omar.

OMANA (oh-MAHN-ah) Hindi: "a woman."

OMEGA (oh-MAY-gah) Greek: "ultimate." The last letter in the Greek alphabet.

ONA (OH-nah) Lithuanian: "full of grace." Variant of Hannah.

ONAONA (oh-NAH-oh-nah) Hawaiian: "sweet smell."

ONATAH (o-NAH-tah) Native American. Iroquois: "earth child and spirit of the stalk." Relates to a native legend about the abduction of the corn spirit by a demon. Not until the sun rose again was the corn spirit freed.

ONAWA (oh-NAH-wah) Native American: "awake."

ONDINE (on-DEEN) Latin: "wavelet." Literature: Undine is a character in Edith Wharton's *Custom of the Country*. *Ondina, Ondyne, Undine.*

ONDREA (ohn-DREE-ah) Czechoslovakian: "fierce woman." Variant form of Andrea. *Ondra.*

ONELLA (oh-NELL-ah) Hungarian: Equivalent of the English Nellie, from Greek for "light."

ONI (OH-nee) Nigeria. Benin: "requested" or "prayed for." Usually refers to a child who arrived in a family only after many years of prayer.

ONIDA (oh-NEE-dah) Native American: "eagerly awaited."

OONAGH (oo-NAGH) Irish: Variant form of the English Una. *Oona.*

OPAL (oh-PAL) Sanskrit: "jewel." A gemstone known for its healing capacities.

OPHELIA (oh-FEEL-yah) Greek: "aid." Literature: Woman whose love for the title character in Shakespeare's *Hamlet* sends her to destruction. Span: *Ofelia.*

OPHIRA (oh-FEER-ah) Greek: "gold."

OPHRAH (OH-prah) Hebrew: "light."

ORA (oh-RAH) English: "beautiful seacoast."

ORAH (OH-rah) Israel. Hebrew: "illumination." *Ora, Oralee, Orit, Orlice, Orly.*

ORALEE (OH-rah-lee) Hebrew: "lord is my light."

ORALIA (oh-RAHL-ee-ah) Hebrew: "light." Latin: "golden."

ORANE (oh-RAHN) French: "rising." From the same Latin source as Oriana. *Orania, Oriane.*

ORENDA (oh-REN-dah) Native American. Iroquois: "spirit force." Refers to the power of life force innate to all beings and objects—one that can be used either for good or evil. A true understanding of this force leads one to the realization that all life is interrelated. In Sioux tradition the name is Wakanda.

ORIANA (oh-ree-AHN-ah) Latin: "as realization dawns"; Celtic: "gold-laden." Journalism: Oriana Falacci, Italian journalist. Fr: *Oraine, Oralia, Orelda, Orelle, Orlann, Orlene.*

ORINDA (oh-RIN-dah) Latin: Seventeenth-century poetic name.

ORINO (oh-REE-noh) Japanese: "workman's meadow."

ORIOLE (OH-ree-ole) Latin: "golden." A gold-flecked bird. Sports: A Baltimore baseball team. *Auriel, Oriel, Orella, Oriola.*

ORLA (or-LAH) Irish: "golden." *Orlaith, Orlaithe.*

ORLANDA (or-LAHN-dah) Latin: "bright sun."

ORLANTHA (or-LAHN-thah) Old German: "from the land."

ORLI (OR-lee) Hebrew: "the light is mine."

ORMANDA (or-MAHN-dah) German: "of the sea."

ORNETTA (or-NET-tah) Hebrew: "cedar tree."

ORNICE (or-NEES) Israel. Hebrew: "cedar" or "fir tree." Hebrew: *Orna, Ornit.*

ORPAH (OHR-pah) Israel. Hebrew: "fawn" or "dusty space." A biblical place name. Movies and Television: Oprah Winfrey, TV talk-show host and actress made this name familiar. *Ophra, Oprah.*

ORQUIDEA (or-KWEE-day-ah) Spanish: "orchid."

ORVA (or-VAH) French: "worth gold."

ORZORA (or-ZOR-ah) Hebrew: "God's strength."

OSANNA (oh-ZAHN-ah) See Hosanna.

OSEYE (oh-SEH-yeh) Nigeria. Benin: "merry person."

OTHA (OH-thah) Anglo-Saxon: "little wealthy one."

OTILIE (OH-til-ee) German: "fortunate heroine." *Otka, Otthild, Otthilda, Otthilde, Otila, Otilia, Otylia.*

OUIDA (oh-WEE-dah) French: "warrior woman."

OVE (oveh) Norse: "awe" or "the spear's point."

OYA (oh-YAH) Native American. Miwok: "to call forth." Refers to the practice of naming or speaking of a creature by name, thus uniting it with its power.

PABLA (PAH-blah) Spanish. From the name Pauline.

PACIENCIA (pah-SEE-en-see-ah) Spanish: "patient."

PADMA (PAHD-mah) Hindi: "lotus." National flower of India and once considered the birthplace of the god Brahma.

PAGE (payge) French: During medieval times, a page was a boy who served as a knight's right hand. Most recently used as a girl's name. Music: Paige O'Hara, singer of Belle in the Disney movie *Beauty and the Beast*. ***Padget, Padgett, Paget, Pagette, Paige.***

PAIVA (PIE-vah) Scandanavian: "god of the sun."

PALESA (pal-EE-sah) African: "flower."

PALILA (pah-LY-lah) Hawaiian: "bird."

PALLAS (PAHL-iss) Greek: "understanding." Mythology: Alternate name for Athena, Greek goddess of wisdom, of the city, and civilized life.

PALMA (PAHL-mah) Latin: "palm tree." *Palima, Pallimirah, Pallmyra, Palmer, Palmira, Palmyra.*

PALOMA (pah-LOH-mah) Spanish: "dove." International symbol for peace. The name is given to a baby who coos. Arts: Paloma Picasso, designer and daughter of Pablo Picasso.

PAMELA (PA-muh-la) Greek: "honey-coated." History: Sir Phillip Sidney, a poet, originated the name in the 1700s. Literature: Pamela Johnson, British novelist (*This Bed Thy Centre*); Pamel Painter, Harvard professor and author of short stories. Sports: Pam Shriver, tennis champion. *Pam, Pamala, Pamalia, Pamella, Pamelina, Pamella, Pammi, Pamilla, Pammela, Pammie, Pammy.*

PANDITA (pahn-DEE-tah) Hindi: "learned one."

PANDORA (pan-DOR-rah) Greek: "bestowed with talents." Pandora was the first mortal woman created by the gods and endowed with innumerable gifts. Unfortunately, she is more famous for opening her dowry box, which released all the world's evils as well as hope. *Panda, Pandorra, Pandy.*

PANIZ (pahn-IZ) Persian: "sugar."

PANSY (PAN-zee) French: Flower name originating in the late nineteenth century and possibly derived from *pensee* meaning "to think." *Pansey, Pansie.*

PANYA (PAHN-yah) Russian: "enthroned." Variant of Stephanie. Popular in Russia.

PAOLA (pah-OW-lah) Italian: "small."

PAPILLON (pap-EE-yon) French: "butterfly."

PAPINA (pah-PEE-nuh) Native American. Miwok: "crawling ivy."

PAQUITA (pah-KWE-tah) Spanish: "free."

PARIS (per-ISS) French: The name of the French capital used as a given name for both girls and boys. *Parisa, Parris, Parrish.*

PARISA (pahr-EE-sah) Persian: "angelic face."

PARMIDA (pahr-MEE-dah) Persian: "princess."

PARNELLA (par-NEL-lah) French: "rock."

PARTHENA (par-THEEN-ah) Greek: "virgin." A name that refers to the Parthenon, Athena's temple in Athens.

PASCALA (pas-CAL-ah) French: "born at Easter." *Pascale, Pascaline, Pasclina.*

PASHA (PAH-shah) Greek: "from the sea." Very popular in Russia. *Palasha, Pashka, Pelageya.*

PASTORA (pah-STOR-ah) Spanish: "shepherdess."

PATI (pah-TEE) Native American. Miwok: "to wring." Refers to a native custom of wrapping freshly caught fish in willow tree leaves.

PATIA (pah-TEE-uh) Spanish Gypsy: "fresh green leaf." A poetic reminder of life's external renewal after a harsh winter.

PATIENCE (PAY-shintz) Latin: "steadfast." One of the virtue names.

PATRICIA (pah-TREE-shah) Latin: "highly honorable" or "royal." History: Patricia Harris, Secretary of Housing and Urban Development under President Jimmy Carter. Sports: Pat Moss, race car driver who won Liege [Rome] Rally (1969). Eng: *Pat, Patric, Patsy, Pattie,* Fr: *Patrice, Patty, Patsy, Patria, Tricia, Trish, Trisha.*

PAULA (PAWL-ah) Latin: "petite." Popular worldwide particularly in Spanish-speaking countries and Poland. Arts: Paula Modersohn Becker, German painter. Journalism: Paula Zahn, host of *TV's Paula Zahn NOW.* Music: Paula Abdul, singer. Eng: *Pauletta, Paulette, Paulina, Pauline, Pollie, Polly;* Bulg: *Paulina;* Czech: *Paula, Paulina;* Ital: *Paolina;* Pol: *Pawlina, Pola, Polcia;* Russ: *Pavia, Pavlina, Pavlinka;* Span: *Paulita.*

PAUSHA (PO-shah) Hindi: Month in the Hindu calendar. Astrology: Equivalent to the sun sign of Capricorn.

PAVLA (PAHV-lah) Russian: "petite." Variant of Paula. Also popular in Czechoslovakia.

PAYTON (PAY-ton) English: Surname used as a given name. *Peyton.*

PAZ (pahz) Latin, Spanish: "peace."

PAZIA (pah-ZEE-uh) Israel. Hebrew: "full of gold." *Paz, Paxice, Pazit.*

PEARL (purl) Latin: A jewel name. Literature: Pearl Buck, U.S. novelist, won the Pulitzer Prize for *The Good Earth* (1932). Music: Pearl Bailey, singer. Sports: Pearl Moore, scored a record 4,061 points in her college basketball career. *Pearla, Pearlie, Pearlinda, Pearline, Perle.*

PEDRA (PED-rah) Spanish: "stone."

PEGGY (PEG-ee) Latin: Short name for Margaret, dating back to the Middle Ages. Arts: Peggy Bacon, painter and illustrator. Music: Peggy Lee, singer. Sports: Peggy Fleming, Olympic gold medalist in figure skating.

PENDA (PEN-dah) Swahili: "love."

PENELOPE (peh-NELL-o-pee) Greek: "she who weaves her dreams." History: Penelope Devereaux, daughter of the first Earl of Essex, subject of Sir Philip Sidney's love poems. Literature: Wife of Odysseus in Homer's *Odyssey*. Mythology: Wife of Ulysses who, during her husband's long absence, warded off suitors by pretending to weave her father-in-law's robe but unraveled it each night. Eng: *Pen, Penina, Penney;* Gk: *Pinelopi, Pipitsa;* Pol: *Pela, Pelcia, Penelopa.*

PENINA (pen-EE-nah) Hebrew: "jewel" or "coral."

PENSEE (pen-SAY-ee) French: "thoughtful."

PEONY (PAY-uh-nee or PEE-uh-nee) Greek: "praise-giving." A flower name. Connotes great honor.

PEPIN (pep-IN) Old German: "perseverance."

PEPITA (pep-EE-tah) Spanish: From Hebrew "multiply." A reference to the child's future prosperity. A variant of Josephine, popular in Spain since the 1700s.

PEPPER (PEP-er) English: "from the pepper plant."

PERAHTA (per-AH-tah) German: "glorious."

PERDITA (per-DEE-tah) Latin: "she who is lost." Literature: A Shakespearean invention, used in his romance *The Winter's Tale.*

PEREGRINE (per-EG-rin) English: "wanderer." *Perri.*

PERI (PER-ee) Greek: "nymph of the mountains and caves"; Hebrew: "from *perah* meaning blossom." Mythology: In Persian fable, an angel who fell.

PERKE (pehr-KEE) Hebrew: "devoted to God." *Perzi, Persike.*

PERLA (PER-la) Slavic: "immaculate pearl." Derived from Margaret.

PERSIS (PER-sees or PER-siss) Greek: "woman of Persia." Bible: First-century Christian woman who won Paul's praise.

PETA (PET-ah) Native American: "golden eagle."

PETRA (PET-rah) Greek: "stone." Variant form of Peter. *Petrina, Peta, Pier, Pierette, Petronella.*

PETRONILLA (pet-ROWN-eel-lah) German: "rock." *Petronille.*

PETULA (pet-ULAH) Latin: "impatient."

PHAEDRA (FAY-dra) Greek: "glowing." Mythology: Phaedra is derived from Phebus, another name for Apollo, who is closely identified with the sun. *Phedre, Phadra, Fedra.*

PHAILIA (phae-LEA) Thai: "sapphire."

PHIALA (phee-ALAH) Irish saint.

PHILA (phee-LAH) Greek: "love."

PHILADELPHIA (phee-LAH-dell-fee-ah) Greek: "brotherly love." History: The city of Philadelphia is a historic site in the creation of the United States.

Founded in 1854, Philadelphia has since been known as the City of Brotherly Love.

PHILANA (phee-LAHN-ah) Greek: "adoring."

PHILANTHA (phee-LAHN-tha) Greek: "lover of flowers."

PHILBERTA (fil-BER-tah) English: "brillant."

PHILENA (phee-LEN-ah) Greek: "lover of mankind."

PHILIPA (phee-LEE-pah) Greek: "horse-groomer" or "horse-lover." Masculine form of Phillip. History: Phillipa Hainaut, fourteenth-century queen of Edward III of England. Eng: *Phil Phillipa, Philli, Phillie, Pippa, Pippy;* Fr: *Filipote, Philippine;* Ital: *Flippa, Pilipa, Pippa;* Pol: *Ina, Inka.*

PHILOMENA (phee-lo-MEE-nah) Greek: "lover of the moon," "song lover," or "friend."

PHILYRA (phee-LYE-rah) Greek: "lover of music."

PHINEAS (phi-NEE-ahs) Greek: "oracle." Egyptian: "dark skinned."

PHOEBE (FEE-bee) Greek: "untainted" or "glowing." Bible: Christian woman who assisted some of the Apostles. Literature: Phoebe Cary, poet and hymn writer, "Nearer Home." Music: Phoebe Snow, singer. Mythology: Phoebe's daughter Leto gave birth to Apollo and Artemis. Span: *Phebe.*

PHOENA (foe-EE-nah) Greek: "mythical bird" or "purple."

PHYLICIA (fee-LEE-see-ah) Contemporary: Combination of Felicia and Phyllis. Movies and Television: Phylicia Rashad, actress (TV's *The Cosby Show*). *Philicia.*

PHYLLIS (FILL-iss) Greek: "green branch." Literature: Phyllis Bentley, novelist, *Spinner Years.* Music: Phyllis Curtis, operatic soprano and teacher. *Phillida, Phyliss.*

PIA (PEE-uh) Latin: "of deep faith." Movies and Television: Pia Zadora, actress and singer.

PIERA (pee-ER-ah) French: "small rock."

PIERETTA (pee-ER-etah) French. Feminine form of Pierre. *Pierette.*

PILAR (pee-LAHR) Spanish: "foundation" or "support beam," refers to the Virgin Mary, foundation of the Christian religion. Dance: Pilar Riohar, flamenco dancer.

PILIALOHA (pee-lee-ah-LO-ha) Hawaiian: "beloved."

PILISI (pi-LEE-see) Greek: "swaying branch." Variant of Phyllis in the United States.

PINGA (PEEN-gah) Hindi: "bronze" or "black." One of the many sacred names of Shakti, the Hindu goddess.

PIPER (PYE-per) English, French: "pipe or organ player." Movies and Television: Piper Laurie, actress.

PIXIE (PIKS-ee) Celtic: "small elf."

PLACIDA (plah-SEE-dah) Spanish: "tranquil."

POLLY (POL-ee) Hebrew: "bitter." Literature: Pollyanna, title character of Eleanor H. Porter's popular children's book, which was later made into a movie. *Poll, Polli, Pollyana.*

POPPY (POP-ee) Latin: "poppy flower." A red flower with cross-cultural meanings: It represents the month of August in the West and December in the East. Astrology: It is associated with the lunar forces of the astrological sign of Cancer. Movies and Televison: Poppy Montgomery, actress (TV's *Without a Trace*).

PORTIA (POR-sha) Latin: Derived from a Roman clan name. Business: The similar-sounding name Porsche is a popular sports car. Literature: Portia is a resourceful noblewoman in Shakespeare's comedy *The Merchant of Venice*. *Porsha, Porsche, Porcha, Porscha, Porschia.*

POSALA (po-SAH-lah) Native American. Miwok: "to explode." Refers to the energy of seeds bursting into life during the springtime.

PRADEEPTA (prah-DEEP-tah) Hindu: "glowing."

PRAMA (prah-MAH) Hindu: "knowing truth."

PRANATI (prah-NAH-tee) Hindu: "prayer."

PRECIOUS (PRESH-us) English, French: "of tremendous value" or "much beloved." Name of endearment. Bible: In Catholic tradition also a reference to the "precious blood of Christ." Music: Precious Wilson, singer. Sports: Precious Mackenzie, weight lifter. *Precia, Preciosa.*

PREETI (PREE-tee) Hindu: "love."

PREITA (preh-ETA) Finnish: "most loving one."

PRIMA (PREE-mah) Latin: "first." *Primavera.*

PRINCESS (PRIN-cess) A "title" name. Fr: *Princesa;* Ital: *Princessa.*

PRISCILLA (pris-SILL-ah) Latin: "from long ago." Priscilla was a favored name with the Puritans of England. Arts: Priscilla Dalmas, architect. Literature: Longfellow gave the name to the heroine of his poem *The Courtship of Miles Standish. Pricilla, Pris, Priscila, Prissie, Priss, Prissy.*

PRISMA (PRIZ-mah) Greek: "cut" or "sawed." Prisms are cut pieces of glass that can be used to separate light into the rainbow spectrum. *Prysma.*

PRITA (PRE-tah) Hindu: "dear one."

PRUDENCE (PROO-dintz) Latin: "using reason to govern one's affairs." One of the virtue names. Education: Prudence Crandall, nineteenth-century school teacher who admitted black students to her girls' school. Music: The Beatles song "Dear Prudence." *Prudy, Prue.*

PRUNELLA (prun-ELL-ah) French: "color of plum." *Prunellie.*

PUALANI (poo-AH-lan-ee) Hawaiian: "heavenly flower." This name refers to the wild ginger blossom or the bird-of-paradise in bloom. *Puni.*

PUEBLA (PUEW-blah) Spanish: "from the city."

PURA (purah) Spanish: "pure." *Pureza, Purisima.*

PURITY (pur-IT-ee) English: "unsullied" or "clean."

QAMRA (KWAM-rah) Arabic: "moon."

QETURAH (KET-ur-ah) Hebrew: "incense."

QI (kwee) Chinese: "fine jade."

QUANDA (KWAN-dah) African-American: "a companion."

QUARTILLA (kwar-TIL-ah) Latin: "fourth." Feminine form of Quartus, a saint's name.

QUBILAH (KWUB-ee-lah) Arabic: "concord."

QUEENA (KWEE-nah) English: Variant of the English title used as a given name. *Queenie, Queen, Queene.*

QUELLA (KWEL-lah) English: "pacify."

QUENBY (KWEN-be) Scandanavian: "womanly."

QUERIDA (kare-EE-dah) Portuguese: "much loved."

QUESTA (KWES-tah) French: "forever seeking."

QUETA (KAY-tah) Spanish: "mistress of the house." Nickname for Enriqueta and Henrietta.

QUINN (kwinn) Gaelic: "advisor." *Quincy.*

QUINTESSA (kwinn-TESS-ah) Latin: "essence."

QUORRA (kwo-OR-ah) Italian: "heart."

RA (rae) English: "doe." *Rae.*

RABEA (rah-BEA) German: "raven."

RABI (rah-BEE) Arabic: "sweet wind." This name suggests one will have a calm, soothing effect on others.

RABIAH (rah-BEE-ah) Arabic "spring."

RACHANA (rah-CHA-nah) Hindi: "creation."

RACHEL (RAY-chill) Israel. Hebrew: "sheep." Arts: Rachel Ruysch, eighteenth-century Dutch court painter. Bible: Sister of Leah and wife of Jacob, who was the son of Isaac. The Puritans used this Old Testament name. It remained popular up to the 1960s and 1970s. Science: Rachel Carson, author and biologist. Theater: Rachel Crothers, playwright. Eng: *Rachele, Rachelle, Rae;* Bulg: *Rahil;*

Fr: *Rachelle;* Ger: *Rahel;* Hawaiian: *Lahela;* Span: *Raquel;* Russ: *Rakhil, Rashel;* Swed: *Rakel;* Yiddish: *Ruchel, Raychell, Rachael, Rachele, Raquella, Raquelle, Rashell, Rashelle, Shell, Shelley, Shellie, Shelly.*

RADELLA (rah-DEL-lah) Old English: "elfin advisor."

RADHIYA (rah-THEE-yah) Swahili: "agreeable."

RADINKA (ra-DINK-ah) Slavic: "full of life."

RADMILLA (rahd-MILL-ah) Slavic: "devoted to others" or "hard worker." Refers to one who works for the benefit of others.

RAE (ray) Israel. Hebrew: "ewe." Used independently in contemporary times. *Raeann, Raelene, Ray, Raye, Rayette, Raylene.*

RAEKA (RAH-eh-kah) Spanish: "beautiful" or "unique."

RAFA (RAH-fah) Arabic: "happy."

RAFAELA (rah-fah-ELL-ah) Spanish, Hebrew: "mended by God." Raphael is one of God's four archangels. *Raphaella.*

RAGNHILD (RAHGN-hild) Norse: "one who is wise in battle."

RAHI (rah-HE) Arabic: "spring."

RAHIL (rah-HILL) Hebrew: "innocent."

RAI (ray) Japanese: "trust."

RAIMUNDA (rah-ee-MUN-dah) Spanish: "wise defender."

RAINBOW (RAYN-boh) English: Used to denote a color spectrum formed by the sun's rays reflecting in drops of water. Used as a given name.

RAISA (rah-EE-sah) Russian: "rose." *Raiza, Raissa.*

RAIZEL (RAY-zel) Yiddish: "rose." *Rayzil, Razil*

RAJA (RAH-jah) Hindi: "hope."

RAMAH (rah-MAH) Israel. Hebrew: "high."

RAMLA (RAHM-lah) Swahili: "soothsayer" or "one who knows the future."

RAMONA (rah-MO-nuh) Spanish: "all-knowing defender."

RANA (RAH-nah) Arabic: "behold."

RANAIT (RANA-it) Irish: "wealthy" or "charming." *Ranalt.*

RANDI (RAN-dee) Old English: "wolf shield." Popular in medieval times and today as a contemporary variant of Randolph. *Randee, Randie, Randy.*

RANE (RAH-neh) Latin: "royal" or "chaste." Popular in Scandinavian countries.

RANI (RAH-nee) Hindi: "queen."

RANITA (rah-NEE-tah) Israel. Hebrew: "joyful noise" or "chant." Popular in Israel. Isr: *Ranice, Ranit, Ranith, Ranitra, Ranitta.*

RASHA (RAH-sah) Arabic: "young gazelle."

RASHIDA (rah-SHEE-dah) Arabic: "righteous." *Rasheedah, Rasheeda.*

RASIA (RAH-see-uh) Greek: "rose blossom."

RATANA (rah-TAHN-ah) Tai: "crystal."

RAVEN (RAY-ven) English: "dark haired" or "wise." *Rayvn.*

RAWNIE (RAW-nee) English Gypsy: "fine lady."

RAYNA (RAY-nah) French: Short form of Lorraine and Reynalda. *Raina, Reyna, Rayne, Raine, Raynee, Rainey, Rainee, Rainie.*

RAZILEE (rah-zi-LEE) Israel. Hebrew: "my secret." *Razili.*

REA (ray) Greek: "brook" or "poppy." Astrology: Good for those born under one of the water signs such as Cancer, Scorpio, and Pisces.

REANNA (ree-ANN-ah) Contemporary combination name. *Reanne, Reannon, Reannah, Reeanne.*

REBECCA (re-BECK-ah) Hebrew: "bound." Bible: Wife of Isaac and mother of Jacob, Rebekah was known for her humility and beauty. Journalism: Rebecca West, British suffragette and journalist. History: Rebecca King, first woman appointed to the U.S. Senate (1922). Music: Reba McEntire, country singer. Eng: *Becca, Beckie, Becky, Bekka, Bekkie, Reba, Rebekka;* Bulg: *Reveka;* Czech: *Rebeka;* Fr: *Rebeque;* Ger: *Rebekke;* Span: *Rebeca;* Rum: *Reveca;* Russ: *Revekka;* Yiddish: *Rifka, Rheba, Riva, Rivah, Rivalee, Rivi, Rivy.*

REGAN (REE-gan or RAY-gan) Gaelic: "ruling." *Reagan, Ragan.*

REGINA (reh-JEEN-ah) Latin: "queenly." Bible: Allusion to the Virgin Mary. History: Heavily influenced by Queen Victoria's full name, Victoria Regina. Theater: *Victoria Regina,* a 1930s play starring Helen Hayes. Eng: *Gina, Raina, Regan, Reggie, Reggy, Regin, Reyne, Rina;* Fr: *Reine, Reinette;* Ger: *Gina, Regine;* Ital: *Reina;* Norw: *Rane;* Pol: *Ina, Renia, Reine, Rayna, Rina.*

REIKO (RAY-koh) Japanese: "very pleasant child." *Rei.*

REMY (REM-ee) French: "from Rheims."

REN (rehn) Japanese: "water lily."

RENA (REE-nah) Hebrew: Name ending used as an independent name. *Reena, Renne, Rina.*

RENEE (reh-NAY) French: "born again" or "resurrected." Sports: Renee Richards, tennis star. Literature: Rene Tardivaux, novelist, *Mademoiselle Cloque.* Eng: *Rene, Renelle, Reni, Renie, Renni, Rennie;* Span: *Renita, Renata, Renisha, Reneisha, Renne.*

RESEDA (reh-ZEE-dah) Latin: "mignonette flower."

RESI (REH-zee) German: "one who reaps." Variant of Theresa.

REVA (RAY-vah) Hindi: "Narmada River." An Indian place name of one of the seven sacred Hindi rivers in India.

REXANNE (rex-ANN) Contemporary: Blend of Rex and Anne. *Rexanna, Rexana, Rexine.*

RHEA (REE-ah) Greek: "flowing." Mythology: Rhea was the mother of Zeus, among others. She was the goddess of the earth and fertility. *Rhia, Rhaya, Rhae, Reya.*

RHIANNON (ree-ANN-an) Welsh: "magic maiden." Mythology: Horse goddess in Welsh mythology. *Rhianna, Rheanna, Rheanne, Rhiann, Rhiannan, Rhianon, Rhiana, Rhyan, Riana, Rianna, Rianne, Riane, Riannon, Riona.*

RHODA (ROH-dah) Greek: "rose." Name of a flower. Rhodes, a Greek island, is known for its roses. Bible: New Testament name revived in the 1700s. Literature: Rhoda Broughton, British novelist, *Cometh Up as a Flower*. **Rhodia, Rhodie, Rhody, Roda, Rodi, Rodie, Rodina.**

RHONDA (RON-dah) Welsh: "powerful seas." Music: Beach Boys' song, "Help Me, Rhonda." **Ronda, Rhonette, Rhona.**

RHOSLYN (ROES-lyn) Welsh: "lovely rose."

RHOSWEN (ROES-wen) Gaelic: "white rose."

RIA (REE-ah) Spanish: "river's origin." **Rie.**

RICARDA (ree-CAR-dah) English: "ruler."

RICHELLE (ri-SHELL) Contemporary: Combination of Rachelle and Richard. **Rikki, Ricki, Riki, Rikkie, Ricci, Ricca.**

RIHANA (ree-HAN-ah) Arabic: "sweet basil."

RILLA (RIL-ah) German: "brook." **Rille, Rillia, Rillie.**

RIMA (REE-mah) Spanish: "rhyme"; Arabic: "antelope."

RINI (REE-nee) Japanese: "little bunny."

RISA (REE-sah) Spanish: Short form of names ending in "rita," especially Margarita.

RITA (REE-tah) Spanish: Short form of Margarita. Literature: Rita Turow, nonfiction author, *Daddy's Little Girl*, and mother of Scott Turow. Movies and

Television: Rita Hayworth, actress; Rita Moreno, singer and actress who has won Oscar, Emmy, Grammy, and Tony awards. Music: Rita Coolidge, singer. Science: Rita Levi-Montalcini, Italian Nobel Prize winner for her discoveries of growth factors (1986).

RIVA (REE-vah) French: "on the bank of a river." *Reva.*

RIVKA (riv-KAH) Hebrew: "servant of god."

ROBERTA (ruh-BUR-tah) English, French, German: "dazzlingly known." Music: Roberta Peters, opera star; Roberta Flack, pop singer; title character in Jerome Kern's light opera *Roberta.* Eng: *Bobbet, Bobbett, Bobbi, Bobbie, Bobby, Robby, Robine, Robina, Robinia, Robinette;* Czech: *Berta, Roba;* Fr: *Robine;* Pol: *Berta;* Span: *Bertunga, Ruperta, Robertha.*

ROBIN (RAH-binn) English: "famous." Used as a boy's name in medieval times. Today it is popular for both sexes. *Robyn, Roynn, Roynne, Robena, Robina.*

ROCH (rock) German: "glory."

ROCHELLE (ra-SHELL) French: "stone." Literature: Rochelle Distelheim, short-story writer and nonfiction author. *Rochele, Rochella.*

RODERICA (roe-DER-ikah) Old German: "famous one."

ROHANA (roh-HAH-nah) Hindi: "sandalwood."

ROLANDA (roe-LAN-dah) German: "from the famous land." *Rolande.*

ROLDANA (ROL-dah-nah) Spanish: "famous."

ROMANA (roe-MAHN-ah) Italian: "from Rome."

ROMHILDA (rom-HIL-dah) German: "glorious battle maiden." *Romhilde, Romhild, Romilde, Romilda.*

RONALDA (ron-ALD-ah) Old Norse: "mighty."

RONIA (ron-EE-ah) Latin: "my lord is my joy."

RONLI (rohn-LEE) Israel. Hebrew: "my own joy." *Rona, Roni, Ronia, Ronice, Ronit, Ronlia.*

ROSALEEN (ROH-za-LEEN) Irish: "love." Another name for Rose. Literature: Roslyn Rosen Lund, novelist, *The Sharing.* Science: Rosalyn Yalow, physician, first U.S. woman to win the Nobel Prize for medicine.

ROSALIA (roe-SAHL-ee-ah) Spanish: "rose garland."

ROSALINE (roe-SAH-lind) Spanish: "beautiful rose." Literature: Rosalind, main female character in Shakespeare's play *As You Like It* who is a fun-loving and playful woman who enjoys speaking about the idea of love. *Rosalinde, Rosalinda, Rosalyn.*

ROSE (rohze) Greek: "rose." Plant name beloved for centuries. The rose is a symbol of Valentine's Day and eternal love. Arts: Rose O'Neill Wilson, illustrator, designed Kewpies. History: Rose Greenhow, Confederate spy; Rosa Parks, refused to move to the back of bus on December 1, 1955, beginning 382-day boycott led by Martin Luther King, Jr. Literature: Rose Hartwick Thorpe, poet, "Curfew Must Not Ring Tonight." Sports: Rosie Casals, winner of six Wimbledon tennis doubles titles. Eng: *Rhoda, Rosa, Rosalie, Rosella, Roselle, Rosette, Rosie;* Czech: *Ruzena, Ruzenka;* Hung: *Razalia, Rozsi, Ruzsa;* Ital: *Rosetta;* Lith: *Rozele, Rozyte;* Pol: *Roza, Rozalie;* Russ: *Ruzha;* Span: *Charo, Rosana, Rosita, Shaba, Zita.*

ROSEANNE (ro-ZANN) Combination of Rose and Anne. Movies and Television: Made popular by actress Roseanne Barr and her highly successful TV series, *Roseanne.* Rosanna Arquette, actress. *Ranna, Roanna, Roanne, Rosanagh, Rosanna, Rosannah, Rosanne, Roseann, Roseanna, Rose-hannah, Rozanna, Rozanne, Rozeanne.*

ROSELANI (roh-suh-LAH-nee) English, Hawaiian: "rose from the heavens." Derived from a red rose native to Hawaii.

ROSEMARIA (rohze-MAH-ree-ah) Spanish: "bitter flower." Eng. *Rosemary.*

ROSEMUND (rohze-MUND) German: "a garden of flowers."

ROSLINE (rahs-LYN) Old French: "little red-haired one."

ROWA (roe-WAH) Arabic: "lovely vision."

ROXANNE (roks-ANN) Persuian: "brilliant one." Literature: In Edmond Ronstad's play *Cyrano de Bergerac*, Roxane is Cyrano's unrequited love who falls in love with his poetry instead of the man. Movies and Television: Title of a popular movie based on *Cyrano de Bergerac*, starring Steve Martin and Daryl Hannah. Music: Popular song sung by the The Police. *Roxane*.

ROZENE (ro-ZAY-nuh) Native American: "rose blossom."

RUANA (roo-AH-nah) Hindi: "musical string instrument." Music: In Hindu tradition being named after a musical instrument is a reminder of God's presence in all sounds.

RUBI (ROO-be) French: "jewel." *Ruby*.

RUPETTA (rue-PET-tah) German: "famous." *Rupette*.

RURI (roo-REE) Japanese: "precious emerald." Ancient Japanese people believed emeralds guarded one's home against demons or bad luck. Astrology: Symbol of the sun sign Taurus.

RUSALKA (roo-SAHL-kah) Czechoslovakian: "wood nymph." Popular Slavic name.

RUTH (ruth) Hebrew: "friend." Bible: In the book of Ruth, Ruth dedicates her life to god and through her grace is instrumental in the history of his people.

RYANN (RYE-ahn) Gaelic "kingly." *Ryanne, Ryane, Ryana, Ryanna.*

RYBA (REE-bah) Czechoslovakian: "fish." Astrology: Fish are the symbol of Pisces.

SABA (sah-BAH) Greek: "woman of Sheba."

SABINA (sah-BEE-nah) Latin: "Sabine." An ancient tribe in central Italy around the time the city of Rome was formed.

SABIRAH (sah-BE-rah) Arabic: "of great patience."

SABLE (SAY-bel) Slavic: "black." An animal whose deep brown pelt is much sought-after by fur wearers.

SABRA (SAH-bra) Arabic: "thorny" or "strong as a cactus." Refers to one who is born in Israel. *Sabrina.*

SABRINA (sah-BREE-nah) Latin mythology: A Celtic nymph who lived in England's Severn River. Movies and Televison: Title of 1954 movie starring Audrey Hepburn and Humphrey Bogart. Literature:

Sabrina is a character in works by Milton. Theater: Character in Fletcher's play *The Shepherdess*. *Brina, Sabreena, Sabrena, Sabryna, Sabrinna, Sabreen, Sabrene.*

SACHI (SAH-chee) Japanese: "blessing" or "lucky."

SACHIKO (SAH-chee-koh), "blessed one" or "lucky one."

SADA (SAH-dah) Japanese: "pure one."

SADIE (SAY-dee) Hebrew: "princess."

SADIRA (sa-DEER-ah) Persian: "lotus."

SAERAN (sai-RAHN) Irish saint.

SAFA (sah-FAH) Arabic: "innocent."

SAFFRON (SAH-fron) Middle English: Flower name. Saffron is a Mediterranean and Indian spice that turns food a bright orange. It is also the traditional color worn by monks in some Eastern religions. *Saffren, Saffronia, Saphron.*

SAGE (sayge) English, French: "wise one." Used more for boys than girls. Also the name of a pungent herb used in native traditions to clear negative vibrations.

SAGIRA (sah-GER-ah) Egyptian: "little one."

SAHARA (sah-HAH-rah) Arabic: Variant form of Sarah. Sahara is also an Arabic name meaning "wilderness." *Saharah, Sahra.*

SAJNI (sahj-NE) Hindu: "beloved."

SAKARI (sah-KAH-ree) India. Rodas: "heart of sweetness."

SAKI (SAH-kee) Japanese: "cloak." Also, the popular name of a Japanese rice wine that is highly intoxicating.

SAKURA (sah-KOO-rah) Japanese: "cherry blossom." The Japanese national flower, which blooms profusely in springtime.

SALA (SAH-lah) Hindi: "sala tree." Mythology: A sacred tree in Buddhist lore, under which the Buddah supposedly died. Branches of the sala tree are said to bestow grace and blessings on a household.

SALBATORE (sahl-BAHT-or-ey) Spanish: "savior." *Salvatore, Salbatora.*

SALENE (say-LEN) French: "dignified one."

SALINA (say-LEE-nah) Latin: "by the salt water." French: "solemn."

SALLY (SAL-ee) Hebrew: "princess." Variant form of Sarah. Military: Sally Tompkins, captain in the Confederate Army. Movies and Television: Sally Jessy Raphael, talk-show host; Sally Field, actress, *Norma Rae.* Science: Sally Ride, astronaut. *Sal, Saletta, Sallie, Sallee, Salina, Salena, Saleena, Sallianne, Sallyann.*

SALMA (SAHL-mah) Spanish: "ambitious." Movies and Televison: Salma Hayek, actress (*Frida*).

SALOME (SAL-oh-may) Hebrew, Greek: "bestowing peace." Bible: Mother of James and John, Disciples of Christ. Theater: Title character in play by Oscar Wilde. *Saloma, Salomia.*

SALWA (sahl-WAH) Arabic: "solace" or "comfort."

SAMANTHA (sa-MAN-tha) Hebrew: Blend of Sam plus Anthea. Movies and Television: Lead role played by Elizabeth Montgomery in the popular 1960's TV sitcom *Bewitched*. Sports: Samantha Druce, youngest female to swim English Channel at age twelve (1983).

SAMARA (SAH-marah) Hebrew: "protected by God."

SAMI (SAH-mee) Arabic: "much praised." *Samia, Samina, Sammar, Sammir, Sammie, Sammy.*

SAMIRA (SAH-mee-rah) Arabic: "entertaining. *Samirah.*

SAMUELA (sahmu-ELAH) Hebrew: "her name is God."

SANA (SAH-nah) Persian: "light."

SANCHA (SAHN-cha) Spanish: "holy." *Sancia.*

SANDRA (SAN-dra or SAHN-dra) Greek: "helper of humanity." History: Sandra Day O'Connor, first woman on the U.S. Supreme Court. Movies and Television: Sandra Bernhard, Sandra Dee, Sandrine Bonnaire, actresses. *Sanda, Sandee, Sandi, Sandie, Saundra, Sondra.*

SAPPHIRE (SAF-ire) Arabic: "gorgeous." The gem and the color are both deep purple-blue. Bible: Sapphira was mortally punished by the Lord for failing to tell the truth. *Safira, Saphira, Sapphira, Sephira.*

SARAH (SAYR-uh) Israel. Hebrew: "young royal" or "princess." Bible: Wife of Abraham who gave birth to Isaac in her old age. Education: Sarah Cooper, kindergarten pioneer. History: Sarah Breedlove (a.k.a. Madam C. J. Walker), entrepreneur and first African-American millionaire. Movies and Television: Sarah Jessica Parker, actress (TV's *Sex and the City*). Literature: Sarah Teasdale, poet; Sarah Woolsey, writer of juvenile novels (*Just Sixteen*). Music: Sarah Vaughan, jazz singer. Eng: *Sadie, Sadye, Saida, Sally, Sarene, Sareen, Sarine, Sarina, Sara, Sarabeth, Sarajane, Sarajean, Saralee, Saralyn, Saralynn, Saramae, Sari, Sarrah, Sarra, Saira, Sairah, Sayra, Sariah;* Hebrew: *Sirke;* Fr: *Sarotte;* Hung: *Sari, Sarika, Sarolta, Sasa;* Pol: *Salcia;* Russ: *Sarka, Sarra;* Span: *Charita, Sarita.*

SARAI (sah-REE) Hebrew: "quarrelsome."

SAREA (sar-EY-ah) Hebrew: "name of an angel."

SARILA (sah-RIL-ah) Turkish: "rush of the waters."

SARISHA (sah-RISH-ah) Hindu: "charming."

SAROLTA (SHAW-rohl-tah) Hungarian: Variant form of both Sara and Charlotte.

SASA (SAH-sah) Japanese: "assistance."

SASHA (SAH-sha) Russian: Short form of Alexandra.

SATIN (SAH-tinn) French, English: A classically smooth fabric.

SAURA (SOW-rah) Hindi: "devoted to the sun." Derived from a sect of Hindu worshipers who exalt the sun as their major divinity. Astrology: Good for those born under the sun-ruled Leo.

SAVANNAH (sah-VAN-ah) Spanish: "treeless plain." Name of a city in Georgia. *Savanna, Savanah, Savana, Savonna.*

SAVARNA (SAHV-arn-ah) Hindu: "daughter of the ocean."

SAWA (SAH-wah) Japanese: "swamp." Native American: Miwok: "stone." Both the Japanese and Native American cultures believe that spirits reside in all elements of nature.

SCARLETT (SKAR-litt) English, French: A bold red color. Movies and Television: Scarlett Johansson, actress (*Lost in Translation*). Literature: Scarlett O'Hara, character in Margaret Mitchell's *Gone with the Wind. Scarlet, Scarlette.*

SEANA (SHAWN-ah) Irish, Hebrew: "God's generosity." *Shana, Siana, Shawna, Seanna.*

SEARLAIT (see-AR-lay-ite) French: "tiny and womanly."

SEASON (SEE-sohn) Latin: "planting time."

SEBILLE (seb-ILL) English: "a fairy."

SEDA (SEE-dah) Armenian: "forest voices."

SEKI (seh-KEE) Japanese: "wonderful." An audacious name in a culture that uses "negative" names to avert bad fortune brought on by angry gods.

SELBY (SELL-be) Old English: "of the manor house."

SELIMA (se-LEE-mah) Israel. Hebrew: "that which brings comfort or peace."

SELINA (se-LEE-nah) Greek: "lunar glow" or "parsley." Parsley is a symbol of springtime and renewal. Astrology: Good for those born under the moon-ruled sign of Cancer.

SELMA (SELL-mah) Old Norse: "God watches over," derived from Anselma; Arabic: "protected" or "secure." Arts: Selma Burke, sculptor. Literature: Selma Lagerlöf, Swedish Nobel Prize winner and first woman to win the prize in literature (1909) who is best known for her writings about Nordic myths and legends.

SEMA (SEE-mah) Greek: "divine omen."

SEMINE (sem-EEN) Danish: "goddess of the sun, moon, and stars."

SEMIRA (SEEM-irah) African: "fulfilled."

SEN (sehn) Japanese: "ancient forest elf." Mythology: Japanese lore speaks of a thousand-year-old hermit with magical powers who lives in the mountain forests. The name is said to bestow long life.

SENNETT (SEHN-ett) French: "wise one."

SENONA (sen-OHN-ah) Spanish: "lively."

SENTA (seen-TAH) Old German: "assistant." *Sente.*

SEPTEMBER (sep-TEM-ber) Latin: "seventh month."

SERAFINA (se-rah-FEE-nah) Latin: From the Hebrew *seraphim,* a class of six-winged angels standing in the presence of God. *Sarphina, Sarphine, Serafine.*

SERENA (se-REN-ah) Spanish: "serene." Sports: Serena Wiliams, tennis star and Olympic gold medalist. In 2002-2003, she won the "Serena Slam" by holding all four grand slam titles: French Open, U.S. Open, Wimbledon, and the Australian Open.

SERENITY (se-RENN-ah-tee) English, French: One of the virtue names connoting a peaceful disposition.

SERHILD (SIR-hild) German: "armored battle maiden." *Serhilda, Serihilde, Serihilda.*

SEVITA (sev-EE-tah) Hindu: "beloved."

SHADA (SHAH-dah) Native American: "pelican."

SHAHAR (shah-HAHR) Arabic: "lunar." Astrology: Good for those born under the moon-ruled Cancer.

SHAINA (SHAY-nah) Yiddish: "lovely to behold."

SHAKA (SHAH-kah) United States. English. African-American: "female defender" or "warrioress." Music: Chaka Khan, pop singer. *Chaka, Shakala.*

SHAKILA (shah-KEE-lah) African: "pretty."

SHAKTI (SHAK-tee) Hindi: "divine feminine." Shakti is the supreme manifestation of the active female principle in Hinduism embodying both loving and wrathful forms. The eternal love of Shiva, the male principle. Popular name among New Age adherents.

SHAMITA (SHA-mee-tah) Hindu: "peacemaker."

SHANDY (SHAN-dee) Old English: "rambunctious."

SHANESSA (sha-NES-ah) Irish: "God is gracious."

SHANI (SHAH-nee) Swahili: "tremendous" or "wonderful."

SHANICE (sha-NEESE) Contemporary: *Shaniece, Shaneice, Shanise, Shanese, Shannice.*

SHANLEY (SHAN-lee) Gaelic: "child of the old hero."

SHANNA (SHANN-ah) United States. English: Variant of Shannan. *Shana.*

SHANNON (shann-OHN) Irish: "wise one."

SHANTA (SHAN-tah) Hindi: "peaceful."

SHANTAY (shan-TAY) French: "enchanting."

SHANTELL (shan-TELL) African-American: "song." *Shantelle.*

SHANTON (shahn-TOHN) French: "we sing."

SHAPPA (SHAH-pah) Native American: "red thunder." Commemorates birth that takes place during inclement weather.

SHARAI (shah-RYE) Israel. Hebrew: "queen's daughter." Origin of the English name Sharon.

SHARDE (shar-DAY) Nigeria. Yoruba: "she who honor has made royal." Phonetic variant form of

Sade, the short form of Folasade. Music: Sade, international pop singer. *Shadae, Shardae, Sharday, Shardai.*

SHARIF (shar-EEF) Arabic: "noble."

SHARIK (sha-REEK) African: "child of God" or "child under the sun."

SHARISSA (shah-RISS-ah) United States. English: Unique combination of Melissa meaning "honey" with Sharon meaning "princess." The overall connotation might mean: "one who rules with the sweetness of honey." Movies and Television: Shari Belafonte, actress; Shari Lewis, puppeteer known mostly for her sock puppet, "Lambchop." *Shari, Sharie, Sharice, Sharine, Sheri, Sherie, Sherice, Sherine, Sherissa, Rissa.*

SHARLA (SHAR-lah) French: "little and womanly." Form of Charlotte.

SHARLENE (shar-LEEN) English: "manly." Feminine variant of Charles.

SHARMA (SHAR-ma) United States. English: Unique contemporary combination of Sharon and Mary.

SHARON (SHAR-on) English, Hebrew: "flat plain." Reference to the fertile plain between Jaffa and Mount Carmel, Israel. Movies and Television: Sharon Ritchie, Miss America 1956; Sharon Stone, actress (*Basic Instinct*). Literature: Sharon Falconer, character in Sinclair Lewis's novel *Elmer Gantry.*

SHAWNA (SHAW-nah) United States. English: Contemporary variant of Sean, the English version of John. *Sean, Shana, Shanna, Shauna, Shaunda, Shaundee, Shaunelle, Shawn, Shawni, Shawnee, Shawnna, Shawnice, Shawniece.*

SHEBA (SHEE-bah) Arabic: Name of a kingdom in southwestern Arabia. Bible: The Queen of Sheba sought to prove whether King Solomon was as wise as people believed. She found he was actually wiser.

SHEENA (SHEE-nah) Irish: "grace of God." Variant of Jane. Music: Sheena Easton, singer. Sports: Sheena Thompson, pool-playing endurance record: 363 hours, 9 minutes. *Shena.*

SHEILA (SHEE-lah) Latin: "blind." *Sheelah, Shela.*

SHELBY (SHEL-bee) English: "sheltered town."

SHELLEY (SHEL-ley) English: "from the meadow." *Shelly.*

SHERRI (sheri) Hebrew: "beloved." *Sherry.*

SHERYL (sheryl) English: "charity." Music: Sheryl Crow, American pop singer.

SHIKA (SHEE-kah) Japanese: "sweet deer." The name traditionally honors a calm and gentle nature.

SHINA (SHEE-nah) Japanese: "wealth." The name may connote either material or spiritual wealth.

SHINO (SHEE-no) Japanese: "bamboo stalk." The name connotes great devotion.

SHIRI (SHEE-ree) Israel. Hebrew: "song of my soul." *Shira, Shirah.*

SHIRIN (SHIR-in) Persian: "sweet." History: Shirin Ebadi, Iranian lawyer and human rights activist who won the Nobel Peace Prize in 2003.

SHIRLEY (SHUR-lee) English: "bright clearing." Aristocratic surname. Education: Shirley Hufstedler, Secretary of Education (1971–81). History: Shirley Chisholm, first black woman elected to Congress (1968). Movies and Television: Shirley Temple Black, child film star and later diplomat, youngest actor to receive an honorary Oscar; Shirley MacLaine, actress, writer, and New Age advocate. Sports: Shirley de la Hunty, Australian athlete who won Olympic gold medal for 80-meter hurdles (1952, 1956). *Shirleen, Shirlene, Shirleynn.*

SHIZU (SHEE-zoo) Japanese: "transparent" or "silent." A name currently enjoying popularity in Japan. *Shizue, Shizuka, Shizuko, Shizuyo.*

SHOSANA (shos-ANA) Hebrew: "lily."

SHURA (SHOO-rah) Russian: "protector of humanity." Modern variant of Alexander.

SIANY (see-AN-ee) Irish: "good health."

SIBLEY (sib-LEE) Greek: "prophetess."

SIDRA (sid-RAH) Latin: "star-borne" or "star-directed." Astrology: Good name for a child whose birth seemed to be miraculous.

SIERRA (see-ERR-ah) Irish: "dark."

SIGFREDA (sig-FREE-dah) German: "victorious." *Sigfrieda, Sigfriede.*

SIGNE (SIG-nee) Latin: "singing healer" or "triumphant advisor." Variant of Sigrid commonly used in Norway.

SIGOURNEY (sihg-OR-nee) French: "daring king." Movies and Televison: Sigourney Weaver, actress (*Alien*).

SIGRID (SIG-ridd) Old Norse: "triumphant advisor." Popular modern Scandinavian name used in many parts of the world. Literature: Sigrid Undset, 1928 Nobel Prize Winner.

SIHU (SEE-hoo) Native American: "flower" or "bush."

SILANA (see-LAHN-ah) French: "dignified."

SILIVIA (see-lee-VEE-uh) Hawaiian: "out of the forest." Derived from the Latin *Silva*.

SILVANA (sil-VAHN-ah) Latin: "forest."

SIMONE (sim-OHN) French: "heard."

SIOBHAN (sha-VAHN) Irish: Form of Joan. *Shavon, Shavona, Shavonda, Shavonna, Shavonne.*

SIRENA (ser-EE-nah) Greek: "siren."

SISIKA (si-SEE-kah) Native American: "singing bird."

SISSY (SISS-ee) United States. English: Pet variant of "sister." Movies and Television: Sissy Spacek, actress (*Coal Miner's Daughter*).

SITA (SEE-tah) Spanish: "rose" from *Zita*. Hindu mythology: The name of Rama's wife-goddess of the earth.

SITI (SEE-tee) Swahili: "lady born to respect."

SKYLAR (SKY-lar) English: "eternal life," "strength," or "beauty and love."

SOFIA (soh-FEE-ah) Greek: "wisdom." History: Sophia Smith, founded Smith College; Sophia Jex-Blake, British physician, established London School of Medicine for Women, 1874. Movies and Television: Sophia Loren, actress. Eng: *Sophia, Sophie, Sophy;* Czech: *Zofia, Zofie, Zofka;* Ger: *Sofi, Sophron;* Nor: *Sonja;* Pol: *Zacha, Zofia, Zosia, Zosha;* Russ: *Sofya, Sofka, Sonya;* Span: *Chofa, Fifi, Soficita;* Swed: *Sofi;* Turk: *Sofya;* Ukrain: *Zofia.*

SOLANA (soh-LAH-nah) Latin: "wind from the east."

SOLANGE (soh-LANZH) French: "solitary." *Soledad, Sola.*

SOMA (SO-mah) Hindi: "lunar." Astrology: Good for a child born under the moon-ruled sign of Cancer.

SOMATRA (sohm-AH-trah) Hindu: "excelling the moon."

SONJA (SOHN-jah) Russian: Derived from Sophia. Sports: Sonja Henie, Olympic figure skater and gold medalist (1928, 1932, 1936); Sonia O'Sullivan, pole-vault champion, holds 1991 record; Sonia Morgenstern, German figure skater, performed first triple salchow jump. *Sonia.*

SORA (SO-rah) Native American: "singing bird soars."

SPERANZA (sper-AHN-zah) Italian: "hope."

STACY, STACEY (STAY-cee) Contemporary: Derived from Eustacia, meaning "she who brings peace," or Anastasia, meaning "reborn." Eng: *Staci, Stacia, Stacie;* Czech: *Stasa, Staska;* Latin: *Stasya, Taska, Tasya;* Span: *Tasia.*

STARLA (STAR-lah) English: Astrological name based on "star." *Star, Starr, Starleena, Starlene, Starlena, Starlette, Starlyn, Starlynn.*

STELLA (STEL-lah) Greek, Latin: "a star."

STEPHANIE (STEF-ah-nee) Greek: "wearer of the crown." Sports: Steffi Graf, tennis champion. History: Stephanie, the Princess of Monaco. Literature: Stevie Smith, poet. Movies and Television: Stefanie Powers, Stephanie Zimbalist, actresses. Eng: *Stef, Stefa, Steffi, Steffie, Stepha, Stepania, Stepanie, Stephana, Stevena, Teena;* Czech: *Stefka;* Fr: *Trinnette;* Gr: *Stamatios;* Pol: *Stefa, Stefka;* Russ: *Panya, Stepanyda, Stesha, Steshka, Stepa.*

STINA (STEE-nah) German: Variant of Christel.

STORMY (STORR-mee) English: Adaptation of the weather term popular in the United States. *Stormie, Stormi.*

SUE ELLEN (soo-ELL-inn) United States. English: Popular combination of Sue ("lily") and Ellen ("light" or "torch").

SUELA (soo-EL-ah) Spanish: "to be consoled" derived from Chela. *Suelita.*

SUGI (SOO-gee) Japanese: "cedar." In Japan, the large sugi tree symbolizes the sacred mysteries of the Shinto religion and are often found near shrines.

SUKE (SOO-kee) Hawaiian: Development of Susan, "lily."

SUKI (SOO-kee) Japanese: "loved one"; Native American. Miwok: "hawk with eagle eyes."

SULA (SOO-luh) Icelandic: Variant of Ursula meaning "baby bear with small paws."

SULETU (soo-LEH-too) Native American. Miwok: "soaring without warning." Mythology: Refers to a mischievous jaybird who was reduced to a low status because of his trickeries.

SUMI (SOO-mee) Japanese: "elegant" or "one who sees clearly."

SUMIKO (soo-MEE-koh) Japanese: "lovely child."

SUMMER (SOME-er) English: "born during the summer." *Suma.*

SUNI (SOO-nee) Native American. Zuni: "native one" or "born to tribe."

SUNNY (SON-ee) English: "of bright disposition." Music: "Sunny," a pop song from the 1960s. *Sunnie, Sunni, Sunita.*

SURATA (soo-RAH-tah) Hindi: "divine joy in great measure." Connotes the transcendant joy experienced by the parents during the child's conception.

SURI (SOO-ree) India. Todas: "sheep blade." Refers to an infant born with a pointy nose.

SURYA (SOOR-yah) Hindi: "god who rules the sun." Astrology: Good for girl born under the sun-ruled sign of Leo. Sports: Surya Bonaly, European champion figure skater.

SUSAN (SOO-zinn) Israel. Hebrew: "lily" or "rose." A name with countless variations around the world. Education: Susan Blow, established the first kindergarten (1873). History: Susan B. Anthony, reformer, active in the temperance movement and women's suffrage. Journalism: Susan M. Headan, Pulitzer Prize-winning journalist at the *Indianapolis Star* (1991). Literature: Susan Cheever, author. Movies and Television: Susan Dey, Susan Sarandon, actresses. Sports: Suzee Chaffee, developed new forms of freestyle skiing for women. Eng: *Sue, Suka, Sukee, Sukey, Suki, Sukie, Suky, Susanna, Susannah, Susanne, Susetta, Susette, Susi, Susie, Susy, Suzanna, Suzannah, Suzanne, Suzette, Suzie;* Armenian: *Shoushan;* Bulg: *Suzana;* Czech: *Zuza, Zuzana, Zuzanka, Zuzka;* Fr: *Suzanne, Suzette;* Ger: *Susanne, Suse;* Hawaiian: *Suke, Suse;* Hebrew: *Sonel;* Hung: *Zsa Zsa;* Ir: *Sosanna;* Ital: *Susanna;* Pol: *Zuza, Zuska;* Rum: *Suzana;* Russ: *Susanka;* Scot: *Siusan;* Span: *Susana.*

SUTKI (SHOOT-kee or anglicized to SOOT-kee) Native American. Hopi: "clay in broken chains." May refer to a vision or dream of the parents.

SUZAMMI (soo-ZAHM-mee) French: From the Carrier Indians. Unique combination of Susan and Annie.

SUZU (SOO-zoo) Japanese: "tiny ringer." Refers to a small bell affixed to a child's belt to ward off bad luck. The name is highly popular in contemporary Japan. Suzue ("branch of little bells"), Suzuki ("bell tree"), and Suzuko ("bell child").

SYDNEY (SIDD-nee) Old French: "from the city of St. Denis, France." A place name. *Sy, Syd, Sydny.*

SYLVIA (SILL-vee-yah) Latin: "woods." Variation on Silvia. Literature: Sylvia Beach, bookseller who published James Joyce's *Ulysses;* Sylvia Warner, British novelist, poet, and biographer *(Kingdoms of Elfin);* Sylvia Plath, novelist *(The Bell Jar).* Science: Sylvia Earie, marine biologist. *Sylvie, Sylvina, Sylvana, Sylvonna.*

TABIA (tah-BEE-ah) Swahili: "gifts" or "artistic abilities."

TABITHA (TA-bih-tha) Aramaic: "leaping gazelle." Bible: From the New Testament, it enjoyed popularity in the 1600s. It resurfaced in the second half of the twentieth century.

TABORA (tah-BOR-ah) Spanish: "plays a small drum."

TACEY (TAH-cee) English: "silent" or "calm." *Tacy.*

TACITA (tah-SEE-tah) Latin: "to be silent."

TAFFY (TAF-ee) Welsh: "beloved."

TAIMA (tah-EE-mah) Native American: "thunderbolt." Connotes great power. Particularly suited for a child who was born during a thunderstorm.

TAIPA (tah-EE-pah) Native American. Miwok: "wings spread." Connotes a sense of majesty and personal fulfillment.

TAIT (that) English: "brings joy."

TAKA (TAH-kah) Japanese: "one on whom honor is bestowed."

TAKARA (tah-KAH-rah) Japanese: "beloved jewel."

TAKENYA (tah-KEHN-yah) Native American. Miwok: "fierce falcon."

TAKI (TAH-kee) Japanese: "waterfall returning home."

TAKODA (tak-OH-dah) Native American: "friend to all."

TAJA (TAH-zha or TAY-zha) Hindi: "crowned."

TALA (TAH-lah) Native American: "stalking wolf." Connotes qualities of auspicious fortune and cunning.

TALIA (TAL-ya) Israel. Hebrew: "golden dew from above." *Talor, Talora, Talya, Tahlia, Taliah.*

TALITHA (ta-LEE-thah or TAL-i-thah) Israel. Hebrew: "child." Bible: Reference to the resurrection of Jairus's daughter when Jesus said, "Child, arise."

TALLIS (TAHL-iss) English, French: "forest."

TALULA (tah-LOO-lah) Native American. Choctaw: "water sprays to sky." Also a Georgia place name. Movies and Television: Tallulah Bankhead, actress. *Talli, Tallie, Tallulah, Tally.*

TAM (tom) Vientnamese: "heart."

TAMA (TAH-mah) Japanese: "gleaming" or "globe." Surname. Literature: Tama Janowitz, novelist. *Tamae.*

TAMAKA (TAH-mee-kah and anglicized tah-MEE-kah) Japanese: "child born for the people." Now current in the United States. *Tami, Tamke, Tamiko, Tamiya.*

TAMARA (tah-MAH-rah) Israel. Hebrew: "palm tree." Bible: Tamar was King David's stunning daughter. Another Tamar appears in the Bible; she is known for her perseverance. Sports: Tamara McKinney, skiing champion; *Tamar, Tamra, Tamarah, Tamryn.*

TAMBRE (tahm-BRAY) English: "great joy" or "music."

TAMESIS (tahm-EES-is) Greek: "goddess of the river."

TAMMY (TAH-mee) United States. English: Short form of Tamara and Thomasina. Music: Tammy Wynette, singer. Theater: Tammy Grimes, Tony Award-winning actress. *Tami, Tammi, Tammie, Tamlyn, Tamilyn.*

TANA (TAH-nah) Slavic: "fairy queen."

TANI (TAN-ee) Japanese: "valley." Melanesian: "sweetheart." Tonkinese: "youth."

TANIS (tah-NES) Spanish. Abbreviation of Estanislao, a name made famous by several Slavic kings and three saints.

TANISHA (tah-NEE-sha) Africa. Hausa: "Monday's child." Current in the United States.

TANITH (THAN-eeth) Greek: "goddess of love."

TANYA (TAHN-yah) Russian, Slavic: Diminutive of Tatiana or Titania. Scand: *Tani, Tonya, Tahnee, Tahni, Tahna, Tahnia, Tana, Tanee, Tanamarie.*

TARA (TAH-rah) Irish: "rugged hill." Literature: Scarlett O'Hara's beloved plantation in Margaret Mitchell's epic novel, *Gone with the Wind. Tarrah, Tarra, Taralynn, Taralyn.*

TARANA (tah-RAH-nah) African: "born during the day."

TAREE (tah-ree-EH) Japanese: "arching branch."

TARIANA (tah-RYE-ana) African-American: "holy hillside."

TARYN (TAH-rin) Contemporary blend of Tara and Erin. *Tarin, Tarryn, Tarynn.*

TASHA (TAH-shah) Russian: Pet name for Natasha. *Tashia, Tashi, Tassa, Tassie, Tasis;* Ital: *Tazia, Tosha, Toshina.*

TASSOS (TAH-sohs) Greek: "one who reaps." Derived from Theresa.

TASYA (TAHS-yah) Russian: Pet name. Also popular in United States and Spain.

TATE (tayte) Scandinavian: "ebullient." Movies and Television: Tatum O'Neill, actress. *Tatum.*

TATIANA (tah-sh'AHN-ah or tah-tee-AHN-ah) Russian: Variation on a Roman family clan name. Music: Tatiana Troyannos, opera star. *Tania, Tanya, Tati, Tatie, Tatyana, Tatyanna, Tatianna, Tonya.*

TAURA (tah-OO-rah) Japanese: "numerous rivers or lakes." Astrology: Taurus, pronounced (TAW-rus). *Taurina.*

TAVIA (TAY-vee-ah) Diminutive of Octavia.

TAWNY (TAW-nee) English Gypsy: "babe" or "wee one." *Tawni, Tawnya, Tawnee, Tawney, Tawnie, Tawnia, Tawna.*

TAYLOR (TAY-ler) English: "tailor" Music: Taylor Dayne, pop singer.

TAZANNA (tahz-ANA) Native American: "princess."

TAZU (TAH-zoo) Japanese: "stork." This name bestows long life on the child.

TEAGAN (TEE-gan) English, Irish: "attractive." *Tegan, Teige.*

TEAL (teel) English: Refers to either the river duck or the dark greenish-blue color. *Teela.*

TEKLA (TEEK-lah) Greek: "divine fame."

TELYN (tell-LYN) Welsh: "harp."

TEME (TEHM-ee) Hebrew: "without flaw." *Temima.*

TEMIRA (teh-MEE-ruh) Israel. Hebrew: "of substantial height." *Timora.*

TEMPEST (TEHM-pist) English: "turbulent" or "stormy nature." Theater: Shakespeare's exotic romance, *The Tempest.*

TENDAI (tehn-DAY) African: "be thankful to God."

TERA (TEH-rah) Japanese: "steadily moving arrow." *Terami.*

TERENA (te-REE-nah) Latin: "earthly."

TERESA (te-REE-sah or te-RAY-sah) See Theresa.

TERRI (TER-ee) English: Short form of Teresa. Movies and Television: Teri Garr, actress (*Close Encounters of the Third Kind*). Terri Hatcher, actress

(TV's *Desperate Housewives*). *Teri, Terrie, Terika, Terilynn, Teriann, Teriana, Teryn, Terrin, Terryn.*

TERYL (TEHR-yl) English: "bright and vivacious."

TESSA (TESS-ah) Polish: Form of Theophila, meaning "loved by God." Short form of Theresa. Literature: Character in Len Deighton's *Paris Match* trilogy; character in George Eliot's 1862 novel, *Romoldo;* title character in Thomas Hardy's *Tess of the d'Urberrilles. Tess, Tessia, Tessie.*

TETSU (TET-su) Japanese: "strong as iron." In many folkloric systems, iron is not only a symbol of force, but magical as well, capable of discouraging demons and wild animals.

TEVY (TEV-ee) Cambodian: "angel."

THADINA (thad-EENA) Hebrew: "given praise." *Thadine.*

THALIA (THAYL-yah) Greek: "flowering." Mythology: Thalia was the muse of comedy.

THANA (tha-NAH) Arabic: "gratitude."

THEA (THEE-ah) Greek: "goddess" or "godly." Movies and Television: Tia Carrera, actress. *Tia, Tiah, Teah.*

THELMA (THEL-mah) Greek: "will" or "willful." Literature: Title character from Marie Corelli's 1887 novel. Movies and Television: Thelma Ritter, actress. Span: *Telma.*

THEODORA (thee-oh-DORR-ah) Greek: "granted by the Lord." Span: *Teodora, Theadora.*

THEOLA (thee-oh-LAH) Greek: "divine."

THEOPHILIA (thee-oh-PHIL-ee-ah) Greek: "loved divinely."

THERESA (te-REES-ah) Greek: "from Theresia." History: This name gained great popularity worldwide in the 1600s when parents began naming their babies after Saint Theresa of Avila in Castile, a mystic and nun who performed many miracles; Mother Teresa, Catholic missionary who helped impoverished people in India. She was a pioneer of peace, starting her own order called The Missionaries of Charity and winning the Nobel Peace Prize in 1979. Eng: *Tera, Terese, Teressa, Teri, Terie, Terri, Terrie, Terry, Tess, Tessa, Tessi, Tessie, Tessy, Trace, Tracey, Traci, Zita;* Bulg: *Tereza;* Czech: *Terezia, Terezie, Terezka, Reza, Rezla;* Fr: *Therese;* Ger: *Resi, Trescha;* Gk: *Tassos;* Hung: *Rezi, Riza, Rizus, Teca, Tereza, Terike, Teruska, Treszka;* Ital: *Teresina, Tersa;* Norw: *Terese;* Pol: *Tesa, Tesia, Tereska;* Russ: *Terezilya, Zilya;* Span: *Teresita, Tete, Teresia, Theressa.*

THIRZA (thir-ZAH) Hebrew: "delightful."

THISBE (THIS-bee) Greek: "where the doves live." Mythology: Thisbe was the fairest maiden in Babylon and the lover of Pyramus. As recounted by Ovid, the story of Thisbe and Pyramus is a tragedy, much like Shakespeare's *Romeo and Juliet.* The berries on the mulberry bush are said to be red, instead of the original white, to commemorate the love and death of this couple.

THOMASINA (TOM-ah-SEE-nah) Hebrew, Aramaic: "twin." *Tamsen, Tamsin, Tomasina, Tommi, Tommie, Tommy.*

TIANA (tee-AHN-ah) Contemporary diminutive of Tatiana. *Tani, Tahna, Tandra, Tiane, Tianna, Tianne, Tiona, Tionna.*

TIARA (tee-ARH-ah) Latin: "headdress." The Spanish word "tierra" means earth. *Tiarra, Tierra.*

TIBELDA (tih-BELL-dah) German: "boldest." *Tibelde, Tibeldie.*

TIFFANY (TIFF-ah-nee) Greek: "God revealed." Music: Tiffany, teenage pop singer known for performing in malls. Sports: Tiffany Chin, figure skating champion. *Tiffanie, Tiffney.*

TILLIE (TILL-ee) Old German: "battle maiden." Literature: Tillie Olsen, author of fiction and nonfiction (*Silences*). *Tilley, Tilli, Tilly.*

TIMBERLY (tim-BER-lee) African-American: "tall ruler."

TIMOTHEA (tim-oh-THEA) Greek: "honoring God."

TINA (TEE-nah) United States. English: Name used by itself or as a blend with other names. Music: Tina Turner, rock star, "What's Love Got to Do With

It?" Movies and Television: Tina Louise, actress (TV's *Gilligan's Island*). *Teena, Tinamarie.*

TING (tyng) Chinese: "slim" or "graceful."

TIRZA (TEER-zah) Israel. Hebrew: "attractive" or "cypress."

TISA (TEE-sah) Swahili: "born ninth."

TISHA (TEE-sha) Latin: Independent name created from diminutives of Leticia and Latisha. *Tiesha.*

TITANIA (tye-THAN-ee-ah) Greek: "giant." Theater: Fairy queen in William Shakespeare's play *A Midsummer Night's Dream.*

TIVONA (tee-VO-nuh) Israel. Hebrew: "nature lover" or "eyes for nature." Widely used in contemporary Israel.

TOBIT (to-BEET) Israel. Hebrew: "good." Popular in Israel for both sexes. *Tobi, Tobie, Toby.*

TOKIWA (to-KEE-wah) Japanese: "perpetual."

TOLA (toe-LAH) Polish: "priceless." *Tolla.*

TOMIKO (toh-MEE-koh) Japanese: "child who is content" or "child of riches."

TONI (toh-NEE) Latin: Diminutive of Antonia and Antoinette. Literature: Toni Morrison, Pulitzer Prize winner for fiction and Nobel Prize winner in Literature. *Tonette, Tonia, Tonelle, Tonisha, Toneisha.*

TONYA (TOHN-ya) Russian: "beyond value." Nickname for Antonin.

TOPAZ (toe-PAHZ) Latin: "yellow gemstone."

TORI (TORR-ee) English, Scottish: Short form of Victoria. Arts: Tori Kuratsukuri, Japanese sculptor, created sixteen-foot-high Buddha. *Torey, Toriana, Torre, Torri, Torrie, Torry.*

TORRA (tor-RAH) Scottish: "from the castle."

TOSHI (TOH-shee) Japanese: "image in the mirror." *Toshie, Toshiko, Toshikyo.*

TOVA (TOE-vah) Hebrew: "good." *Tovah, Tove.*

TRACY (TRAY-cee) English, French: Very old surname. Music: Tracy Chapman, singer. Sports: Tracy Austin, youngest woman to win U.S. Open tennis title at age sixteen. *Tracey, Traci, Tracie.*

TRAVA (TRAH-vah) Czechoslovakian: "fresh grasses." The name connotes renewal and fresh beginnings.

TRILLBY (TRILL-bee) Italian: "one who sings musical trills." Literature: French writer and illustrator George du Maurier's novel, *Trilby*, published in *Harper's Monthly* in 1894, romanticized the artist lifestyle by depicting a story about a young artist who gains fame and fortune through his paintings. *Trilby.*

TRINA (TRIH-nah) Latin: "triple"; Greek: "unadulterated." Hindi: "pointy" or "penetrating." Pronounced (TREE-nah). Refers to the needlelike leaves of the sacred grass called kusa. Hindus wear a ring of kusa grass during rituals to purify their mind and body. Also, a short form of the Swedish Katarina. *Treena, Trena, Trinadette, Trini.*

TRISHA (TRE-sha) United States. English: Started out as a diminutive of Patricia, but is an independent name today. History: Tricia Nixon Cox, daughter of Richard Nixon. *Tricia, Trisa, Trish, Trishana, Trissa.*

TRISTA (TRISS-tah) Latin, French: "melancholy." *Tristan, Tristen, Tristin, Tristina, Tristyn, Trysta.*

TRISTEN (tris-TEN) English: "noisy" or "full of sorrows." Feminine of Tristan. *Tristina.*

TRIXIE (TRIK-see) Latin: "one who brings happiness." Short form of Beatrix.

TRUDA (tru-DAH) Polish: "warrior woman."

TRUDY (TROO-dee) German: "might" or "forcefulness."

TULA (TOO-lah) Hindi astrology: Related to the sun sign of Libra, characterized by balance.

TULIA (TOO-lea) Spanish: "destined for glory."

TWYLA (TWYE-lah) English: Meaning unknown. Dance: Twyla Tharp, dancer and choreographer. *Twila, Twylla.*

TYNA (TEE-nah) Czechoslovakian: Short form of Celestyna ("from the heavens") and Kristyne ("devoted to Christ").

TYRA (TEER-ah or TYE-rah) Scandinavian mythology: "of Tyr, god of battle." *Tyla, Tylena.*

UDELA (OO-del-ah) Anglo-Saxon: "wealthy." *Udele.*

UJANA (OO-jah-nah) African: "youth."

ULA (OO-la) Celtic: "jewel of the sea." Diminutive of the Greek Eulalie.

ULANI (oo-LAH-nee) Hawaiian: "happy nature" or "optimistic."

ULDWYNA (uld-WEE-nah) English: "special friend."

ULI (OO-lee) German: "mistress of all." *Ulka, Ulrica, Ulrika.*

UMA (OO-mah) Hindi: "mother." Refers to the Hindu goddess Sakti. Movies and Television: Uma Thurman, actress.

UMEKO (oo-ME-ko) Japanese: "child of the plum blossom." Japanese lore believes the plum blossom symbolizes long-suffering endurance as well as dedicated persistence.

UNA (OO-nah) Native American. Hopi: "good memory." In native lore, the coyote is honored for being able to remember where he has hidden his supper. Remembering one's ancestors is also considered a virtue.

UNDINE (you-DEEN) Latin: "of the wave."

UNIQUE (you-NEEK) Latin: "one of a kind."

UNITY (yu-NIT-ee) Irish: "together." *Uny.*

URA (yu-RAH) Hindi: "heart."

URANIA (yur-AH-nea) Greek: "heavenly." Mythology: In Greek mythology, Urania is the muse of space, astronomy, and astrology.

URSULA (UR-soo-lah) Latin: "female bear" or "mother bear." Popular today in Slavic, Spanish-speaking and English-speaking countries. Science: Ursa Major and Minor, star constellations meaning Great and Little Bear, are more commonly known as Big and Little Dipper. Movies and Television: Ursula Andress, actress. History: Ursula Benencasa, established Oblate Sisters of Immaculate Conception (1583) and Contemplative Hermit Sisters (1617). Literature: Character in Shakespeare's *Much Ado About Nothing*. *Ora, Orsola, Ursa, Urse, Ursel, Ursie, Ursley, Ursola, Ursuline, Ursy;* Czech: *Vor-*

sila; Est: *Sula, Ulli, Urmi*; Fr: *Ursule;* Ger: *Ulla;* Rum: *Ursule;* Span: *Ursulina.*

USHI (oo-SHEE) Chinese: "the ox." Recurrent symbol in Chinese astrology.

USOA (oo-SO-ah) Spanish: "dove."

UTINA (oo-TEE-nah) Native American: "female compatriot."

VADIT (VAD-iyt) Hebrew: "rose."

VAIL (vayl) Old French: "from the valley."

VALA (VAH-lah) English: "chosen."

VALDA (VAL-dah) Old Norse: "leader." Common in Scandinavia. *Valida, Velda.*

VALENTINA (vahl-lin-TEE-nah) Latin: "powerful"; English: From Valentia. History: Valentina Visconti, Italian, grandmother of King Louis XII. Science: Valentina Tershkova, Russian astronaut, first woman to orbit the earth. Sports: Valentina Zakorestskaya, Russian, holds women's title for the most parachute jumps: 8,000. *Val, Valentine.*

VALERIE (VAL-ah-ree) Old French: "one who is fierce." From a Roman clan name. Movies and Television: Valerie Harper, Valerie Bertinelli, Valerie Perrine, actresses. Eng: *Vairy, Val, Valaree, Valaria, Valerye, Valery, Valli, Vallie, Vally;* Pol: *Wala, Waleria;* Russ: *Lerka, Valka, Valya;* Span: *Valeriana.*

VALMA (VAL-mah) Finnish: "devoted defender." Variant of Wilhelmina.

VALONIA (vah-LOHN-ee-ah) Latin: "of the vale."

VALTINA (vah-TEE-nah) Latin: "health" or "love."

VANDA (VAHN-dah) Slavic: "seeker" or "wayfarer." Variant of Wanda. *Vande.*

VANESSA (vah-NESS-ah) Greek: "butterflies." Jonathan Swift, who wrote *Gulliver's Travels,* may have invented the name in his poem *Cadenus arid Vanessa.* Movies and Television: Vanessa Redgrave, actress; Vanna White, TV's *Wheel of Fortune.* Music: Vanessa Williams, briefly Miss America and later Grammy Award-winning pop singer. Literature: Vanessa Bell, wife of British critic Clive Bell. *Ness, Nessa, Nessi, Nessie, Nessy, Van, Vana, Vania, Vanna, Vanni, Vannie, Vanya.*

VANNA (vah-NAH) Hebrew: "God's gift." *Vania.*

VANORA (VAHN-or-ah) Scottish: "white wave."

VARDIS (vahr-DEES) Israel. Hebrew: "rose." Highly popular in Israel.

VARINA (vah-REE-nah) Slavic: "unknown" or "yet to be discovered." Variant of Barbara.

VARSHA (var-SHAH) Hindu: "rain."

VASHTI (VASH-tee) Persian: "beautiful."

VEDA (VAY-dah) Sanskrit: "divine realization." The Vedas are the most sacred of Hindu teachings.

VEGA (vay-GAH) Arabic: "falling."

VELMA (VEL-mah) Greek: "protector."

VENETIA (vehn-EH-teah) Celtic: "blessed."

VENTURA (vehn-TOR-ah) Spanish: "good fortune."

VENUS (VEE-nuss) Greek: "goddess of love." In Roman mythology, Venus is the goddess of love and beauty, equivalent to the Greek Aphrodite, who was considered the most desirable of the Greek gods. Science: The planet Venus is the brightest object in the sky, other than the Sun and Moon. Sports: Venus Williams, American tennis star and Olympic gold medalist (2000).

VERA (VAR-ah) Latin: "that which is true" or "devoted." A worldwide name, popular in English, Slavic, and Spanish countries. Business: Vera Wang, fashion designer known for her sleek, sophisticated designs. Literature: Vera B. William, author, 1990 Notable Children's Book (*More, More, More Said the Baby!*); Vera Brittain, British, wrote feminist and pacifist works. History: Vera Finger, Russian revolutionary, involved in the assassination of Czar Nicholas II. Eng: *Verena, Verne, Verina, Verla;*

Czech: *Verka, Viera;* Pol: *Wera, Wierka;* Russ: *Verasha, Verinka, Verunka, Verusya;* Swed: *Wera.*

VERENE (ver-EN-ee) German: "protector."

VERONICA (ver-RON-ni-kah) Latin: "true face." Vernice and Verenice are Spanish variants of Bernice. Eng: *Berenice, Bernice, Roni, Ronnie, Ronny, Veronika;* Czech: *Verona, Vernka;* Fr: *Verenice, Veronique;* Ger: *Veronike;* Gk: *Berenike.*

VESPER (VEHS-per) Latin: "evening."

VESTA (VES-tah) Latin: "guardian of the sacred fire." History: The temple of the Roman goddess Vesta housed the sacred fire of Rome, which was renewed at the start of the Roman New Year of March 1.

VEVINA (VEV-ee-nah) Irish: "sweet lady."

VICKIE (VIK-ee) United States. English: Short form of Victoria meaning "victory." Theater: Vickie Baum, playwright. *Vicki, Vicky, Viki, Viky.*

VICTORIA (vik-TORE-ee-ah) Latin: "victorious." History: Queen Victoria, who ruled England from 1837 to 1901; Victoria Woodhull, social reformer, first woman to run for president of the United States (1872). Literature: Victoria Sackville-West, British poet, novelist, and biographer, who wrote under first name of Vida. Eng: *Vicki, Vickie, Vicky, Ciki, Ciky;* Bulg: *Victoria;* Czech: *Viktorka;* Fr: *Victoire;* Gk: *Nike;* Ital: *Vittoria;* Port: *Vitoria;* Russ: *Victoriana, Victorina, Vitoria;* Swed: *Viktoria.*

VIDA (VEE-dah or VYE-dah) Spanish: "life." Hebrew: "beloved." *Veda, Vita.*

VIENNA (vee-EN-ah) Latin: Name of the Austrian city used as a given name. A place name.

VIOLET (VI-oh-let) English: The purple flower. Literature: Violet Paget, British writer and art critic; Violet Jacob, Scottish poet and novelist. Music: Violetta, the tragic heroine of Verdi's opera, *La Traviata.* Theater: Viola is a crafty character in Shakespeare's comedy *Twelfth Night.* Span: *Violeta;* Ital: *Violetta;* Fr: *Violette, Viola.*

VIRGINIA (ver-JIN-yah) Latin: "in a pristine state." History: The first English child born on American soil was Virginia Dare in 1597. Literature: Virginia Woolf, English novelist and critic. Science: Virginia Apgar, American anesthesiologist, developed test to assess newborns' development (Apgar Score). Eng: *Ginger, Ginney, Ginni, Ginnie, Ginny, Jinny, Vergie, Virgy;* Fr: *Virginie;* Hawaiian: *Vegenia;* Span: *Gina, Ginanata, Ginia, Virginai, Virgena, Virgene* (ver-JEEN).

VIVECA (VIV-eh-kah) Latin: "full of life." Movies and Television: Vivica A. Fox, actress (*Kill Bill*). *Vivica, Vivika, Viveka.*

VIVIAN (VIH-vee-ahn) Latin: "lively." Literature: Character in Sir Thomas Malory's *Morte d'Arthur.* Movies and Television: Vivian Leigh, Academy Award-winning actress. Eng: *Viviana, Vivianna;* Fr: *Vivanne, Viviane, Vivien, Vivenne;* Hawaiian/Ital: *Vivana.*

VOLETTA (VOH-let-ah) French: "veiled." *Voleta.*

VONDRA (VAN-drah) Czechoslovakian: "the love of a woman."

VRINDA (ver-IN-dah) Hindu: "virtue and strength."

WALDA (WAHL-dah) German: "ruler."

WALLIS (WAHL-is) English: "from Wales." *Waleis.*

WALTA (wahl-TAH) African: "shield."

WANDA (WAHN-dah) Old German: "wayfarer." Music: Wanda Landowska, Polish harpsichordist. Eng: *Wandi, Wandie, Wandis, Wenda, Wendi, Wendy, Wendeline;* Czech: *Vanda;* Pol: *Wandzia;* Swed: *Wanja.*

WANETA (wah-NAY-tah) Native American: "shape-shifter." *Wannetta.*

WANGARI (wahn-GAR-ee) African: "leopard." History: Wangari Maathai, 2004 Nobel Peace Prize winner who founded the Kenyan Green Belt movement, which plants trees to prevent soil erosion and to provide firewood.

WESESA (weh-seh-SAH) Uganda. Musoga: "imprudent."

WHITLEY (WIT-lee) English: "blonde field."

WHITNEY (WIT-nee) English: "beautiful island." Music: Whitney Houston, singer.

WILHELMINA (will-hell-MEEN-ah) Old German: "devoted defender of justice." The name found some popularity as the name of a famous New York modeling agency. History: Wilma Mankiller, first woman elected principal chief of the Cherokee Nation. Literature: Willa Cather, Pulitzer Prize-winning novelist (*One of Ours*). Eng: *Billi, Billie, Helma, Helmine, Mina, Minna, Minnie, Minny, Valma, Velma, Wilhelmine, Willamina, Wiletta, Wilette, Willi, Willie, Wilma, Wilmette, Wylma;* Fin: *Valma;* Russ: *Vilma.*

WILLOW (WILL-oh) Middle English: "willow tree" or "liberated spirit." In the Bible, willows are associated with weeping or mourning. Many cultures believe willows to be a symbol of healing.

WILONA (whil-OHN-ah) Anglo-Saxon: "hoped for." *Wilone.*

WINDA (WEEN-dah or anglicized to WIN-dah) Swahili: "chasing for food."

WINEMA (wee-NEH-mah) Native American. Miwok: "female chieftain."

WINIFRED (WIN-ah-FRED) Welsh: "reconciled" or "blessed." History: Winifred Holt, social worker who aided the blind. Science: Winifred Blackman, anthropologist who spent fifteen years traveling through Egypt. Theater: Winifred Ashton, British playwright and novelist. *Winnie.*

WINONA (weh-NO-nah) Native American: "first-born daughter." Movies and Television: Winona Ryder, actress.

WISIA (VEE-shuh or anglicized to WI-shuh) Polish: "victorious." Variant of Victoria.

WYANET (wee-AH-net) Native American: "one whose beauty is legend."

WYNNE (WIN) Old Welsh: "fair lady." *Winne, Winnie, Winny, Wyn, Wynn.*

XANDRA (ZAN-drah) Spanish: "protector of the world." *Zandra.*

XANDY (ZAN-dee) Greek: "protector of man."

XANTHE (ZAN-thah) Greek: "sun-kissed" or "golden bright."

XAVIER (zah-vee-AYRE) Arabic: "bright"; Spanish Basque: "new house." A boy's name now gaining popularity in the United States for girls. *Xaviera, Javier.*

XENIA (ZAYN-yah) Greek: "gracious" or "generous." Eng: *Xena;* Fr: *Chimene.*

XIA (zea) Chinese: "glow of the sun rise."

XYLONA (ZYE-lon-ah) Greek: "from the forest."

YACHI (YAH-chee) Japanese: "eight thousand." Japanese parents still follow ancient lore by naming a child after a round number; it is said to bring good luck. *Yachiko, Yachiyo.*

YACHNE (YAHK-ne) Hebrew: "hospitable." Well used by Jews in Poland and Lithuania.

YAFFA (YAH-fah) Hebrew: "beautiful."

YAMKA (YAHM-kah) Native American. Hopi: "time for blossoms."

YANA (YAH-nah) Hebrew: "he answers."

YANABA (yah-NAH-bah) Native American. Navajo: "she who meets the battle head-on."

YANAMARIA (YAHN-ah-ma-rea) Spanish: "bitter grace." *Yanamarie.*

YANKA (yahn-KAH) Slavic: "God is good."

YARMILLA (YAHR-mil-luh) Slavic: "she who sells at market."

YASMIN (YAS-meen) Arabic: "jasmine flower." *Jasmin, Jasmeen, Jasmine, Yasiman, Yasmine, Yazmin, Yasmeen.*

YASU (YAH-soo) Japanese: "that which bestows peace and calm."

YEDDA (EED-dah) Old English: "singing."

YELENA (yeh-LAY-nah) Russian: "illumination." Variant of Helen.

YEMENA (yeh-MEE-nah) Israel. Hebrew: "dexterous" or "capable."

YEPA (YAY-pah) Native American: "winter princess."

YESNIA (yeh-ZNEE-uh) Latin: "from the Essenes." *Yessenia, Yecenia.*

YETTA (ETT-ah) English: "generous."

YEVA (YEH-vah) Russian: "nurturing" or "life-enhancing." Adaptation of Ena.

YNES (ee-NEZ) Spanish: "chaste." Variant form of Ines and Inez from Agnes. *Ynez.*

YOKI (YOH-kee) Native American: "valley bird."

YOKO (YOH-koh) Japanese: "feminine energy" or "child of the open seas" or "good girl." In Asian philosophy, "yo" is the feminine principle. Music: Yoko Ono, singer and widow of Beatle John Lennon.

YOLANDA (yoh-LAHN-dah) Spanish: Variant form of Yolande; French form of Violet. Astrology: Symbol for the month of February and the sun sign of Aquarius. History: Yolande Polignac, wealthy close friend of Marie-Antoinette. Eng: *Eolanda, Eolande, Iolande, Iolanthe, Yolande, Yolane;* Hung: *Jolan, Jolanka;* Fr: *Jolie;* Pol: *Jolanta;* Span: *Yola, Yoli.*

YOLUTA (yo-LOO-tah) Native American: "good-bye spring."

YONINAH (yoh-NEE-nah) Israel. Hebrew: "little dove." *Jona, Jonati, Jonina, Yona, Yonit, Yonita.*

YOSHINO (YO-shee-no) Japanese: "field with good prospects." The Japanese suffix "no" means "field" and can be attached to many other words. For example, Ume*no,* meaning "fields of plum trees."

YOVELA (yo-VAY-luh) Israel. Hebrew: "joyful heart."

YUKI (YOO-kee) Japanese: "snow" or "lucky." *Yukie, Yukiko, Yukiyo.*

YURIKO (yu-REE-koh) Japanese: "lily child" or "village of birth."

YVETTE (ee-VETT) French: "arrow's bow." The name has become popular in the United States as an adaptation of Yvonne. Movies and Television: Yvette Mimieux, actress. Pol: *Iwona, Iwonka;* Port: *Ivone;* Russ: *Ivona.*

YVONNE (ee-VAHN) French: "yew wood," used to make bows. Sports: Tennis player Evonne Goolagong; Yvonne Van Qennip, Dutch medalist in three Olympic speed skating events (1988). Movies and Television: Yvonne De Carlo, actress. *Yvonna.*

ZABRINA (zah-BREE-nah) English: "a princess."
A form of Sabrina. *Zavrina.*

ZADA (ZA-dah) Arabic: "good fortune." Popular
in Syria. *Zaida, Zayda.*

ZAFIRAH (zah-FIR-ah) Arabic: "she who wins."

ZAGIRI (zah-GIR-iy) Armenian: "flower."

ZAHAR (ZA-har) Hebrew: "morning light."

ZAINA (zah-IY-nah) Arabic: "beautiful."

ZAIRA (ZARE-ah) Irish: "princess." Form of Sara.

ZAKIYA (zah-KEE-yah) Swahili: "very smart
one."

ZAMORA (zah-MORE-ah) Hebrew: "praised."

ZANTA (ZAHN-tah) Swahili: "beautiful girl."

ZARA (ZAH-rah) Arabic: "daughter of the king"; Hebrew: "dawn's light."

ZARIFA (zah-REE-fah) Arabic: "moves with grace."

ZAWADI (zah-WAH-dee) Swahili: "precious present."

ZAYIT (zye-EET) Israel. Hebrew: "olive." May be used for both sexes. *Zeta, Zetana.*

ZEA (ZAY-uh) Latin: "wheat" or "crop."

ZELDA (ZELL-dah) Contemporary variant of Griselda in the United States. Literature: Zelda Fitzgerald, wife of F. Scott Fitzgerald, also a writer. Her glamorous jet-setting life ended tragically with her incurable mental illness and his breakdown.

ZELENKA (zeh-LENN-keh) Czechoslovakian: "like a budding green plant." An appropriate name for those born in the springtime.

ZENDA (zen-DAH) Persian: "womanly."

ZENOBIA (zeh-NOH-bee-ah) Greek: History: Queen Zenobia (third century B.C.) was ruler of the wealthy city of Palmyra in the Arabian Desert. *Zena.*

ZIA (ZEE-ah) Arabic: "light" or "splendor."

ZINERVA (zin-ER-vah) Celtic: "pale."

ZITA (ZEE-tah) Spanish: Short form of Rosita.

ZOE (ZO-ee) Greek: "life." Theater: Zoe Caldwell, actress.

ZSA ZSA (Zha Zha) Hungarian: Nickname for Susan.

ZULEMA (zoo-LEE-mah or zoo-LAY-mah) Hebrew, Arabic: "peace." *Zulima.*

ZURI (ZUR-ay) French: "white and lovely."

MALE NAMES

FROM [A] TO [Z]

AARIC (ayr-IK) English: "rule with mercy." *Aric.*

AARON (AYR-un) Hebrew: "illuminated." Arts: Twentieth-century painter Aaron Douglas is called the father of black American art. Bible: Aaron, the first high priest of the Jews, was the mouthpiece for his brother Moses who stuttered. Popular in various spellings worldwide. Business: Aaron Montgomery Ward established the first mail-order firm. Science: Aaron Ciechanover, Israeli Nobel Prize winner in Chemistry (2004). Arab: *Haroun, Harun;* Ger: *Aronne;* Heb: *Aharon;* Ital: *Aronne;* Pol: *Arek;* Port: *Aarao;* Russ: *Aronos.*

ABARRON (ab-ARE-on) Hebrew: "father of a multitude."

ABAYOMI (ah-BAH-yoh-mee) Nigeria. Yoruba: "born to bring me joy."

ABBAN (A-bahn) Irish: "abbot."

ABBAS (ahb-BAS) Arabic: "lion."

ABBOTT (ABB-it) Aramaic: "father." Derived from "Abba," which was a title of respect in Aramaic. Jesus and the apostles spoke a form of Aramaic. *Abbey, Abbie, Abby, Abba.*

ABBUD (ah-BOOD) Arabic: "devoted." Popular among Arabs.

ABDALLA (ab-DAHL-lah) East Africa. Swahili: "servant of God."

ABDUL (Ahb-DOOL) Arabic: "servant of Allah." A Moslem favorite, the name may be used with another name or independently. Example: Abdul Karim, "servant of the generous one." *Abdel, Abdullah.*

ABEJIDE (ah-beh-JEE-deh) Nigeria. Yoruba: "winter's child."

ABEL (A-bull) Hebrew: "breathing spirit." Bible: Second son of Adam and Eve, killed by his brother Cain. Literature: The hero of W. H. Hudson's novel *Green Mansions. Abe, Abell.*

ABELARD (ah-beh-LARD) Old German: "high born" and "committed." *Ab, Abbey, Abby, Abe, Abel.*

ABIR (ahb-EER) Hebrew: "strong."

ABISHA (ahb-EE-shah) Hebrew: "the lord is my father."

ABNER (AB-ner) Hebrew: "he who bestows light." Bible: The commander of King Saul's army. *Ab, Abbey, Abbie, Abby, Avner, Eb, Ebbie, Ebby, Ebner.*

ABRAHAM (ABE-rah-ham) Hebrew: "patriarch of many." Bible: The first Hebrew patriarch. He was first named Abram. After accepting the concept of God, his name was changed to Abraham. (The Hebrew letter H, the symbol for God, was added to his name as a reward.) Science: Avram Hershko, Israeli Nobel Prize winner in Chemistry (2004). Eng: *Abe, Abram;* Arab: *Ibrahim;* Bulg: *Avram;* Dutch: *Bram;* Fr: *Abram;* Ital: *Abramo;* Port: *Abrão;* Russ: *Abram;* Span: *Abran;* Swahili: *Arram;* Yiddish: *Avram, Avrum.*

ABSALOM (AB-sa-lom) Hebrew: "peace-bringer." Bible: Favored, but not rebellious son of King David. Literature: Chaucer used the name for a clerk in his *Miller's Tale*; *Absalom, Absalom,* a novel by William Faulkner.

ACAIR (ah-KARE) Scottish: "anchor." *Acaiseid.*

ACKLEY (ACK-lee) Old English: "meadow of oakes."

ACUZIO (ack-OOZ-ee-oh) Latin: "sharp."

ADAIR (ah-DARE) Scottish: "noble" or "exalted."

ADALRICO (add-al-REE-ko) Latin: "noble." Old German: "powerful and rich."

ADAM (AD-am) Hebrew: "he who sprang from the earth." Bible: Since Adam is the name of the progenitor of the human race, it is a favorite among all Judeo-Christian traditions. Education: Adam Smith, author of *The Wealth of Nations*, founded the science of political science. Literature: *Adam Bede*, a novel by George Eliot. Eng: *Ad, Ade;* Ital: *Adamo;* Pol: *Adamek, Adok;* Port: *Adao;* Russ: *Adamka;* Scot: *Adhamh;* Span: *Adan;* Yiddish: *Adi.*

ADDAI (ADD-aye) Hebrew: "man of god."

ADDISON (ADD-eh-son) Old English: "son of Adam."

ADE (aid) African: "crown" or "royal."

ADEBAYO (ah-DEH-bah-yoh) Nigeria. Yoruba: "he came at a joyful time."

ADELBERT (AID-el-bert) Old German: "famous for nobility."

ADELINO (AID-el-eeno) Old German: "noble."

ADELPHOS (ah-del-FOS) Greek: "brother."

ADERET (ah-dehr-ETT) Israel. Hebrew: "crown." A name used in Israel.

ADIL (ah-DEAL) Arabic: "judicious."

ADIR (ah-DEER) Israel. Hebrew: "noble." Israeli favorite.

ADISH (ADD-ish) Persian: "fire."

ADIV (ah-DEEV) Israel. Hebrew: "lovely" or "soothing." Popular today in Israel.

ADLAI (AD-lie) Hebrew: "refuge of God." Bible: Father of Shaphat, overseer of David's flocks. History: Adlai Stevenson, U.S. vice president under Grover Cleveland.

ADLAR (add-LAIR) German: "eagle." *Adler, Adne.*

ADMON (ahd-MOHN) Hebrew: "peony." Refers to a native Israeli flower, bright red in color, which is usually found in the upper Galilee. A name used in Israel.

ADOLPH (A-dolph) Old German: "noble wolf or "noble hero." Once a name favored by German nobility and royalty. History: Adolph Hitler, German dictator. Movies and Television: Adolph Zukor, producer. Eng: *Adolphus;* Span: *Adolfo;* Fr: *Adolphe;* Latin: *Adolphus.*

ADON (AH-don) Phoenician: "lord." In Hebrew, a form of the word Jehovah, meaning "God." Also a form of the Greek *adonis,* meaning "lord." Mythology: In Greek mythology, Adonis was a young man of godlike beauty, beloved by Aphrodite. His name became synonymous with beauty. Eng: *Adonis;* Gk: *Adonis, Adonnis.*

ADRI (AH-dree) Hindi: "fortress" or "stone." Mythology: A Hindu god who protected mankind.

According to legend he once rescued the sun from evil spirits who tried to extinguish it.

ADRIAN (AY-dree-inn) Latin: "black." A short form of the Latin name Hadrian. Widely used in Latin America, Spain, and the United States. The seaport of Adria, which gave its name to the Adriatic Sea, was known in ancient times for its black sand. Eng/Latin: *Hadrian;* Fr: *Adrien;* Ital/Span: *Adriano;* Russ: *Andreian, Adrik, Andri;* Swed: *Hadrian.*

ADRIEL (AY-dree-el) Israel. Hebrew: "of God's flock." Used in Israel. *Adri, Adrial.*

ADVENT (add-VENT) French: "born during Advent."

AEARY (AYE-ry) Irish: "scholar."

AEGNUS (AYEN-gus) Celtic: "exceptionally strong."

AENEAS (ah-NEE-us) Greek: "praised." Mythology: Aeneas, the defender of Troy, was a famed Trojan hero of Greek and Roman legend. His saga was told in Virgil's *Aeneid.* Eng/Span: *Eneas;* Fr: *Enee.*

AETOS (ah-TOES) Greek: "eagle."

AGATHON (AG-ah-thon) Greek: "the godly."

AGNI (AHG-nee) Hindi: "fire deity." Mythology: Deity depicted with three heads, either four or seven arms, and seven tongues to lap up the butter offered as a sacrifice.

AGOSTINO (ahg-OH-stee-noh) Italian: "respectable."

AHANU (ah-HAH-noo) Native American: "coughing spirit."

AHARON (ah-hah-RON) Israel. Hebrew: "noble" or "divinely honored." A popular name in Israel.

AHEARN (AYE-hern) Celtic: "lord of the horses." *Ahern.*

AHMED (ah-HMED) East Africa. Swahili: "praiseworthy."

AHMED (AH-med) Arabic: "most highly adored." An alternative name of Muhammad, the founding prophet of the Islamic religion. Ancient belief states that any house with an Ahmed or Muhammad is blessed. Science: Ahmed Zewail, Egyptian Nobel Prize winner in Chemistry (1999). *Ahmad.*

AIBNE (ABE-nee) Scottish: "river."

AIDAN (AY-dinn) Gaelic: A form of Aed, meaning "fire." Name of an Irish-born monk sent from Scotland to convert the English to Christianity. Movies and Television: Aidan Quinn, actor. *Aiden.*

AIKANE (ah-ee-KA-nee) Hawaiian: "friend, friendly."

AIKEN (ay-KEN) Anglo-Saxon: "oaken." *Aikin.*

AIN (ayen) English: "merciful."

AINSLEY (AYENS-lee) English: "from Ann's meadow." *Ainslie.*

AJANI (AYE-jahn-ee) African: "he who wins the struggle."

AJAX (ay-JAKS) Greek: "strong."

AKAR (ah-KAHR) Turkish: "rushing stream."

AKEMI (ah-KEE-me) Japanese: "beauty at dawn."

AKIHITO (ah-kee-HEE-toh) Japanese: "bright child." Popularized by the accession of Japanese Emperor Akihito in 1989.

AKIL (ah-KEEL) North Africa. Arabic: "astute" or "smart."

AKIM (ah-KEEM) Hebrew: "God will establish."

AKIO (AH-kee-o) Japanese: "smart child." *Akira.*

AKIRA (ah-KI-rah) Japanese: "intelligent."

AKRAM (AHK-rahm) Arabic: "generous."

AKSEL (AHK-sel) Hebrew: "father of peace." A name used in Norway.

AKULE (ah-KOOL) Native American: "he looks up." Most likely refers to one of the many precious gestures babies do that delight their parents.

ALADDIN (a-LAD-inn) Arabic: "height of faith." Literature: Name became popular after the publication of *The Arabian Nights,* in which the story of Aladdin is told.

ALAIN (al-AY-een) French: "handsome."

ALAIR (al-AIRE) English: "merry" or "cheerful."

ALAJOS (AH-lah-yos) Teutonic: "famous holiness." Name used in Hungary.

ALAN (A-linn) Celtic: "harmony" or "peace"; Gaelic: "fair" or "handsome." The name was introduced into England in the eleventh century during the Norman Conquest. Aeronautics: Alan Shepard, Jr., first U.S. astronaut. Movies and Television: Alan Alda, actor. Theater: Alan Jay Lerner, lyricist of the Lerner-Lowe team who wrote *My Fair Lady* and *Camelot.* Eng: *Allen, Allan, Allyn, Allin, Allon;* Fr: *Alain;* Hawaiian: *Alena;* Ir: *Ailin;* Port: *Alao;* Span: *Alano.*

ALAOIS (A-leesh) Teutonic: "mighty battle." Popular in Ireland. *Aloys, Aloysius.*

ALASTAIR (A-liss-tare) Gaelic: Derivation of the Greek. See Alexander.

ALBAN (ALL-ban) Latin: From *Albanus,* meaning "white." Used in England as far back as the seventeenth century. The city of Albany, in New York, is derived from the name. Eng: *Alba, Albin, Alva, Alby;* Fr: *Aubin;* Pol: *Albek, Albinek;* Ital: *Albino.*

ALBERT (AL-burt) Germanic: "bright" or "noble." This name became popular in England after the marriage of Queen Victoria and Prince Albert in 1840. Literature: Albert Camus, French novelist and philosopher. Science: Albert Einstein, Albert Schweitzer, scientists. Eng: *Adelbert, Al, Bert, El-bert;* Czech: *Albertik, Ales;* Fr: *Aubert;* Pol: *Albek;* Ital: *Alberto;* Ger: *Albrecht, Bechtel, Bertchen.*

ALBIE (AL-bee) United States. English: Adaptation of Albert. See Albert.

ALBURN (AL-byrn) German: "noble warrior."

ALCANDER (al-CAN-der) Greek: "strong."

ALCOTT (al-COT) Old English: "old cottage."

ALDEN (all-DEN) English: "wise friend" or "from the old manor."

ALDO (ALL-doe) English: "archaic." Business: Aldo Bensadoun, French businessman and founder of the successful, international company ALDO Shoes.

ALDRED (all-DREED) English: "wise."

ALDRIC (all-DRIK) English: "wise ruler." *Aldrich.*

ALERON (al-EER-on) French: "knight armor."

ALEXANDER (al-ig-ZAN-der) Greek: "protector of humanity." The name was popularized by Alexander the Great (356–323 B.C.). It has been used steadily worldwide and was a royal name in Scotland. History: Alexander Hamilton, first U.S. treasurer (1789); Alexander Haig, U.S. Secretary of State; Aleksandr Solzhenitsyn, Soviet dissident and writer; Alexander Graham Bell invented the telephone. Literature: Alexandre Dumas, author of *The Three Musketeers* and *The Count of Monte Cristo*; Alexander Pope, a British poet famous for "The Rape of the Lock." Movies and Television: Sir Alec Guinness, actor, who won the Academy Award for the movie *The Bridge on the River Kwai* (1957). Music: Alessandro Scarlatti (1659–1725), composer, considered the founder of modern opera. Science: Sir Alexander Fleming (1881–1955), scientist who shared the Nobel Prize for the discovery of penicillin. Eng: *Alec, Alek, Alex, Alexis, Sander, Sandy;* Fr: *Alexandre;* Ger: *Alik, Axel;* Gk: *Alexandros, Alekos;* Hawaiian: *Alika;* Hung: *Elek, Sandor;* Ir: *Alasandir;* Ital: *Alessandro;* Russ: *Olesko, Sanya, Sasha, Sashenka, Shura, Shurik;* Scot: *Alasdair, Alastair, Alister;* Span: *Alejandro, Alejo, Jando;* Yiddish: *Aleksander.*

ALF (alf) Norwegian: "one who lives in the world beyond."

ALFONSO (AL-fone-soh) Italian: "eager."

ALFRED (AL-fred) Old English: "wise counsel." *Alfredo.*

ALGERNON (AL-ger-non) French: "with mustache." Literature: Oscar Wilde used the name for a character in his play *The Importance of Being Earnest.* Algernon Swinburne, British critic and poet who wrote "Songs Before Sunrise." *Al, Alger, Algie, Algy.*

ALI (ah-LEE) East Africa. Swahili: "exalted."

ALMER (al-MER) English: "infamous."

ALON (ah-LON) Israel. Hebrew: "oak." Popular in Israel.

ALONSO (ahl-ON-soh) Spanish: "eager for battle." *Alonzo.*

ALPHONSE (al-FONS) Old German: "prepared for war." Alfonso is a Spanish royal name. Literature: Alphonse Daudet, French writer who wrote *Le Nabob.* Eng: *Al, Alfie, Alfons, Alphonso, Fons, Fonsie, Fonz, Fonzie;* Fr: *Alfonse, Alphonse;* Ital: *Alfonzo.*

ALSON (ALL-son) English: "son of all."

ALSTON (ALL-ston) Anglo-Saxon: "from the old manor."

ALTMAN (ALT-mahn) German: "wise man." *Altmann.*

ALVAH (ALL-vah) Arabic: "sublime." Bible: Alvah was a biblical place and tribal name. *Alva, Alvan.*

ALVARO (ahl-VAR-oh) Spanish: "extremely cautious."

ALVIN (AL-vin) Old German: "friend to all" or "honored friend." Dance: Alvin Ailey, choreographer. Eng: *Alvie, Alwin, Alwyn, Elvin;* Fr: *Aloin;* Ital: *Alvino;* Pol: *Albin;* Port: *Alwin.*

AMADEUS (ah-ma-DAY-us) Latin: "loves God." Theater: Name was given prominence by the long-running Broadway play and 1984 film about Mozart called *Amadeus.*

AMADI (AH-mah-dee) Nigerian: "general rejoicing."

AMANDO (ah-MAHN-do) Latin: "lover of the divine." Popular name in Spanish-speaking countries.

AMAR (AH-mar) Hindu: "forever."

AMARUS (am-ARE-us) Greek: "unfading love."

AMBERLY (am-BER-lee) Greek: "ruler of the jewels."

AMBROSE (AM-broze) Greek: "immortal." Name comes from the same Greek root for *ambrosia* meaning "food of the gods." Literature: Ambrose Bierce, American journalist and short-story writer. Military: Ambrose E. Burnside, Civil War general. *Ambie, Ambrogio, Ambroise, Ambrosi, Ambrosio, Ambrosius, Amby, Brose.*

AMEER (ah-MEER) Arabic: "young ruler," "regent," or "prince."

AMERY (ay-MER-ee) German: "divine."

AMET (am-ETT) German: "power of an eagle." *Amett, Amhold.*

AMIEL (ah-me-EHL) Israel. Hebrew: "of the family of God." Common in Israel.

AMICHAI (ah-me-KHI) Israel. Hebrew: "my people live." Popular in Israel.

AMIKAM (ah-mee-KAHM) Israel. Hebrew: "empowered nation." Popular in Israel.

AMIL (AM-eel) Hindi: "worthy."

AMIR (ah-MEER) Iran. Persian: "king."

AMITA (ah-MEET-ah) Hebrew: "truth." *Amiti.*

AMON (AY-mon) Hebrew: "trustworthy" or "faithful." Bible: Amon was one of the gods of Thebes in Egypt.

AMORY (AYM-o-ree) German: "renowned leader" or "divine ruler." Literature: Amory Elaine, hero of F. Scott Fitzgerald's *This Side of Paradise. Amery, Emery, Emmery.*

AMOS (AY-muss) Hebrew: "one with many responsibilities." Bible: Amos appears in the Old Testament as a prophet.

AMRAM (AHM-rahm) Israel. Hebrew: "mighty nation." Popular Israeli name today.

AN (ahn) Chinese: "peace." Viet: *An.*

ANANDO (ahn-ahn-DOE) African: "bliss."

ANANT (AHN-ahnt) Celtic: "from the stream."

ANASTASIO (ah-nah-STAH-see-oh) Spanish: "resurrected."

ANATOLI (AH-na-TOH-lee) Greek: "from the East." A favorite name in Russia.

ANDREI (AHN-dray or ahn-DRAY) Latin: "manly." A popular name in Russia.

ANDREW (AN-drew) Greek: "manly" or "love." Bible: Andrew was the first apostle whose relics were allegedly brought to Scotland, where he is the patron saint. The name was common in medieval times and by the 1970s was one of the most frequently used names in the English-speaking world. Arts: Andrew Wyeth, Andy Warhol, painters; Andreas Feininger, photographer and writer. Business: Andrew Carnegie, industrialist who founded U.S. Steel and financed over 2,800 libraries. History: Andrew Jackson, seventh president of the United States (1829–37). Literature: Andre Malraux, author of *Man's Fate*; Andre Gide, winner of the Nobel Prize for Literature (1947). Music: Andreas Segovia, guitarist. Eng: *Andi, Andy, Drew;* Bulg: *Andrei, Andres;* Czech: *Andrej, Bandi, Ondro;* Nor: *Anders;* Gk: *Andreas;* Hawaiian: *Analu;* Hung: *Andi, Andor, Andris;* Lith: *Andrius;* Pol: *Aniol, Jedrek, Jedrus;* Rum: *Dela;* Russ: *Andreyka, Andrik;* Scot: *Aindreas;* Span: *Andres, Necho, Nesho.*

ANGEL (AHN-hail, AIN-jel) Greek: "divine assistant" or "heaven's messenger." Bible: Name for the spirit creatures sent by God to men as messengers. Angelo is most often used now because Angel is considered a girl's name. Literature: Shakespeare used the name for a character in *Measure for Measure*. Sports: Angel Cordero, jockey who has won over 6,000 races in his career. Span: *Angelo, Anjelo, Ange, Angell, Angy.*

ANKER (AHN-ker) Greek: "manly."

ANOKI (ah-NO-kee) Native American: "decisive" or "performer."

ANSEL (AN-sel) Old French: "he who follows nobility." Arts: Ansel Adams, landscape photographer. *Ancel, Ancell, Ansell, Ansil, Ansill.*

ANSGAR (AHNS-gar) Celtic: "warrior."

ANTAL (ahn-TAL) Latin: "prince."

ANTARES (an-TARE-ees) Greek. Astrology: The name for the giant red star in the constellation of Scorpio.

ANTHONY (AN-tho-nee) Latin: "praiseworthy" or "priceless." St. Anthony founded the first Christian monastic order and is the patron saint of the poor. A favorite variation—Anton—is used today in the United States and some European countries. Literature: Anton Chekhov, short-story writer and dramatist. Movies and Television: Anthony Quinn, Anthony Hopkins, Anthony Perkins, Tony Curtis, actors. Music: Anton Bruckner, composer. Science: Anthony Leggett, winner of the Nobel Prize in Physics (2003). Eng: *Antony, Tony;* Czech: *Antek, Antonin, Tonik;* Fr: *Antoine;* Gk: *Andonios, Andonis;* Hawaiian: *Akoni;* Hung: *Antal, Toni;* Ir: *Antoine, Antoin;* Ital: *Antonio;* Latin: *Antos;* Lith: *Antavas;* Pol: *Antek, Antonin, Tolek, Tonek;* Russ: *Antinko, Tosya;* Scan: *Anders.*

ANTOAN (AN-twan) Vietnamese: "safe, secure."

ANTON (AHN-ton) Latin: "inestimable." Popular name in Russia. Russ: *Antosha, Antinko, Tosya, Tusya;* Czech: *Antonin.*

ANWAR (AHN-war) African: "the brightest." History: Anwar al-Sadat, former president of the Arabic Republic of Egypt who won the Nobel Peace Prize in 1978.

ANWELL (ann-WELL) Celtic: "beloved." *Anwyll.*

APENIMON (ah-PEE-nimon) Native American: "reliable."

APOLLO (ah-POL-oh) Greek: "destroyer." Mythology: Apollo was the Greek and Roman god of light, music, and poetry. Apollo was also the name of one the early Christian disciples. *Apolonis, Apollos.*

APSEL (AAP-sell) German: "father of peace."

ARAM (AH-rahm) Assyrian: "high place."

ARAMIS (AYRE-a-miss) French. Meaning unknown. Literature: The famous swordsman from Alexandre Dumas's *The Three Musketeers*.

ARASH (AH-rash) Persian: "hero."

ARAV (AHR-ahv) Hindi: "peaceful."

ARCHANA (are-CHAH-nah) Hindi: "worshipping one."

ARCHER (ARCH-er) Teutonic: "the archer."

ARCHIBALD (AHRCH-e-bald) Old German: "bold." Literature: Archibald MacLeish, poet and playwright, winner of three Pulitzer Prizes. Eng: *Arch, Archie*; Fr: *Archaimbaud, Archambault;* Span: *Archibaldo.*

ARDAL (ahr-DAHL) German: "intelligent" or "noble."

ARDEN (ahr-DEN) Celtic: "lofty" or "eager." Literature: The beautiful forest of Arden in Shakespeare's *As You Like It. Ard, Ardie, Ardin, Ardy.*

ARDON (ahr-DOHN) Israel. Hebrew: "bronzed."

AREN (ARE-en) Nigerian: "eagle."

ARGUS (ARE-gus) Greek: "bright" or "watchful."

ARIC (AYRE-ik) English, Norse: "merciful ruler." *Arek, Arick, Asric, Ric, Rick, Rickie, Ricky.*

ARIEL (ahr-ee-EHL) Hebrew: "God's lion." Literature: Name of a sprite who can disappear in Shakespeare's *The Tempest.* Politics: Ariel Sharon, Prime Minister of Israel. *Aeriell, Airel, Airyel, Arel, Arie, Aryet, Aryeli.*

ARIES (AIR-eez) Latin: "ram." Astrology: Aries is one of the signs of the zodiac, represented by the ram. Mythology: Greek god of war.

ARIF (AH-reef) Arabic: "acquainted" or "knowledgeable." Common today in Arab countries.

ARION (AYR-eye-on) Greek: "musician."

ARISTO (AYR-eye-stoh) Greek: "best."

ARKIN (are-KIN) Norwegian: "the eternal king's son."

ARLAND (are-LAND) Celtic: "pledge." *Arlen, Arlando, Arlin, Arlyn.*

ARMAND (AR-mahnd) Old German: "soldier." Movies and Television: Armand Assante, actor in *The Mambo Kings.* Eng: *Arman, Armin, Armon, Armond, Ormond;* Fr: *Armand;* Span: *Armando;* Latin: *Armands;* Pol: *Arek, Mandek;* Russ: *Arman, Armen.*

ARMEN (AYR-men) Armenian: "Armenian."

ARMON (ahr-MOHN) Israel. Hebrew: "high fortress" or "stronghold." Used in contemporary Israel. *Armin.*

ARNAN (AR-nan) Hebrew: "quick" or "joyful." A biblical name.

ARNOLD (AR-nohld) Old German: "eagle's power." Name was brought to Britain with the Norman invasion. Education: Arnold Toynbee, British historian who wrote the ten-volume work *A Study of History.* Movies and Television: Arnold Schwarzenegger, actor and governor of California. Sports: Arnold Palmer, golf's first one-million-dollar winner. Span: *Arnoldo;* Ital: *Arno, Arnie, Arnel, Arnell, Arnett, Arne.*

ARNON (ahr-NON) Israel. Hebrew: "roaring river." Popular Israeli name.

ARPIAR (ahr-pee-AHR) Armenian: "sun reigns down."

ARSENIO (ar-SEH-nee-oh) Greek: "manly." History: Saint Arsenius, teacher in the Roman Empire.

ARTAIR (ar-TARE) Anglo-Saxon: "like an eagle."

ARTHUR (AR-thur) Celtic: "bold." King Arthur led the Round Table of Knights of the sixth century. Journalism: Art Buchwald, columnist. Literature: Arthur Conan Doyle, author of *The Adventures of Sherlock Holmes.* Sports: Arthur Ashe, tennis star. Theater: Arthur Miller, playwright who won the Pulitzer Prize for his drama *Death of a Salesman* (1949). Eng: *Art, Arte, Artie, Arty;* Hung/Ir/Norw/Russ: *Atur;* Czech: *Artis;* Gk: *Athanasios, Thanos;* Fin: *Arto, Artur;* Fr: *Artur;* Ital/Span: *Arturo;* Pol: *Artek;* Scot: *Artair.*

ARTHUS (AR-thus) Welsh: "bear hero" or "a rock."

ARUN (AH-run) Cambodian: "sun."

ARVAD (ARV-ahd) Hebrew: "wanderer."

ARVE (ahrve) Norwegian: "heir." Popular name in Norway.

ARVID (AHR-ved) Norwegian: "eagle-tree." *Arve.*

ARVIN (AHR-vin) German: "friend to all."

ARYEH (AIR-yeh) Israel. Hebrew: "lion." Common in contemporary Israel.

ASA (AY-sah) Hebrew: "doctor" or "healer." Bible: Asa was a king in the Old Testament. *Ase.*

ASADEL (A-sa-del) Arabic: "greatly successful." Used throughout Arab countries.

ASHER (AH-sher) Hebrew: "felicitous" or "divinely gifted." Bible: Jacob's eighth son.

ASHLEY (ASH-lee) English: "Ash tree field." English place name. According to an old superstition, the ash brings good luck. Ashley and its many variations are English surnames now used as given names. Ashley is used almost exclusively as a girl's name. Literature: Ashley Wilkes, hero of Margaret Mitchell's novel *Gone with the Wind.*

ASHO (ah-SHO) Persian: "pure of heart."

ASUMAN (ahs-OO-man) Hindu: "lord of vital breaths."

ASWAD (ahs-WAHD) Arabic: "dark." Usually refers to the color of skin. Common in Arab countries.

ATA (ah-TAH) Ghana. Fante: "twin."

ATALO (ah-TAH-loh) Greek: "youthful."

ATHAN (ah-THAHN) Greek: "immortal."

ATID (ah-TEED) Thai: "sun."

ATIF (ah-TEEF) Arabic: "caring," or "understanding." Popular in Arab countries.

ATMAN (AHT-muhn) Hindi: "the self" or "soul."

ATTICUS (att-IK-us) English: "father like." Literature: Atticus Finch, main character in Harper Lee's famous novel *To Kill a Mockingbird*. Atticus is a lawyer in the depression-era South who defends his children and client against prejudice.

AUBREY (AW-bree) Old French: "leader of the elves." A name that first arrived in England with the Norman Conquest, it is now used for girls as well. Arts: Aubrey Beardsley, British illustrator, famous for "Lysistrata."

AUGUST (AW-gust) Latin: "highly respectable." Arts: Auguste Rodin, sculptor, famous for "The Thinker"; Auguste Renoir, French impressionist painter. Theater: August Wilson, playwright. Fr: *Auguste;* Ger: *Augustus.*

AUGUSTIN (ah-goo-STEEN) Latin: "ruled by Augustine." A common name in Spanish-speaking countries. *Augustine, Augustus.*

AUKAI (AH-oo-KAH-ee) Hawaiian: "seafarer."

AUREK (AW-rek) Latin: "blond tresses." Contemporary adaptation of the ancient Polish name Aurelius. Czech: *Aurel;* Fr: *Aurele;* Ger: *Aurelius;* Ital: *Aurelio;* Pol: *Aureli, Elek;* Rum: *Aurelian;* Russ: *Avreliy, Avrel.*

AVERILL (AY-ve-rill) Old English: "boar warrior." History: Averell Harriman, U.S. diplomat. *Ave, Averel, Averell, Averil, Averyl, Averyll, Avrel, Avrell, Avrill, Avryll.*

AVERY (AY-ver-ee) English: "ruler of the elves."

AVI (ah-VEE) Israel. Hebrew: "divine father." One of the most popular Israeli names. *Avidan, Avidor, Aviel, Avniel.*

AVIDAN (ah-vee-DAHN) Israel. Hebrew: "God's just ways."

AVINOAM (ah-vee-NO-ahm) Israel. Hebrew: "father who is likeable." Popular in Israel.

AVIV (ah-VEEV) Israel. Hebrew: "nature's renewal" or "springtime." Popular in Israel.

AWAN (AH-wahn) Native American: "somebody."

AXEL (AX-ul) Scandinavian: "divine reward." Also a Scandinavian form of Absalom, meaning "father of peace." Popular name in Sweden and Norway. Literature: Axel Munthe, Swedish author. *Axell.*

AZARYAH (ah-ZAHR-yah) Israel. Hebrew: "God assists." Frequently used in Israel. *Azaria, Azarahu.*

AZIZI (ah-ZEE-zee) Swahili: "precious."

AZRIEL (ahz-ree-AHL) Israel. Hebrew: "the Lord is my salvation." Used often in Israel.

BAE (bye) Korean: "inspiration."

BAHARI (BAA-hari) African: "sea man."

BAILY (BAY-lee) English: "bailiff." During medieval times, a bailiff managed an estate or farm. Science: Baily Willis, geologist known for his studies of earthquakes and erosion; Baily Ashford, surgeon who discovered hookworms. *Bail, Baillie, Bailie, Bailey, Bayley.*

BAINBRIDGE (BAYNE-bridge) Old English: "bridge crosses rushing waters." Place name. *Bain, Bridger.*

BAJNOK (BAJ-nook) Hungarian: "victor."

BAKARI (bah-KAH-ree) East Africa. Swahili: "of noble promise."

BALDER (BAHLD-er) Old Norse: "lord of all illumination." Mythology: Ancient people in the Norse culture worshiped Balder as the son of Odin, the god of war. Norse: *Baldur;* Fr: *Baudier.*

BALDRIC (BAHLD-rik) German: "bold."

BALDWIN (BAHLD-win) Old German: "brave defender." Royal name in Belgium. *Bald, Baldovino, Balduin, Baldwinn, Baldwyn, Baldwynn, Balldwin, Baudoin.*

BALENDIN (BAH-lehn-deen) Latin: "fierce."

BALI (BAH-lee) Hindu: "mighty warrior."

BALIN (BAH-len) East India. Hindi: "powerful warrior." Mythology: Balin is a monkey king. He is said to be able to extract half the strength from anyone who opposes him. *Bali, Valin.*

BALTASAR (bahl-TAH-sar) German: "protected by god." Politics: Baltazar Garzón, Spanish investigating judge who gained international acclaim through his indictment of the former leaders of the Chilean military junta.

BANAN (BAN-ahn) Irish: "white."

BANCROFT (BAN-croft) Old English: "bean field."

BARAK (BARE-ek) Hebrew: "lightning bolt." Bible: Barak and Deborah combined forces toward military success. *Barrak.*

BARAM (BAH-ram) Israel. Hebrew: "son of the people" or "nation's heir." Popular in Israel.

BARCLAY (BARK-lee or BARK-lay) English, Scottish: "birth-tree meadow." Place name. *Barcley, Bartley.*

BARD (bahrd) Irish Gaelic: from *Baird* meaning "bard" or "minstrel."

BARDO (bahrd-OH) Danish: "son of the earth."

BARNABAS (BAHRN-ah-bas) Hebrew: "comfort's son." Bible: Barnabas was a close associate of Paul. Barnaby is most often used in Britain. Eng: *Barnaby, Barnie, Barny, Barn;* Fr: *Barnabe;* Hawaiian: *Bane;* Hung: *Barna;* Span: *Barbebas.*

BARNETT (bar-NET) Old English: "noble man." *Baron, Barnet.*

BARRAK (bahr-ROCK) Hebrew: "flash of lightning." Bible: In the Bible, Barak, a warrior, cooperated with Deborah, the prophetess, to win battles against overwhelming odds. *Barak.*

BARRETT (BARE-ett) Teutonic: "bear-like." *Barret.*

BARRINGTON (bare-ING-ton) English: "fairhaired."

BARRY (BARE-ee) English, Irish: "sword" or "sharp point." In modern usage the name is often a popular substitute for, and diminutive of, names like

Bernard, Barney, Baruch. Music: Barry Gibb, song-writer and member of the Bee Gees; Barry Manilow, singer and songwriter. *Barrie, Barrington.*

BART See Bartholomew.

BARTHOLOMEW (bahr-THOL-oh-MYOO) Hebrew: "son of Tolmai." Bible: Bartholomew was an alternative name for the apostle Nathaniel. Nathaniel was the patron saint of the tanners and leather-workers. Sports: Bart Starr, quarterback and coach of the Green Bay Packers; Bart Connor, U.S. Olympic gymnast. Eng: *Barth, Bart, Bartel;* Czech: *Bartek, Barto, Bartz;* Dan: *Bardo;* Fr: *Bartholome;* Ger: *Bartel, Bartol;* Hung: *Berti;* Span: *Bartoli, Bartolome, Toli* Swed: *Barthelemy.*

BARTRAM (BAHR-tram) English: "brilliant renown." Mythology: The raven was sacred to Odin, the Norse god of war.

BARUCH (BARR-ook or ba-ROOK) Hebrew: "blessed." Philosophy: Baruch Spinoza, Dutch rationalist philosopher.

BARUTI (bah-ROO-tee) Botswana. Tswana: "tutor."

BASIL (BAZZ-il or BASS-il or BAZE-ill) Greek: "royal" or "powerful like a king." Saint Basil (329–379) was one of the learned men of the early Christian church. Movies and Television: Basil Rathbone, actor, famous for his role as Sherlock Holmes. Eng: *Bas, Vas, Vastly;* Bulg: *Vasil;* Czech: *Bazil, Vasil;* Fr: *Basile;* Ger: *Basle;* Gk: *Vasilis;* Hung:

Bazel, Vazul; Ital/Span: *Basilio;* Pol: *Bazek;* Russ: *Basili, Vasilek, Vasya;* Swed: *Basilius, Basle.*

BASIR (buh-SEER) Turkish: "astute" or "discriminating wisely."

BASSAM (bah-SAHM) Arabic: "smiling." Used in Arab countries. *Basim.*

BAXTER (BAK-stir) English: "baker."

BAYANAI (bye-AHN-ey) Filipino: "hero."

BAYARD (BYE-erd or BAY-erd) French: "auburn-haired." History: Bayard Rustin, civil-rights activist who organized the 1963 March on Washington. Military: The name of a sixteenth-century French knight who was a warrior for King Francis I. A national hero of France, he is the symbol of the peerless knight. *Bay, Bayarde, Baylen.*

BAYZLI (BAYZ-lye) Polish: "royalty."

BEAU (boh) French: "highly attractive." Movies and Television: Beau Bridges, actor in *The Fabulous Baker Boys.* Music: Beau Williams, gospel singer. Sports: Bo Jackson, football and baseball player. *Beal, Beale, Bo.*

BEAUMONT (boh-MONT) French: "beautiful mountain."

BECK (bek) Swedish: "brook."

BEINISH (BEH-ee-neesh) Israel. Yiddish: "the right hand's son." Used in Israel.

BEIRCHEART (BEHR-khart) Ireland. Anglo-Saxon: "shining forces." *Bertie.*

BELEN (BELL-en) Greek: "an arrow."

BELTRAN (bel-TRAHN) Spanish: "bright raven."

BEM (behm) Nigeria. Tiv: "peace."

BEN (behn) See Benjamin and Benedict.

BEN-AMI (ben-ah-MEE) Israel. Hebrew: "my people's son." Popular in Israel.

BENEDICT (BEN-eh-dikt) Latin: "graced by God" or "one." Name used by fifteen popes. Saint Benedict established the Benedictine Order of Monks. Military: Benedict Arnold (1741–1801), American Revolutionary War general who became a traitor. Eng: *Ben, Benedic, Bendix, Bennett, Benny, Dick;* Czech/Ger: *Benedikt;* Fr: *Benoit;* Hung: *Benedik, Benci, Benke, Bence;* Ital: *Benedetto, Betto;* Russ: *Venedikt, Venka, Venya, Benedo;* Swed: *Bengt.*

BENICIO (ben-EE-cheo) Latin: "benevolent one." Movies and Television: Benicio del Toro, actor (*Sin City*).

BENITO (ben-EE-toh) Latin: "blessed."

BENJAMIN (BEN-jah-min) Hebrew: "the right hand's son." Puritans brought it to this country. Bible: Benjamin was the youngest son of Jacob and Rachel. History: Benjamin Harrison, twenty-third president of the United States (1889–93). Music:

Benny Goodman, jazz clarinet player. Science: Benjamin Franklin, inventor of the bifocal lens and the lightning rod; Benjamin Spock, pediatrician and child-care expert. Sports: Benjamin Raich, Austrain Olympic medalist in alpine skiing (2002). Eng: *Ben, Benjy, Benny;* Hung: *Beni, Beno;* Ital: *Beniamo;* Pol: *Benek, Beniamin;* Scot: *Beatham;* Span: *Benja, Mincho;* Yiddish: *Binyamin.*

BENJIRO (ben-jee-ROH) Japanese: "be in peace."

BENROY (ben-ROY) Hebrew: "son of a lion."

BENTLEY (BENT-lee) Old English: "grassy meadow." Place name that brings to mind the expensive English car. *Ben, Bentlea, Bentlee, Bentlie, Bently, Lee.*

BER (behr) Israel. Yiddish: "bear." Although Yiddish names are rarely used in Israel today, this name is a popular exception.

BERDY (BAIR-dee) Russian: "genius" or "brilliantly intelligent."

BERGER (BUR-ger) French: "shepherder." Gaining popularity in the United States as a given name, though common in Austria as a surname.

BERK (burk) Turkish: "solid and firm." *Berke.*

BERKLEY (BUR-klee) Irish: "birch-tree meadow." *Berl, Berle, Burlin.*

BERNARD (BUR-nahrd or bur-NAHRD) Old German: "with bearlike might." Business: Bernard Arnault, French businessman and one of the richest men in the world. History: Bernard Baruch, U.S. financier and government adviser. Literature: Bernard Malamud, novelist and short-story writer who wrote *The Fixer*. Sports: Björn Borg, Swedish tennis champion who holds the record for greatest number of singles (five consecutive) wins. Theater: George Bernard Shaw, playwright who wrote *Pygmalion*. Eng: *Barn, Barney, Bern, Bernie;* Czech: *Bernek, Berno;* Fr: *Bernardin, Bernon, Bernot, Bernard;* Ger: *Beno, Berend, Bernardino;* Lat: *Bernhards;* Lith: *Bernadas;* Pol: *Benek;* Russ: *Berngards;* Swed: *Bjorn;* Ir: *Bearnard;* Span: *Bernal, Bernardo.*

BERT Short form of Albert. See Albert.

BERTHOLD (BURT-hold) German: "bright ruler." *Bertholde.*

BERTO (BAIR-to) Spanish: "bright and distinguished." *Veto.*

BERTRAM (BAIR-tram) Old German: "brilliant raven." Literature, Philosophy: Bertrand Russell, considered one of the founders of modern logic who won the Nobel Prize for Literature (1950). Science: Bertram N. Brockhouse, Canadian Nobel Prize winner in Medicine (1994). Eng: *Bart, Bartram;* Czech: *Berty;* Fr: *Bertrand.*

BERWIN (BUR-win) Middle English: "harvest son." Astrology: Appropriate for those born under the earth signs of Virgo, Capricorn, or Taurus.

BERYL (buryl) Hebrew: "dazzling jewel."

BETZALEL (BEH-tsah-lehl) Israel. Hebrew: "in God's shadow."

BEVIN (BEV-in) Celtic: "young soldier." *Bevyn.*

BINGHAM (BING-ham) German: "kettle-shaped hollow."

BINH (beun) Vietnamese: "peace."

BIRCH (burch) Old English: "grove of birch trees." *Birk, Burch.*

BIRGER (BIHR-ger) Norwegian: "rescue."

BITTAN (bit-TAHN) German: "desire." *Bitten.*

BJARNE (byuhrn) Old Norse: "bear." Used in Denmark.

BJORN See Bernard.

BLACKBURN (BLAK-burhn) Old English: "brook of black water."

BLAINE (blayne) English, Scottish: "trim" or "sleek." *Blayne, Blane, Blaney.*

BLAIR (blayre) Irish Gaelic: "meadow child." Astrology: Appropriate for those born under earth signs. More often used as a girl's name. *Blaire, Balyre.*

BLAISE (blayze) Latin: "one who stammers." Philosophy, Science: Blaise Pascal, seventeenth-century French philosopher who invented the calculating machine and hydraulic press. Eng: *Blase;* Fr: *Blaisot;* Ger: *Blasius;* Hung: *Ballas;* Ital: *Biagio;* Pol: *Blazek.*

BLAKE (blayke) Old English: "pale, shining one" or "black." Movies and Television: Blake Edwards, film producer and director famous for *The Pink Panther* series. *Blayke.*

BLYTHE (blyth) English: "merry." *Blyth.*

BOAZ (BO-ahz) Israel. Hebrew: "mighty and quick." Favorite in Israel. *Boas.*

BODAWAY (bo-DAH-way) Native American: "one who makes fire."

BODIL (BO-del) Norwegian, Danish: "ruling with power and might."

BODUA (bo-DOO-ah) Ghana. Akan: "creature's tail." Bodua is an African sacred day called "Akan" in the native calendar, corresponding to Sunday.

BOHUSLAV (BOH-oo-slav) Slavic: "God's glory." Widely used in Czechoslovakia.

BOMANI (boh-MAM-ee) Malawi. Ngoni: "fierce soldier."

BOND (bond) Old English: "farmer" or "he who cultivates the earth." *Bonde, Bondon, Bonds.*

BORDEN (BORE-den) Old English: "near the boar's den."

BORIS (BORE-iss) Russian: "fighter." Popular name in most Slavic countries as well as Russia, where Boris is the patron saint of Moscow. Literature: Boris Pasternak, author of the novel *Doctor Zhivago*, and winner of the Nobel Prize for Literature (1958). Movies and Television: Boris Karloff, actor known for his portrayal in *Frankenstein*. *Borya, Boryenka, Boriss, Borris, Borys.*

BORKA (BOR-kah) Slavic: "fighter."

BORT (bort) English: "fortified." *Bourke.*

BOTAN (bo-TAHN) Japanese: "blossom." The peony flower heralds the arrival of summer.

BOUREY (BU-ree) Cambodian: "country."

BOWEN (BOW-en) Welsh: "youth's son." *Bow, Bowie.*

BOWIE (BOO-ee) Scottish Gaelic: "yellow-haired." *Bow, Bowen, Boyd.*

BOYD (boyd) Celtic: "blond." Business: Boyd Bears, company famous for its collection of stuffed animals.

BRAC (brak) Welsh: "free."

BRAD (brad) Old English: "wide expanse." Adaptation of Bradley and Bradford, often used independently. Movies and Television: Brad Pitt, actor. *Bradd*.

BRADFORD (BRAD-ford) Old English: "from the broad river." Place name. *Brad*.

BRADLEY (BRAD-lee) Old English: "from the expansive field." Place name. *Brad, Brady, Lee, Bradlee, Bradshaw*.

BRAM (bram) English, Scottish: "bramble." Literature: Bram Stoker, author of *Dracula*.

BRANDEIS (BRAN-dies) German: "dwells on a burned clearing."

BRANDON (BRAN-din) Old English: "he who hails from the beacon hill." Journalism: Brendan Gill, columnist. Theater: Brendan Behan, Irish playwright who wrote *The Hostage*. *Brand, Brandan, Branden, Brannon;* Ir: *Bran, Bram, Broin, Brendan, Brennan*.

BRANT (brant) English: "proud." Military: Joseph Brant, Native American from the Mohawk tribe, who fought for the British during the Revolutionary war and was renowned for his strategic military efforts.

BRAXTON (BRAKS-ton) Anglo-Saxon: "brock's town."

BREDE (BREH-deh) Scandinavian: "iceberg." One of the most beloved names in Denmark.

BREEN (breen) Irish: "sadness."

BREN (bren) German: "flame."

BRENT (brent) Old English: "he who hails from the high peak."

BRETT (bret) Old English: "a native of Brittany." Sports: Brett Hull, Olympic medalist in ice hockey (2002). *Bret.*

BRIAN (BRI-an) Celtic: "he rises." Movies and Television: Brian Dennehy, actor; Brian DePalma, director of the movie *Wise Guys.* Music: Brian Wilson, singer in the Beach Boys. Sports: Brian Boitano, Olympic figure skating champion (1988). Eng: *Briant, Bryant, Bryon;* Ital: *Briano.*

BRICE (bryce) Anglo-Saxon: "son of a nobleman." *Bryce.*

BRIGHTON (BRYE-ton) Hebrew: "the one who is loved."

BRISHEN (BREE-shen) English Gypsy: "storm baby" or "child who brought the rain."

BROCK (brahk) Old English: "badger."

BRODERICK (BRAHD-rik) Scottish, Norse: "brother." Name once given to a second son. *Brody, Brodi, Brodie.*

BRODY (BROO-dee) Scottish: "ditch." Brodie is the name of a castle in Scotland. *Brodie.*

BRONISLAW (BRAHN-iss-lahv) Slavic: "glorious weapon." Popular in Poland. Education: Bronislaw Malinowski, considered the father of anthropology.

BRONSON (BRAHN-son) English, German: "brown son." Theater: Bronson Howard, playwright. *Bron.*

BROOKS (brooks) English: "running water" or "stream." Theater: Brooks Atkinson, theater critic for the *New York Times.*

BRUCE (broos) Old French: "brushwood grove." History: King Robert Bruce successfully battled to make Scotland a sovereign nation (1327). Literature: Bruce Catton, historian and writer on the Civil War. Music: Bruce Springsteen, rock star. *Brucey, Brucie.*

BRUNO (BROO-noh) Old German: "brown-skinned." Music: Bruno Walter, orchestral conductor. *Braun.*

BUCK (buk) Old English: "male deer." First used as a nickname, it now stands independently. Movies and Television: Buck Henry, TV writer. Sports: Buck Freeman, baseball player who played 534 consecutive games for the Boston Red Sox, a record prior to 1987. *Buckey, Buckle, Buckley, Bucky.*

BUD (bud) English. Slang word for "buddy" or "brother," it has been in existence since the Middle Ages. Movies and Television: Buddy Ebsen, actor; Bud Abbott, Buddy Hackett, comedians.

BURBANK (BUR-bank) English: "lives on the castle's hill."

BURGESS (BUR-ges) Old English: "free citizen."

BURL (burl) English: "strengthened." Movies and Television: Burl Ives, actor and singer who won an Oscar for his supporting role in *The Big Country*. *Burlie, Burleigh, Burle.*

BURR (boor) Swedish: "youth."

BURT Short form of Burton. See Burton.

BURTON (BUR-tin) English: "hill" or "borough town." Place name. Movies and Television: Burt Reynolds, Burt Lancaster, actors. *Bert, Berton, Burt.*

BUZZ (buz) Celtic: "village in the woods." Aeronautics: Buzz Aldrin, astronaut who flew a mission on Apollo 11 and was one of two men to first step foot on the moon.

BYRON (BYE-rin) Old English: "cow barn." Literature: Lord Byron, romantic poet; Biron was a character in Shakespeare's *Love's Labours Lost*. *Biron.*

CABLE (KAY-bel) English: "one who makes ropes." *Cabe.*

CADAO (ka-DA-o) Vietnamese: "folk song."

CADDA (ka-DAH) English: "warring." *Cadell.*

CADELL (kay-DELL) Celtic: "warring ethos." *Kade, Cade, Caden, Cayen.*

CAEDMON (kayd-MON) Anglo-Saxon: "poet."

CAELAN (KAY-lin) Irish Gaelic: "strong fighter." *Caelin, Calin, Caylan.*

CAESAR (SEE-zar) Latin: "he with the long hair." History: The title of the emperor of Rome from Augustus to Hadrian. Movies and Television: Cesar Romero, actor. Music: Cesar Auguste Franck, classical composer. Eng: *Cesar, Cesare;* Bulg: *Cezar,*

Kaiser; Pol: *Arek, Cezar, Czeck;* Russ: *Kesar, Checha, Sarito.*

CAHIL (kah-HIL) Turkish: "ingenuous" or "yet to experience."

CAIN (kayn) Hebrew: "spear." Bible: Cain was Adam and Eve's firstborn son who killed his brother in anger and spent the rest of his life as a wanderer in exile.

CALBERT (kal-BURT) English: "cowboy."

CALDER (kahl-DER) Old English: "river of stones."

CALEB (KAY-lib) Hebrew: "spontaneous" or "devoted" or "brave." Bible: Caleb and Moses led their people through the wilderness. This name has recently become popular again in the United States. Eng: *Cal, Cale, Kale, Kaleb.*

CALISTO (kal-IST-oh) Greek: "most beautiful."

CALLAGHAN (KAL-uh-khahn) Irish: Name of two Irish saints.

CALLIS (KAL-is) Latin: "cup."

CALLUM (kal-LUM) Celtic: "dove." *Calum.*

CALVIN (KAL-vin) Latin: "bald." History: Originally a Roman family clan name, it was popularized in the United States during the presidency of John Calvin Coolidge. *Cal, Kalvin, Vinnie.*

CAM (kahm) English Gypsy: "one who is deeply loved."

CAMDEN (KAHM-den) Scottish: "from the winding valley."

CAMERON (KAHM-er-run) Scottish Gaelic: "nose askew." Theater: Cameron Mackintosh, producer. *Cam, Camron, Kameron.*

CAMILLUS (kah-MILL-us) Latin: "noble youth aiding in religious services." Patron saint of nurses and patients. Music: Camille Saint-Saens composed the opera *Samson and Delilah.* Fr: *Camille;* Ital: *Camillo.*

CAMLIN (KAM-lyn) Celtic: "crooked line."

CAMPBELL (KAM-bull) Irish: "mouth askew." *Cam, Camp.*

CANDAN (kan-DAHN) Turkish: "sincerely."

CARADOC (kara-DOK) Celtic: "dearly loved."

CARDEN (KAR-den) Celtic: "from the black fortress."

CAREY (KAR-ee or KARE-ee) Welsh, Celtic: "close to the fortress." Movies and Television: Cary Grant, actor.

CARL German: Short form of Charles. See Charles.

CARLO (KAR-loh) Italy, Old French: "masculine and muscular." History: Carlos Filipe Ximenes Belo, Nobel Peace Prize winner for his work in finding a peaceful resolution in East Timor (1999). *Carlino, Carlos.*

CARMEL (KAHR-mel) Israel. Hebrew: "garden." Popular in Israel, it is also the name of a coastal resort town in California.

CARMELO (KAHR-melo) Hebrew: "fruitful orchard." Refers to Mount Carmel in Palestine.

CARMINE (kahr-MEE-neh or KAR-mine) Hebrew: "vineyard." Italian: "song." Common in Italy.

CARNIG (KARN-ig) Armenian: "small lamb."

CARR (kar) Norwegian: "from the marsh."

CARROLL (KARE-ol) Celtic: "champion." *Carrol.*

CARSON (KAR-sin) Old English: "son of the marsh-dwellers." *Karsen, Karson.*

CARTER (KAR-ter) Old English: "cart driver." Sports: Carter Rycroft, Canadian Olympic medalist in curling (2002).

CASEY (KAY-see) Irish: "alert" or "vigorous." Music: The name was made famous by the song about the engineer of the Cannonball Express train, Casey Jones. Sports: Casey Stengel, New York Yankees baseball manager who managed the team to ten pennants and seven championships (1949–60).

CASIMIR (KAH-zah-meer) Slavic: "enforces peace." Eng: *Castimer;* Ger/Russ: *Kazimer;* Hung: *Kazmer;* Pol: *Kazik, Kazio;* Span: *Casimiro, Cachi, Cashi.*

CASPER (KAS-per) Persian: "keeper of the riches." History: Caspar Weinberger, U.S. Defense Secretary under Ronald Reagan. Eng: *Cas, Caspar, Cass, Gaspar, Jasper;* Ger: *Jasper, Kasper;* Fr: *Gaspard;* Hung/Russ/Span: *Caspar.*

CASSIDY (kas-SID-ee) Gaelic: "clever."

CASSIUS (KASH-us) Old Norman French: "casse," and the Latin "capsa" meaning "box" or "protective cover." Roman clan name. History: Gaius Cassius Longinas, first-century Roman general behind the plot to murder Julius Caesar. Literature: Co-conspirator in Shakespeare's tragedy, *Julius Caesar.* Sports: Cassius Clay was the birth name of the heavyweight boxing champion Muhammad Ali. *Cash, Cass, Cassio.*

CASTEL (kah-STEL) Latin: "of the castle." Most often used in Spain and Latin America.

CATHAL (KA-thal) Ireland. Celtic: "battle-mighty." *Cahal.*

CATON (kah-TOHN) Latin: "knowing." Favorite in Spanish-speaking countries. *Cato.*

CAVAN (KAV-ahn) Gaelic: "handsome."

CAYDEN (KAY-den) Gaelic: "spirit of battle."

CECIL (SEES-ul) Latin: "one who does not perceive." Movies and Television: Cecil B. DeMille, producer of the film *Cleopatra*. *Cecil, Cecillo, Cecillus, Cello.*

CEDRIC (SEDD-rik or SEED-rik) Welsh: "wonderful present." Literature: Guardian of Rowena in Sir Walter Scott's novel *Ivanhoe*. Boy hero in the novel *Little Lord Fauntleroy* by Frances Hodgson Burnett. Movies and Television: Cedric the Entertainer, popular African-American comedian and actor. *Caddaric, Ced, Cedrick, Rick.*

CESARO (seys-ARO) Spanish: "long-haired." *Cesar.*

CHAD (chad) Old English: "fierce." Began in England during the Middle Ages and burst in popularity during the 1960s. Movies and Television: Chad Everett, Chad Lowe, actors. Music: Chad Stuart, singer who made "Yesterday's Gone" with Jeremy Stuart. *Chadd, Chaddie.*

CHADBURN (CHAD-byrne) English: "from the wildcat brook." *Chadburne, Chadbyrne.*

CHADWICK (CHAD-wik) English: "Saint Chad's village."

CHAIM (KHY-yum) Hebrew: "living spirit" or "life." Hebrew: *Hyam;* Pol: *Chaimek, Haim;* Russ: *Khaim.*

CHAL (chahl) English Gypsy: "young man" or "kid" or "laddie."

CHANCE (chans) French: "fortune" or "gamble." Variant of Chauncey.

CHANDER (CHAN-der) Hindu: "moon."

CHANEY (CHAN-ee) Old French: "oak wood."

CHANN (chan) English: "young wolf." *Channe, Channing, Channon.*

CHANON (HAHN-on) Hebrew: "cloud."

CHAPIN (CHAP-in) French: "clergyman."

CHAPMAN (CHAP-man) English: "merchant."

CHARLES (CHARHL-z) Latin: "masculine and powerful." A strong name with popular variations used worldwide for hundreds of years. It has been particularly favored by the royalty of several countries, including England's present Prince of Wales. In 800 A.D., the name signified great power as Charlemagne (Charles the Great) was crowned Holy Roman Emperor. Aeronautics: Chuck Yaeger, pilot. Business: Charles Walgreen, founder of the drugstore chain that bears his name. History: Charles De Gaulle, French president. Journalism: Carl Bernstein, journalist who co-authored the book *All The President's Men* about the Watergate scandal. Literature: Charles Dickens, novelist; Carl Sandburg, poet who wrote *Chicago Poems*. Movies and Television: Charlie Chaplin, actor; Charlie Kaufman, 2005 Oscar winner for Best Screenplay (*Eternal Sunshine of the Spotless Mind*). Music: Chuck Mangione, trumpeter. Science: Carl Sagan, astronomer, author.

Eng: *Carl, Cary, Chad, Charlie, Carlton, Chas, Chick, Chip, Chuck;* Russ: *Karl;* Czech: *Karel, Karlik, Karol;* Swed: *Kalle;* Fr: *Charlot;* Ger: *Karal;* Hung: *Kari, Karoly;* Ital: *Carlino, Carlo;* Latin: *Karlen, Karlin;* Span: *Carlo, Carlos.*

CHASE (Chayce) Old French: "one who hunts." Astrology: Appropriate for those born under Sagittarius, which is symbolized by the archer. *Chace;* Fr: *Chaise.*

CHATWIN (chat-WIN) English: "warring friend." *Chatwyn.*

CHAUNCEY (CHAHN-see) French: Place name, village near Amiens. Arts: Chauncey A. Day, cartoonist. Music: Chauncey Olcott, songwriter who composed "My Wild Irish Rose." *Chan, Chance, Chaunce, Chauncy.*

CHAVEZ (CHA-vez) Spanish: "dream maker."

CHEN (chen) Chinese: "immense" or "tremendous."

CHENG (cheng) Chinese: "to become."

CHESTER (chess-TER) English: "lives at the camp of the soldiers." *Chet.*

CHEVALIER (she-VALL-e-air) French: "chivalrous" or "knight-like." Movies and Television: Chevy Chase, actor, comedian, one of the original stars of the TV show *Saturday Night Live. Chev, Chevi, Checy.*

CHEVEYO (chev-AY-oh) Native American: "spirit warrior."

CHI (chee) Chinese: "younger energy."

CHIAMAKA (chee-AH-mah-kah) African: "God is splendid."

CHIOKE (CHEE-oh-keh) Nigeria. Ibo: "gift of God."

CHONI (HOON-ee) Hebrew: "gracious."

CHRISTIAN (KRIS-chin) Greek: "follower of the anointed." Originally a girl's name that became a male name. Ten Danish kings have been called Christian. Literature: Hero of John Bunyan's *Pilgrim's Progress*. Science: Christian Barnard, M.D., surgeon who performed the first heart transplant. Eng: *Chris, Christy, Christen, Kit, Kristian;* Est: *Jaan, Kristjan, Krists;* Fr: *Christophe;* Ger; *Krischan;* Gk: *Christiano, Cretien, Kristos;* Hung: *Kerestel;* Pol: *Chrystian, Crystek, Krystek;* Port: *Christao, Christiano.*

CHRISTOPHER (CHRIS-toe-fer) Greek: "he who carries Christ." Saint Christopher, who is said to have carried the Christ child across a river, is the patron saint of travelers. The name was little used until a revival in the 1940s. Arts: Christopher Wren, architect. History: Christopher Columbus, explorer who discovered the Americas. Literature: Christopher Robin, human hero in A. A. Milne's *Winnie the Pooh.* Movies and Television: Christopher Reeve, Christopher Plummer, actors. Music: Christoph

Willibald Gluck, composer. Eng: *Chris, Kit, Kris, Kriss;* Czech: *Christofer, Kristof;* Den: *Christoffer;* Fin: *Risto;* Fr: *Christophe;* Ger: *Christoph, Stoffel;* Gk: *Christophoros;* Hung: *Kristof;* Ital: *Christoforo;* Latin: *Kriss, Krisus;* Port: *Cristovao;* Russ: *Chrisof, Christofer;* Span: *Cristobal, Tobalito;* Swed: *Kristofor, Kristoffer.*

CHUMA (CHOO-mah) Zimbabwe. Shona: "wealth" or "beads."

CICERO (SIS-eroh) Greek: "the historian." History: Marcus Tullius Cicero, Roman author, orator, and politician.

CILLIAN (SIL-leon) Gaelic: "war."

CLARENCE (KLARE-ince) Latin: "shining" or "acclaimed." Place name, Clare, used as a first name. History: Clarence Darrow, lawyer in Scopes evolution trial. Clarence Thomas, U.S. Supreme Court Justice. *Clair, Clarance, Clarrance, Klarance.*

CLARK (klark) Old French: "one committed to studies or spiritual practice." Centuries ago, men of learning in England were usually members of a clerical order. (The word clerk is still pronounced "clark" in England.) Literature: Clark Kent, alter ego of Superman. Movies and Television: Clark Gable, actor. *Clarke, Clerc, Clerk.*

CLAUDE (klawd) English, Latin: "limping." Arts: Claude Monet, impressionist painter. Music: Claude Debussy, French composer. Science: Claudius

Ptolemy, second-century Alexandrian astronomer who proposed that the solar system revolves around the earth.

CLAYTON (KLAY-tin) Old English: "earth." *Clay, Clayborne, Clayburn, Claiborne, Klayton.*

CLEAVON (KLEE-von) English: "cliff."

CLEMENT (KLEM-int) Latin: "compassionate" or "accommodating." Saint Clement is the patron saint of lighthouses. Business: Clement Studebaker, wagon and carriage manufacturer. Literature: Clement Moore, poet who wrote "The Night Before Christmas." Eng: *Clem, Clemens, Clemmie, Clemmy, Clemmons;* Bulg: *Kliment;* Czech: *Klema, Klement, Klemo;* Den: *Clemens;* Ger: *Klemens, Menz;* Hung: *Kelemen;* Ital: *Clemenza;* Pol: *Klemens, Klimek;* Russ: *Kliment, Klimka, Klyment;* Span: *Cleme, Clemen, Clemente, Clemento.*

CLIFFORD (KLIF-ferd) Old English: "ford aside the cliff." Music: Cliff Richard, singer. Clifford Curzon, concert pianist. Theater: Clifford Odets, playwright. *Cliff, Clyff, Clyfford.*

CLIFTON (KLIF-tin) Old English: "town aside the cliff." Education: Clifton Wharton, Jr., first black president of a major university and chancellor of the largest university system in the United States. *Cliff, Clift, Clyfton.*

CLINTON (KLIN-tin) Old English:" "town aside the hills." English place name. Movies and Television: Clint Eastwood, actor and director.

CLIVE (kleeve or klive) English: "cliff." Place name. Journalism: Clive Barnes, theater and dance critic. History: Clive W. J. Granger, Nobel Prize winner in economics (2003). Military: Originally a last name, Clive became popular as a first name because of the fame of Robert Clive, British conqueror of India. *Cleve, Clyve.*

CLOVIS (KLO-vis) German: "renowned fighter." Variant of Louis.

CLYDE (klyd) Welsh: "heard from afar."

COLBY (KOLE-bee) Old English: "dark-haired." *Colbey, Colbert.*

COLE (kole) Old English: "coal." Greek: "victory of the people."

COLIN (KOH-lyn) Celtic: "youth" or "child." Greek: "victor." *Collin.*

COLM (kolm) Celtic: "dove." *Colman, Colum.*

COLVER (KOLE-ver) English: "dove." *Colvyr.*

COMAN (ko-MAHN) Arabic: "highborn" or "royal." A name used in Arab countries.

COMFORT (KOHM-fort) Latin: "strength."

CONAN (KOHN-an) Celtic: "wise." Movies and Television: Conan O'Brian, comedian and actor. *Conant.*

CONARY (KOH-ner-ee) Irish: Ancient Irish name. Old Irish names are very popular in Ireland now.

CONLEY (kohn-LEE) Celtic: "hero." *Conlan.*

CONNER (KAHN-er) Celtic: "desire."

CONNOR (KAHN-or) Celtic: "much wanted." *Conor.*

CONRAD (KAHN-rad) Old German: "boldly sagacious." Business: Conrad Hilton, international hotel chain founder. Literature: Kurt Vonnegut, popular novelist. Science: Kurt Wüthrich, Swiss Nobel Prize winner in Chemistry (2002). Eng: *Con, Conn, Conni, Connie, Cort, Curt, Konrad, Kurt;* Fr: *Conrade;* Ger: *Cord, Cort, Conny, Konni, Konrad, Kurt;* Ital: *Conrado;* Swed: *Konrad.*

CONROY (KAHN-roy) Celtic: "persistent."

CONSTANTINE (KOHN-stan-teen) Latin: "faithful." History: Constantine the Great, Roman emperor who converted the Roman Empire to Christianity.

CONSUELO (KOHN-swal-oh) Spanish: "consolation."

CONWAY (KAHN-way) Welsh: "river." Music: Conway Twitty, country singer.

CORBAN (KORE-ban) Greek: "a gift devoted to God."

CORBIN (KORE-bin) Old French: "raven" or "black hair." *Corbyn.*

CORDELL (KORE-del) Latin: "small rope."

COREY (KOHR-ee) Irish Gaelic: "hollow cove." *Cori, Correy, Cory, Korey, Kory.*

CORNELIUS (kor-NEEL-yus) Latin: "horn-like." Latin clan name, often used in the Roman Empire. Business: Cornelius Vanderbilt, railroad and steamship magnate. Sports: Cornelius Bennet, football player. *Con, Connie, Cornall, Cornel, Cornelious, Cornell, Cornelus, Corney, Cornilius, Neel, Neil, Neely.*

CORWIN (KOHR-win) English: "friend of the heart." *Corwine, Corwyne, Corwan.*

COSMO (KOZ-moh) Greek: "in good order." Saint Cosmas was the patron saint of the city of Milan, Italy. *Cosimo, Cosme, Cos.*

COTY (KO-tee) Old French: "small slope." *Koty.*

COURTNEY (KOR-than-ee) Anglo-Saxon: "dweller by the stream." *Courtnay.*

COYAN (koy-AHN) French: "modest."

CRAIG (krayg) Scottish Gaelic: "of the craggy rock." Literature: Craig Kennedy, character in Arthur B. Reeves's detective stories. Sports: Craig Morton, football player. *Cragg, Kraig.*

CRISPIN (KRIS-pen) Latin: "curly tresses." Saint Crispin is a patron of shoemakers. Eng: *Chris, Chrispin, Cris;* Ger: *Krispin;* Fr: *Crepin;* Ital: *Crispino;* Span: *Crispo.*

CROSBY (CROZ-bee) English: "dweller near the town crossing."

CURTIS (KUR-tehs) Old French: "polite" or "imbued with courtesy." Music: Curtis Mayfield, pop musician. Eng: *Curt, Kurt, Kurtis;* Span: *Curcio.*

CYRANO (SYR-ahn-oh) Greek: "from cyrene." History: Cyrano de Bergerac, French soldier, dramatist, and satirist who lived during the mid-1600s. Theater: *Cyrano de Bergerac,* play written by Edmond Rostand based on the real person.

CYRIL (SIRR-il) Greek: "with the presence of the lord." Saint Cyril was the inventor of the Cyrillic alphabet, based on the Greek, which is now used in Russia and parts of the Balkans. Military: Cyril Newall, British general who governed New Zealand in the early 1940s. Movies and Television: Cyril Richard, actor. Eng: *Cy, Cyrill;* Bulg: *Kiril;* Fr: *Cyrille;* Ital: *Cirillo;* Russ: *Kirill, Kirl;* Span: *Cirilo, Ciro.*

CYRUS (SYE-rus) Persian: "throne." Bible: Founder of the Persian empire, Cyrus allowed the Jewish people to rebuild Jerusalem. History: Cyrus Vance, U.S. Secretary of State under Jimmy Carter. Sports: Cy Young, baseball pitcher, in whose honor the Cy Young Award is given to "the major league pitcher of the year." Eng: *Cy;* Russ/Bulg: *Kir;* Span/Ital: *Ciro.*

CZESLAW (shez-LAW) Polish: "glory and honor." Literature: Czeslaw Milosz, Polish Nobel Prize winner in Literature (1980).

DABIR (dah-BEER) Arabic: "tutor" or "record-keeper." Used in Algeria and Egypt.

DACEY (DAY-see) Irish Gaelic: "southern." Span: *Dacio, Dace, Dacey, Dacian, Dacy.*

DADA (DAH-dah) Nigeria. Yoruba: "curly-haired child."

DAFYDD (DAF-eth) Hebrew: "much loved." Welsh favorite. *Dafid.*

DAG (dahg) Scandinavian: "light of day." History: Dag Hammarskjöld, former United Nations Secretary General and Nobel Prize winner for Peace. Mythology: Dag is a Norse god, light's son. *Dagen, Daeg, Deegan, Daegan.*

DAI (dah-EE) Japanese: "big."

DAIRE (DEH-ruh) Irish: An ancient usage. Old Irish names are now very popular in Ireland.

DAKARAI (dah-KAH-rah-ee) Zimbabwe. Shona: "happiness."

DAKOTA (da-KOH-tah) Native American. Dakota: "amiable partner." Tribal name. *Dakotah.*

DALE (dayl) Old English: "valley." Place name that referred to those who built their homes or pitched their tents near a valley. Eng: *Dal, Daley, Daly, Dayle;* Czech: *Dalibor.*

DALLAS (dahl-LYS) Celtic: "dwells by the waterfall."

DALLIN (DAY-lyn) Old English: "people who are proud." Place name. Education: Dallin Oakes, lawyer and Mormon church leader. *Dallon, Dallen, Dallan, Dalan, Dalon, D'Alan.*

DALTON (DOLL-tin) English: "the village in the valley."

DAMARIO (DAH-mar-ee-oh) Spanish: "gentle." Masculine variant of the Greek Damaris.

DAMEK (DAH-mek) Czech: "earth."

DAMIAN (DAYM-yan) Greek: "sweet and harmless." Saint Damian (third century) is known as the patron saint of physicians. Literature: Damon Runyon, author and journalist who wrote *Guys and Dolls.* Eng: *Damian, Damon;* Hung: *Damjan;* Fr:

Damien; Ital: *Damiano;* Russ: *Damian, Damyan, Dema, Demyan;* Span: *Damion, Daminao.*

DAMON (DAY-mun) Greek: "one who inspires gentleness." *Damone, Daymen.*

DAN (dan) Hebrew: "judge."

DAN (vung) Vietnamese: "yes."

DANE (dagn) Old English: "he who hails from Denmark." Movies and Television: Dana Carvey, comedian; Dane Clark, actor. *Dana, Dain.*

DANIEL (DAN-yul) Hebrew: "the Lord is my judge." Bible: Daniel's deeply held faith in God saved him from the lion's den in Babylon. History: Daniel Boone, Kentucky pioneer and frontiersman. Literature: Daniel Defoe, author of *Robinson Crusoe*; Dan Brown, author of the acclaimed *Da Vinci Code*. Movies and Television: Danny Thomas, Danny Kaye, comedians; Daniel Day Lewis, Danny De Vito, Danny Aiello, actors. Eng: *Dan, Dannie, Danny;* Bulg: *Danil;* Czech: *Dano, Danko;* Dutch: *Dane;* Fin: *Taneli;* Fr: *Donois;* Hung: *Dasco, Danniel, Dani;* Ital: *Daniele;* Latin: *Daniels;* Lith: *Dane, Danukas;* Pol: *Danek;* Russ: *Daniela, Danila, Danilka, Danya, Danylets, Danylo;* Serb: *Dusan;* Slovenian: *Dani;* Span: *Danilo, Nelo.*

DANNO (DAH-noh) Japanese: "gathering in the meadow."

DANTE (DAHN-tay) Italian, Spanish: "eternally enduring." Literature: Dante Aligheri, considered one of the greatest poets of all time, wrote *The Divine Comedy,* in which the medieval version of Hell known as Dante's Inferno is described.

DAOUD (dah-WOOUD) Hebrew: "much loved." Used in Afghanistan.

DAR (dahr) Hebrew: "pearl."

DARBY (DAHR-bee) Irish Gaelic: "liberated" or "free." *Dar, Darb, Derby.*

DARCY (DAHR-see) Irish Gaelic: "of dark skin." *Dar, Darce, Darcey, Darse, Darsey, Darsy.*

DAREK (DAHR-ek) German: "gifted ruler." Variant of Theodoric.

DAREN (DAH-rehn) Nigeria. Hausa: "night child" or "born after dusk."

DARIN (DARE-in) Greek: "precious present" Eng: *Dare, Darren, Daron, Darrin, Darron;* Ital: *Darren;* Span: *Dario.*

DARIO (DAHR-ee-o) Spanish: "affluent." Literature: Dario Fo, Italian Nobel Prize winner in Literature (1997).

DARIUS (DARE-ee-us) Persian: "he who upholds the good." Music: Darius Millhaud, famed French composer who wrote *Deliverance of Theseus.* Sports: Darius Kasparaitis, Russian Olympic medalist for ice hockey (2002). *Darrius, Darrio.*

DARNELL (DAHR-nell) Middle English: "hidden nook." Education: Darnell Hawkins, sociologist. *Darnel.*

DARREN (DAHR-in) Irish Gaelic: Variation of Darin. See Darin.

DARRION (DARE-ree-in) Contemporary blend of Damion and Dareren. *Darian, Darien, Darion, Darian, Derrian.*

DARRYL (DARE-el) Old French: "small one." Music: Daryl Hall, pop singer. Sports: Darryl Strawberry, baseball player. *Darel, Darrel, Darrell, Daryl, Darroll, Darrol.*

DARTAGNAN (dar-TAIN-ee-on) French: "leader." Literature: D'Artagnan, character in Alexander Dumas's *The Three Musketeers*. *D'Artagnan.*

DARWESHI (dahr-WEH-shee) East Africa. Swahili: "blessed companion." *Dar, Derwin.*

DASAN (DAH-sahn) Native American. Pomo: "ruler." Mythology: In the mythical lore of the Pomo Indians, the bird clan that gave birth to the world was led by Dasan and his father.

DAUDI (dah-OO-dee) Kenya. Swahili: "adored friend." *Daudy.*

DAVID (DAY-vid) Hebrew: "beloved." Bible: King David of Israel wrote the Book of Psalms, and as a young boy killed Goliath the giant with a slingshot. His beloved reputation has made the name a worldwide favorite. A perennial favorite for Christians and Jews. Education: David Ricardo, British economist (1772–1823) who advocated free international trade. History: David Brewster, former U.S. Supreme Court Justice; David Dinkins, New York City's first black mayor (1990–93). Literature: Dave Barry, humorous author who wrote *Dave Barry Slept Here*. Military: David Farragut, admiral who captured New Orleans (Mobile Bay) for the Union forces in the Civil War. Movies and Television: David Niven, actor; David Letterman, TV talk-show host. Music: David Bowie, pop musician; Dave Brubeck, jazz pianist and composer. Sports: Dave Winfield, baseball player. Theater: David Mamet, Pulitzer Prize winner for the drama *Glengarry Glen Ross* (1984). Eng: *Dave, Davie, Davy*; Czech: *Davidek;* Pol: *Dawid;* Port: *Davi, Danya, Daveed, Dodya;* Yiddish: *Dawid, Dowid.*

DAVIN (DAH-vin) Old Scandinavian: "brilliant Finnish." Refers to the representation of high intelligence enjoyed by the Finnish people.

DAVU (DAH-vue) African: "the beginning."

DAWUD (dah-OOD) Hebrew: "much loved." A popular name in Arab countries.

DAYTON (DAY-ton) Old English: "bright town."

DEACON (DEE-ken) Greek, English: "one who serves." *Deke, Dekle, Dekel.*

DEAN (deen) Old English: "one from the valley." Also a name reflecting one's position in church or school administration. Movies and Television: Dean Jones, actor. *Deane, Dene.*

DEANDRE (dee-AHN-drey) United States. English: African-American blend of De and Andre. *D'Andre, Deondre, Diondre.*

DEANGELO (dee-AHN-jello) Italian: "Angelo's son." *D'Angelo, DiAngelo.*

DECHA (deh-CHAH) Thai: "strength."

DECLAN (DEK-lan) Irish: Name of Irish saint. *Deaglan.*

DEDRIK (DED-rik) German: "people's ruler." *Dedrick, Dedric.*

DEION (DEE-on) African-American: "God." Variant of Dion. Sports: Deion Sanders, football star.

DEJUAN (dee-HWAN) United States. English: African-American blend of De and Juan. *D'Juan, DaJuan, Dawon, Dewaun, Dewon, D'Won.*

DEKEL (DEH-kehl) Arabic: "swaying palms" or "date-bearing trees."

DEL (del) French: "of the." Used today as an independent name. Music: Del Shannon, singer, best known for "Runaway."

DELANEY (de-LANE-ee) Irish Gaelic: "born to a warrior." *Del, Delan, Delainey.*

DELANO (del-AHNO) Old French: "of the night."

DELFINO (del-FEE-noh) Latin: "dolphin."

DEMARCUS (dee-MAHR-cus) United States. English: African-American blend of De and Marcus. *Damarcus, Demarkis, Demarkus, D'Marcus.*

DEMETRIUS (dee-MEE-tree-us) Greek: "belonging to Demeter." Dance: Choreographer Demetrius A. Klein. Mythology: Demeter is corn and harvest goddess and represents fertility. Theater: Character in Shakespeare's play *A Midsummer Night's Dream*. Eng: *Demeter, Dimitry;* Bulg: *Dimitr;* Fr:*Demetre;* Gk: *Demetrios, Dimitrios, Dimos, Demetri, Dimetre, Mimis, Mitsos, Takis;* Hung: *Demeter, Domotor;* Ital: *Demetrio;* Pol: *Dymek, Dymitry, Dzeck;* Russ: *Dima, Dimitre, Dmitri, Dmitrik.*

DEMOTHI (deh-MO-tee) Native American: "walks and talks."

DEMPSEY (DEMP-see) Gaelic: "proud." Used in Ireland.

DENIZ (de-NIZ) Turkish: "flowing seas." Popular today in Turkey.

DENNIS (DEN-is) English: Variation of Dionysus. See Dionysus.

DENZEL (DEN-zel) English. Place name in Cornwall. Movies and Television: Denzel Washington, Academy Award-winning actor (*Training Day*). *Denzell, Denzil.*

DEONTAE (dee-ON-tay) United States. English: African-American creation, blend of Deon and Donte. *Donte, D'Ante, Deante, Deonte, Diante, Diontay, Dionte.*

DEREK (DEH-rehk) German: Variation of Theodoric. See Theodoric.

DERMOT (DER-mot) Celtic: "free of envy." *Dermott, Dermod.*

DERON (dee-RON) United States. English: African-American combination of De and Ron. *Daron, Daronn, Deronne.*

DERWIN (DUR-win) Old English: "much loved ally."

DEROR (deh-ROHR) Israel. Hebrew: "that which loves freedom." A name used in Israel. *Dare, Darrie, Derori.*

DERRY (dery) Celtic: "great lover."

DERVIN (der-VIN) English: "gifted friend." *Dervon.*

DESHAWN (dee-SHAWN) United States. English: African-American combination of De and Shawn. Especially popular in the United States. *DaShaun, Dashawn, DeSean, DeShaun, D'shawn.*

DESHI (d-UH-shee) Chinese: "virtuous man."

DESMOND (DEZ-mund) Irish Gaelic: "from South Munster," an old Irish kingdom. History:

Desmond Tutu, South African civil rights activist. *Desmund, Dezmond.*

DESTIN (DESS-tin or dess-TEEN) French: "fate." *Deston.*

DEVANTE (dev-AHN-tay) Spanish: "fighter of wrong."

DEVIN (DEH-vin) Latin, French: "heavenly." Also an English county. *Devinn, Devon, Devyn.*

DEVLIN (DEHV-lin) Irish Gaelic: "courageous" or "showing great valor." *Dev, Devland, Devlen, Devlyn.*

DEWEI (de-UH-weh) Chinese: "truthful."

DEWITT (DEH-wit) Welsh: "blond."

DEXTER (DEKS-ter) Latin: "dexterous" or "right side."

DIDIER (di-DYEH) French: "desired" or "beloved."

DIETER (DEE-ter) German: "the people's ruler."

DIMA (DEE-muh) Russian: "strong soldier." *Vladimir.*

DIN (din) Vietnamese: "calm."

DINO (DEE-noh) Italian: "little sword."

DINOS (DI-nos) Latin: "continuous support." Dinos is among the most popular names in Greece today. *Costa, Kastas, Gus, Konstandinos, Kostas, Kostis.*

DIONYSUS (DI-oh-NEE-sus) Latin mythology: Name for the god of wine, equivalent to the Roman god Bacchus. The popular name "Dennis" is an English variant. Dion is a short form. Education: Dionysus Thrax, second-century Greek who wrote the first Greek grammar book; Denis Diderot, eighteenth-century encyclopedist. History: The name of two tyrannical leaders of Syracuse, a city in the Roman empire (405–343 B.C.). General Dwight D. Eisenhower, thirty-fourth president of the United States (1953–61). Music: Dion, rock musician. Eng: *Den, Denis, Denney, Denny, Deon, Dion, Dwight;* Fr: *Denis, Denys, Dione;* Hung: *Denes, Dennes;* Ir: *Denis;* Ital: *Dionigi, Dionisio;* Russ: *Debnis, Denys, Denka, Denya;* Span: *Dionis, Dionisio, Nicho.*

DIRK (deerk or durk) Teutonic: "dagger." Used in Denmark.

DMITRI (DIM-ee-tree) Slavic: "lover of the earth."

DOBRY (DO-bree) Polish: "lovely" or "nice."

DOLAN (DOLE-an) Celtic: "dark haired."

DOMINICK (DAHM-ih-nik) Latin: "Sunday's child" or "in God's hands." History: Dominique Pire, cleric and humanitarian who won the Nobel Prize for Peace (1958) for postwar aid to displaced persons. Eng: *Dom, Domenic, Nick, Nickie, Nicky;* Czech:

Dominik, Domek, Dumin; Fr: *Dominique;* Hung: *Deco, Dome, Domo, Domokos, Domonkos;* Ital: *Domenico, Domingo, Menico;* Pol: *Dominik, Donek, Niki;* Port: *Domigos;* Span: *Chuma, Chumin, Chuminga, Dominco, Domingo, Mingo.*

DONALD (DOHN-ald) Scottish Gaelic: "leader among the world's peoples." Common as a clan name in Scotland for centuries. Business: Donald Trump, real estate developer. Movies and Television: Donald Sutherland, actor who starred in *Klute;* Donald O'Connor, actor and dancer. Eng: *Don, Donal, Donnie, Donny;* Fin: *Tauno;* Ital: *Donaldo;* Norw: *Donalt;* Span: *Pascul;* Ukrain: *Bogdan, Bohdan, Danya.*

DONATO (doh-NAH-toh) Spanish, Italian: "divine present." Arts: Donatello, fifteenth-century Florentine sculptor who created the renaissance style. Eng: *Donat, Donatus;* Fr: *Donatien;* Ital: *Donatello.*

DONNELLY (don-AL-ly) Celtic: "brave." *Donnell, Donel.*

DORIAN (DORR-ee-in) Greek: "from Doris" or "present." Doris is located in Greece. Literature: A character in Oscar Wilde's novel *The Picture of Dorian Gray. Dorion, Dorien, Dorean.*

DORON (DOH-one) Israel. Hebrew: "divine gift." Common in Israel and becoming popular in the United States. *Doren.*

DOUGALD (DOO-gald) Celtic: "mysterious stranger." Popular in Scotland. *Dougal.*

DOUGLAS (DUG-liss) Scottish: "flowing from the black river." History: Douglas Wilder became Virginia's first black governor (1989). Literature: Name of a powerful clan family in Scottish history, legend, song, and poetry. Military: General Douglas MacArthur led the Pacific forces in World War II. Music: Douglass Moore, composer who wrote the opera *The Devil and Daniel Webster*. Movies and Television: Douglas Fairbanks, actor. Science: Douglas Mawson, Australian who explored the Antarctic. Sports: Doug Weight, Olympic medalist in ice hockey (2002). *Doug, Douglass, Duglad.*

DOUR (dour) Scottish: "from the water."

DOV (duv) Israel. Yiddish: "bear." Popular name in Israel.

DOYLE (DOI-el) Irish Gaelic: "descendant of the dark foreigner."

DRAKE (drayk) Middle English: "owner of the Dragon Inn." Hundreds of years ago, the dragon was a common emblem of stores or lodges; the name refers to the proprietor of such businesses.

DUANE (D'WAYNE) English, Irish: "richly dark." Duante is a contemporary derivative. Music: Duane Allman, musician in The Allman Brothers and The Doobie Brothers. Sports: Duane Bickett and Duane Thomas, football players. *Dewain, Dewayne, Duwayne, Dwain, Dwayne.*

DUC (yuke) Vietnamese: "upright."

DUDLEY (DUD-lee) Old English: "man of the fields." Military: Dudley DeChair, British naval officer during World War I. Movies and Television: Dudley Moore, actor. *Dudly.*

DUGAN (DOO-gin) Irish Gaelic: "dark-colored." *Doogan, Dougan, Douggan, Duggan.*

DUKKER (DOOK-kuhr) English Gypsy: "to foresee the future" or "to entrance." *Duke.*

DUNCAN (DUNN-kin) Scottish Gaelic: "dark chieftain." Arts: Duncan Phyfe, nineteenth-century woodworker noted for excellent chairs, tables, and couches. *Dun, Dune, Dunn.*

DUNIXI (doo-NEE-shee) Greek: "god of wine." Used in the Basque regions of Spain and France.

DURAND (DUR-and) Latin: "enduring." *Duran.*

DURGA (der-GAH) Hindu: "unreachable."

DURRIKEN (DOO-ree-ken) English Gypsy: "soothsayer" or "prophet."

DURRILL (DOO-reel) English Gypsy: "the gooseberry." *Dur, Durril.*

DUSTIN (DUSS-tin) Old English: "valiant fighter." Movies and Television: Dustin Hoffman, actor.

DWIGHT See Dionysus.

DYAMI (dee-AH-mee) Native American: "soaring eagle."

DYLAN (DILL-in) Welsh: "with great influence." Literature: Dylan Thomas, poet. *Dilan, Dillie.*

DYRE (DEE-reh) Norse: "priceless one" or "dear heart." Beloved name in Norway.

EADIG (EE-dig) Anglo-Saxon: "blessed."

EAGAN (EE-gin) Irish: "extremely mighty." *Egan, Egon.*

EAGON (EE-gone) Irish: "fiery."

EALLARD (EEL-lard) English: "brave." *Ealhhard.*

EAMON (EH-mon) Anglo-Saxon: "affluent protector." Used in Ireland.

EARL (url) English: "nobleman." Name commemorates the aristocracy. History: Earl Warren, former chief justice of the U.S. Supreme Court. Literature: Erie Stanley Gardner, mystery writer who created the character Perry Mason. Music: Earl Scruggs, bluegrass musician; Earl Powell, bebop jazz pioneer. Sports: Earl ("the Pearl") Monroe, basketball star. Early Wyn, baseball pitcher. *Earle, Earlie, Early, Erl, Erie, Errol, Erryl.*

EARVIN (EER-vin) English: "friend." Variant of Irving.

EATON (EE-tin) Old English: "village beside the riverbanks." Place name. *Eatton, Eton, Eyton.*

EBAN (ee-BAHN) Hebrew: "stone."

EBENEZER (EBB-eh-NEE-zur) Hebrew: "rock of salvation." Bible: In the Old Testament, it is the name of the statue Samuel erected to commemorate his defeat of the Philistines. Literature: Ebenezer Scrooge, character in Charles Dickens's *A Christmas Carol. Eb, Ebbaneza, Ebeneezer, Ebeneser, Ebenezar, Eveneser.*

EBERHARD (EBB-er-hard) Old German: "boar's brunt." A more popular variation is Everett. *Eberhardt, Everard, Everhardt, Evrard.*

EDEN (EE-din) Hebrew: "glorious paradise." Bible: Name of the garden where Adam and Eve first lived. *Eaden, Eadin, Edin, Edyn.*

EDER (EE-der) Hebrew: "flock." Bible: The biblical tower of Eder was a watchtower where shepherds watched their flock. Over time, Eder symbolized God's watchfulness over His people.

EDGAR (ED-ger) Old English: "prosperous swordsman." An old English royal name. Arts: Edgar Degas, French painter. Journalism: Edgar

Snow, reporter who wrote extensively on China. Literature: Edgar Cayce, author and psychic; Edgar Allan Poe, who wrote the famous poem "The Raven"; in Shakespeare's *King Lear* there is a character called Edgar. Eng: *Ed, Eddie, Ned, Neddy, Ted, Teddy;* Czech: *Edko, Edus;* Ir: *Edgard;* Ital: *Edgardo;* Latin: *Edgars;* Pol: *Edek, Garek.*

EDISON (ED-i-son) Old English: "son of Edward."

EDMUND (ED-muhnd) Old English: "rich defender." Literature: Edmund Spenser, poet; Edmondo De Amicis, a nineteenth-century writer known for children's stories. Science: Edmond H. Fischer, Nobel Prize winner in Medicine (1992). Eng: *Ed, Eddie, Eddy, Edmon, Ned, Neddy, Ted, Teddy;* Fr: *Esmond;* Hung: *Odi, Odon;* Ir: *Eamon;* Ital: *Edmondo;* Latin: *Edmunds;* Pol: *Mundek;* Russ: *Edmon, Edmond;* Span: *Edmundo, Mundo.*

EDRIC (ed-RIK) English: "prosperous ruler." *Eddric, Eddrik.*

EDSEL (ED-sell) German: "noble" or "bright."

EDWARD (eh-DWARD) Old English: "prosperous protector." Favorite name of British royalty. Arts: Edward Steichen, photographer; Edouard Manet, French painter who mixed realism and impressionism. Journalism: Edward R. Murrow, TV journalist. History: Edward, Duke of Windsor. Literature: Edward Gibbon, author of *The Decline and Fall of the Roman Empire*; Edward Lear, poet who wrote "The Owl and the Pussycat." Movies and Television: Edward G. Robinson, actor. Eng: *Ed, Eddie, Ned, Ted, Teddy;* Czech: *Edko, Edus, Edo, Edvard;* Fr: *Edouard;* Hawaiian: *Ekewaka;* Ital: *Edoardo, Eduards;* Pol: *Edek, Edzio;* Port: *Eduardo, Duarte;* Rum: *Edgard;* Scot: *Eidard;* Span: *Eduardo.*

EDWIN (ED-win) Old English: "brimming with friends." Aeronautics: Edwin "Buzz" Aldrin, astronaut who became the second man on the moon (July 21, 1969). History: Edwin Meese III, former U.S. attorney general. Literature: Edwin Arlington Robinson, poet and three-time winner of the Pulitzer Prize for poetry. *Edwyn.*

EFRAT (EEF-raht) Hebrew: "honored" or "distinguished."

EGBERT (EGG-burt) German: "sword," "shiny," or "famous."

EGON (EE-gun) English: "powerful." *Egan.*

EHREN (EH-wren) German: "honorable."

EIMAR (EE-mar) Irish: "swift."

EINAR (EYE-ner) Scandinavian: "leading warrior." Widely chosen name in Iceland and Norway. Eng: *Inar;* Dan: *Ejnar.*

EINHARD (EYEN-ard) German: "strong with a sword."

EISIG (eey-SIG) Hebrew: "he who laughs."

ELAN (eh-LAHN) Israel. Hebrew: "tree." A popular name in Israel.

ELDEN (el-DEN) Old English: "older."

ELDRIDGE (ELD-ridge) German: "wise ruler." History: Eldridge Cleaver, civil rights activist.

ELEAZAR (el-ee-AY-zer) Hebrew: "God has aided us." Bible: Eleazar was Aaron's son. Span: *Eliezer, Eliazar, Elazaro, Eli, Elie, Eliezer, Elazar, Ety.*

ELEK (ell-EK) Hungarian: "helper and defender of mankind."

ELGAN (ELL-gan) Welsh: "bright circle."

ELI (EE-lye or ay-LEE) Hebrew: "He who is on high." Bible: Eli was the high priest who trained the prophet Samuel. History: Eloy Alfaro, former president of Ecuador. Science: Eli Whitney, inventor of the cotton gin (1793). *Eloy, Ely, Eloi, Elie.*

ELIJAH (ee-LYE-ja) Hebrew: "Jehovah is my God." Bible: Elijah was a powerful Old Testament prophet. Education: Elijah Levita, sixteenth-century Italian Jewish scholar who wrote on Hebrew grammar and the Torah. History: Elijah Muhammad, black nationalist leader; Elijah White, physician and pioneer who led over one hundred immigrants to Oregon (1842). Literature: Elie Wiesel, writer. Movies and Television: Elliott Gould, actor. Eng: *Elliot, Eliot, Eliott, Ellison, Elliston, Ellis, Elias, Elis;* Czech: *Elias, Elya, Ilja;* Fr: *Elie, Elihu;* Ger/Span/Hung: *Elias;* Pol: *Elek, Eliasz;*

Swed: *Elihu;* Yiddish: *Eli, Elias, Elija, Elihu;* Zuni: *Elia.*

ELISHA (eh-LEE-shah) Israel. Hebrew: "God is my salvation." A popular name in Israel. *Eli, Elisee, Elisio, Elisher, Lisha.*

ELIYAHU (eh-lee-YA-hoo) Israel. Hebrew: "the Lord is my God."

ELKI (EL-kee) Native American. Miwok: Derived from the word *elkini,* meaning "bear displays."

ELLERY (EL-luhr-ee) Middle English: "elder of the isle." Place name. Literature: Ellery Queen, the pen name of a team of detective writers who wrote over forty novels. *Ellary, Ellerey.*

ELMER (EL-mur) Old English: "aristocratic and famous." Literature: *Elmer Gantry,* the popular novel by Sinclair Lewis that was later made into a movie. Theater: Elmer Rice, playwright and author who won the Pulitzer Prize for *Street Scene* (1929). *Aylmar, Aylmer, Aymer, Ellmer, Elmir, Elmo, El-more.*

ELOY (eh-LOY) Spain. Old German: "famous fighter."

ELRAD (AHL-rad) Israel. Hebrew: "God's sovereign reign." A name used in Israel.

ELROY (el-ROY) French: "the king." *Elrod, El-rick, Elric.*

ELSU (EHL-soo) Native American. Miwok: "falcon swoops low and rises high."

ELTON (ELL-tun) Old English: "of the ancient village." Place name. Music: Elton John, singer and musician. *Elston, Elson, Elon, Elden, Elder.*

ELVIS (EHL-vis) Scandinavian: "knowing all." Music: Elvis Presley, Elvis Costello, singers.

EMERY (EH-mur-ee) Old German: "industrious leader." Eng: *Emerson, Emmery, Emory;* Czech: *Imrich;* Hung: *Imrus;* Ger: *Emery, Amery, Emmerich, Emory, Emmo.*

EMIL (AY-meel or ay-MEEL) Latin: "seeking to please." Education: Emile Durkheim (1858–1917), considered the founder of modern sociology. Literature: Emile Zola, French novelist who wrote *The Dram Shop.* Movies and Television: Emilio Estevez, actor. Ital: *Emiliano;* Fr: *Emil, Emile;* Span: *Emilio;* Welsh: *Emlyn, Aymul, Emelen, Emilianm, Emilion, Emilyan, Emlin.*

EMIR (EE-meer) Arabic: "charming prince."

EMMANUEL (ee-MAN-yoo-ul) Hebrew: "God is with us." Bible: The name given to a son who will be born of a young woman as a sign to King Ahaz in a time of national crisis in Judea (Isaiah 7:14), and quoted in the Gospel of Matthew about Jesus. Music: Emmanuel Ax, pianist. Philosophy: Immanuel Kant (1724–1804), author of *Critique of Pure Reason.* Czech: *Eman;* Hebrew: *Emmanuil;*

Span: *Emanuel, Maolo, Mano, Manuel, Manolito;* Yiddish: *Immanuel, Manny.*

EMMET (EM-it) Old German: "mighty." Emmitt Smith, star football running back.

EMRICK (em-RIK) Welsh: "immortal."

ENGELBERT (EN-gul-burt) Old German: "angelic light." Music: Engelbert Humperdinck, singer. *Bert, Bertie, Berty, Englebert, Ingelbert, Inglebert.*

ENOCH (EE-nok) Hebrew: "devoted" or "scholarly." Bible: Enoch was the father of Methuselah and the model of righteousness.

ENRICO (en-REE-ko) Italian: "ruler of the house." Music: Enrique Iglesias, popular Latino singer. *Enrique, Enzo.*

ENYETO (en-YEH-to) Native American: "how the bear walks."

EOGHAN (YO-wun) Greek: "of noble birth." Used in Ireland.

EOGHAN (oh-GAHN) Irish: "generous gift of the Lord." *Eoin.*

EPHRAIM (EFF-ram) Hebrew: "very bountiful." Bible: Ephraim was a son of Joseph. Music: Efrem Zimbalist, violinist. Span: *Efrain, Ephrain, Efren, Efrem.*

ERASMUS (e-RAS-mus) Greek: "beloved" or "lovable." Saint Erasmus (fourth century), also known as Elmo, is the patron saint of sailors. Education: Desiderius Erasmus, assumed name of the Dutch, humanist philosopher Gerhard Gerhards (1466–1535). Science: Erasmus Reinhold, sixteenth-century German astronomer second only to Copernicus in importance. *Erasme, Erasmo, Ras.*

ERIK (AYRE-ick) Old Morse: "potent forever" or "external strength." Ericson, child of the Viking leader Eric the Red, may have beaten Columbus to North America by five hundred years. Journalism: Eric Severeid, TV newscaster. Literature: Eric Ambler, suspense writer; Erich Segal, novelist who wrote *Love Story.* Music: Eric Clapton, rock musician known for "Layla"; Erich Leinsdorf, conductor. Sports: Eric Dickerson, football player; Eric Heiden, speed skater who won five Olympic medals (1980); Eric Bedard, Canadian Olympic gold medalist (2002). Eng: *Erek, Eric, Erick, Ric, Ricki, Ricky;* Czech/Ger: *Erich;* Ital/Port: *Erico;* Fr: *Eriq;* Latin: *Eriks;* Scan: *Erickson, Ericksen, Ericson, Erikson.*

ERNEST (UR-nest) Germanic: "vigor" or "intent." Literature: Ernest Hemingway, author and winner of the Pulitzer Prize in 1953 for his story *The Old Man and the Sea.* Movies and Television: Ernest Borgnine, actor and Oscar winner for his role in *Marty* (1955). Science: Ernest Rutherford, British physicist who discovered atomic nuclei and won the Nobel Prize for chemistry (1908). Theater: Lead character in Oscar Wilde's play *The Importance of Being Earnest.* Eng: *Ernie, Ernst, Earnest;* Span: *Ernesto.*

ERON (EEH-ron) Hebrew: "peace" or "enlightened."

ERROL (eh-ROLL) English: "to wander."

ESMOND (ESS-mond) Old English: "protective grace."

ETHAN (EE-than) Hebrew: "powerful" or "unswavering." Bible: Ethan, a sagacious Israelite. History: Ethan Allen was a soldier during the American Revolution. *Etan.*

ETU (AY-too) Native American: "glowing sun." Astrology: Appropriate for those born under Leo, which is ruled by the sun.

EUCLID (YOO-klid) Greek: "son of glory." Science: Euclid was a Greek pioneer in geometry circa 300 B.C.

EUDOR (YOO-dor) Greek: "good gift."

EUGEN (YOO-gen) Greek: "noble." A name used in Sweden.

EUGENE (YOO-geen) English, Greek: "highborn." Aeronautics: Eugene Cernan, astronaut. Arts: Eugene Delacroix, nineteenth-century French painter. Dance: Gene Kelly, choreographer and dancer. Education: Eugenio de Ochoa, nineteenth-century scholar who translated the complete works of Virgil. Literature: Eugenio Montale, Italian poet who won the Nobel Prize for Literature (1975). Music: Eugene Ormandy, Hungarian violinist and conductor. Theater: Eugene O'Neill, playwright who wrote *Desire Under the Elms* and *A Long Day's Journey into Night.* Eng: *Gene;* Czech: *Eugen, Zenda;*

Ger: *Eugen, Eugenius, Eugenios, Evgenios;* Gk: *Evgenios;* Hung: *Jano, Jenci, Jensi, Jenoe;* Pol: *Genek, Genio;* Russ: *Eugeni, Genka, Genya, Yevgeniy, Zheka, Zhenka;* Span: *Eugenio, Gencho;* Swed: *Egen.*

EUSTACE (YOOS-tiss) Greek: "bountiful." Name was brought to Great Britain with the Norman invasion. Stacy is a popular short form. Movies and Television: Stacy Keach, actor. *Stacy, Stacey, Eustache, Eustachius, Eustasius, Eustazio, Eustis.*

EVAN (EV-ehn) Welsh: "God's favor." See John.

EVANDER (eev-AND-er) Greek: "benevolent ruler."

EVERARD (EV-er-ard) Old English: "courageous." Norman name more common as a surname. Everett is derived from the name. Eng: *Everet, Everton, Everett, Everitt;* Ger: *Eberhard, Everhart, Evrad.*

EVERETT (EV-er-ett) English: Variation of Everard. See Everard.

EVERLY (EVER-lee) English: "grazing meadow." *Everley.*

EWAN (YOU-wan) Gaelic: "well born." Movies and Television: Ewan McGregor, actor (*Big Fish*).

EZEKIEL (ee-ZEEK-yel) Hebrew: "God fortifies." Bible: While held captive in Babylon, Ezekiel became a prolific writer. His work is contained in the Old Testament's Book of Ezekiel. Span: *Ezequiel, Esquiel, Zeke, Ezechiel, Eziequel.*

EZER (EH-zehr) Israel. Hebrew: "assistance." Popular name in Israel. *Azrikam, Azur, Ezri, Azariah, Ezra.*

EZHNO (EHZH-no) Native American: "by oneself."

EZRA (EZ-ra) Hebrew: "aid." Bible: The Book of Ezra was written by the same man who wrote I and II Chronicles. Business: Ezra Cornell, headed Western Union and established Cornell University. Literature: Ezra Pound, poet who wrote "Cantos." Fr/Span: *Esdras;* Ger: *Esra;* Hawaiian: *Ezera.*

FABIAN (FAY-bee-in) Latin: "one who sows beans." Music: Fabian Forte, pop singer known by his first name only. Sports: Fabio Carta, Italian Olympic medalist (2002). Eng: *Fabyan;* Fr: *Fabien, Fabert;* Ital: *Fabio, Fabiano;* Latin: *Fabius;* Pol: *Fabek;* Russ: *Fabi, Fabiyan.*

FABRIZIO (fah-BREET-see-o) Latin: "one with skillful hands." Fr: *Fabrice.*

FADEY (fah-DAY) Russian: "bold." *Faddei, Fadeyka, Fadeyushka.*

FADIL (FAH-dehl) Arabic: "generous."

FAEGAN (FAYE-gan) English: "joyful." *Fain, Fane.*

FAI (faye) Chinese: "brilliant light."

FAIRFAX (FARE-faks) Old English: "blond-haired." Name of a city in Virginia.

FARID (fah-REED) Arabic: "the only one." Popular name in Arab countries.

FARIS (FAH-rees) Arabic: "horseman" or "knight." Commonly used in Arab countries.

FARLEY (FAR-lee) Old English: "sheep's meadow." Movies and Television: Farley Granger, actor in *Strangers on a Train*. **Fairley, Fairlee, Fairleigh, Fairlie, Farlee, Farleigh, Farlie, Farly, Lee, Leigh.**

FAROLD (FAR-old) English: "powerful traveler."

FARRELL (FARE-el) Irish Gaelic: "of proven courage." **Farall, Farel, Farrel.**

FARUQ (fah-ROOK) Arabic: "he, who knows truth." Popular name in Arab countries.

FATHI (FAH-thee) Arabic: "victory."

FAUSTUS (FAHW-stus) Greek: "lucky." Theater: *Doctor Faustus*, a famous play written by Christopher Marlowe in which the main character, Faustus, a brilliant German scholar, makes a deal to forfeit his soul for supernatural powers. **Fausto.**

FAVIAN (FAV-ean) Latin: "brave man."

FEIVEL (FYE-full) Israel. Yiddish: "God assists."

FELICIANO (fell-EE-see-ahn-oh) Spanish: "happy."

FELIX (FEE-licks) Latin: "merry." History: Felix Frankfurter, former U.S. Supreme Court Justice. Sports: Felix Jose, baseball player; Felix Gottwald, Austrian Olympic medalist (2002). Bulg/Russ: *Feliks;* Czech: *Fela;* Fr: *Felix;* Hung: *Bodog;* Span: *Felo, Pitin, Pito.*

FEORAS (FEE-uh-rus) Greek: "smooth rock." Used in Ireland. *Pierce.*

FERDINAND (FUR-dih-nahnd or FUR-dih-nand) Germanic: "courageous traveler or explorer." The name was imported by the Goths into Spain and became popular there as Fernando and Hernando. Education: Ferdinand de Saussure (1857–1913) was a founder of modern linguistics. History: Ferdinand Magellan discovered the straits that are named after him. It was under the auspices of King Ferdinand and Queen Isabella of Spain that Columbus set sail for the New World; Hernando Cortez conquered Mexico; Ferdinand Marcos, former Philippines president. Literature: Ferdinand was the lover of Miranda in Shakespeare's *The Tempest.* Sports: Fernando Valenzuela, baseball player. Span: *Fernando, Hernando, Ferdinando;* Fr: *Fernand;* Ger: *Ferde, Ferdie, Ferdand.*

FERGUS (fer-GUS) Celtic: "of manly strength." *Fergal.*

FEROZ (FEE-roos) Persian: "lucky." Used in Iran.

FERRIS (FERR-is) Celtic: "rock." Latin: "iron."

FIACHRA (FEE-uh-khruh) Irish: The name of an Irish saint popular today in Ireland. *Feary.*

FICO (fee-KOH) Italian: "fig."

FIDEL (fee-DELL) Latin: "faithful" or "devoted." History: Fidel Castro, Cuban dictator. *Fidal, Fidello, Fidele.*

FILBERT (FILL-burt) English: "brilliant." *Filbuk.*

FILMER (FILL-mer) English: "famous." *Filmarr, Filmore.*

FINN (finn) Irish Gaelic: "fair." Business: Finn E. Kydland, Norweigian Nobel Prize winner in Economics (2004). History: Finn MacCumhail, early Irish hero. Literature: *Finnegan's Wake,* the title of a novel by James Joyce. *Finnegan, Finian.*

FINLEY (FIN-lee) Irish Gaelic: "golden ray of sun" or "fair-haired warrior." *Fin, Findlay, Finn.*

FIONAN (FIN-ee-ahn) Irish: "fair." *Finnian, Fionn.*

FIORELLO (fee-oh-REL-loh) Italian: "little flower."

FIRTH (ferth) Scottish: "arm of the sea."

FISK (fisk) Middle English, "fish" or "sea creature." Astrology: Appropriate for those born under Pisces, symbolized by the fish. *Fiske.*

FITZ (fits) Latin: "son."

FLANNERY (FLAN-ery) Old English: "sheet of metal" or "flat land."

FLETCHER (FLET-chur) Middle English: "he that feathers well." Refers to the important medieval skill of feathering one's arrows. Astrology: Sagittarius is symbolized by the archer. History, Literature: Fletcher Christian led a mutiny against Captain William Bligh on the *H.M.S. Bounty* in 1789. This incident became the basis for the historical novel *Mutiny on the Bounty*. Music: Fletcher Henderson, pianist and jazz band leader. *Flecher, Fletch.*

FLINT (flint) Old English: "brook" or "firm as flint." Flint is a hard quartz that produces a spark of fire when struck by steel.

FLORIAN (FLOOR-ee-in) Latin: "blossoming." Most common in Middle European countries. Education: Florian de O'Campo was a sixteenth-century historian to Charles V.

FLOYD (floyd) Old English: "the hollow."

FLYNN (flin) Irish Gaelic: "male heir to the auburn father." *Flin, Flinn, Flyn.*

FOLUKE (fo-LOO-keh) Nigeria. Yoruba: "given to God."

FONTAINE (FOHN-tane) French: "fountain." *Fontane, Fontayne, Fonteyne.*

FORBES (forbes) Scottish: "headstrong."

FORREST (FORE-est) English: "woodland." *Forest, Forrester.*

FORTUNE (for-too-NEH) French: "given to luck."

FRANCIS (FRAN-sis) Latin: "free man" or "Frenchman." Originally, a nickname referring to a person of French descent or proficient in speaking French. Saint Francis of Assisi was the founder of the Franciscan Order and is the patron saint of animals. Aeronautics: Frank Borman, astronaut. Arts: Frank Lloyd Wright, architect known for his "Prairie Style." Business: Frank Woolworth, who opened the first five-cent store. History: Francis Drake, British explorer first to circumnavigate the globe (1577–80). Literature: Francis Bacon, essayist (1596–1626); Franz Kafka, Austrian writer. Movies and Television: Francis Ford Coppola, Francois Truffaut, film directors. Music: Francis Scott Key, composer of the "Star Spangled Banner." Frank Sinatra, singer; Frank Zappa, rock musician; Franz Josef Haydn, Franz Shubert, Franz Liszt, classical composers. Philosophy: Franz Rosenzweig, German-Jewish existentialist. Sports: Franco Harris, football player. Eng: *Fran, Frank, Frankie, Franky, Frani;* Bulg: *Franc;* Dutch: *Frants;* Fin: *Frans;* Fr: *Francois, Franchot, Franc;* Ger: *Franz, Franzl;* Hawaiian: *Plani;* Ital: *Francesco, Franco;* Pol: *Franio, Franus, Franek;* Span: *Farruco, Francisco, Franco, Fracuelo;* Swed/Norw: *Frans, Franzen.*

FRANKLIN (FRANK-lin) Germanic: "free-man." In the fourteenth and fifteenth centuries the title "Franklin" designated a landowner of free but not noble birth. History: Two U.S. presidents have borne this name: fourteenth president Franklin Pierce and thirty-first president Franklin Delano Roosevelt. Literature: Franklin Pierce Adams, famous columnist and humorous poet.

FRASER (FRAY-ser) Old English: "strawberry." *Fraiser, Frazer, Fraizer.*

FREDERICK (FRED-rik) Old German: "one who leads peacefully." Name brought to Britain by the Hanoverian kings. It became very popular and has remained so for over two hundred years. Aeronautics: Fred Noonan, navigator on the first San Francisco-Honolulu flight (1935). Arts: Frederick Remington, painter of scenes of the Old West. History: Frederik Willem de Klerk, Nobel Peace Prize winner for his work in ending apartheid in South Africa (1993); Frederick II of Prussia (1712–86), known as Frederick the Great; Frederick Douglass, African-American abolitionist speaker and writer. Movies and Television: Fred Savage, Fred MacMurray, actors. Music: Frederic Chopin, composer. Philosophy: Friedrich Nietzsche, German philosopher. Eng: *Fred, Freddie, Freddy, Rick, Rickie, Ricky;* Czech: *Bedrich, Fridrich;* Ger: *Friedel, Friedrich, Fredi, Fritz;* Hung: *Fredek;* Ital: *Federico, Federigo;* Norw: *Fredrik, Fredek;* Pol: *Fredek;* Russ: *Fridrich;* Span: *Federico, Federoquito, Fico, Lico;* Swed: *Frederik, Fritz.*

FREMONT (FREE-mont) Old German: "guardian of freedom."

FULLER (FULL-ur) English: "one who shrinks and thickens cloth."

GABRIEL (GAY-bree-el) Hebrew: "power in God." Bible: An archangel and messenger of God whose trumpet will announce Judgment Day, in Christian theology. History: Gabriel Prosser, American slave who planned a rebellion to form a black state in 1800. Literature: Gabriel Garcia Marquez, novelist. Science: Gabriel Fahrenheit, German physicist who introduced the Fahrenheit scale for thermometers. Eng: *Gabe, Gabie, Gabby;* Bulg: *Gavril;* Czech: *Gabko, Gabris;* Hung: *Gabi,* **Gabor;** Hebrew: *Gavi, Gavriel;* Ital: *Gabrielli, Gabriello;* Span: *Riel*

GADI (GAH-dee) Arabic: "my fortune." Popular in Israel.

GADIEL (GAH-dee-el) Arabic: "God is my wealth."

GAGE (gayj) Old Norman French: "a token of defiance." Arts: Gage White, photographer. *Gaige.*

GALEN (GAY-len) Greek: "calm." Arts: Galen Rowell, photographer. Science: Galen, a second-century physician who founded experimental physiology. Eng: *Gale, Gayle;* Span: *Galeno.*

GALENO (gah-LEH-no) Spanish: "illuminated child."

GALIP (GAL-ip) Turkish: "winner."

GALVIN (gal-VIN) Irish: "sparrow."

GAMALIEL (ga-MAY-lee-el) Hebrew: "the Lord's prize."

GANIT (gahn-IT) Hebrew: "defender."

GANNON (GAHN-on) Irish: "fair complexion."

GAO (gow) Chinese: "tall" or "high." Literature: Gao Xingjian, Nobel Prize winner in Literature (2000).

GARAN (gar-AHN) French: "guardian." *Garen, Garin, Garion.*

GARETH (GAHR-eth) Welsh: "gentle." Norse: "enclosure." French: "watchful."

GARRET (GAH-reht) English: Variation of Gerald. See Gerald.

GARRICK (GA-rik) English: "leads by the spear." Journalism: Garrick Utley, TV newscaster. *Garrik.*

GARRIDAN (GAH-rih-duhn) English Gypsy: "you hid."

GARTH (garth) Old Norse: "defended homestead" or "protected gardens." Arts: Garth Williams, illustrator. Music: Garth Brooks, country and western singer. *Garrett.*

GARY (GAR-ee) Germanic: "spear carrier." The name is sometimes used as a short form of Gerald, or to Americanize names like Garibaldi. Arts: Garry Trudeau, cartoonist who created "Doonesbury." Movies and Television: Gary Cooper, actor. *Gari, Garey, Garrie, Garry.*

GAUTE (GAU-teh) Norwegian: "great man."

GAUTIER (GOH-tyeh) Teutonic: "mighty leader." *Gauthier.*

GAVIN (GAV-in) Old Welsh: "white hawk." One of King Arthur's knights. Literature: Gavin Maxwell, British novelist. *Gav, Gavan, Gaven, Gawain, Gawen.*

GAVRIL (gav-REEL) Russian: "believer in God." *Ganya, Gav, Gavrel.*

GEDALYA (geh-DAHL-yah) Israel. Hebrew: "God's great creation." Popular in Israel. *Gedaliah, Gedalyahu.*

GELLERT (GELL-ert) Hungarian: "powerful soldier."

GENE (jean) English: "born to nobility."

GEOFFREY (JEFF-ree) Germanic: "God's peace." History: Jefferson Davis, president of the Confederate States of America. Literature: Geoffrey Chaucer, author of *The Canterbury Tales.* Eng: *Geoffery, Geoffey, Jeffrey, Jeffree, Jefferson, Jeff;* Fr: *Geffroi, Geffroy, Jeffroi;* Ger: *Gottfried;* Hung: *Gottfrid;* Ital: *Geoffredo, Giotto;* Latin: *Gotfrids;* Pol: *Fotfryd, Fred;* Rum: *Geofri, Godoired;* Russ: *Gottfrid;* Serb: *Bogomir;* Span: *Godofredo, Godfredo.*

GEORGE (jorj) Greek: "farmhand" or "farmer." Saint George, patron saint of England, supposedly conquered a fire-breathing dragon. A name of kings. Dance: George Balanchine, choreographer. History: George Washington, first president of the United States (1789–97); George Bush, forty-first president (1989–93). Literature: George Orwell, author of *Animal Farm.* Military: General George Custer, U.S. general. Music: George Frederick Handel, George Gershwin, composers. Science: George Washington Carver, known for his research on the uses of peanuts; Georges J.F. Köhler, German Nobel Prize winner in Medicine (1984). Sports: George Herman (Babe) Ruth. Theater: George Bernard Shaw, playwright and critic. Arab: *Gevorak;* Den: *Georg, Joren;* Eng: *Georgie;* Bulg: *Georg, Georgi;* Czech: *Durko, Juraz, Jiri, Jurko, Jurik;* Fr: *Georges;* Ger: *Jeorg, Juergen, Jurgen;* Gk: *Georgios, Giorgis, Giorgos;* Lith: *Jurgis;* Pol: *Jurek;* Russ: *Egor, Georgii, Yegor, Yura, Yurchik, Yurik, Yusha, Zhorka;* Span: *Jorge, Yoyi;* Swed/Norw: *Georg, Goran, Jorgen.*

GERALD (JAYR-ild) Old German: "he who rules by the sword." History: Gerald Ford, thirty-eighth president of the United States (1974–77). Literature: Gerald Manley Hopkins, poet. Movies and Television: Geraldo Rivera, TV talk-show host; Gerald Depardieu, Jerry Van Dyke, actors. Science: Gerardus't Hooft, Nobel Prize winner in Physics (1999). Eng: *Gerhard, Gerrard, Gerry, Jerry, Garret;* Fr: *Geralde, Geraud, Giraud, Girauld;* Hung: *Gellart, Gellert;* Ital: *Geraldo, Giraldo;* Pol: *Gerek;* Russ: *Gerald, Garold, Garolds, Kharald;* Span: *Geraldo, Gerando.*

GERIK (GEHR-ik) Polish: "swords and riches." *Edek.*

GERMAIN (jer-MAYN) French: "a German." Arts: Germain Pilon, leading French Renaissance sculptor. Music: Jermaine Jackson, pop singer. *Germaine, Jermain, Jermaine, Jermayne.*

GERSHOM (GEHR-shumm) Yiddish: "a stranger there." Popular in Israel.

GIBOR (gee-BORH) Israel. Hebrew: "powerful." Common in Israel.

GIDEON (GIDD-ee-un) Hebrew: "mighty battler." Bulg/Fr: *Gedeon;* Ital: *Gideone;* Russ: *Hedeon.*

GIFFORD (GIF-ford) French: "chubby cheeks."

GIL (geel) Israel. Hebrew: "joy." Beloved name in Israel.

GILAD (GILL-ad) Arabic: "hump of a camel." Israeli favorite. *Giladi, Gilead.*

GILBERT (GILL-burt) English, Old German: "bright oath." Science: Gilbert Lewis, chemist who developed theories on names of atomic bonds. Sports: Gil Hodges, baseball player. *Gil, Gilberto.*

GILCHRIST (GIL-kreest) Irish: "Christ's servant." *Gil, Gilley.*

GILES (jilz or gylz) Greek: "baby goat." Saint Giles was the patron saint of beggars. Military: Giles Smith, Civil War general who fought with General Sherman through the Carolinas. Fr: *Giles;* Ger: *Egidius;* Span: *Gil.*

GINO (JEE-noh) Italian: "born noble."

GIOVANNI (jee-OH-vanni) Italian: "God is gracious."

GITANO (hee-TAHN-oh) Spanish: "gypsy."

GIVON (GIH-von) Arabic: "hill" or "heights."

GLEN (glen) Celtic: "from the valley." *Glenn, Glyn, Glynn.*

GODDARD (god-ARD) German: "hard spear."

GOFRAIDH (GO-free-y) Irish: "God's peace." *Godfrey, Gorry.*

GOMER (GOH-mer) English: "good fight."

GORDON (GOR-din) Anglo-Saxon. English: "round hill." Place name. Music: Gordon Lightfoot, singer. Scot: *Gordie, Gordy.*

GOZAL (go-SAHL) Israel. Hebrew: "bird" or "soaring." Popular in Israel.

GRAHAM (GRAY-um) Old English: "one who lives where the earth is gray." Graham crackers were named after an American, Dr. Sylvester Graham (1794–1851). Education: Graham Kerr, chef called "The Galloping Gourmet." Literature: Graham Greene, British novelist who wrote *The Power and the Glory. Graeme, Graeham, Gram, Grahame.*

GRANT (grant) French. Variation of the French word *grand,* meaning "great." Arts: Grant Wood, famous for his painting *American Gothic. Grantland.*

GRANVILLE (GRAN-vill) Old French: "large village." *Granvil, Granvile, Granvill, Grenville.*

GRAYSON (GRAY-sun) Middle English: "having grey hair." *Greyson, Gray, Grey, Graysen.*

GREGORY (GREG-a-ree) Greek: "keeping watch." Sixteen popes have had this name. Gregorian calendar was created by Pope Gregory the Great in 1582. Movies and Television: Gregory Peck, Gregory Hines, actors. Sports: Greg Louganis, Olympic gold medalist diver. Eng: *Greg, Gregg, Greig, Greggory;* Bulg: *Grigoi, Grigorou;* Du: *Gregoor;* Ital/Span: *Gregorio;* Gk: *Gregorios, Grigorios;* Latin: *Gregors;* Russ: *Grigori, Grigor, Grisha;* Swed: *Gries.*

GRIFFIN (GRIFF-in) Welsh: "fierce." Mythology: A legendary creature that was half lion and half eagle. *Griffen, Griffith, Griff.*

GROVER (GROH-vur) English: "grove dweller" or "gardener." History: Grover Cleveland, twenty-second and twenty-fourth president of the United States (1885–89, 1893–97). Sports: Grover Alexander, Hall of Fame baseball player who pitched sixteen shutouts in 1916.

GUADALUPE (gwah-da-LOO-pay) Spanish: "valley of the wolf." Used in Spanish-speaking countries. History: Guadalupe Victoria, first president of the Mexican republic (1824–1829).

GUANG (GWANG) Chinese: "light."

GUILLAUME (gee-YOM) Teutonic: "resolute soldier." French form of William. Common in France.

GUNNAR (gun-NER) Teutonic: "bold warrior."

GUNTHER (GUN-ther) English. Old Norse: "brave soldier." Literature: Günter Grass, German Nobel Prize winner in Literature (1999). Science: Günter Blobel, American Nobel Prize winner in Medicine (1999). Eng: *Gun, Guntar;* Fr: *Gunter;* Ger: *Gunter, Guenter;* Ital: *Guntero;* Norw: *Gunnar.*

GUR (goor) Israel. Hebrew: "baby lion." Many variations are common. *Guri, Guriel, Gurion.*

GUSTAF (goo-STAHF) Swedish: "lord's cane" or "support of the Goths." Arts: Gustave Moreau, nineteenth-century French symbolist painter. Literature: Gustave Flaubert, nineteenth-century French novelist. Eng: *Gus, Gussie, Gustave;* Czech: *Gustav, Gustik, Gusty;* Dutch: *Gustaff;* Fin: *Kosti;* Ital: *Gustavo;* Span: *Gustavo, Tabo.*

GUY (gahy) Latin: "living spirit." Arts: Guido di Pietro, fifteenth-century Renaissance painter. Literature: Guy de Maupassant, French short-story writer and novelist. Sports: Guy Chamberlin, member of the Pro Football Hall of Fame. Eng: *Guyon;* Fr; *Gui, Vitus;* Span: *Guido.*

GYASI (JAH-see) Ghana. Akan: "marvelous baby."

HABIB (ha-BEEB) Arabic: "beloved one."

HACKETT (HAK-ett) German: "little woodsman." *Hacket.*

HADAR (hah-DAR) Hebrew: "glory."

HADDEN (HAHD-en) English: "child of the heather-filled valley." *Haden, Haddon, Hadon.*

HAGAN (HAY-gan) Irish: "little Hugh." *Hagen.*

HAGLEY (HAG-lee) English: "from the hedged enclosure." *Hagly.*

HAIDAR (HIGH-dahr) Arabic: "lion." Used in India, and in Moslem countries.

HAKAN (HAHK-an) Norse: "noble." Turkish: "fiery."

HAKEEM (HA-keem) Arabic: "knows every-thing." Sports: Hakeem Olajuwon, basketball player. *Hakim, Haakim, Hakiem.*

HAKON (HAH-kon) Old Norse: "of the chosen race." Many Norwegian kings have had this name. *Haakon, Hako.*

HALBERT (HAL-burt) English: "brilliant hero." *Halbart, Halburt.*

HALI (HAH-lee) Greek: "sea."

HALEN (HAY-len) Swedish: "hall."

HALIM (hah-LEEM) Arabic: "mild" or "gentle." Popular name in Moslem countries.

HAMAL (hah-MAHL) Arabic: "lamb." Astrology: Hamal is also a bright star in the constellation of Aries.

HAMDEN (hahm-DEN) Arabic: "praised." *Hamdun.*

HAMIDI (hah-MEE-dee) Kenya. Swahili: "com-mendable."

HAMILTON (HAM-ill-ton) Old English: "fortified castle." Place name that was the surname of several aristocratic British families. It began to be used as a first name in the early nineteenth century. Literature: Hamilton Basso, novelist who wrote *Sun In Capricorn*. *Hamel, Hamelton, Hamill, Hamil.*

HAMLIN (HAM-lin) Old English: "lover of home."

HANBAL (HAHN-bal) North Africa. Arabic: "purity." Hanbal was a founder of an Islamic school of thought.

HANI (hah-NEE) Arabic: "cheerful and happy."

HANIF (HAH-neef) Arabic: "true believer." Refers to a true believer in the Moslem religion. Afr: *Hanif.*

HANLEY (HAN-lee) Old English: "meadow on the cliff." English place name. *Handlea, Handleigh, Handley, Hanlea, Hanly, Henlea, Henley.*

HANSEL (han-SELL) Scandinavian: "God is gracious." Literature: Character in popular children's nursery rhyme *Hansel and Gretel.* **Hans, Hanz.**

HANUMAN (han-noo-MAHN) Hindi: "monkey chief." Mythology: One of the favorite characters in Hindu literature, Hanuman the monkey chief could fly and had a fantastically long tail.

HARDY (HAHR-dee) Old German: "courageous" or "audacious."

HARI (HAH-ree) Hindi: "like a prince."

HARITH (HAH-reeth) North Africa. Arabic: "cultivator." Popular in Arab countries.

HARLAN (HAHR-lin) Old English: "grounds of warrior." Place name. Business: Harlan Sanders, founder of Kentucky Fried Chicken restaurants. History: Harian Stone, former chief justice of the United States. Literature: Harian Ellison, science-fiction author. *Harland, Harlen, Harlenn, Harlin, Harlyn, Harlynn.*

HARLEY (HAHR-lee) Old English: "spacious meadow." Theater: Harley Granville-Barker, playwright. *Arlea, Arleigh, Arley, Harlea, Harlee, Harleigh, Harly.*

HARLOW (HAHR-low) Old English: "troops on the hill." Music: Arlo Guthrie, singer. Science: Harlow Shapely (1885–1972), astronomer noted for his studies of the galaxy. *Arlo.*

HARMON (HAR-mon) German: "soldier." *Harman, Harmen.*

HAROLD (HAYRE-ild) Old Morse: "chief of the troops." Harold was the name of three Saxon kings of England. Journalism: Harold Ross, founder and editor of *The New Yorker* magazine. Movies and Television: Hal Holbrook, actor. Science: Harold Urey, who discovered heavy hydrogen and won the Nobel Prize in Chemistry (1934). Theater: Harold Pinter, playwright. Eng: *Hal, Harry;* Czech: *Jindra;* Fr: *Arry;* Gk: *Haralpos;* Hung: *Henrik;* Hawaiian: *Hale;* Ir: *Aralt;* Ital: *Araldo, Aroldo, Arrigo;* Lith: *Haroldas;* Pol: *Heronim, Hieronim;* Port: *Haroldo;* Rum: *Enric;* Russ: *Garaald, Garold, Gerahd;* Scot: *Harailt;* Span: *Haraldo;* Swed/Norw: *Harald.*

HAROUN (hah-ROON) Arabic: "lofty" or "exalted." *Harun.*

HARPER (HAR-per) English: "harp player."

HARRELL (HAR-ell) Hebrew: "mountain of God."

HARRISON (HAYR-ih-sun) Old English: "son of Harry." Movies and Television: Harrison Ford, actor who starred in the *Indiana Jones* trilogy. *Harris, Harrisen, Harriss.*

HART (hahrt) Old English: "male deer." Literature: Hart Crane, poet. *Hartman, Harte.*

HARU (HA-roo) Japanese: "born in the spring."

HARUKI (ha-ROO-key) Japanese: "shining brightly."

HARVEY (HAHR-vee) Germanic: "army battle." Name brought to England with the Norman conquest. Business: Harvey Firestone, industrialist who founded Firestone Tire Company. Literature: Harvey O'Higgins, novelist who wrote *Smoke Eaters.* Movies and Television, Theater: The giant rabbit in the Pulitzer Prize-winning play and movie, *Harvey.* Science: Harvey Wiley, chief chemist in the Department of Agriculture (1883–1912), who led the campaign against food adulteration; Harvey Cushing (1869–1939), surgeon and brain specialist.

HASAD (huh-SUHD) Turkish: "harvest" or "reaping."

HASSAN (hah-SAHN) Arabic: "handsome." Journalism: Hassan Sabra, print journalist. Literature: Hassan ibn Thabit, Arab poet.

HASTIN (hah-STEEN) Hindi: "elephant." Mythology: The name of a hero in Hindu mythology who was born in a lake frequented by elephants.

HASTINGS (HAST-ings) German: "swift one."

HAVARD (hah-VARD) Scandinavian: "guardian of the home."

HAVEN (HAY-ven) English: "a secure, safe place."

HAYDEN (HAY-dinn) Old English: "the rosy meadow." Literature: Hayden Carruth, poet. *Haydn, Haydon.*

HEATH (heeth) Old English: "land covered with shrubs." English surname and place name. Movies and Television: Heath Ledger, actor.

HEBER (HEE-bir) Hebrew: "ally." Bible: Founder of tribal family. Science: Heber Curtis, astrophysicist who researched extragalactic nebulae. *Hebor.*

HECTOR (HEK-tor) Greek: "persevering steadily." Literature: Hector was the Trojan hero of Homer's *Iliad.* Movies and Television: Hector Elizondo, actor. *Ettore, Heck, Hektor.*

HEDEON (heh-DEH-on) Russian: "destroyer" or "tree cutter." Used in the Ukraine.

HELAKU (heel-AH-koo) Native American: "sunny day."

HELLER (HELL-er) Old German: "the sun."

HEMAN (heh-MON) Hebrew: "faithful."

HENRY (HEN-ree) English, German: "master of his domain." Frequently used by nobility, it is now the name of Prince Charles's youngest son. Arts: Henri Matisse, Henri de Toulouse-Lautrec, Henri Rousseau, French painters. Business: Henry Ford, industrialist. History: Henry Hudson, navigator after whom a river, bay, and strait were named; Harry S. Truman, thirty-third president of the United States (1945–53). Journalism: Henry L. Mencken, editor and essayist. Literature: Henry Wadsworth Longfellow, poet; Henry James, Henry David Thoreau, writers. Military: Henri Winkelman, Dutch general who defended his country against Nazi invasion. Movies and Television: Henry Fonda, Hal Linden, actors. Music: Hank Williams, country and western singer and songwriter; Harry Belafonte, singer. Science: Harry Rosenbusch, German geologist who laid foundations of microscopic petrography. Sports: Hank Aaron, baseball player. Theater: Henrik Ibsen, playwright and author of *A Doll's House*. Eng: *Hagan, Hal, Hank, Harry, Hendrik, Henryk, Henri;* Bulg: *Henrim;* Czech: *Hinrich, Jindra, Hindrich;* Fr: *Henri;* Ger: *Heiner, Heinrich, Heinz, Hinrich;* Gk: *Bambis, Enrikos, Khambis, Lambos;* Hawaiian: *Hanale, Haneke;* Ir: *Hanraoi;* Hung/Fin: *Henrik;* Ital: *Arrigo, Enrico, Enzio;* Pol: *Heniek, Henier, Honok;* Port: *Henrique;* Rum: *Enric;* Span: *Enrique, Kiki, Quico, Quinto, Quiqui;* Yiddish: *Hersz.*

HERBERT (HER-burt) Old German: "proud soldier." History: Herbert Hoover, thirty-first president of the United States (1929–33). Literature: Herbert Wells (H.G. Wells), British novelist who wrote *The Time Machine.* Science: Herbert Kroemer, German Nobel Prize winner in Physics (2000). *Bert, Bertie, Erberto, Herb, Herbie, Heibert.*

HERCULES (HER-kyoo-leez) Greek: "wonderful gift" or "Hera's servant." Mythology: Zeus's incredibly strong son. Fr: *Hercule, Herakles.*

HERMAN (HER-min) Old German: "soldier." Literature: Herman Melville, author of *Moby Dick*; Herman Hesse, Nobel Prize-winning author of *Steppenwolf.* Science: Herman Snellen, Dutch ophthalmologist who developed the test for acuteness of vision. Fr: *Armand;* Ital: *Ermanno, Ermano, Armanno, Armino;* Span: *Armando;* Swed: *Hermann, Harman, Harmon, Hermie.*

HERMES (HER-mees) Greek: "messenger." Dance: Hermes Pan, dancer and choreographer. Mythology: To the Greeks, Hermes was the messenger for the gods and the guardian of souls to the lower world.

HERN (hurn) English: "mythical hunter." *Herne.*

HEROMIN (hehr-oh-MEEN) Teutonic: "ruler of an estate." Used in Poland.

HERRICK (HAIR-rik) Old German: "war ruler." Literature: Robert Henick, seventeenth-century poet.

HERSH (hersh) Yiddish: "deer." Used in both Israel and the United States. Movies and Television:

Herschel Bernardi, actor. *Hersch, Hersehel, Herzl, Hirsch, Hirschel.*

HEWITT (HEW-it) English: "little smart one." *Hewett.*

HIBAH (hee-BAH) Arabic: "present."

HIDALGO (EE-dahl-goh) Spanish: "noble one." Movies and Television: Movie based on a true story dating from 1890 about a Pony Express rider and his horse, Hidalgo, traveling to Arabia to compete in a racing tournament.

HIDEAKI (HI-day-kee) Japanese: "smart one." Science: Hideki Yukawa, Japanese Nobel Prize winner in Physics (1949). Sports: Hideki Matsui, famous Japanese baseball player for the New York Yankees. *Hideki.*

HIEU (huh-OO) Vietnamese: "respect."

HIGGINS (HIGG-ins) Irish: "intelligent."

HILARY (HILL-a-ree) Latin: "happy." A popular boy's name before the seventeenth century, more common today among girls. Span: *Hilario, Hilery, Hillary, Hillery, Hilaire.*

HILEL (hye-LEL) Arabic: "quarter moon." Astrology: Appropriate for those born under the sign of Cancer, ruled by the moon.

HINUN (hee-NOON) Native American: "spirit of the storm."

HIRAM (HYE-rum) Hebrew: "my exalted brother." History: An ancient king of Tyre. *Hi, Hirom, Hy, Hyrum.*

HIROSHI (hi-ROH-shee) Japanese: "giving."

HIRSI (HIRE-sye) African: "amulet."

HISOKA (hee-SO-kah) Japanese: "holding back" or "waiting before talking."

HOAI (hoe-AYE) Vietnamese: "always" or "eternal."

HOBART (HOE-bart) German: "high" or "bright." *Hobard.*

HOGAN (hoe-GAN) Celtic: "youth."

HOLDEN (HOLD-en) Old English: "deep valley." Literature: Holden Caulfield, the central character in the novel *The Catcher in the Rye. Holman, Holdan, Holdyn, Holdin.*

HOLIC (HO-lik) Czech: "hair-cutter."

HOLT (holt) English: "son of the unspoiled forest."

HOMER (HO-mur) Greek: "pledged or promised." Literature: Homer wrote the two epics the *Iliad* and the *Odyssey*. Movies and Televison: Character on TV's *The Simpsons. Homere, Homeros, Homerus, Omer.*

HONDO (HOHN-doh) Zimbabwe. Shona: "war."

HONOVI (ho-NO-vee) Native American: "power-ful."

HORATIO (ho-RAY-shee-oh) Latin. Roman clan name. History: Horace Greeley, political leader and journalist. Literature: Quintas Horatius Flaccus, Roman poet usually referred to as Horace; Hamlet's friend in Shakespeare's *Hamlet* was named Horatio. Military: Horatio Nelson, British naval hero. Science: Horace Wells, nineteenth-century dentist who pioneered the administration of nitrous oxide. *Horace, Horatius, Horaz, Oratio, Orazio.*

HORST (horst) Old German: "dense grove." Arts: Horst P. Horst, photographer.

HOUSTON (HEW-stun) Scottish: "Hugh's town." Military: Sam Houston, Texas general whose namesake is the city of Houston.

HOWARD (HOW-ird) Old English: Meaning unknown. Business: Howard Hughes, industrialist and aviator. Science: Howard Aiken, mathematician credited with designing the forerunner of the digital computer. *Howie, Ward;* Hawaiian: *Haoa.*

HOWELL (how-WELL) Welsh: "alert one." *Howel.*

HOWI (HO-wee) Native American. Miwok: "turtle-dove."

HOYT (hoyt) Irish: "spirit" or "mind." Music: Hoyt Axton, country and western singer.

HUBERT (HYOU-bert) German: "genius." Saint Hubert is the patron saint of dogs. History: Hubert Wilkins, polar explorer (1888–1958). Eng: *Bert, Bertie, Berty, Hobart, Hubbard, Huber, Hubie, Huey, Hugh, Hugo;* Czech: *Hubert, Hubertek;* Russ: *Berdy;* Span: *Berto, Hubi, Huberto, Uberto.*

HUGH (hyou) Old German: "heart" or "mind." Hugh was a popular medieval name. Journalism: Hugh Downs, TV journalist. Movies and Television: Hugh Grant, actor. Eng: *Huey, Hughie;* Dutch: *Hugo;* Span: *Hugon, Hutch, Huw, Ugo.*

HUGO (OO-go) Teutonic: "bright spirit" or "smart." Name used in Spanish-speaking countries. Business: Hugo Boss, popular men's designer company.

HUME (hume) English: "supporter of peace."

HUMPHREY (HUMPH-ree) English. Meaning unknown. Movies and Television: Humphrey Bogart, actor. Science: Humphry Davy, chemist specializing in electrochemistry, isolated potassium and sodium. *Humfrey, Humfrid, Humfried, Humfredo, Onfre, Onfroi, Onofredo, Onofrio.*

HUNTER (HUNT-er) Old English: "hunter." Occupational name. Journalism, Literature: Hunter Thompson, journalist and author.

HUNTLEY (HUNT-lee) Old English: "hunter's field." *Huntlea, Huntlee, Huntleigh, Huntly.*

HURLEY (HER-lee) Irish Gaelic: "born from the seas." *Hurlee, Hurleigh.*

HURST (herst) Middle English: "grove." *Hearst, Hirst.*

HUSAIN (hoo-SAYN) Arabic: "glory child." Hussein was a descendant of the prophet Muhammad, founder of Islam. *Hussein, Husein.*

HUXLEY (HUX-lee) Old English: "Hugh's field." *Huxlea, Huxlee, Huxleigh, Huxly, Hux, Lee, Leigh.*

IAN (E-en) Scottish: A popular Scottish variation of John. See John. *Iain.*

IBRAHIM (EE-brah-heem) Nigeria. Hausa: "my father is exalted."

ICHABOD (IK-ah-bod) Hebrew: "glory fled." Literature: Ichabod Crane, the name of the schoolmaster in Washington Irving's novel *The Legend of Sleepy Hollow.*

IDEN (EYE-den) Celtic: "wealthy."

IFE (EYE-fee) African: "wide" or "love."

IGASHO (ee-GAH-sho) Native American: "seeker."

IGNATIUS (ig-NAY-shus) English: "burning passionately." History: Saint Ignatius of Loyola, founder of the Jesuits. Music: Ignace Paderewski, Polish concert pianist. Fr: *Ignace;* Ital: *Ignazio;* Latin: *Ignacio, Ignatio, Iggie, Ignac, Ignace, Ignatious, Ignatz, Ignaz, Inigo.*

IGOR (EE-gor) Russian, Scandinavian: "peace-loving soldier." Music: Igor Stravinsky, composer of well-known ballets: *The Rites of Spring, The Firebird, Petrushka.* Scan: *Ingvar;* Russ: *Igoryok, Inge, Ingemar, Ingmar.*

ILARIO (ill-ARE-ee-oh) Italian: "cheerful."

IMARAN (EYE-mahr-an) Hindu: "strong."

IMRE (EM-ray) German: "great king." Literature: Imre Kertész, Hungarian Nobel Prize winner (2002).

INCE (EEN-tseh) Latin: "innocent." Used in Hungary.

INCENDIO (in-sen-DEE-oh) Spanish: "fire."

INDIVAR (in-DIHV-are) Hindi: "blue lotus."

INGALL (in-GAHL) German: "angel." *Ingal, Ingalls, Ingel, Ingelbert.*

INGEMAR (ING-geh-mar) Scandinavian: "son of Ing." Mythology: Ingemar is the Norse fertility god. Movies and Television: Ingmar Bergman, film director. Sports: Ingemar Johansson, Swedish heavyweight boxing champion (1959). *Ingamar, Ingemur, Ingmar.*

INGRAM (ING-ram) English, Old German: "Anglian raven." *Ingraham, Ingrim.*

INGVAR (ING-var) Scandinavian: "soldier under Ing." Mythology: Referring to the Norse mythological god Ing. See Ingemar. *Ingevar.*

INIKO (ee-NEE-ko) Nigeria. Ibo: "bad times." African parents often choose this name if the baby is born during political unrest or debacle of nature.

INNIS (EE-nis) Scottish Gaelic: "isle." *Innes, Iness, Inness, Inniss, Iniss.*

INNOCENZIO (ee-no-CHEHN-tsee-o) Spanish: "innocent." Used in Spanish-speaking countries.

INTEUS (een-TAY-oos) Native American: "unashamed" or "proud."

IOAKIM (joh-AH-keem) Hebrew: "Lord creates." Used in Russia. *Akim, Jov, Yov.*

IOV (jove) Hebrew: "God will establish."

IRA (EYE-rah) Hebrew: "ancestors." Bible: Ira was the name of a priest and a captain at the time of King David. History: Ira Allen, political leader who helped draft the Constitution of the United States. Music: Ira Gershwin, lyricist who won the first Pulitzer Prize awarded to a lyricist (1931). Science: Ira Bowen, astronomer.

IRAM (EYE-rahm) Hebrew: "shining."

IRVING (UR-ving) Old English: "friend of the ocean." Music: Irving Berlin, composer of such popular songs as "White Christmas" and "Alexander's Ragtime Band." Science: Irving Langmuir, winner of the Nobel Prize for Chemistry (1932). *Earvin, Erv, Ewin, Irv, Irvin, Irvine.*

IRWIN (UR-win) Old English: "friend of the boar." Literature: Irwin Shaw, author. Science: Irwin Rose, Nobel Prize winner in Chemistry (2004). *Erwin, Erwinn, Erwyn, Irwinn, Irwyn, Irv.*

ISAAC (EYE-zik) Hebrew: "she laughed." Bible: In the Old Testament, Abraham was 100 years old when his son Isaac was born. Literature: Isaac Bashevis Singer, Nobel Prize-winning novelist; Isaac Asimov, science fiction author. Music: Isaac Stern, Itzhak Perlman, violinists. Science: Isaac Newton discovered the laws of motion and gravity. Eng: *Ike, Ikie;* Czech: *Izak;* Ger/Gk: *Isaak;* Hung: *Izasak;* Yiddish: *Aizik, Isaak, Izik, Isac, Itzak, Izaak, Zack, Zak.*

ISADORO (ee-sah-DOR-oh) Spanish: "strong gift."

ISAIAH (eye-ZAY-ah) Hebrew: "saved by God." Bible: Isaiah was a major prophet who foresaw the destruction of Israel. History: Isaiah Dorman, an African-American U.S. Army interpreter, fought with General Custer in the Battle of the Little Bighorn (1876). Sports: Isaiah Thomas, basketball player. Span: *Isaias, Isa, Isaia, Isia, Isiah, Issiah.*

ISHAQ (EESE-hahk) North Africa. Arabic: "a child who laughed when he was born."

ISHMAEL (ISH-mah-ehl) Hebrew: "God listens." Bible: One of Abraham's sons by Hagar. Literature: The first line of Herman Melville's *Moby Dick:* "Call me Ishmael." Span: *Ismael.*

ISIDORE (IZ-eh-dorr) Greek: "Isis' blessing." Science: Isidor Isaac Rabi, scientist who won the Nobel Prize for his work on atoms (1944). Gk: *Isadorios;* Pol: *Izydor;* Span/Port: *Isidro, Dore, Dorian, Dory, Isadore, Isidor, Isidoro, Issey, Izidor, Izzy, Ysidro.*

ISMET (EYES-met) Turkish: "honor."

ISRAEL (EES-rah-el) Hebrew: "contended with God." Bible: God named Jacob Israel after they battled for three days. History: Name of the Jewish state founded in 1948. Literature, Theater: Israel Zangwill, British playwright and novelist who wrote *Children of the Ghetto;* Israel Horovitz, playwright. Military: Israel Putman, commander and hero of the American Revolution. Science: Israel White, geologist. *Yisrael, Iser, Izzie.*

ISSA (ee-SAH) Kenya. Swahili: "God is our salvation."

ISTVAN (EESHT-vahn) Greek: "crowned." Used in Hungary.

ITTAMAR (EE-tah-mahr) Israel. Hebrew: "island of palms." Popular name in Israel. *Itamar.*

IVAN (eye-VAHN) Slavic: "God is good."

IVAR (eye-VAHR) Norwegian: "archer."

IVES (eevz) Old English: "young archer." Astrology: Sagittarius is the archer. Fr: *Yves*.

IVO (EE-voh) Old German: "wood from the yew tree." Yew wood is the principal material used in making archery bows. *Ifor, Ivar, Iven, Iver, Ives, Ivon, Yves, Yvo, Yvor.*

IYAPO (ee-YAH-po) Nigeria. Yoruba: "multiple obstacles."

IXAKA (ee-SHAH-kah) Hebrew: "laughter."

IYE (EE-yeh) Native American: "smoky clouds."

IZZY (ee-ZEE) Hebrew: "he will laugh."

JA (jah) African: "magnetic."

JABARI (jah-BAH-ree) Swahili: "courageous."

JABBAR (jahb-BAR) Arabic: "mighty."

JABILO (jah-BILE-oh) African: "medicine man."

JABIN (JAY-bin) Israel. Hebrew: "God has created."

JACINTO (hah-SEEN-to) Spanish: "hyacinth flower." *Giacintho, Clacinto, Jacindo, Jax.*

JACKSON (JAK-sun) Old English: "Jack's son." Arts: Jackson Pollock, abstract expressionist who created "Autumn Rhythm." *Jakson.*

JACOB (JAY-cub) Hebrew: "supplanting one." English variant: "James." Bible: Jacob is the patriarch of the book of Genesis whose children founded the twelve tribes of Israel. History: Madison, Polk, Buchanan, Garfield, and Carter. Literature: Iago, a character in Shakespeare's *Othello*. Movies and Television: James Earl Jones and James Stewart, actors. Music: James Taylor, musician. Science: James Watt, inventor of the steam engine. Eng: *Cob, Cobb, Cobby, Jake, Jakob, Jaime, Jago, Jameson, Jamieson, Jamison, Jamie, Jaimie, Jay, Jayme, Jaymes, Jaymie, James, Jim, Jimmy, Jimmie, Jakes;* Bulg: *Ikov;* Czech: *Jakub, Jokubas, Kuba, Kubes, Kubik, Kubo;* Den: *Jakob;* Dutch: *Jaap;* Fr: *Jacques, Jacque, Jacquet, Coco;* Ger: *Jakob, Jocek;* Gk: *Iakov, Iacovo, Iacopo;* Hung: *Jakab, Kobi;* Ir: *Seamus;* Ital: *Iago, Giacomo, Giacobo, Giacopo, Giamo;* Latin: *Jeks, Jeska, Jacobus;* Lith: *Jecis, Jokubas;* Pol: *Jakub, Jakubek, Jalu, Kuba;* Port: *Jaime, Tiago, Diogo;* Russ: *Jakob, Jasha, Yakov, Yanka, Yashko;* Span: *Jaime, Santiago, Diego, Diaz, Chago, Chango, Chanti, Tiago.*

JADON (JAY-don) Israel. Hebrew: "God has heard." Used in Israel. *Jaydon, Jaedon, Jaden.*

JADRIEN (JAY-dree-en) Contemporary combination of Jay and Adrien.

JAEGAR (JAY-ger) German: "hunger."

JAEL (YAH-ehl) Israel. Hebrew: "mountain goat." *Yael.*

JAFARI (jah-FAR-ee) Swahili: "dignified."

JAGGER (JAG-gar) English: "to cart things around."

JAHI (JAH-hee) Swahili: "character" or "honor."

JAIRUS (HYE-rus) Hebrew: "God makes clear." *Jairo.*

JAJA (JAH-jah) Nigeria. Ibo: "honored."

JAKEEM (ya-KEEM) Hebrew, Arabic: "exalted."

JAMAL (jah-MAHL) Arabic: "attractive." Movies and Television: Malcolm-Jamal Warner, actor. Science: Jamel Chelly, geneticist. Sports: Jamaal Wilkes, basketball player. *Jameel, Jamele, Jamelle, Jamaal, Jamahl, Jamall, Jamaul, Jhamal, Jahmal, Jamael, Jamel, Jamil, Jamlle, Jamiel.*

JAMAR (jah-MAHR) United States. English: African-American blend of Jamal and Lamar. *Jamarr, Jemar, Jimar.*

JAMES See Jacob.

JAMESON (JAYM-ee-son) Old English: "son of James." *Jamieson, Jamison.*

JAMIE (JAY-mee) United States. English: Originally a pet name for James. Now used independently. Movies and Television: Jamie Farr, actor. *Jaimay, Jaime, Jayme, Jaymie.*

JAMIL (zhah-MEEL) Arabic: "beautiful." Used in Arab countries.

JAN (yahn) Dutch: Variation of John. See John.

JAPHET (YAH-fet) Israel. Hebrew: "young" or "appealing."

JAPHETH (JAY-feth) Hebrew: "he expands." Bible: Japheth was the oldest of Noah's three sons.

JARAH (JAY-rah) Hebrew: "he gives sweetness." Bible: Jarah was a descendant of Jonathan. *Jarrah.*

JARED (JARE-ed) Hebrew: "down to earth." Derived from the Old Testament and later adapted by the Puritans. Education: Jared Sparks, historian who was among the first to conduct research from original documents. *Jarad, Jarid, Jarod, Jarrad, Jarred, Jarrod, Jaryd, Jerrod, Jerryd, Jered, Jerod, Jerad, Jerrod.*

JAREK (YAH-rek) Polish: "born during the month of January." *Janiusz, Januarius, Janiuszck.*

JARELL (JARE-el) Contemporary combination of Jar and Darell. *Jarrell, Jarrel, Jarel, Jaryl.*

JARETH (JARE-eth) Contemporary combination of Jar and Gareth. *Jarreth, Jerth.*

JARON (JARE-on) Hebrew: "to shout out." Many of its contemporary variations are based on the sounds of Jared and Darren. *Gerron, Jaren, Jarin, Jarren, Jarron, Jaran, Jarran, Jerrin, Jeran, Jeren, Jeron, Jerron.*

JAROSLAV (YA-ro-slahf) Slavic: "springtime's beauty." Popular name in Czechoslovakia. Education: Jaroslav Pelikan, historian. Science: Jaroslav

Heyrovsky, Czech physical chemist who won the Nobel Prize in 1959 for his polargraphic analysis. Czech: *Jarda*.

JARVIS (JAHR-vis) Old German: "man who leads with a spear." Sports: Jarvis Brown, baseball player; Jarvis Williams, football player. *Jervis*.

JASER (jah-SER) Arabic: "fearless."

JASON (JAY-son) Greek: "one who cures." Bible: Jason was the author of the Book of Ecclesiastes. Mythological: Jason led the Argonauts to find the Golden Fleece. Movies and Television: Jason Robards, actor. *Jayson, Jasen, Jase, Jaison, Jaysen, Jaycen, Jace, Jayce, Jacen, Jay*.

JASPER (JAS-per) Persian: "treasurer."

JAVAN (jah-VAN) Latin: "angel of Greece."

JAVAS (JAH-vis) Sanskrit: "fleeting" or "swift-footed." Used in the United States and India.

JAVIER (hah-vee-AIR) Basque: "new home-owner." Found in the Basque regions of Spain and France.

JAVON (JAY-von) United States. English: African-American combination of Ja and Von. Music: Javon Jackson, jazz musician. *Javonne, Jevon*.

JAY (jay) Old French: "blue jay." Used as an independent name. Also a form of James, Jason, and other names beginning with J. Movies and Television: Jay Leno, comedian and talk-show host; Jaye Davidson, actor. Hindi: *Jai, Jaye, Jae.*

JEBADIAH (je-bah-DYE-ah) Hebrew: "beloved friend." *Jeb.*

JEDEDIAH (je-deh-DYE-ah) Hebrew: "God's beloved." *Jed, Jedd.*

JEDREK (JEDD-rick) Polish: "mighty man." *Jedrick, Jedrus.*

JELANI (jeh-LAH-nee) East Africa. Swahili: "strong."

JEREMIAH (jare-ah-MYE-ah) Hebrew: "God exalts." Bible: In the Old Testament, Jeremiah was a prophet who believed that religion's source was in the human heart. Movies and Television: Jeremy Irons, actor. Eng: *Jerimiah, Jem, Jeromy, Jeramee, Jeramey, Jeramie, Jere, Jeremy, Jereme, Jeromy, Jeremey, Jemmie, Jemmy, Jerr, Jerrie, Jerry;* Basque: *Jeremi;* Den: *Jeremias;* Dutch/Ger/Port/Swed: *Jeremias;* Fr: *Jereme, Jeremie;* Hung: *Ember, Katone, Nemet;* Ital: *Geremia;* Russ: *Jeremija, Yeremey;* Swed: *Jeremia, Dermot, Dermott, Diarmid, Jeremiya, Yirmeyah.*

JERIAH (jer-RYE-ah) Hebrew: "Jehovah has seen."

JERIC (JERR-ik) English: "strong" or "gifted ruler."

JERICHO (JARE-a-ko) Arabic: "moon city." Bible: Jericho was destroyed when its walls came tumbling down. Span: *Jerico.*

JERMAINE (jer-MANE) English: "brotherly." *Jermain, Jermayne, Jermane.*

JEROME (jer-ROHM) Greek: "blessed name" or "calling." Saint Jerome is the patron saint of archaeologists and scholars. Dance: Jerome Robbins, choreographer. Literature, Theater: Jerome K. Jerome, British novelist and playwright. Music: Jerome Kem, composer who wrote the music for *Showboat. Jerrome, Jeroen, Jeronimo, Jerry, Jerrie, Gerome, Gerrie, Gerry, Girolamo.*

JERRELL (JER-rel) Contemporary combination of Gerald and Darryl. *Gerrell, Jarell, Jarrel, Jarrell, Jeryl, Jeriel, Jerriel.*

JERRICK (JER-rik) Contemporary combination of Jer and Derrick. *Jerick, Jerrie.*

JESSE (JESS-ee) Hebrew: "wealthy one." Bible: David's father. History: Jesse Jackson, civil rights activist. Sports: Jesse Owens, Olympic track and field legend. *Jessey, Jessie, Jessy, Jesiah, Jess.*

JETHRO (JETH-ro) Hebrew: "in great supply." Bible: Moses' father-in-law. Music: Jethro Tull, rock group.

JIBRIL (jih-BRIL) Arabic: "archangel Gabriel."

JIN (jin) Chinese: "gold." Korean: "truth," "treasure," or "pearl."

JIRAIR (JIR-aire) Armenian: "hard working."

JOAQUIN (WAA-kee) Spanish: "God will establish." Literature: Joaquin Miller, nineteenth-century writer of the American west. Movies and Televison: Joaquin Phoenix, actor (*Ladder 49*).

JOB (jobe) Hebrew: "oppressed." Bible: After being tested relentlessly by God, Job proved his heavenly faith. *Jobe, Joby, Joab.*

JOEL (JO-el) Hebrew: "the Lord is God." Bible: Joel was a prophet and writer of the Book of Joel.

JOHN (jonn) Hebrew: "God is giving." The most prevalent first name in the West, John has been the name of twenty-five popes. Aeronautics: John H. Glenn, astronaut. Bible: Name of one of the twelve disciples. History: Four United States presidents were named John—Adams, Quincy Adams, Tyler, and Kennedy. Literature: John Donne, poet; John Updike and John Steinbeck, Pulitzer Prize-winning authors. Movies and Television: John Wayne, actor; Johnny Carson, longtime host of TV's *Tonight Show*. Music: Beatle John Lennon; Johnny Cash, country singer; three great composers bore this name: Johann Sebastian Bach, Johannes Brahms, and Johann Wolfgang von Goethe. Science: Johannes Wislicenus, German chemist. Sports: Johnny Weissmuller, champion swimmer. Theater: John Gielgud, Shakespearean actor. Eng: *Jack, Jackie, Jock, Johnnie, Johnny, Jon.* Basque: *Iban;*

Belg: *Jan, Jehan;* Bulg: *Ioan, Ivan;* Czech: *Hanus, Johan, Hanschen;* Dutch: *Jan, Jantje;* Fin: *Janne, Juhana;* Fr: *Jean, Jeannot, Jehan;* Ger: *Hanno, Anno, Haensel, Hans, Hansel, Hansl, Johann, Johannes;* Gk: *Giannes, Giannos, Ioannis;* Hung: *Jacsi, Jani, Janika, Janko, Janos;* Ir: *Sean, Seann, Shane;* Ital: *Gian, Gianetto, Giannini, Giovanni, Vanni;* Latin: *Janis, Jancis, Janka, Zanis, Ansis;* Lith: *Jonas, Jonelis, Jonukas, Jonutis;* Pol: *Iwan, Jan, Janek, Jankiel, Jas, Jasio;* Port: *Joao;* Rum: *Iancgnac, Iu, Ioan, Ionel;* Russ: *Ioann, Ivan, Ivano, Ivas, Vanek, Vanka, Vanko, Vanya, Yanka;* Scot: *Ian;* Span: *Juan;* Swed: *Hans, Hansel, Hasse, Hazze, Jan, Jens, Johan, Jonam;* Turk: *Ohannes;* Welsh: *Evan, Jone.*

JOJI (JO-ji) Japanese: "plantation owner" or "one who sows."

JOMEI (joe-MAY) Japanese: "spread light."

JONAH (JO-nah) Hebrew: "dove." Bible: In the famous Bible story, Jonah lived inside a whale's belly for three days. Eng: *Jonas;* Ital: *Giona, Giuseppe;* Russ: *Iona, Yona.*

JONATHAN (JOHN-a-than) Hebrew: "gift from God." Bible: In the Old Testament, Jonathan was the friend of King David and the son of King Saul. Literature: Jonathan Swift, author of *Gulliver's Travels.* *Jon.*

JONTE (jahn-TAY) Contemporary invention combining Jon and Dante. *Johnte, Jontae, Johntay.*

JORDAN (JOR-dan) Hebrew: "to come down" or "descend from heaven." Name of a river flowing through the Holy Land. *Jordan, Jorden, Jordin;* Fr: *Jourdan, Jourdon, Jordain, Jourdaine, Jordy, Jordi, Jordyn, Jori.*

JORN (jorn) German: "vigilant watchman."

JOSEPH (JO-seph) Hebrew: "Jehovah supplants." Bible: Joseph was the son of Jacob and Rachel. He wore the "coat of many colors." Another Joseph was Jesus' earthly father. Dance: Jose Greco, flamenco dancer. Literature: Joseph Conrad and Joseph Wambaugh, authors. Music: Josef Haydn, composer. Science: Joseph Lister, surgeon who founded antiseptic surgery; Joseph Priestly, British scientist who discovered oxygen. Theater: Joseph Papp, producer. Eng: *Jodi, Jody, Joe, Joey, Jojo;* Basque: *Joseba;* Bulg: *Yosif;* Czech: *Josef, Joza, Jozka, Pepa, Pepik;* Fin: *Joosef, Jooseppi;* Fr: *Josephe;* Ger: *Beppi, Josef, Peppi, Sepp;* Gk: *Iosif;* Hung: *Joska, Jozsef, Jozsi;* Ital: *Guiseppe, Pino;* Japan: *Jo;* Latin: *Josephus;* Latv: *Jazeps;* Pol: *Josef, Jozio, Juzef, Juziu;* Port: *Jose, Josef, Zeusef;* Russ: *Iosif, Osip, Osya, Yusif, Yusup, Yuzef;* Serb: *Josep, Josip, Joze, Jozef, Jozhe, Jozhef;* Span: *Che, Cheche, Chepe, Jobo, Jose, Pepe, Pepillo, Pepin, Pipo;* Swan: *Yusuf;* Swed/Norw: *Josef.*

JOSHUA (JOSH-oo-a) Hebrew: "God saves." Bible: In the Old Testament, Joshua was Moses' commander and successor and led the Israelites into the Promised Land. Eng: *Josh;* Dutch: *Josua, Jozua;* Fr: *Josue;* Ger: *Josua;* Hung: *Jozsua;* Ital: *Giosia;*

Port: *Joaquim;* Rum: *Iosua;* Span: *Josue, Jesus;*
Swed: *Josua;* Yiddish: *Yehosha.*

JOSIAH (jo-SYE-ah) Hebrew: "God has
mended." Bible: Ancient child-king of Judah. Business: Josiah Wedgwood, founder of the company
that makes china. Education: Josiah Tucker,
eighteenth-century British economist who argued
against monopolies. Science: Josiah Willard Gibbs,
nineteenth-century physicist and chemist who discovered chemical thermodynamics. *Josh, Josia,
Josias.*

JOVAN (jo-VAHN) Latin: "the sky's father." *Jo-
vanus, Jovin, Jovon, Jovi, Jovito, Jovani, Jovany,
Jovanni, Jovanny, Jeovany, Jervani, Jeovanni, Jo-
vanus.*

JUBAL (JOO-bull) Hebrew: "ram." Bible: Jubal
invented music. Military: Jubal Early, Confederate
general who led the raid on Washington in 1864.

JUDAH (JOO-dah) Hebrew: "the praised one."
Bible: Judah was the fourth of Jacob's twelve sons.
Movies and Television: Jude Law, actor. *Judas,
Jude, Judd, Jud, Juda, Judson.*

JULIAS (JOO-lee-as) Latin: "young" or "faint
beard." Julian was the family clan name of several
of the most powerful Roman emperors. History:
Julius Caesar, Roman emperor after whom the
month of July was named. Literature: Jules Verne,
author. Music: Julio Iglesias, singer. Science: Julius
Mayer, German physician and physicist. Eng: *Jule,
Jules;* Basque: *Julen;* Dutch: *Jules, Julianna;* Pol:

Juliusz, Julian; Span: *Julio, Julian, Juliano;* Fr: *Julien;* Latin: *Julius;* Zuni: *Haiian.*

JUN (joon) Chinese: "verities of life" or "wisdom"; Japanese: "follower of the law."

JURO (joo-ROH) Japanese: "tenth son" or "best wishes."

JUSTIN (JUS-tin) Old French: "just and righteous." Music: Justin Timberlake, popular singer. Science: Justus Byrgius, Swiss mathematician who invented logarithms. Eng: *Justen, Justis;* Bulg: *Justin;* Czech: *Jusa, Justyn;* Fr: *Juste;* Ger: *Just, Justus;* Ital: *Guistino;* Lith: *Justas, Justinas, Justukas;* Pol: *Inek, Justek, Justyn;* Russ: *Iustin, Ustin, Yusts, Yustyn;* Span: *Justino, Justo, Tuto;* Swed/Norw: *Justinus.*

K

KACEY (KAY-see) Contemporary name based on the initials "K.C."

KADAR (KAH-dahr) Arabic: "strong" or "imposing presence."

KADE (kayd) Scottish Gaelic: "from the wetlands."

KADEEM (kah-DEEM) English form of the Arabic word *khadeem* meaning "servant." Movies and Television: Kadeem Hardison, actor. *Kadim.*

KADEN (KAY-dehn) Armenian: "fighter."

KADIN (kah-DEEN) Arabic: "beloved companion." *Kadeen.*

KADIR (kah-DEER) Arabic: "fresh greening." *Kadeer.*

KADO (KAH-do) Japanese: "gateway."

KAELAN (KAY-lan) Gaelic: "mighty at war." *Kalen, Kalin, Kalan.*

KAEMON (kah-AY-mon) Japanese: "joyful" or "right-handed." Old Samurai name.

KAFELE (kah-FEH-leh) Malawi. Ngoni: "inestimable worth."

KAGA (KAH-gah) Native American: "scribe."

KAGAN (kaye-GAHN) Irish: "a thinker" or "fiery." *Kagen.*

KAI (kye) Hawaiian: "water from the seas." Also common among girls. Science: Kai Siegbahn, Swedish Nobel Prize winner in Physics (1981). *Cai, Kye.*

KAINOA (kuh-ee-NOH-uh) Hawaiian: "the name." Popular in Hawaii.

KAIPO (KAH-ee-poh) Hawaiian: "the sweetheart."

KAISER (KYE-ser) German: "emperor." Variant of Caesar.

KAJ (kah-EE) Greek: "earth." Used in Denmark. *Kai.*

KALANI (kah-LAH-nee) Hawaiian: "sky" or "chieftain." Very popular in Hawaii.

KALIDAS (kah-LYE-das) Hindu: "poet" or "musician."

KALIL (kah-LEEL) Arabic: "faithful friend" or "trustworthy." Literature: Kahlil Gibran, Lebanese-American poet, essayist, and author of *The Prophet*. *Kahlil, Kalee, Khaleel, Khalil.*

KALIN (KAY-linn) Origin unknown. Perhaps a contemporary form based on Cale or Caleb. *Calen, Calin, Caylon, Kaelan, Kalen.*

KALIQ (KAH-leek) Arabic: "creative."

KALKIN (kahl-KEEN) Hindi: A Hindu deity. The tenth incarnation of Vishnu, Kalkin is expected to appear riding a white horse and arrive during the Age of Darkness.

KAMI (kah-MEE) Hindu: "loving."

KAMIL (kah-MEEL) Arabic: "without error" or "peerless." One of the ninety-nine traits of virtue attributed to God in the Koran. Beloved name among Moslems. *Kameel.*

KAMUZU (KAH-moo-zoo) South Africa. Nguni: "medicinal."

KANA (KAH-nah) Hawaiian: In Hawaiian mythology, Kana could transform himself into a rope and extend his new form from Molokai to Hawaii.

KANE (kayne) Celtic: "beautiful"; Irish Gaelic: "fighter." Used in England. *Kaine, Kayne.*

KANE (KAH-neh) Hawaiian: "man" or "eastern sky."

KANE (KAH-nee) Japanese: "golden."

KANIEL (kah-nee-AYL) Israel. Hebrew: "stalk" or "reed." *Kan, Kani, Kanny.*

KARDAL (KAHR-dal) Arabic: "mustard seed."

KARE (KAW-reh) Norwegian: "enormous."

KAREEM (ka-REEM) Arabic: "very generous." Generosity is one of the ninety-nine divine virtues categorized in the Koran. Sports: Kareem Abdul-Jabbar, basketball legend. *Karim, Karime.*

KAREL (KAHR-el) Old French: "virile." Used in Czechoslovakia. Eng: *Carl, Karol;* Czech: *Karol.*

KARIF (kah-REEF) Arabic: "born in autumn." *Kareef.*

KARL (karl) German: Form of Charles. See Charles.

KARMEL (kahr-MEHL) Israel. Hebrew: "garden of grapes." Popular in Israel for both sexes.

KARNEY (CAR-nee) Irish Gaelic: "winner." *Carney, Carny, Karny.*

KARSA (KAR-sah) Hungarian: "falcon."

KASEN (KAH-sen) Latin: "protected with a helmet."

KASIB (KA-sib or ka-SEEB) Arabic: "earthy" or "productive." *Kaseeb.*

KASIM (kah-SEEM) Arabic: "at odds" or "separated."

KASIYA (kah-SEE-yah) Malawi. Ngoni: "separation."

KASS (cass) German: "like a blackbird." *Kaese, Kasch, Kase.*

KATEB (KAH-teb) Arabic: "writer."

KATO (KAY-toh) Latin: "good judgment."

KAVI (KAH-vee) Hindu: "poet."

KAZUO (KA-zu-oh) Japanese: "man of peace."

KEAHI (keh-AH-hee) Hawaiian: "flames." Popular in Hawaii.

KE'ALA (keh-AH-luh) Hawaiian: "the aroma."

KEANDRE (kee-AHN-dray) Contemporary combination of Ke and Andre. *Keene.*

KEANE (keene) Old English: "sharp." *Kean, Keen.*

KEARN (kurn) Irish Gaelic: "dark."

KEATON (KEE-tun) Old English: "where the hawks go." *Keeton, Keiton, Keyton.*

KEB (keb) Egyptian: The world's greenery grew on the back of this ancient Egyptian deity.

KEDAR (KEH-dahr) Hindi: "god of the mountain peaks." Alternate name for Shiva, Hindu supreme deity.

KEDEM (KE-dem) Hebrew: "ancient" or "old."

KEEFE (keyf) Irish Gaelic: "attractive" or "beloved." *Keifer, Keefer.*

KEEGAN (KEE-gan) Irish Gaelic: "tiny, bold flame." Astrology: Appropriate for a boy born under a fire sign such as Leo, Aries, or Sagittarius. *Keagan, Keegen, Kegan, Kagen.*

KEELAN (KEE-lan) Irish Gaelic: "lean."

KEELEY (KEE-lee) Irish Gaelic: "attractive." *Kealey, Kealy, Keelie, Keely.*

KEENAN (KEE-nun) Irish Gaelic: "little ancient one." Movies and Television: Keenan Ivory Wayans, actor. *Keen, Kienan, Kienen, Keenon, Kenan.*

KEIJI (KAY-jee) Japanese: "lead cautiously."

KEIR (keer) Gaelic: "black." Movies and Television: Keir Dullea, actor. *Keiron, Kieran, Kieron, Kerr.*

KEITARO (kay-tah-ROH) Japanese: "blessed."

KEITH (keeth) Irish Gaelic: "warrior descends." Aeronautics: Sir Keith Smith, Australian who made the first flight from England to Australia. Literature: Keith Douglas, British poet. Music: Keith Richards, Rolling Stone guitarist. Sports: Keith Hernandez, baseball player.

KEKOA (keh-KOH-uh) Hawaiian: "bold one."

KELBY (KEL-bee) Old German: "plantation near the stream." *Keeby, Kelbee, Kelbie.*

KELE (KEH-lee) Native American. Hopi: "sparrow hawk." *Kellie.*

KELE (KEH-leh) Hawaiian: "navigator."

KELII (ke-LEE) Hawaiian: "chief."

KELL (kel) Old Norse: "from the spring."

KELLEN (KELL-en) Irish Gaelic: "mighty warrior." *Kellan, Keelan, Keilan, Kelle, Kelden.*

KELLY (KEL-lee) Irish Gaelic: "spirited."

KELSEY (KEL-see) Old English: "town of the keels." Place name. *Keldon, Kelten, Keltonn.*

KELVIN (KEL-vin) Celtic: "man of the waters." *Kelven, Kelvan, Kelvyn.*

KEMAL (KEH-mahl) Turkish: "greatest honor."

KEMPE (kemp) English: "warrior." *Kemp.*

KENAZ (KEN-azh) Hebrew: "bright."

KENDALL (KEN-dull) English: "valley of the river Kent." Place name referring to Kent, England. *Kendal, Kendel, Kendale.*

KENDRICK (KEN-drik) Welsh Gaelic: "royal chieftain." *Kendrik, Kendric, Kendrix.*

KENLEY (KEN-lee) Old English: "royal field." Place name. *Kenlea, Kenlee, Kenleigh, Kenlie, Kenly.*

KENNEDY (KEN-neh-dee) Irish: "ugly helmet." Sports: Kennedy McKinney won the 1988 Olympic gold medal for bantam-weight boxing. *Canaday, Canzady, Kenneday.*

KENNETH (KENN-ith) Irish Gaelic: "appealing." The first king of Scotland was named Kenneth. Literature: Kenneth Patchen, poet. Movies and Television: Kenneth Branagh, actor and director. Music: Kenny Rogers, country and western singer; Kenny Loggins, pop singer. Eng: *Ken, Kennett, Kennith, Kenny, Kenney;* Russ: *Kenya, Kesha;* Span: *Chencho, Incencio, Inocente.*

KENRICH (KEN-rick) Welsh: "chief hero." Old English: "royal ruler." *Kenriek, Kenrik, Kenryk, Kenric.*

KENT (kent) Old English: A county in England. *Kenton, Kentrell, Kenrick.*

KENTON (KEN-tun) Old English: "castle estate." Place name. Used as a first name since the 1950s.

KEOLA (keh-OH-luh) Hawaiian: "the life."

KEON (key-ON) United States. English: African-American invention. *Keyon, Kion.*

KEREM (keh-REM) Turkish: "virtuous."

KEREY (KEH-ree) English Gypsy: "going home." *Keir, Ker, Keri.*

KERN (kurn) Irish Gaelic: "dark-haired child." *Kearn, Kerne, Kieran.*

KERR (kir) Irish Gaelic: "sword" or "black" or "a spear."

KERRY (KER-ree) Irish Gaelic: "father's dark child." *Keary, Kerrigan.*

KERWIN (KUR-win) Irish Gaelic: "baby with the blackest eyes." Popular in the United States and Ireland. *Kervin, Kervyn, Kerwen, Kerwinn, Kirwin.*

KESIN (keh-SEEN) Hindi: "little beggar with big hair."

KEVE (keev) Hungarian: "pebble."

KEVIN (KEH-vin) Irish Gaelic: "good-looking." Movies and Television: Kevin Costner, actor and director. Sports: Kevin Butler, football player. *Kevan, Keven, Kevon, Kevyn.*

KHALDUN (khal-DOON) North Africa. Arabic: "forever."

KHALFANI (kahl-FAH-nee) East Africa. Swahili: "born to lead."

KHALIL (kahl-EEL) Arabic: "friend."

KHIRY (KEER-ee) Contemporary creation formed from the Arabic word *khayru,* meaning "benevolent." *Khiri, Kiry.*

KIBBE (KEEB-beh) Native American. Nayas: "night bird."

KIEFER (KEE-fer) German: "barrel-maker." Movies and Television: Kiefer Sutherland, actor. *Keefer.*

KIEL (KYE-el) Irish Gaelic: "good-looking." *Kyle.*

KIERAN (KEE-ran) Irish Gaelic: "dark" or "swarthy." *Keiran, Keiron, Keran, Keirnan, Kieron.*

KIHO (CHEE-ho) Uganda. Dutooro: "fog" or "child born on a foggy day."

KILIAN (KIL-ee-an) Irish Gaelic: "problems." *Killian, Killie, Killy.*

KIM (kim) Vietnamese: "precious metal" or "golden ore." History: Kim Dae-Jung, President of South Korea and Nobel Peace Prize winner (2000).

KIMBALL (KIM-bull) Old English: "courageous warrior." *Kimbal, Kimbell, Kimble.*

KIN (kin) Japanese: "made of gold."

KINCAID (kin-KAYD) Celtic: "lead warrior."

KINGSLEY (KINGS-lee) English: "regal meadow." Literature: Kingsley Amis, British novelist. *King, Kingley, Kinsley.*

KINGSTON (KING-stun) Old English: "out of the kingdom." *King, Kinston.*

KINGSWELL (KINGS-well) Old English: "well of the king."

KINNARD (KIN-nard) Irish Gaelic: "tall slope."

KINSEY (kin-SEY) Old English: "victorious prince."

KIPP (kip) Old English: "he who hails from the sharp peak." *Kipper, Kippie, Kippy.*

KIRAL (ki-RUHL) Turkish: "supreme chief."

KIRBY (KUR-bee) Old Norse: "lives in the devoted village." *Kerby, Kerbie, Kerbey, Kirbie, Kirkby.*

KIRI (KEE-ree) Cambodian: "mountain."

KIRK (kurk) Old Norse: "church owned." Science: Kirk Bryan, geologist. Sports: Kirk Gibson, baseball player. *Kirke, Kerk.*

KIRKLEY (KURK-lee) Old English: "meadow by the church." *Kirklee, Kirklie.*

KIRKWELL (KURK-well) Old English: "spring beside the church." Place name.

KIRKWOOD (KURK-wood) Old English: "forest by the church."

KISHO (KYE-show) Japanese: "one who knows his own mind."

KISTNA (KIST-nah) Hindi: Place name. Refers to the Kistna River, a sacred river in the Hindu religion.

KISTUR (KEE-stoor) English Gypsy: "One who rides skillfully."

KIVI (KEE-vee) Hebrew: "defend" or "provide generously." Common in Israel. *Akiba, Akiva, Kiva.*

KIYOSHI (kee-YO-shee) Japanese: "peaceful" or "wordless." *Yoshi.*

KNOTON (K'NO-ton) Native American: "the wind." *Nodin.*

KNOX (noks) Old English: "he who hails from the hills."

KNUTE (noot) Scandinavian: "knotty." English use dates back to the eleventh century. Sports: Knute Rockne, Notre Dame football coach who revolutionized the game by stressing the forward pass. *Knud, Cnut, Knut, Canute.*

KOBE (KOH-bee) Hebrew: "supplanter."

KODY (KO-dee) English: "helpful." *Kodey, Kodie.*

KOEN (KOH-en) German: "brave and gallant."

KOFI (koh-FEE) African: "born on Friday." History: Kofi Annan, Nobel Peace Prize winner from Ghana (2001).

KOI (KO-ee) Hawaiian: "enlist."

KOKAYI (koh-KAH-yee) Zimbabwe. Shona: "gather them together."

KONALA (koe-NAH-lah) Hawaiian: "world ruler."

KONO (KO-no) Native American. Miwok: "squirrel gnaws pine nut through."

KONSTANCJI (kon-STAHNT-syee) Latin: "steadfast." Popular name, especially in Russia. Pol: *Konstanty;* Russ: *Kostantin, Kostya, Kostenka;* Swed: *Konstantin.*

KORBIN (KORE-bin) Latin: "raven."

KRISHNA (KRISH-nah) Hindi: "pleasurable" or "inspiring." Krishna is the name of one of God's divine incarnations into human form in the Hindu religion. *Kistna, Kistnah, Krisha, Krishnah.*

KRISTOS (KREES-tos) Greek: "Christ-bearer."

KUGONZA (koo-GO-'nzah) Uganda. Dutooro: "love."

KUNLE (KOON-leh) Nigeria. Yoruba: "acclaimed home."

KURT (kurt) German: Variation of Conrad. See Conrad.

KUZIH (KOO-zhi) Native American. Carrier: "skillful speaker."

KWACHA (KWAH-chah) Malawi. Ngoni: "morning."

KWENDE (KWEHN-deh) Malawi. Ngoni: "let's go."

KYLE (kile) Scottish: "chief." Sports: Kyle Abbott, baseball player. *Kyler, Kylan, Kylar, Kylen, Kye, Kyrell.*

KYROS (KEEH-ros) Greek: "master."

LABEL (LAAH-bell) Hebrew: "lion."

LACHLAN (LOCK-lin) Scottish Gaelic: "from the land of lakes." Very popular name in both Australia and Scotland. Military: Lachlan McIntosh, American Revolutionary soldier who wintered at Valley Forge with General Washington. *Lachlann, Lachuun.*

LADD (lad) Middle English: "assistant" or "servant." *Lad, Laddie, Laddy, Laddey.*

LADISLAV (LAHDI-slav) Czech: "famous ruler."

LADO (LAH-do) Southern Sudan. Bari: "he that arrives second." Can refer to the second of male twins.

LAFAYETTE (lah-fay-ETT) French: Surname used as a first name. Military: Lafayette du Motier, general under George Washington.

LAIRD (layrd) Scottish: "lord." Scottish land-holder's title.

LAIS (lays) East Indian: "powerful lion." Popular name in India.

LAL (lahl) Hindi: "loved one." Used in India.

LAM (lahm) Vietnamese: "full understanding" or "knowledge."

LAMAR (lah-MAR) Old German: "well-known land." Education: Lamar Alexander, former U.S. Secretary of Education. Sports: Lamar Hunt established the American Football League. *LaMarr, Lamarr.*

LAMBERT (LAM-burt) Old German: "land-bright." *Bert, Lamberto, Lambirt, Landbert.*

LAMONT (luh-MONT) Scandinavian, Gaelic: "man of law." Lamond is a Scottish clan name. *Lamonte, Lamond, Lammond, Monty.*

LANCE (lance) Old German: "land." Sports: Lance Johnson, baseball player, Lance Armstrong Olympic medalist in cycling and five-time winner of the Tour De France. *Lancelot, Launce, Launcelot.*

LANDER (LAN-der) Middle English: "owner of property."

LANDON (LAN-don) Old English: "rolling, green fields." Sports: Landon Turner, basketball player. *Landan, Landen.*

LANDRY (LAN-dree) Anglo-Saxon: "leader."

LANE (layne) Middle English: "one from the narrow road." *Layne, Laine.*

LANG (lang) Old English: "tall."

LANGDON (LANG-don) Old English: "coming from the tall hill." *Land, Landon, Langden.*

LANGFORD (LANG-fird) Old English: "long ford." Place name. Theater: Lanford Wilson, Pulitzer Prize-winning playwright who wrote *Fifth of July. Lanford.*

LANGLEY (LANG-lee) Old English: "from the dense fields." Place name. *Lang, Langly, Langlea, Langlee, Langleigh.*

LANGSTON (LANG-stin) Old English: "giant's village." Literature: Langston Hughes, African-American poet, short-story writer, and lyricist known for reflecting the black experience in the United States. *Lang, Langsdon, Langsden.*

LANGUNDO (lahn-GOON-do) Native American: "calm and trusting."

LANI (LAHN-nee) Polynesian: "heaven." Used in Hawaii.

LANTOS (LAHN-toes) Hungarian: "lute player."

LAP (lapp) Vietnamese: "independent."

LAPIDOS (LAH-pee-dos) Israel. Hebrew: "torches." Used in Israel. *Lapidoth.*

LARRIMORE (LAR-ee-more) Old French: "armorer." *Larmer, Larmor.*

LARS (lars) Latin: "laurel." *Larry.*

LASZLO (LAHZ-loh) Hungarian: "renowned leader." *Laslo, Lazlo.*

LATEEF (lah-TEEF) North Africa. Arabic: "civilized." *Latif.*

LATHAM (LAY-tham) Scandinavian: "barn." Place name.

LATIMER (LAH-tih-mer) Middle English: "interpreter."

LAVAN (LAH-van) Israel. Hebrew: "white." Popular in Israel.

LAVE (LAH-vee) Israel. Hebrew: "roaring lion." Astrology: Appropriate for child born under Leo, represented by the lion. Yiddish: *Leib, Leibel.*

LAWLER (LAW-ler) Irish Gaelic: "one who mutters." *Lawlor, Loller, Lollar.*

LAWRENCE (LAWR-intz) Latin: "laurels." Name of a third-century martyr, Saint Laurence. History: Lorenzo de'Medici, ruler of Florence and patron of literature and art. Literature: Larry McMurtry, Pulitzer Prize-winning novelist (*Lonesome Dove*).

Movies and Television: Sir Laurence Olivier, actor. Science: Laurent Lafforgue, renowned French mathematician. Sports: Larry Bird, basketball player; Lawrence Taylor, football player. Eng: *Larry, Lauren, Laurence, Lon, Lonnie, Lonny, Lorn, Lorne, Loren, Lorin;* Basque: *Lauren, Laurentzi, Lorentz, Loren;* Den: *Lauritz, Lorenz, Lorens;* Fin: *Lauri;* Fr: *Laurent;* Ger: *Lorenz;* Hung: *Lenci, Lorant, Lorinc, Lorenca, Lorencz;* Ir: *Labhras, Lon, Laurence;* Ital: *Lorenzo, Loren, Renzo;* Pol: *Inek, Lorenz, Laivrenty;* Port: *Lourenco, Laurencho;* Russ: *Labrentsis, Laurentiji, Larka, Larya, Lavr, Lavrik, Lavro;* Span: *Chencho, Laurencio, Lencho, Lorenzo;* Swed/Norw: *Lars, Larse, Laurans, Lorens.*

LAWTON (LAW-tun) Old English: "out of the hill village." *Laughton, Law.*

LAZARUS (LAH-zah-rus) Hebrew: "God will assist." Bible: Lazarus, brother of Martha and Mary, was resurrected by Jesus. *Eleazer, Laza, Lazare, Lazaro, Lazzro.*

LEAL (LEE-ahl) English: "loyal."

LEANDER (lee-AN-dir) Greek: "man who is leonine." Mythology: The name of the mythological stalwart who swam the Hellespont strait to see his lady-love. *Ander, Leandre, Leandro, Leandros, Lee, Leo.*

LEAR (leer) German: "of the meadow." Literature: Main character in Shakespeare's play *King Lear.*

LEATHAN (LEE-than) Scottish: "river." *Leith.*

LEB (lay) Hebrew: "heart."

LEBEN (LAY-ben) Israel. Yiddish: "life." Popular in Israel.

LEE (lee) Old English: "pasture." Business: Lee Iacocca, Chrysler Corporation chairman. *Leigh.*

LEGGETT (LEG-it) Old French: "representative of the people." *Legate, Leggitt, Liggett.*

LEIF (leef) Scandinavian: "loved one." According to Norse legend, the Viking Leif Ericson landed his longboat on North American shores some five hundred years before Columbus arrived.

LEIGHTON (LAY-tin) English: "village by the meadow." Place name. *Layton, Leyton.*

LELAND (LEE-lund) English: "grazing ground." Science: Leland H. Hartwell, American Nobel Prize winner in Medicine (2001). *Leeland, Leighland, Leyland.*

LEMUEL (LEMM-you-el) Hebrew: "devoted to God." Bible: Lemuel was a king mentioned in Proverbs. Literature: Lemuel Gulliver, hero of Swift's satire *Gulliver's Travels. Lem, Lemmie.*

LEN (lehn) Native American. Hopi: "flute."

LENNON (LEN-inn) Irish Gaelic: "cape."

LENNOX (LEN-icks) Scottish Gaelic: "with many elm trees." *Lenx.*

LEO (LEE-oh) Latin: "lion." Thirteen popes have been named Leo. Astrology: The sun sign of Leo is represented by the lion. Literature: Leo Tolstoy, Russian novelist. Science: Leo Szilard, nuclear physicist instrumental in ushering in the atomic age. *Lee, Leon, Leontios, Lion, Lyon.*

LEON (LEE-on) Latin: "powerful like a lion." History: Leon Trotsky, Russian Communist who led the Bolshevik seizure of power in 1917. Literature: Leon Uris, novelist. Czech: *Leo, Leosko, Lev;* Gk: *Leonidas;* Ital: *Leone;* Lith: *Leonas, Liutas;* Pol: *Leonek, Leos;* Port: *Leao, Leonardo;* Russ: *Leo, Leva, Levka, Levko.*

LEONARD (LEN-ard) Old German: "lion-hearted." Leonard was the name of a saint in the Middle Ages. He is the patron saint of prisoners. Arts: Leonardo da Vinci, fifteenth-century Italian painter. Education: Leonardo Fibonacci, Italian mathematician who introduced Arabic numerals to Europe in the Middle Ages. Movies and Television: Leonard Nimoy, actor. Music: Leonard Bernstein, composer. Eng: *Lee, Len, Lenny, Leo, Leon, Lon, Lonnie, Lonny;* Fr: *Lienard;* Ger: *Leonhard;* Gk: *Leonidas, Leonides;* Ital/Span: *Leonardo;* Pol: *Leonek, Linek, Nardek;* Russ: *Leonid, Lonya;* Swed/Norw: *Leontes.*

LEOPOLD (LEE-oh-pold) Old German: "daring ones." Music: Leopold Stokowski, conductor who established the American Symphony Orchestra (1962). *Leo, Leupold.*

LEOR (leh-OHR) Israel. Hebrew: "light descends into me."

LERON (leh-ROHN) Israel. Hebrew: "song of my soul." Contemporary Israeli name. *Lerone, Lerato, Liron, Lirone.*

LEROY (LEE-roy) French: "king." Originally an occupational name for pages or servants who reported directly to the king. Business: Leroy Grumann, president of Grumann Aircraft Engineering Company (1929–46). Music: Leroy Jenkins, composer. *Lee, Leeroy, LeeRoy, LeRoi, Roy, Leroi, LeRoy, Elroi, Elroy.*

LESLIE (LEZ-lee) Scottish Gaelic: "gray castle." Place name that was once used by Scottish royalty. Movies and Television: Leslie Howard, Leslie Nielsen, actors. *Leslea, Leslee, Lesley, Lesly, Lezly, Lessie, Les.*

LESTER (LES-tir) Old English: "from Leicester." Leicester is an area in central England. *Leicester, Les.*

LEV (lehv) Israel. Hebrew: "heart." *Leb.*

LEVERETT (LEV-ir-ett) Old French: "young hare." *Leveret, Leverit, Leveritt.*

LEVI (LAY-vee) Hebrew: "joined in harmony." Used widely in Israel. Bible: Levi was the son of Jacob and Leah. Also, the name of a priestly tribe of Israel. Business: Levi Strauss, jeans manufacturer. *Lev, Levey, Levy, Lewi, Levon.*

LI (lee) Chinese: "strength."

LIAM (lee-AHM) Irish. See William.

LIANG (LEE-ahng) Chinese: "superior" or "well done."

LIKO (LEE-koh) Hawaiian: "bud."

LINCOLN (LINK-an) Latin, Welsh: "village by the lake." Journalism: Joseph Lincoln Steffens, leader of the muckrakers. *Linc, Link.*

LINDBERG (LIND-burg) Old German: "mountain where the linden trees flourish." Place name. *Lindbergh, Lindburg, Lindy.*

LINDELL (LIN-dull) Teutonic: "from the linden tree dell." Place name. *Lendell, Lendall, Lindall, Lindel, Lyndall, Lyndell.*

LINDLEY (LIND-lee) Old English: "pasture of linden." Place name. *Lindlea, Lindlee, Lindleigh, Lindly.*

LINDSAY (LINN-zay) Anglo-Saxon: "island of linden trees." Journalism: Lindsey Nelson, sports reporter. *Lindsey, Lind, Lindsee, Lindsy, Linsay, Linsey, Lyndsay, Lyndsey, Lyndale.*

LINFORD (LIN-fird) Old English: "linden tree ford." Place name. *Lynford.*

LINFRED (LIN-freed) Old German: "transcendent peace" or "calm." Contemporary German name.

LINLEY (LINN-lee) Old English: "flax meadow." Place name. *Linlea, Linlee, Linleigh, Linly.*

LINTON (LINN-tin) Old English: "city of flax."
Lintonn, Lynton, Lyntonn.

LINUS (LYE-nus) Greek: "flaxen-haired." Linus
was the second Pope. Arts: Linus, a character in the
cartoon *Peanuts*. Science: Linus Pauling, Nobel
Prize-winning chemist (1954).

LINWOOD (LYN-wood) Old English: "stream forest."

LIONEL (LYE-ah-null) Latin: "lion cubs." Movies
and Television: Lionel Barrymore, actor. Music: Lionel Richie, pop singer. Span: *Lionello, Leonel, Li-
onell, Lonell, Lonnell.*

LISIMBA (lee-SEEM-bah) Malawi. Yao: "lion."

LITTON (LIT-ton) Old English: "hillside town."

LLEWELLYN (loo-ELL-an) Welsh: "leonine."
Llewllyn, Lew.

LLOYD (loid) Welsh: "grey." Movies and Television: Lloyd Bridges, actor. Theater: In 1959, Lloyd
Richards became the first African-American to di-
rect a Broadway play, *A Raisin in the Sun*. *Floyd,
Loyd.*

LOCHLAIN (LOCK-lane) Irish: "home of the
Norse."

LOCKE (lock) Old English: "trench" or "forest."
Lock, Lockwood.

LOGAN (LOH-gun) Irish Gaelic: "small cove." Literature: Logan Pearsall Smith, author. Science: Logan Clendening, medical writer who wrote *The Human Body.*

LOMAN (LO-mahn) Serbo-Croatian: "sensitive" or "tender."

LON (lahn) Irish Gaelic: "unflinching" or "powerful." *Lonnie, Lonny.*

LONATO (lo-NAH-to) Native American: "flint stone."

LONG (lahng) Vietnamese: "hair."

LONO (LOH-no) Hawaiian: "god of the crops."

LONZO (LOHN-zoh) Spanish: "fierce." Variant of Alfonzo.

LORIMER (LORE-eh-mer) Latin: "one who makes harnesses." *Lorrimer.*

LORING (LORR-ing) Old German: Derived from French duchy meaning "famous in war." *Lorring.*

LOUIS (LOO-iss) Old German, Old French: "renowned fighter." History: Name used by eighteen French kings, of whom Louis XIV (1638–1715), called "The Sun King," is the best known. Literature: Louis Untermayer, poet and humorist. Movies and Television: Louis Gossett, Jr., actor. Music: Louis "Satchmo" Armstrong, jazz trumpeter and bandleader. Science: Louis Pasteur, French chemist who developed pasteurization and a vaccine against rabies. Sports: Lou Gehrig, baseball great who played a record 2,130 consecutive games. Eng: *Lew, Lewes, Lewis, Lon, Lou, Louie;* Czech: *Lude, Ludek, Ludko, Ludvik;* Fin: *Ludirk;* Fr: *Clovis, Louis;* Ger: *Lothar, Ludwig;* Ital: *Ludovici, Luigi;* Latin: *Ludis;* Pol: *Ludwik, Lutek;* Port: *Luis;* Russ: *Ludis;* Swed/Norw: *Ludvig.*

LOWELL (LOH-ull) Norman French: "wolf cub." Journalism: Lowell Thomas, radio newscaster. *Lovel, Lovell, Lowe, Lowel.*

LUCIAN (LOO-shan) Latin: "illumination." History: Lucien Bonaparte, president of the Council of Five Hundred who ensured his brother Napoleon's election as French consul. Music: Luciano Pavarotti, opera singer. Ital: *Luciano, Lucio, Lucan, Lucio, Lucca;* Fr: *Lucien, Lucianus, Lucjan, Lukianos, Lukyan.*

LUCIUS (LOO-shus) Latin: "illumination." Used by the Romans. *Luca, Lucas, Luce, Lucias, Lucio, Lukas, Luke.*

LUDLOW (LUD-loh) Old English: "mountain of the chief." Place name. *Ludlowe.*

LUDWIG (LUDE-wig) German: "famous victories." Music: Ludwig van Beethoven, composer famous for his nine symphonies. Philosophy: Ludwig Wittgenstein, pioneer in linguistic analysis.

LUGONO (loo-GOH-noh) Malawi. Ngoni: "sleep."

LUIGI (LOO-ee-gee) Italian: "warrior."

LUKE (luke) Greek: "illuminating." Place name: Luciania, region of Southern Italy. Bible: Luke was a first-century Christian who is the patron saint of doctors and artists. Movies and Television: Luke Wilson, actor. Eng: *Lucus, Lucian, Lucien, Lucius, Luck, Lucky;* Czech: *Lukas;* Fr: *Luce, Lucien, Lucius;* Ger: *Lucius, Lukas;* Gk: *Loukas;* Hung: *Lukacs;* Lat: *Lukass;* Pol: *Lukasz;* Port/Span: *Luccas;* Russ: *Luchok, Luka, Lukash, Lukasha, Lukyan;* Swed: *Lukas;* Zuni: *Lusio, Luc, Lucio.*

LUKMAN (look-MAHN) North Africa. Arabic: "seer."

LUNDY (LUN-dee) Scottish Gaelic: "grove by the island."

LUNN (lun) Irish Gaelic: "always ready for a fight." *Lon, Lonn.*

LUNT (luhnt) Swedish: "from the grove."

LUTHANDO (LUTH-and-oh) Latin: "loving."

LUTHER (LOO-thir) Old German: "warring ones." Music: Luther Vandross, soul singer. Science: Luther Burbank, horticulturist who developed a strain of potato that bears his name. *Lotario, Lothair, Lothar, Lothario, Lutero, Lute.*

LYLE (lile) Old French: "from the isle." Music: Lyle Richards, Lyle Lovett, singers. Sports: Lyle Alzado, football player. *Lisle, Lyall, Lyell, Lysle, Ly.*

LYMAN (LYE-minn) Old English: "man from the valley." Military: Lyman Lemnitzer, U.S. Army general, a World War II hero who later became chairman of the Joint Chiefs of Staff. *Leaman, Leyman.*

LYNCH (linch) Irish Gaelic: "sailor."

LYNDON (LINN-dun) Old English: "from the hill of linden trees." History: Lyndon Baines Johnson, thirty-sixth president of the United States (1963–69). *Lyndell, Lindon, Lyn, Lin, Lindy, Lynn, Linden, Lynden.*

LYRON (lee-ROHN) Israel. Hebrew: "songlike" or "with lyricism." Israeli name. *Liron.*

LYSANDER (lye-SAN-der) Greek: "he who has come to free." Literature: Lysander is one of the main characters in Shakespeare's *A Midsummer Night's Dream.* Span: *Lisandro.*

MAC (mack) Scottish Gaelic: "son of" or "heir to." Also a nickname for longer names starting with "Mac." *Mack, Macklin, Mackie.*

MACARIO (mah-KAR-ee-oh) Spanish: "happy."

MACAULAY (mah-KAW-lay) Scottish: "son of righteousness." Surname used as a first name. Movies and Television: Macaulay Culkin, actor.

MACBRIDE (mak-BRIDE) Irish Gaelic: "son of a devotee of Saint Brigid." Saint Brigid was an influential fifth-century Irish nun. *Macbryde, McBride.*

MACCOY (mah-KOY) Irish Gaelic: "heir of Hugh." *MacCoy, McCoy.*

MACDONALD (mak-DAHN-ild) Scottish Gaelic: "Donald's son." *MacDonald, McDonald.*

MACGOWAN (mak-GOW-in) Irish Gaelic: "son of the blacksmith." *MacGowna, Magowna, McGowan.*

MACHAIR (MAC-aire) Scottish: "plain." *Machar.*

MACKENZIE (mah-KEN-zee) Irish Gaelic: "son of the learned leader." *MacKenzie.*

MACKINLEY (mah-KIN-lee) Irish Gaelic: "wide rulers." *Mackinley, McKinley.*

MACMURRAY (mak-MURR-ay) Irish Gaelic: "sailor's son." *Mac, Mack, Murray, Murry, MacMurray, McMurray.*

MACY (MAY-see) Old French: "from Matthew's land." Old English: "club." *Macie.*

MADDOCK (MA-duck) Old Welsh: "generous." *Madoc, Madock, Madog.*

MADDOX (MA-ducks) Anglo-Welsh: "son of the patron." Contracted form of "Maddock's son." Literature: Ford Maddox Ford, poet, critic, editor, and novelist. *Madox.*

MADISON (MA-dih-sunn) Old English: "son of the brave soldier." Literature: Madison Jones, novelist and short-story writer. *Maddie, Maddy.*

MAED (mayd) English: "meadow."

MAERT (MAYER-et) English: "little famous one."

MAGEE (mah-GEE) Irish Gaelic: "son of Hugh." *MacGee, MacGhee, McGee.*

MAGNUS (MAG-nus) Latin: "excellent." Science: Magnus Mittag-Leffler, Swedish mathematician who derived theorem that bears his name. *Magnes, Manus.*

MAGUIRE (mah-GWIRE) Irish Gaelic: "son of the beige one." *MacGuire, McGuire, McGwire.*

MAHER (mare) Irish: "generous."

MAHIR (mah-HEER) Israel. Hebrew: "industrious" or "expert."

MAHON (MA-hone) Gaelic: "bear."

MAIMUN (mye-MOON) Arabic: "fortunate."

MAJOR (MAY-jir) Latin: "better." Military: Surname that is also a military rank. *Majar, Mayer, Mayor.*

MAKALANI (mah-kah-LAH-nee) Kenya. Mwera: "excellent writer."

MAKALO (mah-kah-LOH) African: "wondering."

MAKAN (mah-KAH-an) Hawaiian: "wind."

MAKARIOS (MA-ka-rios) Greek: "anointed." *Macario, Macarios, Maccario, Maccarios.*

MAKIN (mah-KIN) Arabic: "strong." *Makeen.*

MAKOTO (ma-KOH-toh) Japanese: "good."

MALACHI (MA-la-kye) Hebrew: "God's messenger." Bible: Malachi wrote the last book of the Old Testament. *Malachie, Malachy, Malechy.*

MALCOLM (MAL-cumm) Scottish Gaelic: "follower of Saint Columbus." Business: Malcolm Forbes, publisher of *Fortune* magazine. Theater: Character in Shakespeare's play *Macbeth*. History: Malcolm X was the first black Moslem "national minister." Movies and Television: Title character of the popular TV show *Malcolm in the Middle*. *Malcolum, Malkolm.*

MALIK (mah-LEEK) Arabic: "master." *Malique.*

MALIN (MAY-lin) Old English: "brave, young soldier." *Mallin, Mallon.*

MALLORY (MAL-oh-ree) Old French: "without fortune." Also used for girls. *Mallery, Mallorie, Malory, Mal, Lory.*

MALONEY (mal-LO-nee) Irish Gaelic: "churchgoing." *Malone, Malony.*

MALVIN (MAL-vin) Irish: "leader." *Malvyn.*

MAMO (MAH-mo) Hawaiian: "yellow blossom."

MANCHU (MAN-chew) Chinese: "stainless" or "immaculate."

MANCO (MAHN-ko) Peru. Spanish: "supreme leader" or "high authority."

MANDALA (mahn-DAH-lah) Malawi. Yao: "flowers."

MANDAR (MAHN-dar) Hindi: "tree of heaven."

MANDEL (MAN-dull) German: "almond." *Mandell.*

MANDEK (MAN-dek) Polish: "army man."

MANELIN (MAN-ell-in) Persian: "prince of princes."

MANFRED (MAN-freed) Old English: "one who bestows peace." Aeronautics: Manfred von Richthofen, the name of the World War I aviator called the "Red Baron." Literature: Manfred Lee, one of the team of detectives that assumed the name Ellery Queen. Music: Manfred Mann, pop singer. *Manfrid, Manfried, Mannfred, Mannfryd.*

MANIPI (mah-NEE-pee) Native American: "living marvel."

MANLEY (MAN-lee) Old English: "the man's pasture." Literature: Gerhard Manley Hopkins, poet.

MANN (man) English: "hero."

MANNING (MAN-ing) Old English: "son of man."

MANSA (MAHN-sah) African: "king." In ancient Egypt the mansa rulers always had a large entourage.

MANSEL (MAN-sell) Old English: "from the manse," a cleric's house. *Mansell.*

MANSFIELD (MANS-feeld) Old English: "field by the narrow waters."

MANSOUR (MANS-or) Arabic: "one who triumphs."

MANTON (MAN-tun) Old English: "town of the returning hero." Place name. *Manten, Mannton.*

MANVILLE (MAN-vill) Old French: "wonderful villa." *Mandeville, Manvile, Manvill.*

MANUEL (MAN-u-el) Hebrew: "God in us." Derived from the ancient form Emanuel. The name is most widely used in Spanish-speaking countries. History: Manuel Lisa, eighteenth-century fur trader who established posts along the Missouri River. Czech: *Eman, Emanuel;* Hung: *Maco, Mano;* Lat: *Emek;* Span: *Mango, Manny, Manuel, Minel;* Russ: *Emmanuil, Manuyil;* Yiddish: *Immanuel.*

MARAR (mah-RAHR) Southern Zimbabwe. Wataware: "mud" or "dust."

MARCEL (mar-SELL) French: "little hammer."

MARCELLUS (mar-SELL-us) Latin: "young fighter." One of a group of names that all have their root in Mars, the Roman god of war. Literature: Marcel Proust, Nobel Prize-winning French novelist. *Marceau, Marcelin, Marcelin, Marcello, Marcely, Marcel.*

MARCUS (MAR-cus) Latin: "rebellious." History: Marcus Maximilian, Holy Roman emperors reigned: I (1493–1519); II (1564–76). Sports: Marcus Allen,

Heisman Trophy-winning football player. Czech: *Marko;* Fr: *Marc, Marque;* Ger: *Marcas, Markus, Markel, Markell;* Gk: *Markos;* Hung: *Markus;* Russ: *Marko, Markov, Markusha;* Slav: *Marek;* Span: *Marco, Marcos, Marquez;* Port: *Marques, Markos, Marcio, Marco.*

MARDEN (MAR-den) Old English: "from the valley with the pool." *Mardon.*

MARID (MAH-rid) Arabic: "argumentative" or "revolutionary."

MARINO (ma-REE-no) Latin: "of the sea."

MARIUS (MAR-ee-us) Latin: Roman clan name. Education: Marius Servius, fourth-century Latin grammarian and scholar. Literature: Mario Puzo, novelist. Science: Mario J. Molina, Nobel Prize winner in Chemistry (1995). Ital: *Mario.*

MARK (mark) Latin: "battler." Bible: Saint Mark, one of the four Evangelists, is the patron saint of Venice. Business: Mark Burnett, renowned TV producer for reality TV series. Dance: Mark Morris, choreographer. History: Marcus Garvey, African-American political activist. Literature: Mark Twain (real name Samuel Clemens), writer. Sports: Mark Spitz, U.S. Olympic gold medalist swimmer. Eng: *Marc, Marcus, Markus;* Czech: *Marcus, Marek, Marko;* Den/Dutch: *Markus;* Fr: *Marc;* Gk: *Marinos, Markos;* Port: *Marcos.*

MARLAND (MAR-land) Old English: "settlement near the pond."

MARLEY (MAR-lee) Old English: "pasture beside the pond."

MARLON (mar-LON) Old French: "little hawk."

MARLOW (MAR-low) Old English: "slope beside the pond"; English: "marshy meadow." *Marley, Marlowe.*

MARMADUKE (MAR-mah-duke) Celtic: "leader of the seas."

MARMION (MAR-me-on) Old French: "small." Literature: Title of a poem by Sir Walter Scott. *Marmyon.*

MARNIN (mahr-NEEN) Israel. Hebrew: "joy giver" or "sings with delight."

MARO (MAH-roh) Japanese: "myself."

MARQUIS (mar-KEE) French: Royal rank between duke and earl. Literature: Marquis Childs, journalist and novelist who wrote *The Peacemakers.* Ital: *Marquise;* Port: *Marques, Markeese, Marqui, Markeece, Markese.*

MARQUISE (mar-KEE-say) French: Female equivalent of a marquis, but used as a boy's name by African-Americans. *Markweese, Marquece, Marqueese.*

MARSDEN (MARS-den) Old English: "valley of the marshes." Place name. Arts: Marsden Hartley, painter. *Marsdon.*

MARSH (marsh) Old English: "swampy lands." Place name.

MARSHALL (MARSH-ull) Old French: "groomsman." Also a military title. Business: Marshall Field, department store founder. Journalism: Marshall McLuhan, media theorist. *Marschal, Marsh, Marshal, Marshell.*

MARSTON (MARS-tunn) Old English: "marshside town."

MARTIN (MAR-tin) Latin: "seditious." Originated with the Roman war god, Mars. See Marcus. The fourth-century Saint Martin is the patron saint of beggars. History: Martin Van Buren, eighth president of the United States; Martin Luther founded Protestantism in the sixteenth century. Literature: *Martin Eden*, autobiography by Jack London. Movies and Television: Martin Scorcese, film director. Science: Martin L. Perl, Nobel Prize-winning scientist in Physics (1995). Eng: *Mart, Marten, Marti, Martie, Marton, Marty;* Czech: *Martinka, Tynek;* Fr: *Mertin;* Ger: *Martel;* Gk: *Martinos;* Hung: *Marci, Marcilki, Marton;* Ital: *Martino;* Lith: *Martinas;* Pol: *Marcin;* Port: *Martinho;* Russ: *Martyn;* Span: *Martiniano, Marto;* Swed: *Marten;* Slovenian: *Marti.*

MARVIN (MAR-vin) Celtic: "beautiful sea"; Anglo-Saxon: "sea friend." Music: Marvin Gaye, singer; Marvin Hamlisch, pianist and composer. *Marv, Marve, Marven, Mervyn, Merwyn, Marwynn, Mervin, Merwin, Murvynn.*

MARWOOD (MAR-wood) Old English: "forest pond." Place name.

MASKA (MAYS-kah) Native American: "strong."

MASLIN (MAS-lin) Old French: "young Thomas." *Maslen, Lasling.*

MASON (MAY-son) Old French: "sculptor" or "stone carver." Music: Mason Williams, composer and musician. *Mace, Sonnie.*

MASSIMO (MAH-see-moe) Italian: "greatest."

MASUD (mah-SOOD) Arabic: "lucky." Popular in Swahili culture in Africa.

MATAI (may-TYE) Hebrew: "gift from God." *Matz.*

MATEO (mah-TAY-oh) Greek: "devoted to God."

MATHER (MA-thur) Old English: "advancing troops."

MATT United States. English: Short form of Matthew. See Matthew.

MATTHEW (MATH-yoo) Hebrew: "divine present." Bible: Saint Matthew is the patron saint of accountants and bookkeepers. Literature: Matthew Arnold, poet. Military: Matthew Perry, nineteenth-century naval officer who opened up Japan to the West. Movies and Television: Matthew Broderick, actor. Sports: Mats Wilander, tennis star. Eng: *Mathew, Mathias, Matt, Mattias, Mattie, Matty;* Bulg: *Matei;* Czech: *Matek, Matus;* Fr: *Mathieu, Matthieu;* Ger: *Mathie, Matthaus, Matthias;* Gk: *Matthaios;* Hung: *Mate;* Ital: *Mat-*

teo; Norw: *Matteus;* Pol: *Matheiu;* Russ: *Matfei, Matvey, Mayfe, Motka, Motya;* Scot: *Mata;* Span: *Mathias.*

MAULI (MOW-lee) Hawaiian: "black."

MAURICE (maw-REESE or MORE-iss) English, French: "black Moor." Saint Maurice is the patron saint of infantrymen. Arts: Maurice Sendak, illustrator of children's books. Music: Maurice Ravel, French composer; Maurice Gibb, musician in the Bee Gees, a pop group. Eng: *Morrice, Maurie, Maurey, Maury, Morey, Morie, Morrie, Morry, Morris, Moris, Morice;* Ital: *Maurizio;* Span: *Mauricio, Morrill, Morriss, Moss, Morrison, Morrisson.*

MAVERICK (MAV-rik) United States. English: Name of a fiercely independent western cattle rancher. *Mavrick.*

MAVIS (MAY-vis) English: "a small bird."

MAXFIELD (MAX-feeld) English: "Mack's fields."

MAXIMILLIAN (MAX-ee-MILL-yun) Latin: "supreme quality." Journalism: Max Lerner, newspaper columnist. Movies and Television: Maximillian Schell, actor. Eng: *Mac, Mack, Max, Maxie, Maxy, Maxey;* Czech: *Maxi, Maxim;* Fr: *Maxim, Maxime;* Ger: *Maximalian;* Hung: *Maks, Makszi, Miksa, Maxi;* Ital: *Massimiliano, Massimo;* Ital: *Makimus, Maksymilian;* Port: *Maximilano;* Russ: *Maksim, Maksym, Maksimka, Sima;* Span: *Max, Maxi, Maximo, Maximos, Maximino.*

MAXWELL (MAX-well) Scottish: "well of Maccus." Literature: Maxwell Perkins, editor of Fitzgerald, Hemingway, and Wolfe; Maxwell Bodenheim, poet, novelist, and essayist. Science: Maxwell Close, Irish geologist. Theater: Maxwell Anderson, playwright. *Max.*

MAYER (MAY-ir) English, German: "landlord" or "proprietor." Widely used in Austria. Business: Meyer Guggenheim, merchant who built merchandising and mining empires; Meyer Rothschild, banker who founded the international banking house. *Meir, Meyer, Meyeer, Mayor, Meirer.*

MAYFIELD (MAY-feeld) Old English: "one's field is strong."

MAYNARD (MAY-nard) Old English: "hard strength." Education: John Maynard Keynes, economist who advocated deficit spending. *Meinhard, Mayne, Maynhard, Meinhard, Mendar.*

MAYNOR (MAY-nor) French: "powerful."

MAYO (MAY-oh) Irish Gaelic: "yew tree plain."

MEAD (meed) Old English: "from the pasture." *Meade, Meed.*

MEARA (meer-RAH) Irish: "happy."

MEDWIN (MED-win) Old German: "faithful ally." *Medwine, Medwyne.*

MEHTAR (meh-TAHR) East Indian: "prince." Name used to indicate noble ancestry.

MELBOURNE (MEL-born) Old English: "brook by the mill." *Mel, Melborn, Melburn, Milbourne, Milburn, Millburn, Millburne.*

MELDON (MEL-dun) Old English: "hill by the mill." *Melden.*

MELDRICK (MEL-drik) Old English: "boss of the mill."

MELE (MEL-ee) Hawaiian: "merry."

MELVILLE (MEL-vill) Anglo-Saxon: "town of the mill."

MELVIN (MEL-vin) Irish Gaelic: "Michael's friend." Movies and Television: Mel Gibson, actor; Mel Brooks, filmmaker. *Melvyn, Mel, Malvin, Malvyn, Malvynn, Melwin, Melwinn, Vinnie.*

MENDEL (MEN-del) Semitic: "scholarly accomplishments." *Mendeley.*

MERCER (MER-sir) Middle English: "shopkeeper." Occupational name. Dance: Merce Cunningham, choreographer. *Merce.*

MERLE (murle) French: "blackbird's song." Music: Merle Haggard, country and western singer. *Merlin, Merlyn, Merla.*

MERLIN (MUR-lyn) Middle English: "falcon who flies low." Literature: The original Merlin was a Welsh bard whose story became part of Arthurian legend. He appears in forms of literature as varied as the works of Geoffrey, Mark Twain, and Lerner and Lowe. Sports: Merlin Olsen, Football Hall of Fame member. *Marlin, Marlon, Merle, Merlen, Merlinn, Merlyn, Merlynn.*

MERRICK (MER-rik) English: "ruler of the sea."

MERRILL (MER-ril) English: "gleaming water." *Meril, Merill, Merrel, Merrell, Merril, Meyl.*

MERRITT (MAYR-itt) Old English: "small but famous." *Merrett, Merit, Meritt.*

MERTON (MUR-ton) Old English: "town near the pond."

MERVIN (MUR-vin) Old Welsh: "hill beside the seas." Literature: Mervyn Peake, British novelist, poet, and critic. *Mervyn, Mervynn, Merwin, Merwinn, Merwyn, Murvin, Murvyn.*

MICHAEL (MY-kul) Hebrew: "who compares to God?" Bible: Michael, slayer of dragons, is one of the original four archangels. Arts: Michelangelo, sculptor. Dance: Michael Bennett, choreographer and stage director. History: Mikhail Gorbachev, former President of the Soviet Union and Nobel Peace Prize winner (1990). Literature: Miguel de Cervantes Saavedra, author of *Don Quixote*. Movies and Television: Mickey Rooney, Michael Caine, Michael J. Fox, actors. Music: Michael Jackson and Mick Jagger, pop stars. Science: Michael Faraday, British chemist. Sports: Mickey Mantle, baseball player; Michael Jordan, basketball player, Michael Phelps, American Olympic medalist in swimming

(2004). Eng: *Mickel, Mickie, Micky, Mike, Mitch, Mitchell;* Bulg: *Mihail;* Czech: *Michal, Mychal, Mychael;* Fin: *Mikko;* Fr: *Dumichel, Michau, Michel, Michon;* Gk: *Michail, Mikhail, Mikhalis, Mikhos;* Hung: *Mihaly, Misi, Miska;* Ital: *Michele;* Norw: *Mikkei;* Pol: *Machas, Michak, Michal, Michalek, Mietek;* Port: *Miguel;* Rum: *Mihail, Mihas;* Russ: *Michail, Mika, Mikhalka, Misha, Hischa;* Slav: *Miko;* Span: *Micho, Mickey, Miguel, Migui, Miki, Mique;* Swed: *Mehalje, Mikael, Mikkel;* Ukrain: *Mihailo.*

MILAGRO (MILL-ah-grow) Spanish: "miracle."

MILAN (mee-LAHN) Italian: Place name, city in Italy. *Milano.*

MILEK (mill-EK) Polish: "victorious people."

MILES (myles) German, English: "given to mercy." History: Miles Standish, English colonist in North America, who arrived on the *Mayflower.* Music: Miles Davis, jazz trumpeter. *Milo, Myles.*

MILFORD (MIL-ford) Old English: "protector of the mill." History: Millard Fillmore, thirteenth president of the United States (1850–53). *Millward, Milward.*

MILLER (MILL-ir) Old English: "miller." *Mellar, Mylier.*

MILLS (mills) Old English: "near the mills."

MILO (MYE-loh) English: "merciful."

MILTON (MILL-tin) Old English: "town built around a mill." Movies and Television: Milton Berle, comedian. *Milt, Mylton.*

MINGAN (min-GAN) Native American: "grey wolf."

MINOR (MYE-nir) Latin: "younger." Arts: Minor White, photographer. Business: Minor Keith, railroad magnate who founded the United Fruit Company. *Mynor.*

MIO (MEE-oh) Spanish: "mine."

MIROSLAV (MEER-oh-slav) Slavic: "famous."

MISU (MEE-soo) Native American. Miwok: "rippling water."

MITCHELL American: Form of Michael. See Michael. *Mitch.*

MOE (moe) English: "dark skinned."

MOHAMMED (moh-HAH-mid) Arabic: "highly praised." The name of the prophet and founder of Islam has become one of the most common male names in the world. Sports: Muhammad Ali, heavyweight champion. *Ahmad, Ahmed, Amad, Amed, Hamid, Hamdrem, Hamdun, Hammad, Hamayd, Mahmud, Mehemet, Mehmet, Mohammad, Mohamed, Mohamad, Muhammad, Mahmoud, Mohamet, Mohomet.*

MOHAN (MO-han) Hindi: "wonderful." Another name for Krishna. See Krishna.

MOLAN (MOLE-ahn) Irish: "servant of the storm."

MONAHAN (MON-ah-han) Irish Gaelic: "pious man" or "monk." *Monaghan, Monoghan.*

MONGESKA (MOHN-ges-ka) Native American. Nebraska: "a deer's white breast."

MONGO (MOHN-go) Nigeria. Yoruba: "famous."

MONROE (MON-row or mun-ROH) Irish Gaelic: "mouth of the Roe River." *Monro, Munro, Munroe.*

MONTAGUE (MONT-ah-gyu) French: "sharp cliff." *Montagu.*

MONTGOMERY (munt-GUM-ree) Old English: "prosperity mountain." Movies and Television: Montgomery Clift, actor who starred with Marilyn Monroe in *The Misfits. Montgomerie, Monty, Monte.*

MONTSHO (MOHN-sho) Botswana. Tswana: "black."

MOONEY (MOON-ee) Irish: "wealthy."

MOORE (moor) Old English: "moors." *More.*

MORAN (MOOR-ahn) Irish: "great." *Morain.*

MORDECAI (moor-DEY-caye) Hebrew: "warrior."

MORELAND (MORE-lend) Old English: "moor." The landscape of many Scottish romances, *moor* is the Anglo-Saxon name of an extensive area of un-tamed scrubland. *Moorland, Morland.*

MORGAN (MORE-ginn) Welsh: "gleaming seas." Movies and Television: Morgan Freeman, actor. *Morgen.*

MORLEY (MORE-lee) Old English: "pasture of the moor." *Moorley, Moorly, Morlee, Morleigh, Morly, Morrley.*

MORRIS (MORE-ihs) United States: English: Anglicization of Maurice. See Maurice.

MORSE (morse) Old English: "Maurice's son." *Morrison.*

MORTIMER (MOR-tih-mer) Old French: "calm seas." *Mort, Mortym, Mortmer.*

MORTON (MORE-tinn) Old English: "town of the moor." Place name. *Morten.*

MORVEN (MORE-vin) Old English: "child of the sea."

MOSES (MOH-sez) Hebrew: "drawn from the water." Bible: Moses led the Israelites out of Egypt and received the Ten Commandments on top of Mount Sinai. History: Moshe Dayan, Israeli defense minister. Eng: *Moe, Mose, Moshe, Moss;* Bulg: *Moisei;* Fr: *Moise;* Gk: *Moisis;* Hung: *Mozes;* Ital: *Moise, Mose;* Lith: *Moze;* Pol: *Moshe, Mosze, Moszek;* Port: *Moises, Moisey, Mosya;* Russ: *Moisey, Mosya;* Yiddish: *Moises, Moshe, Mozes.*

MURDOCK (MUR-dock) Scottish Gaelic: "warrior-sailor." *Murdo, Murdoch, Murtagh, Murtaugh.*

MURPHY (MUR-fee) Irish Gaelic: "soldier of the seas."

MURRAY (MUR-ray) Scottish Gaelic: "sailor."

MYRON (MY-run) Greek: "aromatic essence." Science: Myron S. Scholes, Nobel Prize winner in economics (1997). *Miron, Myreon.*

NADAV (nah-DAHV) Hebrew: "noble" or "generous one."

NADIR (nah-DEER) Arabic: "dearly loved."

NAGID (nah-GEED) Israel. Hebrew: "leader" or "kingly." Used in Israel.

NAHELE (NAH-heh-le) Hawaiian: "jungle" or "dense garden."

NALDO (NAHL-doh) Spanish: "strong."

NALREN (NAHL-rehn) Native American. Dene: "melted."

NAMDEV (NAHM-dev) Hindu: "poet" or "saint." *Narsi.*

NAMID (NAH-meed) Native American: "dances with the lights of heaven."

NAMIR (nah-MEER) Israel. Hebrew: "swift cat." Contemporary Israeli name.

NANTAN (NAHN-tan) Native American. Apache: "spokesman."

NAPOLEON (nah-POH-lee-inn) French, Italian: "fierce one from Naples." Napoleon was the name of a fourth-century saint of Alexandria. The name was later used by prominent Italian families. History: Napoleon Bonaparte, nineteenth-century French emperor. Sports: Napoleon Lajoie, baseball player who was one of the earliest entries into the Baseball Hall of Fame (1937).

NARAIN (nah-RYNE) Hindi: "vishnu." In Hindu lore, Vishnu is the supreme deity of the world.

NARCISSE (nahr-SIS-suh) French: "daffodil." Mythology: Name of a beautiful Greek youth who would only love his own reflection. *Narcissus, Markissos.*

NASH (nash) Old English: "cliff."

NASSER (NAS-sir) Arabic: "triumphant." One of the ninety-nine qualities of God listed in the Koran. Favorite among Moslems.

NATHAN (NA-thin) Hebrew: "blessing." Derivative of Nathaniel used as an independent name. Bible: The name of the prophet who rebuked David for his treachery to Uriah. Business: Nathan Strauss, German-born merchant who headed Macy's department store. History: Nathan Hale, American Revolutionary War hero. Music: Nathan Milstein, violinist. Eng: *Nat, Nate, Nathen, Nathon, Natt, Natty;* Hung/Span: *Natan.*

NATHANIEL (na-THAN-yell) Hebrew: "divinely bestowed." Literature: Nathaniel Hawthorne, novelist. Eng: *Nat, Nate, Nathan, Nathon, Natt, Natty;* Fr: *Nathanael;* Ital: *Nataniele.*

NAV (nahv) Hungarian: "nomenclature." Used by English Gypsies.

NAVARRO (nah-VAR-oh) Spanish: "plains." *Navarre.*

NAWAT (NAH-waht) Native American: "on the left."

NAYATI (nah-YAH-tee) Native American: "he who fights or wrestles."

NEESE (nees) Celtic: "choice."

NEHEMIAH (nee-ah-MYE-ah) Hebrew: "God soothes." Bible: Nehemiah was an Old Testament prophet. Science: Nehemiah Grew, British botanist who pioneered the study of plant anatomy.

NEIL (neel) Irish Gaelic: "victor." Aeronautics: Neil Armstrong, astronaut and first man on the moon. Music: Neil Diamond, Neil Young, singers. Theater: Neil Simon, Pulitzer Prize-winning playwright (*Lost in Yonkers*). Eng: *Neal, Neale, Neall, Nealle, Neile, Neille, Neill, Neils, Nels, Nial, Niels,*

Niles, Nigel; Fin: *Nilo;* Russ: *Nil, Nilya;* Scan: *Nels, Niels, Nils;* Scot: *Niall, Nealon.*

NELEK (NEEL-ek) Polish: "like a horn."

NELSON (NEL-sun) English: "son of Neil." English surname used as a first name. History: Nelson Mandela, South African civil-rights leader; Nelson Rockefeller, vice president under President Gerald Ford. Military: Nelson Miles, Civil War officer. Music: Nelson Riddle, composer and conductor. *Nealson, Nells, Nels, Niles, Nils, Nilson, Nilsson.*

NEN (nen) Egyptian: "ancient waters." According to the Egyptian *Book of the Dead,* Nen was the spirit of primal seas, often depicted as half-man, half-frog.

NEPER (NEH-pair) Spanish: "of the new city." *Napier.*

NEPTUNE (NEP-tyoon) Roman mythology: Roman sea god.

NERIAN (neer-EE-ahn) Anglo-Saxon: "protects."

NERO (NEE-roh) Latin: "powerful" or "strict." Bulg/Fr/Span: *Neron;* Ital: *Nerone.*

NESBIT (NES-bit) Old English: "curving like a rose." *Naisbit, Naisbitt, Nesbitt, Nisbet, Nisbett.*

NESTOR (NESS-tir) Greek: "wayfarer" or "sojourner." Nestor was a wise Greek general.

NETO (NEH-toh) Spanish: "serious."

NEVADA (ne-VAH-dah) Spanish: "covered in snow." A western state in the United States.

NEVILLE (NEH-vill) Old French: "new village." Music: Neville Marriner, conductor.

NEVIN (NEH-vinn) Irish Gaelic: "spiritually significant." Science: Nevin Scrimshaw, nutritionist. *Neo, Nevan, Nevins, Nevyle.*

NEWELL (NEW-el) Old English: "new hall." *Newel, Newhall.*

NEWLAND (NOO-lind) Old English: "new land."

NEWLIN (NOO-lin) Old Welsh: "freshly made lake." Place name. *Newlyn.*

NEWMAN (NOO-min) Old English: "new arrival" or "newcomer."

NEWTON (NOO-tin) Old English: "new town." A city in Massachusetts.

NIBAL (NYE-ball) Arabic: "arrows."

NIBAW (NEE-baw) Native American: "upright" or "standing tall."

NICABAR (nee-kah-BAHR) Spanish Gypsy: "stealth" or "secret taking."

NICHOLAS (NIC-oh-las) Greek: "triumph of the people." Saint Nicholas (fourth century) is Russia's patron saint. Dance: Nico Charisse, dancer and choreographer. History: Nicholas II, czar of Russia; Nikita Khrushchev, first secretary of the Communist Party. Literature: *Nicholas Nickleby*, novel by Charles Dickens. Science: Nicolaus Copernicus, sixteenth-century astronomer who developed the heliocentric system. Eng: *Claus, Cole, Nic, Nick, Nicky, Nicol, Nikki, Nikky;* Bulg: *Nikita, Nikolas;* Czech: *Nikula;* Den: *Niels;* Dutch: *Nicolaas, Niko;* Fr: *Colin, Nicole;* Ger: *Claus, Klaus, Nikolaus;* Gk: *Nikolos, Nikos, Niko;* Hung: *Micu, Niki, Niklos;* Ital: *Coloa, Niccolo, Nicolo;* Latv: *Niklaus, Nikolais, Niklas;* Norw: *Nicolai;* Russ: *Kolya, Nikolai, Nikita;* Span: *Nicolas;* Swed: *Niklas, Nils.*

NIGEL (NIGH-gehl) Latin: "dark one."

NIHAR (NYE-har) Hindu: "mist" or "fog."

NIRAN (NIH-rahn) Thai: "eternal."

NIREL (NEE-rell) Hebrew: "God's field."

NISSIM (nee-SEEM) Israel. Hebrew: "heavenly omen." Used in Israel.

NITIS (NEE-tiss) Native American: "trustworthy" or "intimate."

NOAH (NO-ah) Hebrew: "calm" or "quietude." Bible: The hero of a well-known Bible story, Noah was led by God to build an ark that saved him, his family, and the earth's creatures during a disastrous flood. Education: Noah Webster, lexicographer, wrote the first spelling book. Bulg: *Noi;* Dutch: *Noach;* Russ: *Noi, Noy;* Span: *Noel;* Swed: *Noak.*

NOAM (NO-ahm) Hebrew: "pleasant friend."

NODIN (NOH-dinn) Native American: "windy day or spirit that blows the trees." *Noton.*

NOEL (NOH-el) French: "day of Christ's birth." Strongly associated with Christmas. Theater: Noel Coward, playwright who wrote *Private Lives.* Eng: *Nowel, Nowell;* Ital: *Natale;* Span: *Natal, Nata.*

NOLAN (NOH-linn) Irish Gaelic: "well known" and "high-born." Sports: Nolan Ryan, baseball pitcher, first to strike out 5,000 batters. *Noland, Noeln, Nolin, Nollan, Nolyn.*

NORBERT (NOR-birt) Old German: "famous in the north." Science: Norbert Wiener who founded the science of cybernetics. *Bert, Bertie, Betty, Norberto.*

NORMAN (NOR-min) Old English: "northern dweller." Arts: Norman Rockwell, artist, famed for magazine covers. Education: Norman Vincent Peale, clergyman. Journalism: Norman Cousins, editor of the *Saturday Review.* Literature: Norman Mailer, Pulitzer Prize-winning author. Military: Norman Schwarzkopf, former U.S. Army general. Movies and Television: Norman Lear, TV producer. *Norm, Normen, Normie;* Span: *Normand, Normando.*

NORRIS (NOR-iss) Old French: "arrived from northern shores." *Norrie, Norry.*

NORTHCLIFF (NORTH-cliff) Old English: "cliff in the north." Place name. *Northcliffe, Northclyff, Northclyffe.*

NORTHROP (NORTH-rupp) Old English: "farmstead in the north." Place name. Literature: Northrop Frye, critic and author. *Northrup.*

NORTON (NOR-tin) Old English: "northern settlement." Place name.

NORVILLE (NOR-vil) Old Anglo-French: "town up north." Place name. *Norval, Norvel, Norvell, Norvil, Norvill, Norvylle.*

NORVIN (NOR-vin) Old English: "friend from northern plains." *Norvyn, Norwin, Norwinn, Norwyn, Norwynn.*

NORWARD (NOR-wird) Old English: "protector of northerners." *Norwerd.*

NORWOOD (NOR-wood) Old English: "northern woods."

NOWLES (nolz) Middle English: "forest cove" or "thick meadows." *Knolls, Knowles.*

NUMAIR (noo-MARE) Arabic: "panther."

NUNCIO (NOON-see-oh) Latin: "messenger."

NURI (NOO-ree) Israel. Hebrew: "flaming lights." *Nur, Nuria, Nuriel, Nury.*

NURU (NOO-roo) East Africa. Swahili: "illumination."

NUSAIR (noo-SIRE) Arabic: "bird of prey" or "scavenger."

NYACK (NYE-ack) African: "won't give up."

NYE (nye) English: "island." *Nyle.*

OAKES (ohks) Old English: "beside the grove of oak trees." *Oak, Ochs.*

OAKLEY (OHK-lee) Old English: "pasture of oaks." *Oak, Oakes, Oakleigh, Oakly.*

OBA (AW-bah) Nigeria. Yoruba: "king."

OBADIAH (oh-ba-DYE-ah) Hebrew: "one who serves God fully." Bible: An Old Testament prophet. Theater: Obadiah "Sky" Masterson is a character in the musical *Guys and Dolls*. *Obadias, Obed, Obediah, Obie, Ovadiah, Ovadiach.*

OBELIX (OBE-liks) Greek: "pillar of strength"

OBERON (OH-burr-on) Old German: "bear heart." Literature: Oberon is the name of the King of the Fairies, married to Titania, in Shakespeare's *A Midsummer Night's Dream*. *Auberon.*

OCHEN (OH-chen) Ugandan: "one of the twins."

OCTAVIUS (ahk-TAH-vee-us) Latin: "eighth." History: Roman family name, of whom the most celebrated member was Augustus, the first Roman emperor, formerly called Octavius. Literature: Octavio Paz, Mexican writer and Nobel Prize winner in Literature (1990). *Octave, Octavian, Octavien, Octavio, Octavo, Otavus, Ottavio.*

ODELL (OH-dell) Middle English: "hilly forest." *Dell, Ode, Odey, Odie, Ody, Odall.*

ODHRAN (OHD-rahn) Irish: "pale green." *Oran, Odran.*

ODIN (OH-dinn) Scandinavian: A god's name. Mythology: In Norse lore, Odin is the supreme divinity from whom all knowledge flowed.

OFER (OH-fer) Hebrew: "fawn."

OGDEN (OG-dinn) Old English: "he who lives beside the oak grove." Journalism: Ogden Reid, editor and publisher of the *New York Tribune.* Literature: Ogden Nash, poet. *Ogdan, Ogdon.*

OGELSBY (oh-GELS-bee) English: "fearsome." *Oegelsby.*

OGILVY (oh-GILV-ee) Old Scottish: "from the high peak." *Ogilvie.*

OGUN (oh-GOON) Nigeria. Yoruba: In the Yoruban pantheon of divinities, Ogun is the god of war and is invoked for power and fortitude. *Ogunkeye, Ogunsawo, Ogunsheye.*

OISTIN (OHS-teen) Latin: "venerable." Used in Ireland. *Austin.*

OKOTH (oh-KOTH) Uganda. Luo: "born when it was raining."

OLA (AW-lah) Nigeria. Yoruba: "wealth" or "riches."

OLAF (OH-laff) Norse: "family lineage." Saint Olaf was the first Christian king of Norway (1000 A.D.). Literature: Olaf Bull, Norwegian poet. Music: Olaf, baritone singer. Eng: *Olin;* Ice: *Olafur, Olaff, Olav, Olave, Ole, Olie, Olof, Olov.*

OLDRICH (OLD-rick) Czech: "one with riches and power."

OLEG (OH-lehg) Russian: "sacred." Popular in Russia. *Olezka.*

OLIN (OH-lyn) Old English: "holly."

OLIVER (AH-liv-ir) Greek: From *elaia,* meaning olive, the name of a fruit. History: Oliver Wendell Holmes, U.S. Supreme Court justice. Literature: *Oliver Twist,* novel by Charles Dickens. Movies and Television: Oliver Stone, director; Oliver Hardy, half of the comic duo Laurel and Hardy. *Noll, Oliverio, Olivero, Olivor, Olley, Ollie, Olliver, Ollivor;* Fr: *Olivier;* Hawaiian: *Oliwa.*

OMA (OH-mah) Arabic: "commander."

OMAR (OH-mahr) Arabic: "supreme devotee." Astrology: "Omarr," astrologer. Literature: Omar Khayyam, twelfth-century Persian poet. Military: Omar Bradley, former U.S. Army general. Movies and Television: Omar Sharif, actor. *Omarr.*

OMER (OH-mehr) Arabic: "first son."

OHMET (OH-meht) Hebrew: "my light." *Ori.*

ONAN (o-NOHN) Turkish: "wealthy." Popular as a Turkish surname as well.

ONAONA (oh-NAH-oh-nuh) Hawaiian: "appealing aroma."

ONOFRE (oh-NOH-frey) Spanish: "defender of peace."

ONSLOW (OHNS-low) Old English: "hill of the passionate one." *Ounslow.*

ORAN (OH-ran) Irish Gaelic: "green life." *Oren, Orin, Orran, Orren, Orrin.*

ORBAN (OR-bahn) Latin: "knows the city." Used in Hungary.

OREN (OH-ren) Hebrew: "pine tree"; Irish Gaelic: "light-complexioned." *Orin, Orren, Orrin.*

ORESTES (oh-RESS-teez) Greek: "granite heart of man." Mythology: Orestes murdered his mother, Clytemnestra, to avenge his father's death. Theater:

Orestes appears in plays by Aeschylus, Sophocles, and Euripides. *Aresty, Oreste.*

ORION (oh-RYE-inn) Greek: "heir to the flame." A legendary Greek hunter who was transformed into a heavenly constellation. His three-star belt is usually quite apparent in the sky.

ORJI (OR-jee) Nigeria. Ibo: "majestic trunk."

ORMAN (OR-mahn) Old English: "spearman." *Ormond, Ormund.*

ORRICK (OR-rick) Old English: "venerable oak." Literature: Orric Johns, poet and editor. *Orric.*

ORSON (OR-sun) Latin: "bearlike courage." Movies and Television: Orson Welles, actor and director famous for *Citizen Kane. Orsen, Orsin, Orsini, Orsino, Sonny, Urson.*

ORVILLE (OR-vill) French: "village of gold." Literature: Name was invented by Fanny Burney (1779) for the hero of her novel *Evelina.* Aeronautics: Orville Wright, aviation pioneer. *Orv, Orval, Orvell, Orvil.*

ORVIN (OR-vin) Old English: "friend with a sword."

OSAYABA (oh-sah-YAH-bah) Nigeria. Benin: "God forgives."

OSBERT (OZ-burt) Old English: "luminescent divinity." Literature: Osbert Sitwell, English poet, novelist, and satirist.

OSBORN (OZ-born) Old English: "bear of God." Music: Ozzy Osbourne, rock star. *Osborne, Osbourn, Osbourne, Osburn, Osburne, Ozzie, Ozzy.*

OSCAR (OSS-ker) Anglo-Saxon: "sacred sword." The gold-covered statuette given as the award from the Academy of Motion Picture Arts and Sciences was so named when the academy's librarian Margaret Herrick first saw it and exclaimed, "He reminds me of my uncle Oscar." Music: Oscar Hammerstein, legendary lyricist. Sports: Oscar de la Hoya, Olympic medalist in boxing and notable Hispanic boxing champion. Theater: Oscar Wilde, Irish playwright. *Oskar, Osker, Ossie, Ozzy.*

OSGOOD (OZ-good) Old English: "Goth of the heavens."

OSMAN (OZ-minn) Anglo-Saxon: "God's servant." History: Osman was the name of the founder of the Ottoman Empire. *Osmin, Osmond, Osmund, Oswin.*

OSMAR (OZ-mar) Old English: "marvelously sacred."

OSMOND (OZ-mund) Old English: "godly defense." *Osman.*

OSRIC (OZ-rik) English: "divine ruler."

OSWALD (OZ-wald) Old English: "God's omnipotence." *Ossie, Osvald, Oswell, Ozzie, Waldo.*

OSWIN (OZ-winn) Old English: "friend in spirit." *Osvin, Oswinn, Oswyn, Oswynn.*

OTHELLO (oh-THEL-loh) Greek: "prosperous." Literature: Title of a popular Shakespearean drama.

OTIS (OAT-is) German: "wealthy." Greek: "acute."

OTTO (AH-to) Old German: "one with riches." Contemporary adaptation from the ancient German name, Odo. Otto is a favorite name of German and Austrian nobility. Movies and Television: Otto Preminger, film director and producer. Music: Otto Klemperer, conductor. Science: Otto Hahn, chemist who worked on atomic fission. Czech: *Otik;* Fr: *Odon;* Ger: *Otfried, Ottomar;* Gk: *Othon;* Ital: *Otello, Ottone;* Norw: *Audr, Odo;* Pol: *Otek, Otton, Tonek;* Span: *Otilio, Otman, Tilo.*

OURAY (oh-RAY) Native American: "arrow's shot." Astrology: Appropriate for those born under the sign of Sagittarius, symbolized by the archer.

OVED (OH-vehd) Israel. Hebrew: "devotee." Popular name in Israel.

OVID (OH-vid) Latin: "lamb." Literature: Renowned Roman writer whose works are still popular. *Ovidio.*

OWEN (OH-wehn) Greek: "born into fortune." Literature: Owen Wister, novelist. Movies and Television: Owen Wilson, actor. Science: Sir Owen

Richardson, Nobel Prize-winning British physicist (1928). *Ewen, Owain, Owin, Owyn.*

OXFORD (OX-fird) Old English: "river's pass" or "oxen crossing the river." One of England's oldest universities and the name of English city.

PABLO (PAHB-loh) Spanish: "little." Variant of Paul. Literature: Pablo Neruda, renowned Chilean poet who won the Nobel Prize in Literature (1971).

PACHO (pah-CHOH) Spanish: "free." *Paco.*

PACKARD (PAK-ard) Old English: "one who packs."

PADEN (PAD-en) Scottish: "royal."

PAGE (payj) French: In medieval times, a young boy who was the right hand of a knight was called a page. More commonly used for girls. *Padget, Padgett, Paget, Pagett, Paige, Payge.*

PALLATON (pahl-LAH-ton) Native American: "fighter."

PALMER (PAWL-mer) English, Latin: "bearing a palm branch." Refers to the palm branches borne by religious devotees during pilgrimages to shrines.

PALTI (PAHL-tye) Hebrew: "my escape."

PANCHO (PAHN-cho) Spanish: "tuft" or "plume."

PANDITA (pan-DEE-tah) Hindu: "scholar."

PARAS (PAR-ahs) Hindu: "touchstone."

PARIS (PAIR-ess) French: The name of the City of Lights. Arts: Paris Bordone, sixteenth-century Venetian painter. Mythology: Paris fell in love with Helen, causing the Trojan War. He also killed Achilles. *Parris.*

PARKER (PAR-kur) Old English: "protector of the park." Occupational name. Movies and Television: Parker Stevenson, actor.

PARKIN (PAR-kin) Old English: "young Peter."

PARLAN (PAR-lahn) Scottish: "farmer."

PARNELL (PAR-nell) Old French: "young Peter." Politics: Charles Parnell, nineteenth-century Irish activist. *Parnel, Parrnell, Pernel, Pernell.*

PARR (parr) Old English: "garden in the park." Place name.

PARRISH (PAYR-ish) Old French: From the ecclesiastical term parish. A parish is a district of a city or village served by a single priest or minister.

PARRY (PAYR-ee) Old Welsh: "Harry's son." Sports: Parry O'Brien, Olympic gold medalist in track and field (1952, 1956). *Parrey, Parrie.*

PARSIFAL (PARS-if-ahl) English: "valley piercer." *Parsefal.*

PASCAL (PAS-cull) French: "Eastertide's infant." *Pace, Pasqual.*

PATAMON (PAY-tah-mon) Native American: "tempest" or "raging."

PATRICK (PA-trik) Latin: "royal character." According to legend, Saint Patrick cleared Ireland of snakes. History: Patrick Henry, American patriot. Science: Patrick Manson, Scottish parasitologist who discovered that the mosquito is the host of malaria. Eng: *Pat, Paddy, Paddie, Patrik;* Fr: *Patrice;* Ger: *Patricius, Patrizius;* Hawaiian: *Pakelike;* Ir: *Padraic, Padraig, Padhragi;* Ital: *Patrizio;* Pol: *Patek;* Port: *Patricio;* Span: *Ticho.*

PATTON (PAT-tun) Old English: "village of warriors." Military: General George Patton, World War II hero who headed the Third Army invasion of German-occupied France. *Pat, Paton, Patten, Pattin.*

PATWIN (PAT-win) Native American: "contemporary man."

PAUL (pawl) Latin: "small" or "little." Arts: Paul Cezanne, Paul Gauguin, French painters. Bible: Saint Paul, originally named Saul, was the great missionary and apostle of Christianity. History: Paul Revere, American Revolutionary War hero. Movies and Television: Paul Newman, actor. Music: Paul Simon, Paul McCartney, singers and songwriters. Science: Paul Ehrlich, German immunology pioneer who won the Nobel Prize for Physiology (1908). Eng: *Pol, Poll, Paulia, Pauly;* Czech: *Pavel;* Pol: *Inek, Paulin, Pawel;* Russ: *Pasha, Paska, Pavel, Pavlik, Pavlo, Pashenka, Pavlusha;* Span: *Oalo, Pablo, Paulino, Paulo;* Swed: *Pal.*

PAXTON (PAX-tun) Latin, Old English: "village of peace." Movies and Television: Paxton Whitehead, actor. *Pax, Paxon, Packston, Paxten.*

PAYAT (PAY-yaht) Native American: "on his way." *Pay, Payatt.*

PAYNE (payne) Latin: "compatriot" or "comrade." *Paine.*

PAZ (pahz) Spanish: "peace."

PEKELO (pee-KEE-loh) Hawaiian: "stone."

PELL (pell) Old English: "scarf."

PELLEGRIN (pell-LEH-grin) Hungarian: "pilgrim."

PEMBROKE (PEM-broke) Celtic: "highland."

PENLEY (PEN-lee) Old English: "fenced-in field." *Penlea, Penleigh, Penly.*

PENN (pen) Old English: "corral." *Pen.*

PENROD (PEN-rod) Old German: "esteemed commander."

PEPIN (PEP-in) Old German: "determined" or "industrious." *Pepi, Peppi, Peppie, Peppy.*

PERCIVAL (PER-sih-val) Old French: "pierce the vale." Literature: The name was invented by twelfth-century poet Chretien de Troyes for a knight of the Round Table. *Parsifal, Perce, Perceval, Percy, Purcell.*

PERCY (PER-cee) French: "hailing from Percy." French place name for a village near Saint Lo. Percie was the family name of William de Perci who came to England with William the Conqueror. Literature: Percy Bysshe Shelley, nineteenth-century British poet, leader of Romanticism. Music: Percy Faith, conductor and composer. *Pearcy, Percey, Percie.*

PEREGRINE (PER-reh-grin) Latin: "spiritual wanderer." Also the name of a falcon. Literature: Peregrine Worsthome, English editor, journalist, and author of *The Socialist Myth. Peregin, Peregryn.*

PERICLES (PARE-ah-klees) Greek: Name of the Greek leader who democratized Athens. Theater: Title character of a romance by Shakespeare.

PERKIN (PER-kin) Old English: "young Peter." *Perkins, Perkyn, Perrin.*

PERRY (PAYR-ee) French: "pear-bearing grove." Education: Perry Miller, historian who interpreted seventeenth-century New England. Music: Perry Como, singer. *Parry, Perrie.*

PERTH (purth) Celtic: "thorny bush." *Pert.*

PETER (PEE-tur) Greek: "rock" or "foundation." Bible: Peter was one of the twelve apostles, who was known for his unwavering faith. Business: Peter Minuit, businessman who purchased Manhattan from the Indians for twenty-four dollars. History: Peter the Great, Russian emperor; Pierre Trudeau, Canadian prime minister. Journalism: Peter Jennings, TV news anchor. Literature: Peter Taylor, Pulitzer Prize-winning novelist for *A Summons to Memphis* (1987). Movies and Television: Peter O'Toole, actor; Peter Bogdanovich, film director. Music: Peter Ilyich Tchaikovsky, Russian composer; Pete Seeger, folk singer. Science: Peter Agre, Nobel Prize winner in Chemistry (2003). Sports: Pete Rose, baseball player. Theater: James M. Barrie's 1904 play, *Peter Pan.* Eng: *Pete, Petey;* Bulg: *Petr, Piotr;* Dutch: *Pietr;* Fr: *Pierre, Pierrot;* Gk: *Panos, Petros, Takis;* Ital: *Pedro, Pero, Piero, Petro, Perion;* Ir: *Peadar, Peadair;* Norw: *Peder, Petter;* Pol: *Pietrek, Piotr;* Rum: *Petar, Petru;* Russ: *Perka, Petr, Petro, Petruno;* Scot: *Peadair;* Span: *Pedrin, Pedro, Perico, Peyo;* Swed: *Peder, Petrus, Petter.*

PEYTON (PAY-tunn) Old English: "warrior's home." Sports: Peyton Manning, award-winning quarterback for the Indianapolis Colts. *Pate, Payton.*

PHELAN (FEE-lahn) Gaelic: "little wolf."

PHILIP (FILL-ip) Greek: "groom" or "horse lover." Bible: Popular since the beginning of the Christian era because Philip was one of Jesus' apostles. Business: Philip Armour, industrialist and meat packer. Literature: Philip Roth, author. Music: Phil Collins, singer. Science: Philipp Lenard, German physicist who discovered properties of cathode rays. Theater: Philip Barry, playwright. Eng: *Phil, Phillip, Phillipp;* Bulg/Czech: *Filip;* Fr: *Philippe;* Ger: *Philipp;* Gk: *Phillipos;* Ital: *Filippo;* Lat: *Filips;* Pol: *Filipek;* Russ: *Filip, Filya;* Span: *Felipe, Felipino;* Yiddish: *Fischel.*

PHINEAS (FINN-ee-us) Hebrew: "face of piety" or "prophecy."

PHOENIX (FEE-niks) Greek: "mythical bird" or "purple." Mythology: The phoenix is a mythical bird that represents rebirth through its ability to consume itself by fire every 500 years and be reborn from its ashes.

PIERCE (peerce) Old Anglo-French: "rock." Early adaptation used during the Middle Ages. Today, popular in English-speaking countries. Movies and Television: Pierce Brosnan, actor. *Pearce, Piers, Pearson, Pierson.*

PIERRE (PYAIR) French: Form of Peter. See Peter.

PILLAN (pee-LAHN) Native American: "god of stormy weather." *Pilan.*

PINON (pee-NON) Native American. Name for Tupi-Guarani, a god who, according to legend, became the constellation Orion.

PIRRO (PEER-ro) Greek: "hair on fire."

PITNEY (PIT-nee) Old English: "isle of the strongman." Place name. *Pittney.*

PLACIDO (PLAH-si-doh) Spanish: "placid" or "calm." Music: Placido Domingo, opera singer. *Placidus, Placyd, Placydo.*

PLATO (PLAY-toh) Greek: "strong shoulders." Philosophy: Plato, Greek philosopher and author of the *Republic. Platon.*

PLATT (platt) Old French: "ground without slope." *Platte.*

POLLARD (POL-lard) Middle English: "hairless." *Poll, Pollerd, Pollyrd.*

POMEROY (POM-eh-roy) Old French: "apple tree grove." *Pommeray, Pommeroy.*

PONCE (pohntz) Spanish: "fifth." History: Ponce de Leon, Spanish explorer who discovered Florida.

PORTER (PORR-tir) Latin: "one who guards the door." *Porteur, Portier.*

POV (pohv) English Gypsy: "ground" or "mud."

POWA (PO-wah) Native American: "wealthy."

PRANAY (PRAH-naye) Hindu: "love and romance."

PRAVAT (PRAH-vaht) Thai: "history."

PRENTICE (PREN-tiss) Middle English: "one who apprentices to another." *Prentis, Prentiss.*

PRESCOTT (PRESS-kaht) Old English: "home of the priest." *Prescot, Prestcot, Prestcott.*

PRESLEY (PRESS-lee) Old English: "fields of the priest." *Presleigh, Presly, Presslee, Pressley, Prestley, Priestley, Priestly.*

PRESTON (PRESS-tun) Old English: "estate owned by the priest." Movies and Television: Preston Sturges, screenwriter and director.

PREWITT (PREW-itt) Old French: "valiant one." *Pruett, Pruie, Pruitt.*

PRICE (pryce) Welsh: "passion's son" or "son of Rhys." *Brice, Bryce, Pryce.*

PRIMO (PREE-moh) Italian: "first" or "premier quality." Literature: Primo Levi, Italian poet and novelist. *Preemo, Premo.*

PRINCE (printz) Latin: "prince." Music: Prince, rock musician. *Prinz, Prinze.*

PRYOR (PRY-ur) Latin: "head of the monks." *Prior, Pry.*

PUEBLO (PWEB-loh) Spanish: "from the city."

PUTNAM (PUTT-numm) Old English: "beside the lake."

QABIL (kah-BILL) Arabic: "able." *Qadir*.

QAMAR (kah-MAR) Arabic: "moon."

QUAID (kwaid) Irish. Form of Walter. See Walter.

QUANG (kwang) Vietnamese: "clear."

QUANY (kwany) Scottish: "proud." *Quarrie*.

QUENNEL (KWEN-nell) Old French: "dweller by the oak tree."

QUENTIN (KWEN-tin) Latin: "the fifth." Quintus was a popular Roman first name, believed to have been given to a fifth son. Saint Quentin was a Roman fifth-century martyr after whom a town in France was named. Literature: *Quentin Durward*, a novel by Sir Walter Scott. Movies and Television: Quentin Tarantino, film director (*Kill Bill*). *Quent,*

Quenton, Quinn, Quinten, Quintin, Quinton, Quintus, Quintyn.

QUERAN (KWEH-ran) Irish: "dark."

QUIGLEY (KWIG-lee) Irish Gaelic: Meaning unclear.

QUILLAN (KWILL-luhn) Irish Gaelic: "baby lion."

QUIMBY (KWIM-bee) Old Norse: "at the mother's house." *Quenby, Quim, Quin, Quinby.*

QUINBY (KWIN-bee) Scandinavian: "from the queen's estate."

QUINCY (KWIN-see) French: "fifth son's place." A town in Massachusetts. History: The middle name of the sixth president of the United States, John Quincy Adams. Music: Quincy Jones, jazz musician and arranger. *Quin, Quincey.*

QUINLIN (KWIN-lin) Irish Gaelic: "powerful one." *Quinn, Quinley, Quinlan.*

QUINN (kwin) Irish Gaelic: "smart" or "discerning." Also a form of Quinlin, Quintin, and other names starting with Quin. Movies and Television: Quinn Redeker, actor. *Quin.*

QUINTO (KWIN-toh) Latin: "fifth child." *Quito.*

RAANAN (RAH-ahn-ahn) Hebrew: "fresh" or "new."

RABI (ra-BEE) Arabic: "soothing breezes." *Rabbi, Rabee.*

RAD (rahd) Old English: "counselor." *Radd.*

RADBURN (RADD-burn) Old English: "stream colored like blood." *Burnie, Burny, Rad, Radd, Radborn, Radbourne, Radburne.*

RADCLIFF (RADD-cliff) Old English: "cliff of red rocks." *Cliff, Rad, Radd, Radcliffe, Radclyffe.*

RADFORD (RADD-furd) Old English: "ford full of reeds." *Radlea, Radleigh.*

RADMAN (RADD-munn) Slavic: "happiness."

RAE (ray) Old English: "doe."

RAFFERTY (RAFF-ur-tee) Irish Gaelic: "one who brings riches." *Raferty, Raffarty, Rafe, Rafer, Raff, Raffer.*

RAFI (rah-FEE) Arabic: "praising."

RAGNER (RAG-nur) Old Norse: "powerful forces." Common in Scandinavia. *Ragnor, Rainer, Rainier, Rayner, Raynor.*

RAHMAN (rah-MAHN) Arabic: "understanding" or "forgiving." Moslems often use this name, which corresponds to one of the many attributes of God.

RAIMI (raye-MEE) African: "compassionate."

RAINART (RAYNE-art) German: "powerful decision." *Rainhard, Reinart, Reinhard, Reinhardt, Reinhart, Renke.*

RAINER (RAYNE-er) German: "strong counselor." Literature: Rainer Maria Rilke, renowned German poet (*Letters to a Young Poet*). *Rainier, Rainor.*

RALEIGH (RAHL-ee) Old English: "meadow of the swift deer." Old English place name that is now the name of a city in North Carolina. *Rawleigh, Rawley, Rawly.*

RALPH (ralf) Old English: "wolf advisor." Popular in many variations for centuries. Education: Ralph Nader, consumer advocate. History: Ralph Abernathy, civil-rights leader. Literature: Ralph Waldo Emerson, poet and essayist. *Rafe, Raff, Ralk, Raoul, Raul, Rold, Rolph.*

RALSTON (RAHL-stin) Old English: "homestead of Ralph."

RAMBERT (RAHM-burt) German: "mighty" or "intelligent." *Ramhert.*

RAMIRO (rah-MEE-roh) Portuguese: "supreme judge." *Ramirez.*

RAMSAY (RAM-see) Old English: "valley of the ram." *Ramsey.*

RANDALL (RAN-duhl) English: A form of Randolph from the Middle Ages. See Randolph.

RANDOLPH (RAN-dolf) Old English: "warrior's wolf." Literature: Randall Jarrell, poet and novelist who wrote *Losses.* Movies and Television: Randy Quaid, actor. Sports: Randy White, basketball player; Randall Cunningham, football player. *Rand, Randall, Randell, Randy, Randie, Randolf.*

RANGER (RAIN-gher) Old French: "keeper of the grove." *Rainger, Range.*

RANIT (RAH-neet) Israel. Hebrew: "song." *Ronit, Rani.*

RANKIN (RAN-kin) Old English: "small armor." Used as a surname in Ireland and Scotland, but sometimes adopted as a given name.

RANSFORD (RANS-ford) Old English: "ford of the raven."

RANSLEY (RANS-lee) Old English: "field of ravens." *Ransleigh, Ransly.*

RANSOM (RAN-som) Old English: "son of armored one." *Rance, Ransome, Ranson.*

RAPHAEL (RA-fee-el) Hebrew: "God cures" or "God has helped." Arts: Raffaello Sanzio, Italian Renaissance painter, better known as Raphael. Science: Raphael Meldola, British chemist who produced the first oxazine dye. *Rafaello, Rafe, Rafel, Rafello.*

RAPIER (RAPE-ee-air) Middle French: "sharp as a blade."

RASHAUN (RAH-shawn) United States. English: African-American creation of Ray and Shawn. *Rayshawn, Rayshaun.*

RASHIDI (rah-SHEE-dee) East Africa. Swahili: "trustworthy advisor." Popular African name in the United States. *Rashid.*

RAVI (rahvi) Hindu: "sun" or "benevolent." Music: Ravi Shankar, renowned Indian sitar musician.

RAVIV (rah-VEEV) Hebrew: "mist."

RAY (ray) English, French: "king" or "royal." Once a short form of Raymond, now used as an independent name and in contemporary blends such as Rayce and Raylen. Business: Ray Kroc, who established McDonald's hamburger chain in 1955. Literature: Ray Bradbury, science fiction writer. Movies and Television: Ray Milland, actor. Music: Ray

Charles, jazz musician and singer. Sports: Sugar Ray Leonard, boxer. *Rayce, Rayder, Raylen, Raydon, Raynell, Raydell, Rayford.*

RAYBURN (RAY-bum) Old English: "stream where the deer roam." *Raeborn, Raeburn, Rayborn, Rayburne.*

RAYMOND (RAY-mund) Old German: "knowing defender." Literature: Raymond Chandler, novelist who wrote the Phillip Marlowe series. Military: Raymond Spruance, World War II admiral who was victorious in Midway Island. Movies and Television: Raymond Massey, Raymond Burr, actors. Science: Raymond Davis, Jr., American Nobel Prize winner in Physics (2002). Eng: *Ray, Raymund;* Czech: *Rajmund;* Ger: *Raimund;* Ital: *Raimondo;* Ir: *Redmond, Radmond;* Port: *Raimundo;* Rum: *Reimond;* Span: *Raimundo, Ramon, Mundo.*

RAZI (RAH-zee) Aramaic: "hidden truth." *Raz, Raziel.*

READING (RED-ing) Old English: "son of the auburn wanderer." Place name, a city in Pennsylvania. *Redding, Reeding, Reiding.*

RECENE (ree-SEEN) Anglo-Saxon: "quick."

REDFORD (RED-furd) Old English: "red ford."

REDLEY (RED-lee) Old English: "red fields." *Radley, Redlea, Redleigh, Redly.*

REECE (rees) Old Welsh: "passionate" or "spontaneous." *Reese.*

REED (reed) Old English: "auburn" or "flushed." Science: Reid R. Keays, geologist. *Reid, Read, Reade, Reid, Reyd, Reide.*

REEVE (reeve) Middle English: "bailiff." A representative of a king or lord in medieval times, a reeve administrated property and collected rents. *Reave, Reeves.*

REGAN (RAY-gan) Irish Gaelic: "would-be king." *Reagan, Reagen, Regen, Reaghan.*

REGINALD (REH-gin-ald) Germanic: "mighty advisor." A favorite warrior's name throughout history. Aeronautics: Reginald Mitchell, designed the Spitfire fighter in 1936. Science: Reginald Pollock, first to classify animals by their external features. Sports: Reggie Jackson, baseball player. *Naldo, Rainault, Rainhold, Reg, Reggie, Reginalt, Reginauld, Reginault, Reinald, Reinaldo, Reinhold, Reinwald, Renault, Rene, Reynaldo, Reynaldos, Reynold, Reynolds.*

REGIS (REE-jis) Latin: "rules." Movies and Televison: Regis Philbin, actor (TV's *Live with Regis and Kelly*).

REI (RAY-ee) Japanese: "law, rule" or "strive."

REIDAR (REY-dar) Scandinavian: "warrior."

REMINGTON (REM-ing-ton) Old English: "town of ravens." *Remy, Remi, Remo.*

REMUS (REE-mus) Latin: "fleet-footed." Remus and his brother Romulus are said to have founded

Rome. Literature: Joel Chandler Harris's *Uncle Remus* stories.

REMY (REE-me) French: "of the town of Rheims." The name of a central French town that is famous for its fine brandies made from champagne. *Remee, Remi, Remie, Remmy.*

REN (wren) English: "raven."

RENARD (ruh-NARD) Teutonic: "counsel."

RENATO (REN-ah-toh) Spanish: "rise again."

RENAUD (ruh-NOH) Teutonic "sagacious strength."

RENDOR (REN-dohr) Hungarian: "police officer."

RENE (ruh-NAY) Latin, French: "born again." Span: *Renato, Renny, Rennie, Renne, Renee, Renat, Renato, Renatus.*

RENFRED (REN-fred) Old English: "enduring peace." *Renfrid.*

RENJIRO (ren-jee-ROH) Japanese: "clean" or "virtuous."

RENNY (REHN-ee) Irish Gaelic: "compact strength."

RENSHAW (REHN-shaw) Old English: "forest full of ravens." *Renishaw.*

RETH (reth) African: "king."

REUBEN (RU-ben) Hebrew: "a son before you." Bible: Reuben was the eldest son of Jacob and Leah. Music: Ruben Blades, singer. *Reuban, Reubin, Reuven, Rouvin, Rube, Ruben, Rubin, Ruby, Reubin.*

REX (rex) Latin: "king." Movies and Television: Rex Harrison, British actor. Span: *Rey, Reyes, Rexford.*

REYHAM (REH-hahn) Arabic: "God's choice."

REYNARD (REY-nard) Old French: "fox"; Old German: "cunning." *Raynard, Reinhard, Renard, Renaud, Renauld, Rennard.*

REYNOLD (REN-old) Old English: "counsel power." Aeronautics: Ronald McNair, first African-American astronaut. History: Ronald Reagan, fortieth president of the United States (1981–89). Science: Ronald Norrish, Nobel Prize-winning chemist (1967). Eng: *Ron, Ronnie, Ronni, Raynald, Reynolds, Renald;* Fr: *Renauld, Renault;* Span: *Renaldo, Reinaldo, Rinaldo, Reynaldo.*

RHETT (wret) Welsh: "stream."

RHODES (roadz) Greek: "field of roses." A Greek island. Business: Cecil Rhodes, British philanthropist. *Rhodas, Rodas, Rhoades.*

RICHARD (RICH-urd) Old German: "imposing chieftain." Originally a Teutonic name, Richard and its many variants have been a favorite for over nine hundred years. Business: Richard Sears, nineteenth-century merchant who founded the mail-order catalog company that bears his name. History: Richard I, was dubbed Richard "the lion-hearted." Movies and Televison: Richard Burton, Richard Gere, actors. Music: Richard Wagner, composer. Theater: Richard Rodgers, legendary composer. Science: Riccardo Giacconi, Nobel Prize winner in Physics (2002); Richard Axel, Nobel Prize winner in Medicine (2004). Eng: *Dick, Dickie, Ricard, Rich, Rick, Rickert, Richie, Ricky;* Est: *Arri, Juku, Riki, Riks, Rolli;* Fin: *Reku, Rikard;* Ger: *Richart;* Gk: *Rihardos;* Hung: *Riczi, Rikard;* Ital: *Riccardo, Ricciardo;* Lith: *Risardas;* Norw: *Rikard;* Pol: *Rye, Rysio, Ryszard;* Span: *Ricardo, Richi, Ricky, Rico, Riqui.*

RICHMOND (RICH-mond) Old German: "mighty defender." Place name, Richmond is the capital of Virginia.

RIDA (REH-dah) Arabic: "favor."

RIDDOC (rih-DOCK) Irish: "from the smooth field."

RIDER (RYE-der) Old English: "horse rider." Literature: Rider Haggard, nineteenth-century English novelist. *Ridder, Ryder.*

RIDGE (ridge) Old English: "ridge" or "side of a cliff." *Rigg.*

RIDGEWAY (RIDGE-way) Old English: "path along the ridge."

RIDLEY (RID-lee) Old English: "red pasture." Movies and Television: Ridley Scott, successful film director and film and television producer. *Riddley, Ridlea, Ridleigh, Ridly.*

RIGBY (RIG-bee) Old English: "valley of the ruler."

RIGEL (RYE-jel) Arabic: "foot." Rigel is part of the Orion constellation.

RILEY (RYE-lee) Irish Gaelic: "brave." *Reilly, Ryley, Rylee.*

RIMON (RIH-mohn) Arabic: "pomegranate."

RING (ring) Old English: "ring." Music: Ringo Starr, Beatles drummer. *Ringo.*

RINGO (RIN-go) Japanese: "apple."

RIO (REE-oh) Spanish: "river."

RIORDAN (REER-den) Irish Gaelic: "troubador." *Rearden, Reardon.*

RIPLEY (RIP-lee) Old English: "pasture for loud men." *Ripleigh, Riply.*

RISHLEY (RISH-lee) Old English: "from the wild meadow."

RISLEY (RIZ-lee) Old English: "shrub-like pasture." *Rislea, Risleigh.*

RITTER (RIT-ter) German: "chivalrous" or "knight."

RIVER (RIH-ver) Old French: "river." Movies and Television: River Phoenix, actor.

RIYAD (ree-YAHD) Arabic: "gardens."

ROALD (ROH-ald) Old German: "known for strength." Literature: Roald Dahl, children's book author.

ROARK (ROH-ark) Irish Gaelic: "without peer in strength." *Roarke, Rorke, Rourke, Ruark.*

ROB (rob) Old English: "memorable." Now used independently. Movies and Televison: Rob Lowe, actor; Rob Reiner, actor and director. *Robb, Robbie, Robby.*

ROBERT (ROB-urt) Old English: "glory bright." Made famous in the fourteenth-century by Robert the Bruce, king of Scotland, and has been a favorite ever since. History: Robert Kennedy, U.S. senator. Literature: Robert Frost, poet; Robert Lewis Stevenson, poet and novelist. Military: Robert E. Lee, commander of the southern army in the Civil War. Movies and Television: Robert Redford, Robin Williams, actors. Music: Robert Schumann, German classical composer. Eng: *Bert, Bob, Bobbie, Bobby, Rob, Robb, Robbie, Robby, Robertson, Robin, Robyn, Robinson;* Czech: *Berty, Bobek, Hubert;* Fr: *Robers, Robin, Robinet;* Ger: *Rudbert, Ruprecht;* Hung: *Robi;* Ir: *Riobard;* Ital: *Roberto, Ruberto, Ru-*

perto; Lith: ***Rosertas;*** Rum: ***Robin;*** Span: ***Berto,
Bobby, Rober, Roberto, Ruperto, Tito.***

ROCCO (ROK-oh) German, Italian: "rest." ***Roxxo,
Roch, Roche, Rochus, Roque.***

ROCK (rok) Old English: "from the rock." Movies
and Television: Rock Hudson, actor. Sports: Rocky
Marciano, Rocky Graziano, boxers. Eng: ***Rocky,
Rockford, Rockwell;*** Fr: ***Roel.***

ROCKLEY (ROK-lee) Old English: "pasture of the
rocks." ***Rockleigh.***

RODEN (ROHD-en) English: "red valley."

RODERICK (ROD-rik) Old German: "one whose
leadership is remembered." Eng: ***Rick, Ricky, Rod,
Roddie, Roddy, Roderic, Rodrich, Rodrick, Rory;***
Fr: ***Roidrique;*** Ger: ***Roderich;*** Hung/Ital: ***Rodrigo,
Roderigo;*** Russ: ***Rurich, Rurik;*** Span: ***Rodrigo,
Ruy.***

RODMAN (ROD-minn) Old German: "famous
man." ***Rodd, Roddie, Roddy.***

RODNEY (ROD-nee) Old English: "isle close to the
open land." Last name transferred to a first name.
Sports: Rod Laver, tennis champion who won Wimbledon four times. ***Rod, Roddy, Rodnee, Rodnie.***

RODOR (ROW-door) Anglo-Saxon: "sky."

ROE (row) Middle English: "roe deer." ***Row, Rowe.***

ROGER (ROD-jur) Old German: "famous swordsman." History: Roger Williams, advocate of democracy and religious tolerance who founded Rhode Island. Journalism: Roger Mudd, TV news correspondent. Movies and Televison: Roger Moore, Rutger Hauer, actors. Sports: Roger Maris, baseball player, first to hit sixty-one home runs in a single season. Eng: *Rodge, Rodger, Rutger, Ruttger, Dodge;* Ger: *Rudiger;* Hung: *Rogerios;* Ital: *Ruggero;* Pol: *Gerek;* Span: *Rogelio, Rogerio.*

ROHAN (RO-han) Hindi: "sandalwood."

ROHIN (ro-HEEN) East Indian: "skybound."

ROKA (ROH-kah) Japanese: "foamy wave."

ROLAND (ROH-lund) Old German: "from the famous land." Dates from the Dark Ages. Orlando is a common variant in several European languages. Aeronautics: Roland Garros, aviator, who was the first to fly over the Mediterranean Sea. History, Literature: A nephew of King Charlemagne of France whose courageous deeds during the Crusades are described in *The Song of Roland.* Movies and Televison: Orlando Bloom, actor. Music: Orlando Di Lasso, sixteenth-century Flemish composer. Eng: *Orland, Orlan, Rolland, Rollin, Rollins, Rollo, Rolly, Rollie, Rowe, Rowland;* Ger: *Orlando, Rudland, Ruland;* Hung: *Lorand, Lorant;* Ital/Span: *Orlando, Rolando;* Pol: *Rolek;* Span: *Lando, Olo, Orlo, Roldan, Rolon, Rollon.*

ROLF (rohlf) Old German: "wolf wisdom." Science: Rolf M. Zindernagel, Nobel Prize winner in Medicine (1996). *Rolfe.*

ROLON (ro-LOHN) Spanish: "famous wolf."

ROMAN (ROH-man) Latin: "Roman." Movies and Television: Roman Polanski, director. *Romano, Rome, Romeo, Romulo;* Fr: *Romain.*

ROMEO (ROH-mee-oh) Italian: "pilgrim to Rome." Literature: Romeo Montague, title character in Shakespeare's play *Romeo and Juliet.*

ROMNEY (rohm-NEE) Welsh: "winding river."

ROMULUS (ROHM-ul-us) Latin: "he that dwells in Rome." Romulus and his brother Remus are said to have been the founders of Rome. Theater: Romulus Linney, playwright.

RON (rahn) Israel. Hebrew: "sing." Popular in Israel.

RONALD (RAHN-ild) Form of Reynold. See Reynold.

RONAN (ROWN-ahn) Celtic: "oath."

ROONEY (ROO-nee) Irish Gaelic: "auburn locks." *Rowan, Rowen, Rowney.*

ROOSEVELT (ROO-zeh-velt) Dutch: "field of roses." Roosevelt used as a first name honors twentieth-century presidents Theodore and Franklin Delano Roosevelt. Sports: Roosevelt Grier, football player.

RORY (ROAR-ee) Irish Gaelic: "red." History, Literature: Rory O'More was the name of one of three Irish rebel chieftains celebrated in song and ballad. *Rorey, Rorry.*

ROSARIO (roe-ZAR-ee-oh) Spanish, Portuguese: "rosary."

ROSCOE (ROSS-coh) Scandinavian: "deer woods." Sports: Roscoe Tanner, tennis star. *Ross.*

ROSS (ross) Scottish Gaelic: "high station." Theater: Terence Rattigan's play, *Ross*, is about Lawrence of Arabia, who had once used this name. *Rosse, Rossell.*

ROSWELL (ROZ-well) Old English: "springtime of roses."

ROTH (rawth) Old German: "red."

ROWLEY (ROW-lee) Old English: "hastily mowed pasture." *Rowlea, Rowlee, Rowleigh, Rowly.*

ROWTAG (rowe-TAG) Native American. Algonquin: "fire."

ROXBURY (ROKS-bury) Old English: "rooks of crown alight." *Roxburghe.*

ROY (roy) Gaelic: "ruler." History: Roy Wilkins, civil-rights leader. Music: Roy Orbison, rock singer. *Roi, Rey.*

ROYCE (royse) English: "son of the king."

RUDOLPH (RUDE-olf) Old German: "wolf." History: Rudolf Guiliani, former mayor of New York City who governed the city during the 9/11 terrorist attacks on the World Trade Center. Science: Rudolph A. Markus, Nobel Prize winner in Chemistry (1992). *Rudy.*

RUFUS (RUE-fuss) Latin: "red-haired one."

RUNE (rune) German: "secret."

RUPERT (RUE-purt) French: "bright fame." Business: Rupert Murdoch, owner of The News Corporation, one of the largest media groups in the world.

RUTHERFORD (RUHTH-er-ford) Old English: "from the cattle ford."

RYAN (RYE-ahn) Gaelic: "little king." Movies and Television: Ryan Reynolds, actor.

SABER (SAY-bur) French: "spear." A saber was the first choice of weapon during medieval battles.

SABIR (SAHB-ear) Arabic: "patient."

SABOLA (sah-BOH-lah) Malawi. Ngoni: "pepper."

SACHIEL (sah-CHEE-ell) Hebrew: "angel of water."

SADIQ (sah-DEEK) Arabic: "friend."

SAFFORD (SAFF-ord) English: "from the willow ford."

SAHALE (sah-HAH-teh) Native American: "above."

SAHIR (sah-HEAR) Arabic: "wakeful."

SAID (SAH-eed) Arabic: "cheerful." *Saeed, Say-eed, Sayid.*

SAKIMA (sah-KEE-mah) Native American: "king."

SALAMON (sah-LAH-mon) Hebrew: "peaceful." *Saloman.*

SALEM (sah-LEHM) Hebrew: "peace." Place name of an ancient biblical city later identified as Jerusalem. Arabic: *Saleem, Salim.*

SALVATORE (SAL-vah-tor-ee) Italian: "redeemer" or "savior." Arts: Salvador Dali, surrealist painter. Dance: Salvatore Vigano, Italian ballet dancer and choreographer. History: Salvador Allende, elected president of Chile in 1970. Literature: Salvatore Di Giacomo, Italian novelist. *Sal, Salvador, Saloator, Xavier, Xaviero, Zavier.*

SAMIR (SAHM-ear) Hindu: "wind."

SAMSON (SAM-son) Hebrew: "sun." Bible: Samson was a physically powerful judge in the Old Testament. Education: Samson Hirsch, German theologian. Music: Samson Francois, French pianist. Theater: Samson Raphaelson, playwright. Eng: *Sam, Sammie, Sammy, Sampson*; Ital: *Sansone*; Port: *Sansao*; Span: *Sanson*; Swed: *Simson.*

SAMUEL (SAM-you-ull) Hebrew: "God's word." Bible: Samuel anointed Saul and David, the first kings of Israel. History: Samuel Adams, colonial patriot; Samuel Morse, invented Morse code. Literature: Samuel Taylor Coleridge, poet and author. Movies and Television: Sam Waterston, Samuel L. Jackson, actors. Sports: Samuel Gompers, established the American Football League. Theater: Samuel Beckett, playwright. Eng: *Sam, Sammie, Sammy;* Bulg: *Samuil;* Czech: *Sanko, Samo;* Ger: *Zamiel;* Gk: *Samoeul;* Hung: *Samie, Samu;* Ir: *Somhairle;* Ital: *Salvatore, Samuele;* Japn: *Samuru;* Lith: *Samuelis;* Russ: *Samuil, Samuel;* Yiddish: *Shem, Shemuel, Schmuel.*

SANCHO (SAHN-choo) Spanish: "saint."

SANDERS (SAN-durs) Middle English: "Alexander's son." *Sanderson, Sandor, Saunders, Saunderson.*

SANDON (SAHN-dohn) English: "from the sandy hill."

SANFORD (SAN-ford) Old English: "sandy ford." Theater: Sanford Meisner, acting teacher. *Sandford.*

SANTIAGO (sahn-TEE-ah-go) Spanish: "supplanter." Place name. Capital of the Chile.

SANTO (SAHN-toh) Spanish, Italian: "blessed" or "pious one." *Santos.*

SARAD (SAH-rahd) Hindi: "born in autumn."

SARGENT (SAHR-gent) Old French: "officer." Business: R. Sargent Shriver, renowned philanthropist who founded the Special Olympics.

SARKIS (sar-KISS) Armenian: "royalty."

SAROSH (SAR-osh) Persian: "prayer."

SASSON (SASS-ohn) Hebrew: "joy."

SAUL (soll) Hebrew: "petitioned." Bible: Saul was ancient Israel's first king. Literature: Saul Bellow, Pulitzer and Nobel Prize-winning author. *Sol, Sollie.*

SAVILLE (sa-VEEL) French: "willow town." Savite Row, a street in London famous for its tailors. *Savil, Savile, Savill, Savylle.*

SAWYER (SOY-yur) Middle English: "woodworker." Occupational name.

SAXON (SAX-un) Old English: "Wade." The Saxons were an old Germanic tribe. *Saxe, Saxen.*

SAYER (SAY-ur) Welsh: "woodworker." *Sayers, Sayre, Sayres.*

SCANLON (SCAN-lun) Irish Gaelic: "young hunter." *Scanlan, Scanlen.*

SCHUYLER (SKY-ler) Dutch: "learned one" or "armor." Name transported to America by Dutch pioneers in the 1600s. History: Schuyler Colfac, U.S. vice president under Andrew Johnson. *Schyler, Schylar, Schuylar, Skuyler, Skylar, Skyler, Skylior, Sky.*

SCOTT (scot) Old English: "Scotsman." Popular contemporary name. Literature: Scott Turow, author of the novel *Presumed Innocent;* F. Scott Fitzgerald, novelist who wrote *The Great Gatsby.* Music: Scott Joplin composed ragtime music. Sports: Scottie Pippen, basketball player; Scott Hamilton, 1984 Olympic gold medalist in figure skating. *Scot, Scottie, Scotty.*

SCULLY (SCUL-lee) Celtic, Gaelic: "town crier."

SEABERT (SEE-burt) Old English: "gleaming sea." *Seabright, Sebert, Seibert.*

SEABROOK (SEE-brook) Old English: "seaside stream." *Seabrooke.*

SEAMUS (SEE-mus) Celtic: "supplanter." Variant of James. Literature: Seamus Heaney, Noble Prize winner in literature (1995).

SEAN (shawn) Hebrew: "heavenly generosity." Irish form of John from the French *Jean.* History: Sean O'Kelly, president of Ireland (1945–59). Movies and Television: Sean Connery, Sean Penn, actors. Theater: Sean O'Casey, Irish playwright. *Shaine, Shan, Shandon, Shandy, Shawn, Shane, Shayun, Shayne.*

SEARLE (surl) Old English: "shield."

SEATON (SEE-tun) Old English: "village by the sea." *Seeton, Seton.*

SEBASTIAN (seh-BASS-chun) Latin, Greek: "reserved." Saint Sebastian, a third-century Roman soldier, was killed by a shower of arrows, a scene depicted widely in paintings during the Middle Ages. Literature: Viola's twin brother in Shakespeare's *Twelfth Night*. Military: Sébastien de Vauban, French military engineer who invented the socket bayonet. Movies and Television: Sebastian Cabot, actor. Sports: Sebastian Coe, Olympic gold medalist in track. Fr: *Sebastien*.

SEDGE (sedj) English: "swordsman." *Sedgeley*.

SEELEY (SEE-lee) Old English: "graced by God." *Sealey, Seely*.

SEF (seff) Egyptian: "yesterday." Literature: Sef is the name of an Egyptian lion god in the *Book of the Dead*.

SEFTON (SEF-tun) Old English: "village of rushes."

SEIF (sife) Arabic: "religion's saber."

SELBY (SELL-bee) Old English: "estate." *Shelby*.

SELDON (SELL-dun) Old English: "valley of whispering willows." *Selden, Sliden, Shelden*.

SELIG (SELL-ig) Old German: "exalted" or "graced." *Seligman, Seligmann, Zelig*.

SELWIN (SELL-win) English: "good friend." *Selwine, Selwyne, Selwyn*.

SENNETT (SENN-it) French: "old age." *Sennet*.

SENON (SEH-nohn) Spanish: "living" or "given by Zeus."

SERENO (serr-EE-noh) Latin: "calm" or "serene."

SERGEI (sehr-GAY) Latin: "attending helper." Most popular boy's name in Russia today. Dance: Serge Lifar, French dancer, choreographer, and writer on dance. Music: Sergei Rachmaninov, Sergei Prokofiev, Russian composers. Eng: *Serge;* Arm: *Sarkis;* Ger: *Sergius;* Ital: *Sergio, Sergios;* Pol: *Serg, Sergiusz, Sewek;* Russ: *Serge, Sergey, Sergeyuk, Sergo, Sergunya, Serzh, Serhiy, Serhiyko, Syarhey, Serjiro.*

SETH (seth) Hebrew: "substitute" or "compensation" or "appointed." Arts: Seth Thomas, clock maker. Bible: Seth was Adam and Eve's third son. Military: Seth Warner, American Revolutionary War officer.

SEUNG (see-OONG) Korean: "winning."

SEVILEN (seh-veh-LEN) Turkish: "much loved."

SEWARD (SOO-ward) Old English: "protector of the sea." *Sewerd.*

SEXTON (SEKS-tun) Middle English: "church custodian."

SEYMOUR (SEE-moor) Old French: "from the Saint Maur." Use as a name suggested one's family had hailed from Saint Maur, a village in Normandy.

SHADI (shah-DEE) Arabic: "singer."

SHALOM (shah-LOM) Hebrew: "peace." *Sholoom.*

SHANAHAN (SHAH-nah-han) Irish Gaelic: "discerning" or "cunning."

SHANDY (SHAN-dee) Old English: "energetic" or "lively."

SHANE (shane) Irish: "God is gracious." *Shayne.*

SHANNON (SHA-nun) Irish Gaelic: "ages old." Popular in Ireland. The name of a river, county, and airport in Ireland. *Shanan, Shannan, Shannen.*

SHARIF (shah-REEF) Arabic: "widely respected." *Shareef, Shereef.*

SHAW (shaw) Old English: "small forest."

SHEA (shay) Irish Gaelic: "imposing" or "penetrating." *Shaye, Shae, Shai, Shayan, Shae.*

SHEEHAN (SHEE-han) Irish Gaelic: "peaceful and small."

SHEFFIELD (SHEF-feeld) Old English: "winding pasture."

SHELDON (SHELL-dun) English: "deep valley." Journalism: Sheldon Cheney, critic and founder of *Theatre Arts Magazine.* Music: Sheldon Harnick, lyricist. *Shelden, Shelton.*

SHELLEY (SHELL-lee) English: "clearing on a bank."

SHEM (shem) Hebrew: "famous." Bible: Shem was the name of Noah's eldest son in the Old Testament.

SHEN (shen) Chinese: "spirit" or "contemplation."

SHEPHERD (SHEP-herd) Old English: "one who herds sheep." *Shep, Shepard, Shephard, Shepp, Sheppard, Shepperd.*

SHEPLEY (SHEP-lee) Old English: "field of sheep." *Shepply, Shipley.*

SHERBORN (SHUR-born) Old English: "sparkling brook." *Sherborne, Sherburn, Sherburne.*

SHERIDAN (SHARE-eh-dinn) Irish Gaelic: "wild one." Literature: Sheridan Le Fanu, Irish novelist. *Sheridon, Sherridan.*

SHERLOCK (SHUR-lok) Old English: "gleaming tresses." Literature: Sherlock Holmes, Arthur Conan Doyle's fictional detective. *Sherlocke.*

SHERMAN (SHUR-man) Old English: "shireman" or "sheepshearer." Dates back to the medieval wool business. *Scherman, Schermann, Shermann.*

SHERWIN (SHUR-win) Middle English: "smart friend." *Sherwyn, Sherwynn.*

SHERWOOD (SHUR-wood) Old English: "gleaming grove." Literature: Sherwood Anderson, novelist. *Sherwoode.*

SHILIN (shee-LEEN) Chinese: "bright."

SHILO (shy-LOH) Hebrew: "the one to whom it belongs." Bible: Shiloh is the prophetic name for the Messiah. History: Site of a significant battle during the American Civil War. *Shiloh.*

SHING (shee-ING) Chinese: "victory."

SHIPTON (SHIP-tun) Old English: "village of shepherds."

SIDNEY (SID-nee) Old English: "of Saint Denis." Business: Sidney Hillman, labor leader who helped organize the CIO. Literature: Sydney Carton, hero in Dickens's *A Tale of Two Cities.* Movies and Television: Sidney Lumet, director of *Long Day's Journey into Night;* Sidney Poitier, actor. Theater: Sidney Kingsley, Pulitzer Prize-winning playwright. Science: Sydney Brenner, British recipient of the Nobel Prize in Medicine (2002). Eng: *Cid, Cyd, Si, Sid, Syd, Sydney;* Span: *Sidonio.*

SIEGFRIED (SIG-freed) Old German: "calm" or "triumphant." Literature: Siegfried Sassoon, British poet and biographer. Eng: *Seigfried, Sig, Sigfried;* Fr: *Siffre;* Ger: *Siegfried, Seifert, Seifried;* Lat: *Zegfrids;* Norw: *Sigvard, Siurt;* Pol: *Zygfryd, Zygi;* Port: *Fredo, Siguefredo;* Russ: *Zigfrids;* Span: *Sigfrido, Sigfredo.*

SIGMUND (SIG-mund) Old German: "triumphant defender." Education: Sigmund Freud, father of psychoanalysis. Music: Sigmund Romberg, composer of the operetta *The Student Prince*. *Siegmund, Sigismond, Sigmond, Szygmond.*

SILVANUS (SIL-van-us) Latin: "dweller of the forest." The name Silas is a contraction of Silvanus. Bible: Traveled with the Apostle Paul. History: Silas Deane was an eighteenth-century lawyer who was a member of the U.S. Continental Congress. Eng: *Selwyn, Selvyn;* Span/Port: *Silvan, Silverio;* Span: *Silvino.*

SILVESTOR (sil-VES-tor) Latin, German: "tress." Movies and Television: Sylvester Stallone, actor. *Silvestre, Selvestro, Sylvester.*

SIMBA (SEEM-bah) Swahili: "lion." Astrology: Appropriate for those born under the sign of Leo, symbolized by the lion.

SIMCHA (SEEM-khah) Israel. Hebrew: "joy."

SIMON (SYE-munn) Hebrew: "to hear with mercy." Bible: Simeon carried the infant Jesus into the Temple at Jerusalem. History: Simón Bolívar, freed South American countries from Spanish rule; Shimon Peres, former Israeli Prime Minister and recipient of the Nobel Peace Prize (1994). Music: Simon Rattle, conductor. Eng: *Si, Simeon, Symon, Simmonds, Simons, Simms, Simpson, Symon, Symms;* Arab: *Samein;* Fr: *Simion, Simeon;* Ger: *Simeon, Sim, Simmy;* Gk: *Semon;* Ital: *Simone;*

Port: *Simao;* Rum: *Simion;* Russ: *Simeon;* Span: *Jimenes, Jimenez, Ximenes;* Yiddish: *Shimon.*

SINCLAIR (SIN-clair) Old French: "related to Saint Clair." Literature: Sinclair Lewis, Pulitzer Prize-winning novelist. *Sinclare, Synclair.*

SIPHO (see-POH) South Africa. Zulu: "present."

SKAH (skah) Native American: "white."

SKIP (skip) Scandinavian: "ship's authority." Derived from "skipper," meaning the captain of a vessel. *Skipp, Skipper, Skippie, Skippy.*

SLADE (slayd) Old English: "he who hails from the valley." History: Slade Gorton, U.S. senator (Washington, 1981–95). *Slaide, Slayde.*

SLEVIN (SLEE-vin) Gaelic: "mountaineer."

SLOAN (stone) Irish Gaelic: "armed warrior." *Sloane.*

SMITH (smith) Old English: "blacksmith." *Smitty, Smyth, Smythe.*

SNOWDEN (SNOW-den) Old English: "snow-capped mountain." A Welsh mountain. History: Lord Snowden, former husband of Princess Margaret of England.

SOCRATES (SOCK-rah-tees) Greek: Meaning unknown. Philosophy: The name of the famous philosopher of ancient Greece who examined virtue.

SOLOMON (SOL-oh-mahn) Hebrew: "bestowing peace." Bible: In the Old Testament, King Solomon was a symbol of discerning judgment. Eng: *Soloman, Sollie, Solly;* Czech: *Salamun;* Fr: *Lasimonne, Salomon;* Ger/Swed: *Salomo;* Hung: *Salamon;* Ital: *Salomone;* Lith: *Solomonas;* Norw/Span: *Salomon;* Pol: *Salamen;* Yiddish: *Shelomah, Shlomo.*

SOMERSET (SUM-ur-set) Old English: "residence for summer." An English county. Literature, Theater: Somerset Maugham, novelist and playwright who wrote *Of Human Bondage. Sommerset, Summerset.*

SOMERTON (SUM-ur-tun) Old English: "town for summering." *Somervile, Somerville.*

SOREN (SORE-en) Scandinavian: "god of war."

SOUTHWELL (SOWTH-well) Old English: "well in the south."

SPALDING (SPALD-ing) Old English: "measured lands." Theater: Spalding Gray, monologist. *Spaulding.*

SPEAR (speer) Old English: "swordsman." *Spears, Speer, Speers, Spiers.*

SPENCER (SPEN-ser) Middle English: "host." A spencer is the person in a lodge or inn who provided nourishment. Movies and Televison: Spencer Tracy, actor. *Spense, Spenser.*

STACY Short form of Eustace. See Eustace.

STAFFORD (STAF-furd) Old English: "ford where one stops." *Stafforde, Staford.*

STANBURY (STAN-bur-ee) Old English: "stone fort." *Stanberry, Stanbery.*

STANCLIFF (STAN-cliff) Old English: "rocky cliff." *Stancliffe.*

STANFIELD (STAN-field) Old English: "rocky field." *Stansfield.*

STANFORD (STAN-furd) Old English: "ford full of stones." *Stamford, Standford.*

STANISLAUS (STAN-ee-slaws) Slavic: "stand of glory." Regarded as a martyr who died for his ideals, Saint Stanislaus was an eleventh-century bishop who became the patron saint of Poland. Eng: *Stan, Stanislas;* Czech: *Stana, Stando;* Fr: *Stanislas;* Ger: *Stanislau;* Pol: *Stanislaw, Stasio;* Russ: *Slava, Slavik, Slavka, Stas, Staska, Stasko;* Serb: *Stane;* Span: *Estanislao, Lao, Tano, Tilo.*

STANLEY (STAN-lee) Old English: "stony meadow." Aristocratic surname that became a first name at the turn of the century. Movies and Television: Stanley Kubrick, film director. Science: Stanley B. Prusiner, American Nobel Prize winner in Medicine (1997). Sports: Stan "the Man" Musial, baseball great. Theater: Stanley Houghton, British playwright. *Stanleigh, Stan, Stanly.*

STANMORE (STAN-more) Old English: "stony pond." Place name.

STANTON (STAN-tun) Old English: "town of stones."

STANWICK (STAN-wik) Old English: "dweller at the rocky village." *Stanwicke, Stanwyck.*

STARR (star) Middle English: "star."

STAVROS (STAV-rose) Greek: "crowned with wreath."

STEADMAN (STED-man) Old English: "farmer" or "owner of a farmstead." Occupational name. *Steadmann, Stedman.*

STEEL (steel) Old English: "resistant as steel" or "implacable." *Steele.*

STEIN (styne) or (stayne) German: "rock." Sports: Stein Erickson, skiing champion.

STEINAR (STI-nar) Norwegian: "rock-warrior."

STEPHEN (STEE-vunn) Greek: "made royal" or "crowned." Came into prominence with Saint Stephan, the first martyr for Christian beliefs. Also, the name of a Hungarian king in the tenth century. History: Stephen A. Douglas, known as the "little giant," was Abraham Lincoln's opponent during the famous debates. Literature: Stephen Crane, novelist. Movies and Television: Steve Martin and Steve McQueen, actors; Steven Spielberg, filmmaker.

Music: Stevie Wonder, singer. Theater: Stephen Sondheim, Pulitzer Prize-winning composer and lyricist. Eng: *Stef, Steffan, Steph, Steve, Stevie;* Czech: *Stefan;* Fin; *Tapani, Teppo;* Fr: *Etienne, Tiennot;* Ger: *Stefan, Steffel;* Gk: *Stamos, Stefanos, Stefos, Stephanos, Stavros;* Hung: *Isti, Istvan;* Ital: *Stefano;* Lat: *Stefens;* Norw: *Steffan;* Port: *Estevao;* Russ: *Stefan, Stenya, Stepan, Stepanya, Stepka;* Span: *Esteban, Stevan, Tab.*

STERLING (STUR-ling) Old English: "genuine" or "top quality." Early English money was called sterling. Literature: Sterling Brown, twentieth-century African-American poet and critic. Military: Sterling Price, nineteenth-century politician and general in the Civil War. *Stirling.*

STERNE (sturn) Old English: "unwavering" or "strict." *Stearne, Stearns, Stern.*

STILLMAN (STILL-man) Old English: "reserved" or "peaceful."

STOCKTON (STOK-tun) Old English: "village of cut-down tree."

STOCKWELL (STOK-well) Old English: "well near the cut-down tree."

STORM (storm) Old English: "storm."

STRATFORD (STRAT-ford) Old English: "bridge over the river."

STROM (strahm) German: "stream."

STROUD (straud) English: "from the thicket."

STUART (STOO-art) Old English: "steward." In medieval times, feudal estates were managed by stewards. Literature: *Stuart Little*, children's book by E. B. White. *Stewart, Steward.*

STYLES (stiles) Old English: "stairway." Refers to a set of stairs that make it easier to cross over an embankment usually found in the countryside.

SULLIVAN (SULL-ih-venn) Irish Gaelic: "dark, burning eyes." *Sully.*

SULLY (SUH-lee) Old English: "southern field." *Sulleigh, Sulley.*

SULTAN (sool-TAHN) East Africa. Swahili: "ruler."

SUTCLIFF (SUT-clif) Old English: "cliff in the south." *Sutcliffe.*

SVEN (s'VEHN) Scandinavian: "young" or "fresh." Widely used in Norway and Sweden today. Den: *Svbend, Svein, Swen, Swenson.*

SWEENEY (SWEE-nee) Irish Gaelic: "brave, young one."

SWINBURNE (SWINN-burn) Old English: "pig pond." *Swinborn, Swinburn.*

TAB (tab) Old German: "genius." Movies and Television: Tab Hunter, teenage idol in the 1950s whose given name was Arthur. *Tabb, Taber, Tabor.*

TABIB (tuh-BIB) Turkish: "healer."

TABOR (TAY-bor) Hungarian: "coming from the trenches." *Taber, Taibor, Taybor, Tayber.*

TADDEO (tad-DAY-oh) Italian: "courageous" or "one who praises."

TADELESH (tah-DELL-esh) African: "lucky."

TAGGART (TAG-gurt) Irish Gaelic: "priest's heir" or "pastor's son."

TAHIR (TAH-hir) Arabic: "stainless" or "innocent." Beloved Moslem name in Arab countries and India.

542

TAI (TAH-ee) Vietnamese: "talent."

TAIMA (TAY-ee-mah) Native American: "thunder."

TAIT (tite) Swedish: "merry."

TAJ (tahzh) Hindi: "crown."

TAJO (TAH-ho) Teutonic: "day."

TAKEO (TAH-kay-oh) Japanese: "strong like bamboo."

TALBOT (TAL-bot) Middle English: "sculptor of wood." Surname of the English upper classes until adopted as a given name in the last century. *Tal, Talbert, Tallie, Tally.*

TALE (TAH-leh) Botswana. Tswana: "green."

TALIB (TAH-lib) Arabic: "one who searches."

TALON (tall-OHN) French: "sharp."

TAMAL (tah-MAHL) Hindi: "dark tree."

TANEK (tan-EK) Polish: "immortal."

TANELI (than-ELL-aye) Hebrew: "judged by God."

TANI (TAH-nee) Japanese: "dale."

TANNER (TAN-nur) Old English: "tanner or leather worker." *Tan, Tann, Tanney, Tannie, Tanny.*

TANTON (TAN-tunn) Old English: "village by the peaceful waters." Place name.

TAO (tauw) Chinese: "peach." In the Chinese culture, Tao is the symbol of long life.

TAPANI (tah-PAHN-ee) Hebrew: "victorious."

TARAK (tar-AHK) Hindi: "protector."

TARLETON (TAR-el-tunn) Old English: "Thor's settlement." See Thor.

TARO (TAH-roh) Japanese: "first son."

TATE (tate) Middle English: "he who brings cheer." *Tait, Taitt, Tayte.*

TAU (TAH-oo) Botswana. Tswana: "lion."

TAURINO (tau-REE-noh) Spanish: "bull like." Astronomy: The constellation Taurus. *Taurin, Taurinus, Tauro.*

TAVISH (TAH-vish) Irish Gaelic: "twin." *Tavis, Tevis.*

TAYE (taye) African: "he has been seen." Movies and Television: Taye Diggs, actor.

TAYLOR (TAY-lur) Middle English: "tailor." *Tailer, Tailor, Tayler.*

TEDMUND (TED-mund) Old English: "the land's guardian." *Tedmond.*

TELEK (TE-lek) Polish: "ironworker."

TELLAN (TELL-ahn) Anglo-Saxon: "considers."

TEMAN (TAY-muhn) Israel. Hebrew: "on the right."

TEMPLETON (TEM-pull-tunn) Old English: "village near the temple." *Temp, Temple.*

TENNANT (TEN-int) Old English: "tenant" or "one who rents." A surname now used as a given name. *Tenant, Tennent.*

TENNESSEE (TEN-eh-SEE) Native American: Cherokee: Originally an Indian place name, now a state name. Theater: Tennessee Williams (given name, Thomas), playwright.

TENNYSON (TEN-nee-son) Middle English: "heir of Dennis." *Tenny.*

TERENCE (TERR-intz) Latin: Name of a Roman clan. Literature: Terrance Dicks, children's author. Sports: Terry Bradshaw, football player who led the Pittsburgh Steelers to four Super Bowl titles. *Terance, Terencio, Terrence, Terris, Terry.*

TERRILL (TERR-ill) Old German: "devotee of Thor." Mythology: Thor was the Norse god of thunder. *Terrall, Terrel, Terril, Terrell, Terrie, Terry, Tirrell, Tyrrell.*

TERRON English. Contemporary blend of Terrance and Darren. *Darren, Taran, Taron, Teron, Terran.*

THABIT (TAH-bit) North Africa. Arabic: "gratefulness."

THADDEUS (THAD-dee-us) Aramaic: "bold." Bible: Thaddeus was one of the twelve apostles. Eng: *Tad, Tadd, Thadd, Thad;* Czech: *Tadeas, Tades;* Fr: *Thadee;* Ger: *Thaddus;* Hung: *Tade;* Ital: *Taddeo, Thaddeo;* Pol: *Tadek, Tadzio;* Russ: *Faddei, Fady, Tadey;* Span: *Tadeo, Tadzio, Thaddaud.*

THAI (tie) Vietnamese: "many."

THANE (thayne) Old English: "landowner." In medieval hierarchy, a thane was higher than a peasant and lower than royalty; he owned land but paid service to his land. *Thaine, Thayne.*

THANOS (TAHN-os) Greek: "royal." *Thanasis, Athanasios.*

THATCHER (THAT-chur) Old English: "one who thatches roofs." *Thacher, Thatch, Thaxter.*

THEOBALD (THEE-oh-bald) Old German: "brave kin." *Teobaldo, Thebault, Theo, Thebaud, Thibault, Thibaut, Tibold, Tiebold, Tybald.*

THEODORE (THEE-oh-door) Greek: "divine present." Name from the early Christian era and the name of several saints. Arts: Theodore Rousseau, French impressionist painter. History: Theodore

Roosevelt, twenty-sixth president of the United States (1901–09). Literature: Theodore Dreiser, American novelist; Fyodor Dostoyevsky, Russian novelist. Eng: *Ted, Teddie, Teddy, Theo, Theodor, Tudor;* Bulg: *Feodor;* Czech: *Bohdan, Fedor, Tedik, Thodor, Teodus;* Ger: *Tewdor, Theodor;* Pol: *Tivadar, Teos, Teodorek, Tolek, Dorek;* Russ: *Feodor, Feodore, Fedinka, Dyodr, Fyodor, Teodor, Todor, Todar, Todas;* Span: *Teodoro.*

THEODORIC (THEE-oh-doh-rik) Old German: "leader of the masses." Theodoric is an adaptation of Derek and Dirk and Terry. Arts: Thierry Mugler, fashion designer. Fr: *Thierry, Thiery.*

THERON (THAYRE-unn) Greek: "hunter."

THOMAS (TAHM-us) Greek: "twin." Bible: Thomas owes much of its worldwide popularity to Saint Thomas, one of Christ's twelve apostles who was called "Doubting Thomas" because he at first refused to believe in Christ's resurrection. Arts: Thomas Gainsborough, eighteenth-century British portraitist who painted the famous *Blue Boy.* History: Thomas Jefferson, third president of the United States (1801–09); Thomas Edison, inventor of the light bulb. Journalism: Tom Brokaw, TV news anchor. Literature: Thomas Mann, Thomas Wolfe, authors. Movies and Television: Tom Cruise, Tom Hanks, actors. Philosophy: Saint Thomas Aquinas (1225–74). Sports: Tom Seaver, Tommy John, baseball pitchers. Eng: *Thom, Tom, Tommie, Tommy;* Fin: *Tuomas, Tuomo;* Ger: *Thoma;* Hung: *Tamas, Tomi;* Ital: *Tomasso;* Lith: *Tomelis;* Pol: *Tomico, Tomek;* Port: *Tomaz, Tome;*

Russ: *Foma, Fomka;* Scot: *Tavis, Tavish;* Span: *Chuno.*

THOR (thorr) Old Norse: "thunder." Mythology: The Norse god of thunder.

THORALD (THOR-uld) Old Norse: "Thor's devotee." *Terrell, Terrill, Thorold, Torald, Tyrell.* See Thor.

THORBERT (THOR-burt) Old Norse: "Thor's brightness." *Torbert.* See Thor.

THORBURN (THOR-burn) Old Norse: "thunder's bear." Old Anglo-French: *Thorbjorn.* See Thor.

THORNTON (THORN-tunn) Old English: "town of the thorns." Literature, Theater: Thornton Wilder, Pulitzer·Prize-winning novelist and playwright *(The Bridge of San Luis Rey),* 1927. *Thorn, Thorne, Thornley.*

THORPE (thorpe) Old English: "small settlement." *Thorp.*

THURLE (thurle) Irish: "strong fort." *Thurl.*

THURSTON (THURS-tunn) Scandinavian: "thunder's stone" or "stone of Thor." *Thorstan, Thorstein, Thorsten, Thurstain, Thurstan, Thursten, Torsten, Torston.*

TIBOR (tih-BORE) Hungarian: "holy place."

TIER (teer) Irish: "regal." *Tiernan, Tierney.*

TILDEN (TILL-dunn) Old English: "prosperous dale." *Tilford.*

TIMOTHY (TIM-oh-thee) Greek: "to exalt the Lord." Bible: Timothy was a companion to Paul, who addressed two letters to him. Literature: The story of Tiny Tim in Charles Dickens's *A Christmas Carol,* is a perennial Christmas favorite. Movies and Television: Timothy Hutton, actor. Science: Tim Hunt, Nobel Prize winner in Medicine (2001). Eng: *Tim, Timkin, Timmy, Timon;* Bulg: *Timotei;* Fin: *Timo;* Fr: *Timothee;* Ger: *Timotheus;* Gk: *Timotheos;* Hung: *Timot;* Ir: *Tiomoid;* Norw/Swed: *Timoteus;* Pol: *Tymek, Tymon;* Port/Span: *Timoteo;* Russ: *Tima, Timka, Timok, Tisha, Tishka.*

TIMUR (tee-MOOR) Israel. Hebrew: "imposing height."

TIN (tin) Vietnamese: "think."

TITUS (TYE-tuss) Greek: "land of the giants." Bible: Titus was a Greek Christian missionary. Literature: Titus Plautus, Roman playwright and a character in Longfellow's poem *The Golden Legend.* Eng: *Tite;* Gk: *Titos;* Ital: *Tito;* Pol: *Titek, Tytus.*

TIVON (tee-VOHN) Israel. Hebrew: "nature lover."

TOBBAR (TOH-bahr) English Gypsy: "highway."

TOBIAS (toh-BEE-uss) Hebrew: "God is great." Toby is a short form. Bible: Popularized by the Puritans, who obtained it from the Old Testament. Theater: Toby Belch, character in Shakespeare's *Twelfth Night.* **Tobe, Tobiah, Tobie, Tobin, Tobit, Toby.**

TODD (tahd) Middle English: "fox." **Tod.**

TOMI (TOH-me) Japanese: "wealthy."

TONG (tong) Vietnamese: "fragrant."

TOR (toor) Nigeria. Tiv: "ruler" or "royal."

TORIN (TORE-in) Celtic: "chief."

TORIO (toh-ree-OH) Japanese: "bird's tail."

TORRENCE (TORR-intz) Scottish, Irish: "from the ragged hills." Eng: *Tor, Torence, Torey, Torin, Torrance, Torrey, Torre;* Scot: *Torrie, Torry.*

TORU (TOH-roo) Japanese: "sea."

TOSHIRO (toh-shee-ROH) Japanese: "talented" or "intelligent."

TOVI (toh-VEE) Hebrew: "good."

TRACE (trase) Anglo-Saxon: "brave."

TRAVIS (TRA-viss) Old French: "at the road's fort." Music: Travis Tritt, country and western singer. *Traver, Travers, Travus, Travys.*

TREMAIN (tree-MAYNE) Celtic: "house made of rocks." *Tremaine, Tremayne.*

TRENT (trent) Latin: "flowing rivers." A river in England. *Trenten, Trentin, Trenton.*

TRENTON (TRENT-ohn) Latin: "town by the rapids." Place name, capital of New Jersey. *Trentin, Trenten.*

TREVOR (TREV-ur) Welsh: "big estate." Originated in Wales, but spread to other parts of England during the mid-Victorian era. Movies and Television: Trevor Howard, actor. *Trefor, Trevar, Trever.*

TREY (tray) Middle English: "three." Movies and Television: Trey Hunt, actor.

TRISTAN (TRIS-tenn) Celtic: "bold" or "melancholy." In medieval legend, the hero of a tragic love story between a knight and his uncle's wife. Literature: *Tristram Shandy,* Laurence Sterne's eighteenth-century novel; Tristan Tzara, French poet and writer who founded the Dada movement in 1916. Music: Richard Wagner memorialized the tragic story in his opera, *Tristan und Isolde.* Sports: Tristram Speaker, baseball player who was elected to the baseball Hall of Fame (1937). *Tris, Tristram, Tristam.*

TRIPP (trip) Old English: "traveler." *Trypp, Tryp.*

TROY (troy) Irish Gaelic: "trooper." A famous port in ancient Greece, the site of the Trojan War, fought for the beauty of a single woman. Place name, Troy, New York. Movies and Television: Troy Donahue, actor. *Troi, Troye.*

TRUMAN (TROO-munn) Old English: "faithful follower." Literature: Truman Capote, short-story writer and novelist who wrote *In Cold Blood. Trueman, Trumaine, Trumann.*

TRUMBLE (TRUM-bull) Old English: "mighty." *Trumball, Trumbell, Trumbull.*

TUARI (too-ARE-ee) Native American: "young eagle."

TUCKER (TUCK-kur) Old English: "one who pleats wool." Occupational name relating to a popular trade in the Middle Ages.

TUDOR (TOO-door) Welsh: "divine gift."

TULIO (too-LEE-oh) Scottish: "lively."

TULLY (TULL-ee) Irish Gaelic: "calm" or "surrender to God." *Tull, Tulley, Tullie.*

TUMAINI (tu-MAH-nee) Kenya. Mwera: "hope."

TUMO (too-MOE) African: "fame."

TUNG (tehng) Vietnamese: "stately."

TUNU (TOO-noo) Native American. Miwok: "deer waiting to ravage the garden."

TURNER (TURN-ur) Middle English: "woodworking master." "Turning" the lathe was a term referring to a process in the seventeenth-century decorative arts.

TUVYA (TOOV-yuh) Israel. Hebrew: "God's goodness." *Tuvyahu, Tobiah.*

TWAIN (twane) English: "cut in two."

TYEE (TYE-ee) Native American: "chieftains."

TYLER (TYE-lur) Middle English: "one who tiles a roof." Journalism: Tyler Mathisen, financial reporter. *Tilar, Ty, Tylar.*

TYMON (TEE-mahn) Greek: "exalting the Lord." Used in Poland. *Tymek.*

TYNE (tyne) Old English: "river."

TYREE (TY-ree) Scottish: Place name, from Tiree, the name of an island off the west coast of Scotland. *Ty.*

TYRELL (tye-RELL) Latin: Name of a Roman clan. *Terrell, Tirell, Tyrrell.*

TYRONE (ty-RONE) Irish Gaelic: "Owen's property." Tyrone is the name of a county in Ireland. Movies and Television: Tyrone Power, actor. Sports: Ty Cobb, baseball player who had a record .367 lifetime batting average. *Ty, Tyrort.*

TYSON (TY-sunn) Old French: "explosive." *Ti-sort, Ty, Tycen, Tysert.*

TZADOK (TSAA-dock) Hebrew: "just."

TZURIEL (TSOO-ree-ehl) Israel. Hebrew: "God is my rock." Used in Israel.

UDEH (YUD-ay) Hebrew: "praise."

UDELL (you-DELL) Old English: "grove of the yews." *Dell, Eudel, Udel, Udall.*

UDOLF (OOD-olf) English: "wealthy wolf."

UGO (yuh-GOH) Italian: "bright in mind and spirit."

ULANI (YOU-lahn-ee) Polynesian: "cheerful."

ULF (oolf) Old German: "wolf."

ULMER (UHL-mur) Old English: "wolf's fame travels far." *Ulmar.*

ULRIC (UHL-rik) Old German: "power of the wolf" or "power of the home." History: Ulrich Cili, medieval Austrian prince. *Rick, Udo, Ullric, Ulrich, Ulrick, Ulrik.*

ULYSSES (you-LISS-ees) Latin: Form of the Greek name *Odysseus* meaning "angry." Ulysses is the wanderer whose adventures are the subject of Homer's *Odyssey.* History: Ulysses S. Grant, Civil War general and the eighteenth president of the United States. Literature: *Ulysses,* the title of a famous novel by James Joyce. *Ulises, Ulisse.*

UMBERTO (uhm-BERT-oh) Italian: "color of earth."

UMED (OOM-ed) Hindi: "hope."

UMI (oo-MEE) Malawi. Yao: "life."

UNIKA (oo-NEE-kah) Malawi. Lomwe: "brighten."

UPTON (UP-tun) Old English: "village on the hill above." Literature: Upton Sinclair, social reformer and writer.

URBAN (UHR-ban) Latin: "in the city" or "metropolis." The name of eight popes. Eng: *Orban, Urbane;* Fr: *Urbain, Urbaine;* Hung: *Orban;* Ital: *Urbano;* Russ: *Urvan.*

URIAH (you-RYE-ah) Hebrew: "Jehovah is my light." Bible: Uriah was a captain in King David's army. Literature: Uriah Heep is a character in Charles Dickens's novel *David Copperfield.*

URIEL (OOR-ee-el) Hebrew: "angel of light." Bible: Uriel was one of seven archangels. In Moslem tradition, Israfil (Uriel) is the angel of music. Literature: John Milton in *Paradise Lost* describes Uriel as the "Regent of the Sun." *Urie, Uriah, Uri.*

USI (OO-see) Malawi. Yao: "smoke."

VACHEL (VAY-chel) Old French: "keeper of the cows." Literature: Vachel Lindsay, poet and author.

VADIN (VAH-deen) Hindi: "renown lecturer" or "scholar."

VAIL (vale) Old English: "valley." Old English place name, now famous as a ski resort in Colorado. *Bail, Bale, Vaile, Vale.*

VALDEMAR (vahl-DEH-mar) Scandinavian: "ruler." *Valdemarr.*

VALENTINE (VAL-en-tine) Latin: "healthy" or "powerful." February 14, the day Saint Valentine became a martyr, coincided with the observance of the festival of Juno when lots were drawn for lovers. *Balint, Folant, Val, Valentin, Valentino, Veiten, Walenty.*

VALERIAN (vah-LEER-ee-unn) Latin: "potent." *Valerio, Valery, Valeryn.*

VALIN (VAH-leen) Hindi: "monkey king." See Balin.

VAN (van) Dutch: "of" or "heir of." Preposition showing place or origin, related to French and Spanish *de,* Italian *da, de,* and *di,* and German *von.* Movies and Television: Van Johnson, actor. Music: Van Cliburn, pianist; Van Morrison, rock singer. *Vann.*

VANCE (vantz) Old English: "swamp."

VANDYKE (van-DIKE) Dutch: "of the dyke."

VARDEN (VAR-den) Old French: "grassy slopes." *Vardon, Verden, Verdon, Verdun.*

VARICK (VAR-ik) Old German: "chief who defends honorably." *Waric, Warrick, Warrick.*

VARUN (var-UHN) Hindu: "lord of the waters."

VASILIS (vahs-ILL-is) Greek: "kingly."

VAUGHN (vawn) Old Welsh: "reduced size." *Vaughan.*

VAVRIN (VAHV-rin) Czech: "laurel."

VERNON (VER-nunn) Old French: "dense grove" or "springtime." Name brought by the Normans as a surname, developing into a given name in the

1800s. Business: Vernon L. Smith, Nobel Prize winner in Economics (2002). Dance: Vernon Castle, British dancer who originated the one-step and the turkey trot. History: Vernon Walters, diplomat. Literature: Vernon Watkins, Welsh mystic and visionary poet. *Laven, Vern, Verne, Verney.*

VERRILL (VER-ril) Old French: "faithful"; Old German: "virile." *Verill, Verrell Verroll, Veryl.*

VICTOR (VIC-tur) Latin: "he who triumphs." Name that found fame in Christian Rome, and again during the reign of Queen Victoria. Three popes, about thirty-five saints, and a number of Italian kings have borne this name. Literature: Victor Hugo, French novelist who wrote *Les Misérables*. Music: Vic Damone, singer. Eng: *Vic, Vick;* Bulg/Russ: *Viktor;* Fr: *Victoir;* Ital: *Vittore, Vittorio;* Pol: *Wiktor, Witek;* Port: *Vitor;* Russ: *Vika, Vitenka, Vitka, Vitya;* Span: *Victorio, Victorino, Vito, Vitin.*

VIDOR (VEE-door) Hungarian, Latin: "happy."

VILMOS (VEEL-mosh) Teutonic: "steadfast warrior." *Vili.*

VINCENT (VIN-sent) Latin: "subjugate" or "embraces powerfully." Popularity derived from Saint Vincent de Paul, seventeenth-century priest who founded an order of missionary brothers. Arts: Vincent van Gogh, Dutch painter. Movies and Television: Vincent Price, actor. Music: Vincent Youmans, composer. Sports: Vince Lombardi, football coach. Eng: *Bink, Vin, Vince, Vinn, Vint;* Czech: *Vincence, Vinco;* Fr/Ger: *Vincenz;* Gk: *Binkentios;* Hung:

Vinci; Ital: *Enzo, Vicenzo, Vincenzo;* Pol: *Wicek, Wicent, Wicus;* Russ: *Kesha, Vika, Vikent, Vikenti, Vikesha;* Span: *Vicente.*

VINSON (VINN-sun) Old English: "heir of Vincent."

VIRGIL (VURR-jill) Latin: "flourishing." Literature: Virgil (70 B.C.–19 B.C.), poet and author of the *Aenid. Verge, Vergil, Virgilio.*

VITALY (VIT-ahl-ee) Russian: "vital." Science: Vitaly L. Ginzburg, Russian Nobel Prize winner in Physics (2003).

VITO (VEE-toh) Latin: "life." *Vital, Vitale, Vitalis, Vitus, Witold.*

VLADIMIR (v'LA-duh-meer) Russian: "prince of the world" or "glory of the prince." History: Vladimir Lenin, leader of the Russian Revolution (1917). Literature: Vladimir Nabokov, novelist. Music: Vladimir Horowitz, Russian pianist. *Vladamir, Vladimeer, Wladimir, Wladimyr.*

VOLKER (VOLE-ker) German: "people's guard."

WABAN (wah-BAHN) Native American: "breezes from the east."

WADE (wayd) Old English: "ford in the river." Military: Wade Hampton, Civil War Confederate general. Sports: Wade Boggs, baseball player, American League batting champ (1983, 1985–88).

WADSWORTH (WADS-wirth) Old English: "town with a crossing."

WAGNER (WAG-nur) German: "wagonmaker." *Waggoner.*

WAITE (wayte) Middle English: "protector." *Waits, Wayte.*

WAKEFIELD (WAKE-feeld) Old English: "wet meadow."

WAKIZA (wah-KEE-zah) Native American: "determined warrior."

WALCOTT (WAHL-cot) Old English: "cottage near the embankment." *Walcot, Wallcott, Wolcott.*

WALDEMAR (WAHL-de-mar) Germanic: "strong and famous." Journalism: Waldo Frank, publisher. Literature: Ralph Waldo Emerson, poet and essayist. *Valdemar, Waldo.*

WALDEN (WAHL-den) Old English: "valley dense with woods." Literature: Thoreau used the name for a pond and his book *Walden. Waldi, Waldon.*

WALFORD (WAHL-fird) Old English: "ford in the stream." Music: Walford Davies, composer.

WALFRED (WAHL-fred) Old German: "he who rules for the sake of peace."

WALKER (WAHL-ker) Old English: "cloth-walker." Occupational name for one who walked on cloth to cleanse it.

WALLACE (WAHL-iss) Old English: "one from Wales." Term originally used to separate Scots from other foreigners. History: Wallace Fard, revolutionary who established the Black Muslim movement in the United States. Literature: Wallace Stevens, Pulitzer Prize-winning poet. Movies and Television: Wallace Reid, Wallace Beery, actors. *Wallach, Wallie, Wallis, Wally, Walsh, Welch, Welsh.*

WALLER (WAHL-lur) Old English: "wall-maker."

WALTER (WAHL-tur) Old German: "army of the masses." Sir Walter Raleigh, the renowned courtier, gave the name great prominence. Legend has it that Sir Walter Raleigh once put down his cloak on a muddy spot for the Queen to step on and she ordered him to then "wear the muddy cloak till her pleasure be further known." Arts: Walt Disney, cartoonist who won twenty Oscars. Journalism: Walter Cronkite, TV news commentator and former anchor. Literature: Walt Whitman, poet. Science: Walter Adams, astronomer who determined the speed and distance of thousands of stars. Sports: Walter Payton, football great. Eng: *Wallie, Wally, Walt;* Czech: *Valtr, Vladko, Waltr;* Fr: *Gauther, Gautier;* Ger: *Walli, Walther;* Ital: *Gualtiero;* Lat: *Valter, Valters;* Lith: *Vanda, Vandele, Waldemar;* Pol: *Ladislaus;* Russ: *Dima, Dimka, Vadimir, Volga, Vova, Vovka;* Span: *Gualberto, Bualterio, Gualtero, Gualterio, Gutierre.*

WALTON (WAHL-tun) Old English: "reinforced village."

WALWORTH (WAHL-worth) Old English: "fenced-in farm."

WALWYN (WAHL-win) Old English: "friend from Wales." *Walwin, Walwinn.*

WANN (wahn) Anglo-Saxon: "dark."

WAPI (WAH-pee) Native American: "lucky."

WARD (ward) Old English: "one who guards." *Warde, Warden, Worden.*

WARFIELD (WAHR-feeld) Middle English: "meadow near the weir." Pens in a river used to catch fish are called weirs.

WARNER (WAR-ner) Old German: "determined defender." *Werner, Wernher.*

WARREN (WAR-ren) Old English: "warden." A warren was an area designated for the breeding of animals. Business: Warren Buffett, wealthy stock market investor from Omaha, known for his modesty and unrivaled success. History: Warren Harding was the twenty-ninth president of the United States (1921–23). Warren Burger, Chief Justice of the U.S. Supreme Court (1969–86). Movies and Television: Warren Beatty, actor and director. *Ware, Waring, Warrin, Warriner.*

WARWICK (WAR-wik) Old English: "buildings close to the weir." *Warick, Warrick.* See Warfield.

WASHBURN (WASH-burn) Old English: "overflowing river."

WASHINGTON (WASH-ing-tun) Old English. Meaning unknown. Literature: Washington Irving, novelist. See Ichabod.

WATSON (WAT-sun) Old English: "Walter's son." Literature: Sherlock Holmes's partner, to whom he often observed, "Elementary, my dear Watson."

WAVERLY (WAYV-ur-lee) Old English: "grove of aspen trees." *Waverlee, Waverly.*

WAYLAND (WAY-land) Old English: "near the footpath." Music: Waylon Jennings, country and western singer. *Way, Waylan, Waylen, Waylin, Waylon, Weylin.*

WAYNE (wayn) Old English: "one who builds or drives wagons." Originally a short form of Wainwright, but long used as an independent name. Music: Wayne Newton, singer. Sports: Wayne Gretzky, hockey great voted most valuable player (1980–87, 1989). *Wain, Wayn.*

WEBB (web) Old English: "one who weaves." *Web, Weber, Webster.*

WELDON (WEL-don) Old English: "hill with the well." *Welden, Welldon.*

WELFORD (WEL-fird) Old English: "well near the ford."

WELLS (wells) Old English: Place name. Wells, a city located in western England, is well known for its cathedral.

WEMILO (weh-MEE-loh) Native American: "speaks to all."

WENCESLACIS (WENN-sih-sloss) Old Slavic: "marvelous necklace of honor." History: King Wenceslas ruled Bohemia in the tenth century and was later made the patron saint of Czechoslovakia. Music: The well-known Christmas carol using the name Wenceslas was written in the nineteenth century. *Wenceslas, Wenzel, Wiencyslaw.*

WENDELL (WEN-dull) Old German: "seeker." History: Oliver Wendell Holmes, U.S. Supreme Court justice. *Wendall, Wendel.*

WENTWORTH (WENT-worth) Old English: "white man's village."

WESLEY (WES-lee) Old English: "field in the west." Military: Wesley Merritt, chief of West Point (1882–87). Movies and Television: Wesley Snipes, actor. Sports: Wesley Person, basketball player. *Wesly, Wessley, Westleigh, Westley.*

WESTBROOK (WEST-brook) Old English: "brook in the west." Place name that describes where one lives. Journalism: Westbrook Pegler, sports newspaper columnist. *Brook, Brooks, Wesbrook, West, Westbrooke.*

WESTBY (WEST-bee) Old English: "farmer in the west."

WESTON (WES-tun) Old English: "settlement in the west." *Westen, Westin.*

WETHERBY (WETH-ur-bee) Old English: "farm of wethers." *Wetherly.*

WHEATLEY (WHEET-lee) Old English: "fields of wheat." *Wheatleigh, Wheatly.*

WHEATON (WHEE-tun) Old English: "settlement for wheat."

WHEELER (WHEEL-ur) Old English: "one who makes wheels."

WHELAN (WHEEL-ahn) Irish: "joyful."

WHISTLER (WHIS-ler) Old English: "he who whistles."

WHITBY (WHIT-bee) Old English: "farm with white walls." *Whitbey, Whitbie.*

WHITCOMB (WHIT-cum) Old English: "valley of the white light." Literature: James Whitcomb Riley, poet.

WHITFIELD (WHIT-feeld) Old English: "white field."

WHITFORD (WHIT-furd) Old English: "white ford."

WHITLEY (WHIT-lee) Old English: "white meadow."

WIESLAV (WHY-slav) Slavic: "one with great glory."

WILBUR (WIL-burr) Old German. Meaning unknown. Aeronautics: Wilbur and Orville Wright, brothers who pioneered in aviation, flying the first flight at Kitty Hawk, North Carolina (1903). Sports: Wilbur Shaw, race car driver who won the Indianapolis 500 three times. *Wilber, Billbur.*

WILEY (WYE-lee) Old English: "flooded field." Aeronautics: Wiley Post, aviator, who was among the first to fly around the world (1933). *Willey, Wylie.*

WILFORD (WIL-ford) Old English: "ford by the willows." Movies and Television: Wilford Brimley, actor.

WILFRED (WIL-fred) Old English: "peace with reason." Saint Wilfrid (673–709) was a famous English prelate. Literature: The name of the hero in two of Sir Walter Scott's books, *Ivanhoe* and *Rokeby. Wilfredo, Wilfried, Will.*

WILKINSON (WILK-in-sun) Old English: "son of little Will." *Wilkins, Willkins, Willkinson.*

WILLARD (WIL-lard) Old German: "determination." Movies and Television: Willard Scott, TV weatherman.

WILLIAM (WILL-yum) Old German: "determined defense." William is second only to John as the most widely used name in the United States and England. The name became very popular in England because of William the Conqueror (1066) and succeeding English kings. Arts: William Hogarth, painter and engraver. Business: William Lear, founder of the company that sells the Lear jet. Education: Wilson Barrett, anthropologist, who studied religion and science among Indian tribes. History: Four U.S. presidents were named William: Harrison, McKinley, Taft, and Clinton. Literature: William Faulkner, William Kennedy, Pulitzer Prize-winning novelists. Movies and Television: Liam Neeson, William Hurt, and Willem Dafoe, actors. Music: Willie

Nelson, country singer. Science: William Henry (1578–1657), scientist who discovered that blood circulates. Sports: Willie Mays, baseball great who hit 660 home runs in his career. Eng: *Bill, Billy, Will, Willie, Willis, Willy, Wilson;* Bulg: *Vilhelm;* Czech: *Vila, Vilek, Vilem, Viliam, Vildo, Vilous;* Fr: *Guillaume;* Ger: *Wilhelm, Willil, Willy;* Gk: *Vasilios, Vassos;* Hung: *Villi, Vilmos;* Ir: *Ulliam;* Russ: *Vas, Vasili, Vasiliy, Vasilak, Vaska, Vassili;* Swed: *Vilhelm, Ville, Wilhelm, Williw;* Yiddish: *Velvel, Welfel, Wolf.*

WILLOUGHBY (WIL-oh-bee) Old English: "farm of willows." *Willoughbey, Willoughbie.*

WILSON (WIL-son) Variant of William. See William.

WILTON (WIL-tun) Old English: "from the farm with a spring." Sports: Wilt "the Stilt" Chamberlain, basketball great. *Will, Willie, Willy, Wilt.*

WINCHELL (WIN-chell) English: "drawer of water."

WINDSOR (WIND-sor) Old English: "of Windsor." A town and the royal castle in England are named Windsor. The municipal borough of Southern England and seat of Windsor Castle, the principal residence of the British royal family. *Wyndsor.*

WINFIELD (WIN-feeld) Teutonic: "friend of the soil" or "friend of the earth." *Winnfield, Wynfield, Wynnfield, Field, Win, Winn, Wyn.*

WINSLOW (WINS-low) Old English: "hill where friends live." Arts: Winslow Homer, painter famous for his marine scenes.

WINSTON (WIN-stun) Old English: "town where friends live." History: Winston Churchill, prime minister of England. *Winsten, Winstonn, Wynstan, Wynston.*

WINTHROP (WIN-throp) Old English: "village of friends." History: John Winthrop, Puritan governor of Massachusetts.

WOLCOTT (WOHL-cot) Old English: "cottage of the wolf."

WOLFE (wolf) Old English: "wolf." Science: Wolf Szmuness, epidemiologist, who developed studies of the hepatitis B vaccine. *Woolf.*

WOLFGANG (WOLF-gang) Old German: "quarrel of the wolf." Music: Wolfgang Mozart, eighteenth-century Austrian composer. Science: Wolfgang Pauli, Nobel Prize-winning physicist.

WOODROW (WOOD-row) Old English: "row of bushes or trees near the woods." History: Woodrow Wilson, twenty-eighth president of the United States (1913–21). Movies and Television: Woody Allen (born Allen Konigsberg), screenwriter, director, and actor. Music: Woody Guthrie, folk singer. Sports: Woody Hayes, college football coaching great. *Woody.*

WOODWARD (WOOD-ward) Old English: "warden of the woods." *Woodard.*

WOODY (WOOD-ee) English: Short form of Woodrow. See Woodrow.

WORTH (worth) Old English: "farm with fences." *Worthey, Worthington, Worthy.*

WREN (wren) Welsh: "chief."

WRIGHT (rite) Old English: "woodworker" or "carpenter."

WYATT (WHY-it) Old French: "fights little." History: Wyatt Earp, Arizona and Kansas lawman. *Wiatt, Wye.*

WYCLIFF (WHY-kliff) Old English: "cliff with white rocks." Music: Wycliff Jean, popular rap artist. *Wycliffe.*

WYLIE (WHY-lee) Old English: "cunning." *Wiley, Wye.*

WYNDHAM (WIND-im) Old English: "hamlet near the wandering path." Literature: Wyndham Lewis, English writer and painter. *Windham, Wynndham.*

WYNN (win) Welsh: "light-complexioned." *Win, Winn, Wynne.*

WYNONO (wi-NO-no) Native American: "first-born son."

XABAT (zah-BAHT) Spanish: "savior."

XANTHUS (ZAN-thus) Latin, Greek: "blonde tresses." *Xanthos.*

XARLES (ZAR-less) French: "manly."

XAVIER (ZAY-vee-ayre) Arabic: "splendid." Spanish: "new dwelling." Xavier was adopted by the Spanish during the Moorish occupation. Francis (of) Xavier was a Jesuit missionary who took Christianity to the East Indies and Japan. Music: Xavier Cougat, bandleader. Sports: Xavier McDaniel, basketball player. Eng/Span: *Javier;* Ger: *Xavier;* Ital: *Saverio.*

XENOS (ZEE-nos) Greek: "guest." *Zeno, Zenos.*

XERXES (ZERKS-eez) Persian: "royal leader." History: The name of three Persian kings (fifth century B.C.).

YAAKOV (YAH-kov) Israel. Hebrew: "supplanting one." Literature, Theater: Iago is a character in Shakespeare's *Othello*. **Yaacob, Yachov, Yago, Yakob, Yakov;** Ital: *Iago.*

YADID (yah-DID) Hebrew: "beloved."

YAGIL (yah-GEL) Israel. Hebrew: "he will celebrate."

YAIR (YAH-eer) Hebrew: "he will instruct." *Jair.*

YAKEZ (YAH-kehz) Native American. Carrier: "divine skies."

YALE (yale) Old English: "on the side of the slope." Sports: Yale Lary, Hall of Fame football player.

YANCY (YAN-cee) Native American. Disputable origin, but possibly Indian term for "Englishman."

Literature: Yancey Cravat, character in Edna Ferber's *Cimarron*. *Yance, Yancey, Yantsey.*

YANIS (yah-NIS) Hebrew: "gift from god."

YAPHET (YAH-fet) Israel. Hebrew: "good-looking." *Japhet, Japheth, Yapheth.*

YARDAN (yah-DAHN) Arabic: "king."

YARDLEY (YAHRD-lee) Old English: "meadow with fences." *Yardleigh, Yardly.*

YAREMA (yah-REEM-ah) Hebrew: "appointed by God."

YASAR (yah-SAHR) Arabic: "riches." *Yaser, Yassar, Yasser.*

YATES (yates) Middle English: "iron gates." *Yeats.*

YAVIN (yah-VIN) Hebrew: "understanding."

YAZID (YAH-zid) North Africa. Arabic: "ever increasing." This name dates back to ancient Arabic literature. *Zaid.*

YE (yey) Chinese: "light."

YEHUDAH (yeh-HOO-dah) Israel. Hebrew: "exalt." Music: Yehudi Menuhin, concert violinist. *Yehudi, Yechudi, Yechudit, Yehuda, Judah.*

YESHAYA (yeh-SHAH-yah) Israel. Hebrew: "God lends." *Yeshayahu.*

YITZHAK (yiht-ZAHK) Hebrew: "laughter." Variant of Isaac. History: Yitzhak Rabin, Israeli Nobel Peace Prize winner (1994).

YOBACHI (YOHB-ah-chee) African: "pray to God."

YONAH (yoh-NAH) Hebrew: "dove."

YUL (yule) Chinese Mongolian: "beyond the horizon." Movies and Television: Yul Brynner, actor.

YUMA (YOO-mah) Native American: "son of the chief."

YVES (eev) French: Variation of Ivo, which is Teutonic for "archer's yew." A name used in France. Music: Yves Montand, singer.

ZABULON (ZAHB-oo-lahn) Hebrew: "to exhalt, honor."

ZACCHEUS (zak-EE-us) Hebrew: "innocent" or "pure." Bible: Zacchaeus was a disciple of Jesus.

ZACHARIAH (zak-a-RYE-ah) Hebrew: "recalled by the horde." Bible: Zacharias was the father of John the Baptist. History: Zachary Taylor, twelfth president of the United States (1849–50). Eng: *Zach, Zacharia, Zachery, Zack, Zakb, Zechariah, Zeke;* Fin: *Sakari;* Fr: *Zacharie;* Ger: *Sacharja, Zachari;* Hebrew: *Zachary;* Hung: *Zacharias, Zako;* Port/Span: *Zacarias;* Russ: *Sachar, Zakhar;* Swed/Norw: *Sakarias, Sakarja, Zakris.*

ZAFIR (SAH-fer) Arabic: "victorious."

ZAHI (SAH-ee) Arabic: "bright and shining."

ZAIDE (SAH-ee-deh) Israel. Yiddish: "elder."

ZAMIR (zah-MEER) Israel. Hebrew: "bird" or "song."

ZANE (zayne) English: Form of John. See John. *Zayne.*

ZANIEL (ZAHN-ee-ell) Latin: "angel of Mondays."

ZAREK (ZAH-rek) Greek: "may God protect this king." Used in Poland. *Baltek.*

ZEBULON (ZEBB-you-lun) Hebrew: "dwelling place." A variant, Zevulun, is currently a popular name in Israel. History: Pikes Peak was named after General Zebulon Pike. *Zevulun.*

ZEDEKIAH (zed-e-KYE-ah) Hebrew: "God is fair." Bible: Zedekiah, the last king of Judah.

ZEHEB (ze-HEB) Turkish: "gold."

ZEKE (zeek) Hebrew: Contemporary short form of Zachariah, or a short form of Ezekiel. See Zachariah and Ezekiel.

ZEKI (ze-KI) Turkish: "smart."

ZELIG (ZELL-ig) German: "happy."

ZEUS (zoos) Greek: "living." Mythology: The supreme deity of the Olympic gods.

ZIKOMO (zee-KOH-moh) Malawi. Ngoni: "thank you."

ZION (ZYE-on) Hebrew: "protected place." The name was first applied only to an elevated section of Jerusalem, then to the whole city. Bible: David built his palace and Solomon his temple in Zion.

ZIVEN (ZIHV-en) Slavic: "vigorous and alive."

ZUBERI (zoo-BEH-ree) Swahili: "strong."

THE BABY NAME DATA BANK

FEMALE NAMES

AERONAUTICS
Amelia
Amy
Beryl
Blanche
Bonnie
Claire
Jacqueline
Katherine

ARTS
Adelaide
Agnes
Alice
Andrea
Augusta
Bernice
Cameo
Chanel
Clara
Cynthia
Denise
Diana
Dorothy

Edith
Emily
Faith
Freda
Gabrielle
Gelsey
Genevieve
Georgia
Heidi
Isabel
Jeanette
Judith
Kristin
Lisa
Madeline
Madonna
Mary
Maya
Melba
Melvina
Mona
Morgan
Paloma
Paula

Peggy
Priscilla
Rachel
Rose
Selma
Tori

ASTROLOGY
Am
Anona
Arista
Callista
Cara
Cerella
Eartha
Gemini
Gurit
Irisa
Jael
Jean
Jora
Kenda
Kiku
Kona

Leandra
Leya
Livana
Luna
Melba
Mesha
Mina
Naida
Nashota
Nerissa
Pati
Pausha
Poppy
Rea
Ryba
Saura
Selina
Shahar
Sidra
Soma
Surya
Taura
Tula
Ursula
Yolanda
Zea

BIBLE
Abigail
Abira
Bethany
Beulah
Carmen
Chloe
Danna

Deborah
Delilah
Dina
Drusilla
Elizabeth
Emanuele
Esther
Gabrielle
Genesis
Geva
Hannah
Hulda
Janae
Jemima
Jezebel
Judith
Keren
Keturah
Kezia
Lael
Lois
Lydia
Mariam
Martha
Michal
Mirella
Mozelle
Nuria
Persis
Phoebe
Precious
Rachel
Rebecca
Regina
Rhoda

Ruth
Salome
Sapphire
Sarah
Sheba
Tabitha
Talitha
Tamar
Veronica

BOTANY
Alaqua
Amarantha
Amaryllis
Amayeta
Andromeda
Anemone
Anthea
Ayame
Azalea
Azami
Bakula
Behira
Blossom
Bluebell
Brier
Bryony
Cam
Camelia
Celia
Cherry
Chrisann
Dahlia
Daphne
Eglantine

Fern	Mauve	Henrietta
Fleur	Myrta	Ivana
Flora	Netia	Kendall
Gada	Nizana	Martha
Gardenia	Nurit	Mary
Garland	Ogin	Mercedes
Geneva	Oliana	Muriel
Giacinta	Padma	Norell
Gressa	Palma	Portia
Hadassah	Pandora	Vera
Hadley	Peony	
Haley	Poppy	**CALENDAR**
Hana	Pualani	April
Hazel	Raizel	Asa
Hoa	Rasia	Bejide
Honey	Reseda	Chausiku
Hortencia	Roselani	Christmas
Hyacinth	Rozene	Chu Hua
Ianthe	Ruri	Chun
Irisa	Ryba	Easter
Ivy	Thalia	Elidi
Jacinda	Yoluta	Freya
Jasmine	Zahra	Garnet
Jolan		Holly
Jonquil	**BUSINESS**	Jora
Kalanit	Alice	June
Kalina	Aziza	Kiku
Kiele	Claiborne	Lakya
Kuai Hua	Claire	Lenadra
Kusa	Eileen	Masika
Lien	Elizabeth	Migina
Lisette	Estée	Mika
Magnolia	Georgia	Mu Lan
Marganit	Gertrude	Sakura
Melba	Godiva	Tanisha

CUTTING EDGE

Agata
Bree
Burgundy
Chanel
Cherilyn
Darnell
Daryl
Daryn
Deandra
Derica
Diantha
Dorinda
Janae
Jazlyn
Jeanelle
Jenica
Jeovana
Jerica
Jiana
Jiselle
Kacie
Kari
Kassidy
Kaylyn
Kenda
Kendra
Kenisha
Kevina
Kiara
Kismet
Kora
Lakeisha
Latanya

Latasha
Lavonne
Lia
Myla
Nisha
Rainbow
Reanna
Rena
Rexanne
Richelle
Ryann
Shaka
Shanice
Shanna
Sharissa
Sharma
Shawna
Stormy
Taryn
Tiana

DANCE

Agnes
Alberta
Alexandra
Augusta
Carlotta
Cynthia
Darcy
Darnell
Deborah
Doris
Giselle
Grace
Gwen

Isadora
Juliet
Martha
Melissa
Nina
Odette
Pilar
Twyla

EDUCATION

Ada
Ann
Caroline
Cornelia
Ellen
Emma
Frances
Gail
Hannah
Helen
Jane
Juliet
Karen
Kristin
Lucretia
Marvel
Prudence
Sarah
Shirley
Susan

HISTORY

Abigail
Ada
Agnes

Agrippa	Dolores	Inga
Alexandra	Eda	Isabel
Ali	Edana	Jacinda
Alice	Eden	Jackie
Alva	Edlyn	Jacqueline
Amelia	Eleanor	Jemima
Amy	Elizabeth	Joan
Anastasia	Emily	Jody
Angela	Esma	Josephine
Ann	Ethel	Joy
Annette	Eugenia	Karla
Antonetta	Eva	Karolina
Augusta	Evelina	Leonora
Barbara	Evelyn	Lidiya
Beatrice	Faustine	Linda
Belle	Fawn	Lorraine
Bernadette	Felicia	Lucrece
Beryl	Flora	Machiko
Betsy	Florence	Mairead
Blanche	Frances	Margaret
Bobdana	Gemma	Maria
Brunhilda	Genevieve	Marion
Candace	Georgia	Martha
Carly	Geraldine	Mary
Caroline	Gertrude	Mercy
Carrie	Godiva	Molly
Catherine	Golda	Nicole
Cecilia	Grace	Nina
Charlotte	Hannah	Ninon
Clara	Harriet	Noelle
Corazon	Heloise	Olinda
Cynthia	Hilda	Orinda
Delia	Hillary	Pamela
Diana	Imelda	Patricia
Dolly	Indira	Penelope

Philadelphia
Phillipa
Rebecca
Regina
Rose
Sabina
Sarah
Shirin
Shirley
Sofia
Stephanie
Susan
Theresa
Trisha
Ursula
Valentina
Vera
Veronica
Vesta
Victoria
Virginia
Wangari
Wilhelmina
Winifred
Yolanda
Zenobia

JOURNALISM
Abigail
Ann
Bree
Charlayne
Deborah
Diana
Hedda

Helen
Ida
Janet
Joyce
Katherine
Linda
Lorraine
Lucinda
Marcia
Maria
Nellie
Nina
Oriana
Rebecca
Susan

LITERATURE
Ada
Adelaide
Adrienne
Agatha
Agnes
Ali
Alice
Amanda
Amber
Amelia
Amy
Angela
Ann
Anna
Antonia
Arabella
Arden
Ariel

Ashley
Augusta
Aurora
Ayla
Babette
Barbara
Beatrice
Belle
Beulah
Beverly
Bianca
Blythe
Bobbi
Brenda
Bridget
Brier
Caitlin
Calliope
Camille
Candace
Candida
Carson
Cassandra
Catherine
Celeste
Charlotte
Chastity
Chloe
Christabel
Christina
Chryseis
Claudia
Cleo
Constance
Consuelo

Cora	Evelina	Ivy
Cordelia	Evelyn	Jacqueline
Cozette	Faith	Jane
Cynthia	Fanny	Janet
Daisy	Faustine	Janice
Damhnait	Felicia	Jessica
Danielle	Fern	Joanna
Daphne	Fiona	Joanne
Dawn	Fleur	Josephine
Deidre	Frances	Jovita
Delia	Gabrielle	Joy
Dido	Gail	Joyce
Dinah	Galatea	Julia
Dora	Genevieve	Juliet
Dorinda	Germaine	June
Doris	Gertrude	Karen
Dorrit	Gladys	Karina
Dulce	Gloria	Karla
Dylana	Grazia	Karolina
Eavan	Gretal	Kate
Eden	Griselda	Katherine
Edith	Gudrun	Kay
Edna	Guinevere	Kerry
Elaine	Gwendolyn	Kim
Eleanor	Hadley	Kizzy
Elfriede	Harriet	Kora
Elizabeth	Heidi	Laura
Ellen	Heloise	Lenore
Emily	Hilda	Leslie
Emma	Holly	Lillian
Erica	Hortencia	Lois
Erma	Ida	Lolita
Esma	Imogene	Lorna
Esperanza	Irisa	Louise
Eudora	Isabel	Mabel

Madeline
Maggie
Maisie
Margaret
Maria
Mariam
Mary
Matilda
Maya
Maxine
Melanie
Melvina
Mercy
Mimi
Minnie
Miranda
Muriel
Myra
Nadine
Nancy
Naomi
Nelly
Nora
Odessa
Ondine
Ophelia
Orinda
Pamela
Pearl
Penelope
Perdita
Phoebe
Pollyanna
Portia
Priscilla

Renee
Rhoda
Rita
Rochelle
Rosaleen
Rosalind
Rose
Roxanne
Sabrina
Sarah
Scarlett
Selma
Sharon
Sigrid
Stephanie
Susan
Sylvia
Tamara
Tess
Thelma
Tillie
Toni
Trilby
Twyla
Ursula
Vanessa
Vera
Victoria
Violet
Virginia
Vivian
Wilhelmina
Xavier
Zelda

MILITARY
Bridget
Doria
Edwige
Florence
Grace
Gudrun
Leslie
Loretta
Morgan
Sally

MOST POPULAR
Abigail
Alexis
Alyssa
Anna
Ashley
Ava
Brianna
Chloe
Elizabeth
Ella
Emily
Emma
Grace
Hailey
Hannah
Isabella
Kaitlyn
Kaylee
Lauren
Lily
Mackenzie

Madeline
Madison
Megan
Natalie
Olivia
Riley
Samantha
Sarah
Sophia
Sydney
Taylor
Zoe

MOVIES AND TELEVISION

Ali
Anastasia
Angela
Annette
Audra
Audrey
Ava
Bambi
Barbara
Beatrice
Blythe
Bo
Bonita
Bridget
Brooke
Candace
Carmen
Carol
Carrie
Cecilia

Celeste
Charo
Charlize
Chastity
Cher
Chloris
Courtney
Cybil
Dale
Daryl
Dawn
Deborah
Debra
Delmelza
Dinah
Doris
Dorothy
Drew
Elisha
Elizabeth
Ellen
Elvira
Emma
Estella
Esther
Eva
Farrah
Fay
Geena
Genevieve
Geraldine
Gigi
Gilda
Gillian
Gina

Ginger
Glenda
Glenna
Gloria
Glynis
Golda
Grace
Greer
Greta
Gwenyth
Haley
Halle
Heidi
Helwig
Hilary
Holly
Ida
Iman
Imogene
Ingrid
Irene
Isabel
Jacqueline
Jada
Jane
Janet
Jean
Jeanette
Jessica
Jill
Joan
Jodi
Julia
Julianna
Julianne

June
Kate
Katherine
Keira
Keshia
Kim
Laura
Lauren
Lea
Lena
Leslie
Libby
Lillian
Liv
Loretta
Love
Lucy
Mabel
Madeline
Madison
Margaret
Margaux
Marilyn
Marla
Marlene
Marlo
Mary
Maureen
Melaine
Melanie
Melissa
Mercedes
Meredith
Merle
Mia

Michele
Milla
Minnie
Miranda
Mitzi
Morgan
Mulan
Naomi
Natalie
Natasha
Nicole
Nora
Norma
Olivia
Oprah
Paula
Phylicia
Pia
Piper
Poppy
Rita
Roseanne
Roxanne
Sabrina
Sally
Salma
Samantha
Sandra
Sarah
Scarlett
Sharissa
Sharon
Shirley
Sigourney
Sissy

Sofia
Stephanie
Susan
Talula
Tate
Terri
Thea
Thelma
Tina
Uma
Ursula
Valerie
Vanessa
Vivian
Yvette

MUSIC
Adriane
Aida
Alberta
Amy
Ann
Arabella
Aretha
Badu
Barbara
Beverly
Beyonce
Bianca
Birgit
Blanche
Bonnie
Britney
Cadence
Calypso

Camille	Gloria	Martina
Candida	Guinevere	Maureen
Carly	Gwen	Melissa
Carmen	Hilda	Michaela
Chantal	Inga	Michele
China	Isabel	Mimi
Cleo	Isolde	Mindy
Constance	Janet	Minnie
Crystal	Jeanette	Misty
Deborah	Jenny	Myra
Della	Jessica	Naomi
Delta	Jewel	Natalie
Diana	Jezebel	Nellie
Dido	Joan	Nicole
Dionne	Joanna	Norah
Dolly	Jocelyn	Olivia
Dominique	Josephine	Page
Donna	Judith	Paula
Doris	Kirsten	Pearl
Dusty	Laila	Peggy
Eartha	Latifah	Phoebe
Eileen	LaToya	Phyllis
Ella	Leonora	Precious
Ellen	Lillian	Prudence
Erice	Linda	Rebecca
Erin	Lisa	Rhonda
Ethel	Liza	Rita
Faith	Lola	Roberta
Faustine	Loretta	Roxanne
Fiona	Lorna	Ruana
Frances	Madonna	Sarah
Frederica	Maria	Shaka
Galatea	Mariah	Sharde
Gladys	Marilyn	Sheena
Glenda	Marne	Sheryl

Sunny
Tammy
Tatiana
Taylor
Tiffany
Tina
Tracy
Vanessa
Violet
Wanda
Whitney
Yoko

MYTHOLOGY
Adonia
Akako
Alima
Amarantha
Andromeda
Anemone
Araidne
Artemis
Athena
Awanata
Ayame
Brisa
Callista
Calypso
Cassandra
Ceres
Chloe
Chloris
Clemence
Cleo
Cybele

Cybil
Cynthia
Danae
Daphne
Delia
Delmelza
Demetria
Diana
Dido
Dionne
Echo
Elaine
Electra
Elysia
Eudora
Fauna
Flora
Fortuna
Freya
Galatea
Grace
Halcyone
Helen
Helia
Hera
Hyacinth
Ianthe
Indira
Iphigenia
Irisa
Isadora
Isis
Ivy
Jacinda
Jocasta

June
Kama
Kimane
Kolea
Kona
Lara
Leda
Levana
Lorelei
Lucina
Macaria
Mandara
Marcella
Marina
Milada
Minerva
Morgan
Narcissa
Natesa
Nenet
Nimaine
Niobe
Oceana
Odessa
Oifa
Olympia
Pallas
Penelope
Peri
Phaedra
Phoebe
Rhea
Rhiannon
Sabrina
Sala

Sen
Sita
Suletu
Thalia
Thisbe
Tracy
Tyra
Urania
Venus

NATURE
Alauda
Amaya
Amaui
Amethyst
April
Awanata
Baka
Bena
Beryl
Calandra
Ceres
Danika
Delfina
Derora
Diamond
Dyani
Eartha
Esmeralda
Esther
Fiala
Fontane
Gaea
Garnet
Gemma

Hesper
Hinda
Holly
Hoshi
Ilana
Iola
Ivory
Jade
Jael
Jonina
Kalinda
Kallan
Kalli
Keida
Keitha
Kelby
Kezia
Kiku
Kimana
Kimberly
Kirsi
Kuri
Lala
Lark
Laverne
Leanna
Lilia
Linette
Liviya
Lorelle
Mansi
Mavis
Melantha
Mora
Noelani

Noga
Opal
Oriole
Pearl
Rainbow
Raisa
Randi
Rea
Rhoda
Rhonda
Ria
Rihana
Rochelle
Sable
Saki
Sakura
Saffron
Sala
Sapphire
Shappa
Sisika
Sita
Solana
Sora
Starla
Stormy
Sugi
Suki
Sula
Sunny
Tabitha
Taka
Takenya
Taki
Tala

Talia
Tallis
Tama
Tamara
Taree
Tawny
Tazu
Teal
Tempest
Tera
Tetsu
Tirza
Trava
Violet
Willow
Yasmin
Yoki
Yolanda
Yoninah
Zea

PHILOSOPHY
Artha
Augusta
Blaise
Maria
Marilyn
Mary

SCIENCE
Adelle
Agnes
Alice
Anna
Caitlin

Charlotte
Christa
Christen
Christiane
Diana
Dixie
Dorothy
Ellen
Emily
Florence
Gail
Gardenia
Gertrude
Grace
Henrietta
Jane
Jovita
Joy
Katherine
Leona
Lidia
Lilia
Linda
Lois
Lydia
Marcia
Margaret
Maria
Marie
Marion
Mildred
Nova
Rachel
Rita
Rosaleen

Sally
Sylvia
Ursula
Valentina
Venus
Virginia
Winifred

SPORTS
Adriana
Althea
Andrea
Ann
Bonnie
Brandy
Carol
Catalina
Charlotte
Christa
Christina
Dana
Danielle
Dawn
Dorothy
Esther
Evelyn
Fabienne
Fani
Fiona
Florence
Gabrielle
Gertrude
Greta
Hayley
Hazel

Helen	Precious	Eileen
Hilde	Renee	Electra
Ina	Rose	Ethel
Ingrid	Samantha	Faith
Irena	Serena	Fanny
Isabelle	Sheena	Flora
Isolde	Shirley	Gertrude
Jacqueline	Sonja	Gloria
Jane	Stephanie	Gwendolyn
Janet	Surya	Hedda
Janica	Susan	Helen
Jill	Tamara	Inga
Kari	Tiffany	Irene
Karina	Valentina	Joanna
Kaye	Venus	Josephine
Kristin		Lorraine
Laura	**THEATER**	Lucy
Lillian	Ada	Maggie
Lori	Ade	Minnie
Mary	Adelaide	Nora
Maureen	Adrienne	Peggy
Maya	Amanda	Rachel
Mia	Andrea	Regina
Midori	Antonetta	Sabrina
Monica	Arden	Salome
Nadia	Beatrice	Tammy
Nancy	Bernadette	Tempest
Nanna	Blythe	Titania
Noelle	Chava	Vickie
Nona	Cher	Violet
Oriole	Cheryl	Winifred
Pamela	Claire	Zoe
Patricia	Constance	
Pearle	Edith	
Peggy	Effie	

MALE NAMES

AERONAUTICS
Alan
Buzz
Charles
Edwin
Eugene
Frances
Frederick
John
Keith
Manfred
Neil
Orville
Reginald
Reynold
Roland
Wilbur
Wiley

ARTS
Aaron
Andrew
Ansel
Aubrey

August
Chauncey
Christopher
Claude
Donato
Duncan
Edgar
Edward
Eugene
Francis
Frederick
Gage
Galen
Garth
Gary
Germain
Grant
Gustaf
Guy
Henry
Horst
Jackson
Leonard
Linus

Marsden
Matthew
Maurice
Michael
Minor
Norman
Paris
Paul
Raphael
Salvatore
Seth
Theodore
Theodoric
Thomas
Vincent
Walter
William
Winslow

ASTROLOGY
Antares
Aries
Berwin
Blair

Chase
Etu
Fisk
Fletcher
Hamal
Hilel
Ives
Keegan
Lave
Leo
Omar
Ouray
Simba

BIBLE
Aaron
Abel
Abner
Abraham
Absalom
Adam
Adlai
Alvah
Amon
Amos
Andrew
Angel
Arnan
Asa
Asher
Barak
Barnabas
Bartholomew
Benjamin
Cain

Caleb
Cyrus
Daniel
David
Ebenezer
Eden
Eder
Eleazar
Eli
Elijah
Emmanuel
Enoch
Ephraim
Ethan
Ezekiel
Ezra
Gabriel
Heber
Ira
Isaac
Isaiah
Ishmael
Israel
Jacob
Japheth
Jarah
Jason
Jeremiah
Jericho
Jesse
Jethro
Job
Joel
John
Jonah

Jonathan
Joseph
Joshua
Josiah
Jubal
Judah
Lazarus
Lemuel
Levi
Luke
Malachi
Mark
Matthew
Michael
Moses
Nathan
Nathaniel
Nehemiah
Noah
Obadiah
Paul
Peter
Philip
Reuben
Samson
Samuel
Saul
Seth
Shem
Shiloh
Silvanus
Simon
Solomon
Thaddeus
Thomas

Timothy
Titus
Tobias
Uriah
Uriel
Zaccheus
Zachariah
Zedekiah
Zion

BOTANY
Alon
Botan
Carmel
Dekel
Durril
Florian
Jacinto
Karmel
Lennox
Liko
Malawa
Mandala
Miki
Nahele
Narcisse
Oakes
Orji
Riyad
Waverly
Zahur

BUSINESS
Aaron
Aldo

Andrew
Bernard
Boyd
Charles
Clement
Conrad
Cornelius
Donald
Ezra
Finn
Francis
Harlan
Harvey
Henry
Howard
Hugo
Josiah
Lee
Leroy
Levi
Malcolm
Mark
Marshall
Mayer
Minor
Nathan
Peter
Philip
Ray
Rhodes
Richard
Rupert
Sargent
Sidney
Stanford

Vernon
Warren
William

CALENDAR
Abejide
Bodua
Botan
Dominick
Jarek
Karif
Noel
Pascal
Sarad

CUTTING EDGE
Dakota
Darrion
DeAndre
DeJuan
DeMarcus
Deontae
DeRon
DeShawn
Duane
Jamar
Jarell
Jareth
Jaron
Javon
Jerrell
Jerrick
Jonte
Kacey

Kalin	Emil	Carlos
Keandre	Erasmus	Casper
Keon	Eugene	Cassius
Khiry	Ferdinand	Charles
Marquise	Florian	Christopher
Marsh	Graham	Clarence
Rashaun	Jared	Clive
Terron	Jaroslav	Constantine
	Josiah	Cyrano
DANCE	Lamar	Cyrus
Alvin	Leonard	Dag
Demetrius	Marius	Daniel
Eugene	Maynard	David
George	Noah	Desmond
Hermes	Norman	Dionysus
Jerome	Perry	Dominick
Joseph	Ralph	Douglas
Mark	Samson	Earl
Mercer	Sigmund	Edward
Michael	William	Edwin
Nicholas		Eldridge
Salvatore	**HISTORY**	Eli
Sergei	Adlai	Elijah
Vernon	Adolph	Ethan
	Alexander	Felix
EDUCATION	Andrew	Ferdinand
Adam	Anwar	Fidel
Arnold	Arsenio	Finn
Bronislaw	Averill	Fletcher
Clifton	Bayard	Francis
Dallin	Benjamin	Franklin
Darnell	Bernard	Frederick
David	Bruce	Frederik
Dionysus	Caesar	Gabriel
Elijah	Calvin	Geoffrey

George	Nelson	Vladimir
Gerald	Nicholas	Wallace
Grover	Octavius	Warren
Guadalupe	Olaf	Wenceslas
Harlan	Oliver	Wendell
Henry	Osman	William
Herbert	Parnell	Winston
Hiram	Patrick	Winthrop
Horatio	Paul	Woodrow
Hubert	Pericles	Wyatt
Ignatius	Peter	Xerxes
Ira	Ponce	Yitzhak
Isaiah	Quincy	Zachariah
Israel	Ralph	Zebulon
Jacob	Reynold	
Jesse	Richard	**JOURNALISM**
John	Robert	Arthur
Julias	Roger	Brandon
Kim	Rory	Charles
Kofi	Roy	Clive
Lawrence	Rudolf	Edgar
Leon	Salvatore	Edward
Louis	Samuel	Erik
Lucian	Schuyler	Garrick
Lyndon	Sean	Harold
Malcolm	Shiloh	Hassan
Manuel	Shimon	Henry
Marcus	Silvanus	Hugh
Martin	Simon	Hunter
Michael	Snowden	Lincoln
Miles	Stephen	Lindsay
Milford	Theodore	Lowell
Moses	Thomas	Marshall
Napolean	Ulric	Maximillian
Nathan	Ulysses	Norman

Ogden
Peter
Roger
Sheldon
Thomas
Tyler
Waldemar
Walter
Westbrook
Willard

LITERATURE

Absalom
Adam
Aladdin
Albert
Alexander
Algernon
Alphonse
Ambrose
Amory
Andrew
Angel
Anthony
Aramis
Archibald
Arden
Ariel
Arthur
Ashley
Atticus
Axel
Bernard
Bertram
Boris

Bram
Bruce
Byron
Cassius
Cedric
Charles
Christian
Christopher
Cisero
Clark
Clement
Craig
Czeslaw
Damian
Daniel
Dante
Dario
D'Artagnan
David
Derek
Dorian
Douglas
Dylan
Earl
Ebenezer
Edgar
Edmund
Edward
Edwin
Elijah
Ellery
Emil
Erik
Ernest
Eugene

Ezra
Ferdinand
Finn
Fletcher
Francis
Franklin
Gabriel
Gao
Gavin
Geoffrey
George
Gerald
Graham
Gustaf
Guy
Hamilton
Hansel
Harlan
Hart
Harvey
Hassan
Hayden
Hector
Henry
Herbert
Herman
Herrick
Hilary
Holden
Homer
Horatio
Hunter
Ichabod
Irwin
Isaac

Ishmael	Merlin	Robert
Israel	Mervin	Roland
Jacob	Michael	Rory
Jerome	Nathaniel	Salvatore
Joaquin	Nicholas	Samuel
John	Norman	Saul
Jonathan	Northrop	Seamus
Joseph	Oberon	Scott
Julius	Octavius	Sebastian
Kalil	Ogden	Sef
Keith	Olaf	Sheridan
Kenneth	Oliver	Sherlock
Kingsley	Omar	Sherwood
Kurt	Orrick	Sidney
Langston	Orville	Siegfried
Lawrence	Osbert	Sinclair
Lemuel	Othello	Somerset
Lear	Ovid	Stephen
Leo	Owen	Sterling
Leon	Pablo	Stuart
Logan	Percival	Terence
Louis	Percy	Theodore
Lysander	Peregrine	Thomas
Maddox	Peter	Thornton
Madison	Philip	Timothy
Manfred	Primo	Titus
Manley	Quentin	Tobias
Marcellus	Rainer	Tristan
Marius	Ralph	Truman
Mark	Randolph	Ulysses
Marmion	Ray	Upton
Marquis	Raymond	Uriah
Martin	Remus	Uriel
Matthew	Rider	Vachel
Maxwell	Roald	Vernon

Victor
Virgil
Vladimir
Walden
Waldermar
Wallace
Walter
Washington
Watson
Whitcomb
Wilfred
William
Wyndham
Yaakov
Yancy
Yates

MILITARY
Ambrose
Bayard
Benedict
Brant
Clive
Cril
David
Douglas
Dudley
George
Giles
Henry
Horatio
Houston
Israel
Jubal
Lachlan

Lafayette
Lyman
Major
Matthew
Nelson
Norman
Omar
Patton
Raymond
Robert
Sebastian
Seth
Sterling
Wade
Wesley

MOST POPULAR
Aidan
Alexander
Andrew
Caden
Calib
Christopher
Connor
Daniel
David
Dylan
Ethan
Jack
Jackson
Jacob
James
Jayden
Jesse

Jonathan
Joseph
Joshua
Justin
Kyle
Logan
Matthew
Michael
Nathan
Nicholas
Noah
Peter
Philip
Robert
Ryan
Sean
Stephen
Tyler
William
Zachary

MOVIES AND TELEVISION
Adolph
Aidan
Alexander
Alan
Andrew
Anthony
Armand
Arnold
Basil
Beau
Benicio
Blake

Boris	Ewan	Lawrence
Brad	Farley	Leonard
Brian	Francis	Leslie
Buck	Frederick	Liam
Bud	Gary	Lionel
Burl	Gerald	Lloyd
Burton	Gregory	Louis
Caesar	Harold	Luke
Carey	Harrison	Macaulay
Cecil	Harvey	Malcolm
Cedric	Heath	Martin
Chad	Hector	Matthew
Charles	Henry	Maximillian
Charlie	Hersh	Melvin
Chevalier	Hidalgo	Michael
Christopher	Homer	Milton
Clark	Hugh	Montgomery
Clinton	Humphrey	Morgan
Conan	Ingemar	Norman
Cyril	Jacob	Oliver
Dabe	Jamal	Omar
Daniel	Jamie	Orlando
David	Jason	Orson
Dean	Jay	Otto
Denzel	Jeremiah	Owen
Donald	Joaquin	Parker
Douglas	John	Paul
Dudley	Jude	Paxton
Dustin	Kadeem	Peter
Edward	Keenan	Pierce
Elijah	Keir	Preston
Emil	Kenneth	Quentin
Ernest	Kevin	Quinn
Eustace	Kiefer	Randy

Ray
Raymond
Regis
Richard
Ridley
River
Rob
Robert
Robin
Rock
Roger
Roman
Ryan
Samuel
Sean
Sebastian
Sidney
Silvestor
Spencer
Stanley
Stephen
Tab
Taye
Thomas
Timothy
Trevor
Trey
Troy
Tyrone
Van
Vincent
Wallace
Warren
Wesley

Wilford
William
Woodrow
Yul

MUSIC
Alexander
Andrew
Anthony
Barry
Beau
Benjamin
Brian
Bruce
Bruno
Caesar
Camillus
Casey
Chad
Charles
Chauncey
Christopher
Claude
Clifford
Conway
Curtis
Darius
Darryl
David
Del
Dion
Dionysus
Douglas
Duane

Earl
Elton
Elvis
Emmanuel
Engelbert
Enrique
Ephraim
Erik
Eugene
Fabian
Fletcher
Francis
Frederick
Garth
George
Germain
Gordon
Harlow
Hector
Henry
Hoyt
Ignatius
Igor
Ira
Irving
Isaac
Jacob
Javon
Jerome
Jethro
John
Joseph
Julius
Justin

Keith	Ravi	Adri
Kenneth	Ray	Aeneas
Leonard	Reuben	Agni
Leopold	Richard	Apollo
Leroy	Ring	Aries
Lionel	Robert	Balder
Louis	Roland	Balin
Lucian	Roy	Bartram
Ludwig	Samson	Dag
Luther	Scott	Dasan
Lyle	Sergei	Demetrius
Manfred	Sheldon	Griffin
Marvin	Sigmund	Hanuman
Mason	Simon	Hastin
Maurice	Stephen	Hercules
Merle	Travis	Hermes
Michael	Tristan	Ingemar
Miles	Van	Ingvar
Nathan	Victor	Jason
Neil	Vincent	Leander
Nelson	Vladimir	Narcisse
Neville	Walford	Neptune
Olaf	Wayland	Odin
Osborn	Wayne	Orestes
Oscar	Wenceslas	Paris
Otto	William	Terrill
Paul	Wolfgang	Thor
Percy	Woodrow	Zeus
Perry	Wycliff	
Peter	Xavier	**NATURE**
Philip	Yehudah	Akemi
Placido	Yves	Aries
Presley		Arun
Prince	**MYTHOLOGY**	Aryeh
Quincy	Adon	Atid

Bartram
Ber
Birch
Brede
Brock
Brooks
Delfino
Deniz
Dov
Dyami
Etu
Fletcher
Gavin
Giles
Gur
Hai
Haidar
Hali
Hamal
Hart
Hersh
Hilel
Hinun
Howi
Hurst
Ivo
Jael
Jay
Jonah
Jubal
Kele
Kibbe
Kiho
Kiri
Lais

Leverett
Lionel
Lisimba
Lowell
Makani
Mamo
Merle
Misu
Namir
Numair
Nusair
Okoth
Paris
Percy
Peregrine
Pillan
Pinon
Quillan
Raviv
Reynard
Rigel
Ring
River
Roe
Silvestor
Simba
Starr
Tau
Toru
Ulf
Zamir

PHILOSOPHY
Bartholomew
Baruch

Bertram
Emmanuel
Francis
Frederick
Ludwig
Plato
Socrates
Thomas

SCIENCE
Aaron
Albert
Alexander
Ahmed
Anthony
Avram
Baily
Benjamin
Bertram
Blaise
Charles
Christian
Claude
Edmond
Erasmus
Ernest
Euclid
Gabriel
Galen
George
Gerardus
Gilbert
Günter
Harlow
Harold

Harvey	Martin	Arthur
Heber	Maxwell	Bartholomew
Henry	Michael	Beau
Herbert	Myron	Benjamin
Herman	Nehemiah	Bernard
Hideki	Nevin	Brett
Horatio	Nicholas	Brian
Howard	Norbert	Buck
Humphrey	Otto	Carter
Ira	Owen	Casey
Irving	Patrick	Cassius
Irwin	Paul	Cornelius
Isaac	Peter	Craig
Isidore	Philip	Cyrus
Israel	Raphael	Darius
Jacob	Raymond	Darryl
Jamal	Reed	David
Jaroslav	Reginald	Deion
John	Riccardo	Doug
Joseph	Richard	Duane
Josiah	Rolf	Earl
Julius	Rudolph	Emmitt
Justin	Stanley	Erik
Kai	Sydney	Fabio
Kirk	Tim	Felix
Kurt	Vitaly	Ferdinand
Laurent	Walter	Francis
Leo	William	George
Leland	Wolfe	Gilbert
Linus	Wolfgang	Gregory
Logan		Grover
Louis	**SPORTS**	Guy
Luther	Angel	Hakeem
Magnus	Armin	Henry
Mario	Arnold	Herman

Hideki	Rodney	Clifford
Ingemar	Roger	Cyrano
Isaiah	Roosevelt	David
Jamal	Roscoe	Demetrius
Jarvis	Samuel	Elmer
Jesse	Scott	Ernest
John	Sebastian	Eugene
Kareem	Stanley	Faustus
Keith	Stein	George
Kennedy	Terence	Harley
Kevin	Thomas	Harold
Kirk	Tristan	Harvey
Knute	Tyrone	Henry
Kyle	Vincent	Israel
Lamar	Wade	Jerome
Lance	Walter	John
Landon	Wayne	Joseph
Lawrence	Wesley	Langford
Louis	Wilbur	Lloyd
Lyle	William	Malcolm
Marcus	Wilton	Maxwell
Mark	Woodrow	Neil
Matthew	Xavier	Noel
Merlin	Yale	Obadiah
Michael		Orestes
Mohammed	**THEATER**	Oscar
Napoleon	Alan	Pericles
Nolan	Amadeus	Peter
Oscar	Arthur	Philip
Peter	August	Richard
Peyton	Bernard	Romulus
Randolph	Brandon	Ross
Ray	Bronson	Samson
Reginald	Brooks	Samuel
Rock	Cameron	Sanford

Sean
Sidney
Somerset
Spalding
Stanley
Stephen
Tennessee
Thornton
Tobias
Yaakov